Preliminary Studies on the Scholia
to Euripides

CALIFORNIA CLASSICAL STUDIES

NUMBER 6

Editorial Board Chair: Donald Mastronarde

Editorial Board: Alessandro Barchiesi, Todd Hickey, Emily Mackil, Richard Martin, Robert Morstein-Marx, J. Theodore Peña, Kim Shelton

California Classical Studies publishes peer-reviewed long-form scholarship with online open access and print-on-demand availability. The primary aim of the series is to disseminate basic research (editing and analysis of primary materials both textual and physical), data-heavy research, and highly specialized research of the kind that is either hard to place with the leading publishers in Classics or extremely expensive for libraries and individuals when produced by a leading academic publisher. In addition to promoting archaeological publications, papyrological and epigraphic studies, technical textual studies, and the like, the series will also produce selected titles of a more general profile.

The startup phase of this project (2013–2017) is supported by a grant from the Andrew W. Mellon Foundation.

Also in the series:

Number 1: Leslie Kurke, *The Traffic in Praise: Pindar and the Poetics of Social Economy*, 2013

Number 2: Edward Courtney, *A Commentary on the Satires of Juvenal*, 2013

Number 3: Mark Griffith, *Greek Satyr Play: Five Studies*, 2015

Number 4: Mirjam Kotwick, *Alexander of Aphrodisias and the Text of Aristotle's* Metaphysics, 2016

Number 5: Joey Williams, *The Archaeology of Roman Surveillance in the Central Alentejo, Portugal*, 2017

PRELIMINARY STUDIES ON THE SCHOLIA TO EURIPIDES

Donald J. Mastronarde

Berkeley, California

© 2017 by Donald J. Mastronarde.

California Classical Studies
c/o Department of Classics
University of California
Berkeley, California 94720–2520
USA
http://calclassicalstudies.org
email: ccseditorial@berkeley.edu

ISBN 9781939926104

Library of Congress Control Number: 2017916025

CONTENTS

Preface	vii
Acknowledgments	xi
Abbreviations	xiii
Sigla for Manuscripts of Euripides	xvii
List of Plates	xxix

1. The Scholia and the Ancient and Medieval Tradition of Commenting on Euripides	1
1.1. Editing the Scholia	1
1.2. The Development of Annotation on Euripides in Antiquity	7
1.3. The Scholia in the Middle Ages	26
1.4. Glossation	37
Appendix: The Yv Paraphrast and the Periphrastic Scholia in Arsenius	44
2. Teachers' Scholia, Tzetzes, and Planudes	60
2.1. "Grammatical" Scholia or Teachers' Notes	60
2.2. Tzetzes and the Teaching Tradition	77
2.3. Planudes and the Teaching Tradition	89
3. The Extra Exegetical Material in SSa and the Teaching Tradition	107
3.1. The Preliminaries Preceding *Hecuba* in SSa	107
3.2. The Miscellany of Notes on *Hecuba* in S	113
3.3. The Tip of the Iceberg? A Vocabulary List Based on *Hecuba* in Barberinianus graecus 4	148
4. On Venetus Marcianus Graecus 471 (Codex M of Euripides)	161

4.1. The Problem of Dating 161
4.2. General Description and Evidence for Dating 165
4.3. Detailed Description 172
   A. Scribal Tallies and Quires 172
   B. Use of Majuscule 173
   C. Use of Enlarged Letters 173
   D. Comments on Specific Letters 175
   E. Abbreviations 180
   F. The Scholia Reference System 182
   G. Other Oddities 182
Appendix: Numeration Sequence in Scholia References in M 186

Plates 189

5. On Vaticanus Graecus 909 (Codex V of Euripides) 199
   5.1. V and Planudes? 199
   5.2. The Partner Scribes of the Original Production 206
   5.3. Characteristics of the Original Hands 210
   5.4. Other Correctors and the Cursive Hands 214
   Appendix: The Distribution of Work between Hands A and B 217

Bibliography 224
Index of Manuscripts 236
Index locorum 238
General Index 239

PREFACE

When I first began in 2009 to work in earnest on editing the scholia to Euripides as a digital open-access project (EuripidesScholia.org), I believed I could work on discrete chunks in sequence and I chose to concentrate at first on *Orestes* 1–500. The studies presented in this volume are intended to appear shortly before a much expanded sample of scholia on those 500 lines is to be released online. This sample will replace the initial one, available since 2010, which covered only 50 or so lines and was based on fewer witnesses. The intervening years have taught me, however, that it is not practical to limit my purview to such a discrete chunk. The process of collating and the process of interpreting scholia and determining how best to present them have necessitated forays into other areas of the triad. The prospect of new information about the scholia in the Jerusalem palimpsest (H) from the Palamedes Project caused me to collate the other main witnesses for old scholia for the lines of the triad plays covered by scholia in H. When I eventually realized that I would never get adequately accurate collations from the reproductions I had of Marcianus graecus 471 (M) and Vaticanus graecus 909 (V), I obtained new color digital images of M, and the Vatican Library and the Polonsky Foundation kindly acceded to my request that V be digitized and made available online, and it soon became both a priority and a matter of efficiency to collate all the scholia in these witnesses, including those for non-triad plays. A trip to Madrid for the oral defence of a dissertation allowed me to visit Salamanca and see Salamanticensis 31 (S) in person, which set off my interest in the odd collection of annotations published in Chapter 3 of this book. Consequently, in order to understand those annotations, larger samples of scholia on *Hecuba* had to be collated. It has also been a priority to take trips to conduct autopsy examination of problematic manuscripts while I have research funding remaining after retirement and while I am still lucky enough to be able to endure the long flights from California to Europe. Thus my work has proceeded in several directions simultaneously, and it seemed best to push myself, for some topics, to come to conclusions definitive enough to be presented to fellow scholars now, while continuing to work toward a more complete inventory of the scholia, for my online project at EuripidesScholia.org is at this stage primarily an inventory.

I have advisedly included the word "preliminary" in the title for several reasons. First, nobody ever collates with 100 percent accuracy, and in any case collating additional witnesses over time tends to send one back to a manuscript previously collated either to discover an omission or mistake or to solve a puzzle about a damaged or ambiguous reading. Apart from the issue of accuracy, there are many more manuscripts to collate more completely, which will provide fuller context for confirming or questioning hypotheses reached so far. Second, one must work with images of various kinds and various qualities, but the situation is constantly improving. The ideal is to have color digital images of sufficient resolution so that they can be enlarged to make the tiny script of many scholia as legible as possible and the identification of changes of ink clearer. Good-resolution grayscale scans are the second-best option, for those cases in which libraries refuse to provide color (a restrictive holdover that scarcely makes sense in the modern world of digital photography and cheap mass storage) or continue to price color images at an outrageous level (again, in digital imaging the difference between the price of grayscale and color no longer has much justification). Less desirable is digitization from black and white microfilm, but even this can sometimes be adequate when the ink is uniformly dark against a light background of unstained paper. Microfilms themselves are often inadequate for accurate collation of scholia, being impossible to magnify sufficiently and often unable to show clearly inks that are faint. By acquiring better images or because of new online access I have gradually eliminated my need to use the microfilms that I had accumulated. As more years pass, even more manuscripts of Euripides will become accessible in online images. Third, a lot of what interests me depends on a fuller knowledge of other scholia corpora and of Byzantine works that tell us about philological study and teaching in the 11th to the 14th centuries, but much of that material is only partially covered in the published sources and the TLG data. Thus, conclusions I reach here will undoubtedly need revision when others finally provide fuller inventories of the scholia on Sophocles and Aeschylus, or a modern edition of the scholia on Oppian, or authoritative editions of more of the works of Tzetzes, Planudes, Moschopulus, and Thomas Magister.

Despite these imperfections in access to the manuscript source material and in knowledge of the context of the manuscripts, it is an opportune moment for studies of this kind, even for one located so far from the European libraries. As already mentioned, great improvements have been made possible by using digital images. There are many more manuscripts now available online in good images than when I began, and the number will only increase as time goes by. Furthermore, in the past few decades significant advances have been made in medieval Greek palaeography and codicology and in the study of Byzantine, and particularly Palaeologan, scholars and their contexts. Ole L. Smith's edition of the scholia on Aeschylus' *Septem* set a new standard for proper attention to the annotations and glosses in the *recentiores* of tragedy. Hans-Christian Günther's study of the circulation of Palaeologan annotations in a large number of 14th-century witnesses of Euripides provided essential groundwork for even more extensive study. Palaeologan intellectual pursuits have been illuminated in many studies, two notable examples being Daniele Bianconi's *Tessalonica nell'età dei paleologi. Le pratiche intellettuali nel riflesso della cultura civica* (2005) and Niels Gaul's *Thomas Magistros und die spätbyzantinische Sophistik. Studien zum Humanismus urbaner Eliten in der frühen Palaiologenzeit* (2011). The maturation of projects like the *Lexikon zur byzantinischen Gräzität* and *Prosopographisches Lexikon der Palaiologenzeit*, the publication of new catalogues, and the development of sites like Pinakes (pinakes.irht.cnrs.fr) have made research more effective. The study of ancient scholarship and of the phenomenon of scholia in general has been a major focus of research in several countries, particularly in Italy, and the *Lexicon of Greek Grammarians of Antiquity* and the surveys and special studies in *Brill's Companion to Ancient Greek Scholarship* are now important points of reference.

My pursuit of the project of an open-ended online edition of scholia reflects the fact that I am interested in the entire history of intellectual and readerly reception of Euripides. Much of what I have written in these chapters may be of more interest to Byzantinists than to those classicists who believe the only scholia worth editing are those with some chance of being annotations transmitted from a time before the invention of minuscule or, even more strictly, from before 200 CE (or even earlier).

The first chapter reviews the achievements and shortcomings of previous editions of Euripidean scholia and argues for the need for more comprehensive treatment of this and similar corpora of scholia. It also shows the disadvantages of stratifying scholia on a chronological basis and argues for the importance of understanding glosses, which have been impossible to assess properly because of the incomplete and misleading information provided by previous editions. The second chapter argues that the term teachers' scholia may be usefully applied to many of the so-called *scholia recentiora*. It demonstrates key features of manuscripts meant for less ambitious levels of teaching and some characteristic types of teachers' notes. The evidence for the teaching of Ioannes Tzetzes related to Euripides is gathered more completely than previously, as is that for Maximus Planudes. The third chapter analyzes the oddly jumbled (older) prefatory material (including the *Life of Euripides* and scattered teachers' notes on *Hecuba*) transmitted in two *recentiores* and then offers the first edition of, and commentary on, a miscellany of teachers' notes on *Hecuba* found in a manuscript dated 1287 but clearly copied there from an older source. The connection of some of these notes with the teaching of Tzetzes and Eustathius and other middle Byzantine sources is assessed. A third section presents a brief list of notes on vocabulary, which I noticed by chance when looking at Barberinianus graecus 4 for another reason in May 2017 and which I realized was compiled in connection with reading Euripides' *Hecuba*. The fourth chapter marshals the evidence for the dating of the manuscript M, still claimed by some to be from the 12th century rather than the 11th, and provides some palaeographic and codicological details beyond what is in the relevant recent catalogue. The fifth chapter briefly challenges the claim that the original production of the manuscript V and some of the scholia surviving only in V should be connected to new interests that arose only in the period of Planudes. It argues that Planudean elements are verifiable only in the additions made in cursive more than a generation after the original production. It supports the earlier dating (1250–1280) proposed by Nigel Wilson, and then proceeds to a detailed description of the hands in V that are most important for the scholia and a full listing of the respective work of the two partner scribes who produced the original codex.

Something should be said of my decision not to include images of manuscripts in this publication. My reasons are partly practical and partly ideological. In the format of this book, black and white images of whole manuscript pages would not be very satisfactory, especially since my interest is largely in the scholia, and antiquated permissions rules often do not accommodate open-access publication. I applaud the libraries that have made significant numbers of their medieval Greek manuscripts freely visible in good images online and I believe that this is the proper treatment of the patrimony that they protect. No picture I could publish of Vaticanus graecus 909 would be as useful as seeing the images created by the Polonsky Foundation now available at digi.vatlib.it. I hope that the Biblioteca Marciana will someday soon offer images of its treasures, including Marcianus graecus 471. I also intend to request permission to show online some sample pages of certain manuscripts at EuripidesScholia.org. In the fuller descriptions of the manuscripts being used that I present on that site, I provide links to the online images that I know of, and this aspect of the site will be upgraded in 2018; and at some point the site may be able to reference images under the new standard known as IIIF (International Image Interoperability Framework, iiif.io).

Finally, many of the scholia cited from particular manuscripts in this study are presented without iota subscript because the iota is lacking in the source(s); likewise, the accentuation is in places not made to conform with modern conventions. I do not, however, make any attempt to retain the punctuation of the manuscripts.

ACKNOWLEDGMENTS

Many individuals have assisted me with advice and materials, or by sending scans of bibliographic items inaccessible to me, or shooting digital photos for me of manuscript pages. For such help I owe sincere thanks to Robert Allison, Luigi Battezzato, Maria Cannatà Fera, Guglielmo Cavallo, Stephen Daitz, GiovanBattista D'Alessio, James Diggle, Hans-Christian Günther, Timothy Janz, Teresa Martínez Manzano, the late Kjeld Mattheissen, Maria Mavroudi, Fausto Montana, Inmaculada Pérez Martín, Ilias Nesseris, Filippomaria Pontani, Lucia Prauscello, Mario Telò, Nigel Wilson, and Michael Zellmann-Rohrer. Special thanks are due to Maria Pantelia and the Thesaurus Linguae Graecae for providing me with raw files of the scholia as published by Schwartz and Dindorf to save me from inputting them myself.

A number of Berkeley students have assisted me through the Undergraduate Research Apprentice Program, mainly by identifying lines on each digital image and renaming the image for easier consultation, but sometimes also by doing preliminary collations or typing up scholia not in Dindorf or Schwartz. I would like to thank them here: Sara Hobe, Tovah Keynton, YeChan Kwak, Jay Lamb, Brittany Lauber, Juhaie Hannah Lee, Karen MacLaughlin, Ryan Rasmussen, Jeremy Simmons, Josh Smith, and Nathaniel Solley.

I also want to acknowledge the hospitality of the libraries that I have visited so far for this project: Biblioteca Apostolica Vaticana, Biblioteca Angelica, Biblioteca Ambrosiana, Biblioteca Nazionale Marciana, Biblioteca Medicea Laurenziana, Bodleian Library, Cambridge University Library, Biblioteca Nacional de España, Biblioteca General Histórica (Universidad de Salamanca), Real Biblioteca del Monasterio de El Escorial. For provision of images I am grateful to the same libraries, as well as to Biblioteca Nazionale di Napoli, Biblioteca Nazionale Universitaria di Torino, Biblioteca Statale (Governativa) di Cremona, Biblioteca Estense Universitaria di Modena, Bibliothèque Nationale de France, Bibliothèque Municipale Reims, British Library, Herzog August Bibliothek Wolfenbüttel, Bayerische Staatsbibliothek, Oesterreichische Nationalbibliothek, Det Kongelige Bibliotek København, National Bank Cultural Foundation: Center for History and Palaeography, Athens (and Monk Theologos of the Iviron Monastery). For confirming that the partial images of some lines and words of Vaticanus graecus 909 used in the Plates of this book are covered by fair use, I thank Riccardo Luongo of the Reproductions and Rights Office of the Biblioteca Apostolica Vaticana.

I am grateful to the two referees recruited by California Classical Studies for their encouragement and corrections, especially to Filippomaria Pontani, who saved me from many errors of commission or omission. The skilled copy editing of Elizabeth Ditmars has made the final product more accurate and clearer, and Justin Hudak helped with proofreading. For any errors or improbabilities that remain in this final version (somewhat expanded since the draft that was reviewed), I alone am responsible.

Donald J. Mastronarde
Berkeley, October 2017

ABBREVIATIONS

Bibliographic Abbreviations

Most items are referred to by author's name and date as they appear in the Bibliography at the end of the book. But a few key works are referred to by name only, as indicated here together with other standard abbreviations.

BCAGS	Montanari, F., Matthaios, S., and Rengakos, A., eds. 2015. *Brill's Companion to Ancient Greek Scholarship*. Leiden and Boston.
CAG	*Commentaria in Aristotelem Graeca*.
Diggle	Diggle, J., ed. 1981–1994. *Euripidis Fabulae*. 3 vols. Oxford Classical Texts. Oxford.
Dindorf	Dindorf, Guilielmus [Wilhelm], ed. 1863. *Scholia graeca in Euripidis tragoedias ex codicibus aucta et emendata*. 4 vols. Oxford.
DGE	*Diccionario Griego-Español*, redactado bajo la dirección de F. R. Adrados. 1980–. Vols. 1–. Madrid [also available at http://dge.cchs.csic.es/xdge/].
FGrHist	F. Jacoby. 1923–. *Die Fragmente der griechischen Historiker*. Leiden.
Glasgow ed.	[Duncan, A., and Duncan, J. M., eds.] 1821. *Euripidis opera omnia; ex editionibus praestantissimis fideliter recusa; latina interpretatione, scholiis antiquis, et eruditorum observationibus, illustrata: necnon indicibus omnigenis instructa*. 9 vols. Glasgow.
GrammGr	*Grammatici Graeci recogniti et apparatu critico instructi*. 1883–1901. 4 vols. Leipzig.
Kovacs	Kovacs, D., ed. 1994–2002. *Euripides*. 6 vols. Loeb Classical Library. Cambridge, Mass.
Lake	Lake, K. and S. 1934–1939. *Dated Greek Minuscule Manuscripts to the Year 1200*. 10 vols. Boston [text and images online at http://pyle.it/facsmiles/lake-online/].
LBG	Trapp, E., ed. 1994–2017. *Lexikon zur byzantinischen Gräzität besonders des 9.–12. Jahrhunderts*. 8 vols. Vienna [also available at

	http://stephanus.tlg.uci.edu/lbg/].
LGGA	Montanari, F., ed. 2015–. *Lexicon of Greek Grammarians of Antiquity*. BrillOnline Reference Works. Available to subscribers at http://referenceworks.brillonline.com/browse/lexicon-of-greek-grammarians-of-antiquity.
Matthiae	Matthiae, A., ed. 1813–1837. *Euripidis Tragoediae et Fragmenta, recensuit interpretationem Latinam correxit, scholia graeca e codicibus manuscriptis partim supplevit partim emendavit Augustus Matthiae*. 10 vols. Leipzig.
Paroem. Gr.	Leutsch, E. v., and Schneidewin, F. G., eds. 1839–1851. *Corpus Paroemiographorum Graecorum*. 2 vols. Göttingen.
PG	*Patrologia Graeca*.
PLP	Trapp, E., et al., eds. 1976–1996. *Prosopographisches Lexikon der Palaiologenzeit*. 12 fascicles. Veröffentlichungen der Kommission fur Byzantinistik, Bd. 1. Vienna.
P-W	Prinz, R., and Wecklein, N. 1872–1902. *Euripidis Fabulae*. 3 vols. Leipzig.
RE	Pauly, A., and Wissowa, G., eds. 1884–1978. *Realenzyklopädie der classischen Altertumswissenschaft*. Leipzig.
RGK	*Repertorium der griechischen Kopisten 800–1600*. 1981–1997. 3 vols. in 9. Veröffentlichungen der Kommission für Byzantinistik, Bd. 3. Vienna.
SchArist	Koster, W. J. W., Holwerda, D., et al., eds. 1960–2007. *Scholia in Aristophanem*. 4 vols. in 18. Groningen.
Schwartz	Schwartz, E., ed. 1887–1891. *Scholia in Euripidem*. 2 vols. Berlin.
SuppHell	Lloyd-Jones, H., and Parsons, P. J., eds. 1983. *Supplementum Hellenisticum*. Berlin.
TLG	Thesaurus Linguae Graecae. Available to subscribers at http://stephanus.tlg.uci.edu/index.php.
TrGF	Snell, B., Kannicht, R., and Radt, S., eds. 1971–2005. *Tragicorum Graecorum Fragmenta*. 5 vols. in 6. Berlin.

Abbreviations for Scholia References

Abbreviations of ancient authors' names and works are in standard forms. Note that references to particular scholia are made in the format Sch. Hec. 371 (Eur. is not included) or Sch. Arist. Nubes 987 or Sch. T Od. 6.114, all without italics. When Eustathius' commentary on *Iliad* is referred to, it is by relevant book and line number of the epic followed by, in parentheses, the volume number, page, and line numbers in Van der Valk's edition (as in the TLG; the reference by the page and line numbers of the Roman edition is not given).

Abbreviations for Sigla and Apparatus Criticus

The manuscripts to which sigla refer can be identified from the lists in the following section.

In this book a siglum occasionally has a superscript added, according to the following usage (with A used as an arbitrary siglum):

A^s the item is above the line, not in the margins of the codex.

A^2, A^3 hand (or a stage of adding to a manuscript) distinguished from the main hand of the text and scholia (or the stage at which the text and scholia were first written out).

A^a, A^b different instances of the same note written by the same scribe.

When variants are provided in an apparatus, the following abbreviations may appear:

a.c.	before correction
add.	adds, has in addition
p.c.	after correction
prep.	preposes, has added at the beginning
om.	omits, does not attest
scr.	writes, written
s.l.	above the line
κτλ	and the remaining (words to the end of the passage)
( )	at end of a Greek word indicates that the scribe has truncated the word and not provided any explicit information about the intended ending
(ου)	indicates the spelling out of an abbreviation

SIGLA FOR MANUSCRIPTS OF EURIPIDES

In the Euripidean scholia project, I am adopting so far as possible the sigla that have been established over several decades in the discussions of the textual tradition or of the scholia by Turyn 1957, Matthiessen 1974, Mastronarde and Bremer 1982, Diggle 1991, Günther 1995, Merro 2008, Cavarzeran 2016, or in some cases used in the OCT of Diggle. Since Günther's book is such an extensive discussion of the scholia, in several cases I give priority to his sigla over Diggle's for the convenience of those discussing the Palaeologan scholia. In other cases, it has been impossible to maintain consistency with Diggle because he sometimes used the same siglum for different witnesses for different plays.

This is not a complete list of manuscripts of Euripides, but instead includes only those that have been assigned a siglum. The following compilation of the sigla (136 in all) also includes a few new ones created to refer to witnesses not previously designated. For fuller descriptions of manuscripts and the hands and annotations in them, as well as bibliography, see the listing at EuripidesScholia.org, which will be updated as necessary. Note that some of these manuscripts contain only the text of some plays or the plays plus argumenta, but no scholia.

An asterisk after the shelfmark indicates that the manuscript (or edition) can be viewed online (as far as I could determine in summer and fall 2017), and a list of general URLs is appended. (Some of the Vatican images posted in lieu of eventual new high-quality images are old digitizations of microfilm and a few, such as for P, are more or less useless for reading annotations.) Note that for the Laurentian plutei I use numeration in the form 31.10 or 32.09 (as recognized by the online site's search function) rather than the traditional form (31,10 or 32,9). The "numéro Diktyon" is the reference number of the manuscript database at Pinakes (pinakes.irht.cnrs.fr), which provides the quickest way to locate a particular record there.

xviii SIGLA FOR MANUSCRIPTS OF EURIPIDES

List 1: by city

siglum	location, library shelfmark, date	other sigla, or other uses of a siglum	numéro Diktyon
Ja	Athens, Ethn. Bibl. 1057, late 15th c.		3353
Ad	Athos, Dionysiou 334, 15th c.		20302
W	Athos, Iviron (Iberorum) 161 (Lambros) (Monastery shelf no. 209), ca. 1300	E Diggle; used by P-W for Π² of *Rhesus*	23758
Si	Athos, Iviron (Iberorum) 185 (Lambros = Monastery shelf no. 438), 15th c.		23782
gV	Athos, Vatopediou 36 (Lamberz), (early?) 12th c.	Ga Matthiessen	18183
At	Athos, Vatopediou 671 (Arkadios-Eustratiades), 1420–1443		18815
Pk	Cambridge, Corpus Christi College 403*, 15th c. (end)	Xc Diggle; C.C.C. Matthiae, C Porson	11831
Co	Cambridge, Univ. Libr. Dd.11.70, 16th c.		12149
Zx	Cambridge, Univ. Libr. Mm.1.11, ca. 1330–1340	Cant. Porson, Matthiae; Mm Mastronarde and Bremer, Diggle	12225
J	Cambridge, Univ. Libr. Nn.3.13, ca. 1480		12243
Z	Cambridge, Univ. Libr. Nn.3.14, 1320–1330	fol. 1–121 only	12244
Zd	Cambridge, Univ. Libr. Nn.3.14, 1450–1500	fol. 122–207 only	12244
Hn	Copenhagen, GKS 417, ca. 1475	Haun Diggle, C P-W	37158
Zc	Copenhagen, GKS 3549, early 14th c.	H Schwartz (*vita*)	37215
Cr	Cremona, Bibl. Gov. 130, ca. 1350 (or 1330–1340)		13187
gE	El Escorial, X.I.13, early 14th c.	Ge Matthiessen	14971
Ae	El Escorial, Ω.I.9, 16th c.		15059
Xc	Florence, Laur. conv. sopp. 11, 1320–1330	Flor. 56 Matthiae, Dindorf	15785
K	Florence, Laur. conv. sopp. 66, ca. 1291	used by P-W and Diggle *Hipp.* for codex P. Berol. 5005	15814
Xb	Florence, Laur. conv. sopp. 71, early 14th c. (perhaps 1310–1320)	Flor. 76 Matthiae, Dindorf	15817
Yf	Florence, Laur. conv. sopp. 98, 14th c.	Flor. 59 Matthiae, Dindorf	15830
P	Florence, Laur. conv. sopp. 172, 1320–1325	G P-W	15874

SIGLA FOR MANUSCRIPTS OF EURIPIDES   xix

Sb	Florence, Laur. plut. 31.03*, 1287		16234
Lb	Florence, Laur. plut. 31.06*, 15th c. (end)	Fl. 6 Matthiae, Dindorf (who use same for La)	16237
O	Florence, Laur. plut. 31.10*, ca. 1175 (or earlier?)	Flor. 10 Matthiae, Dindorf; c P-W	16241
D	Florence, Laur. plut. 31.15*, 14th c.	d P-W	16245
Lr	Florence, Laur. plut. 31.17*, 1431	Flor. 17 Matthiae, Dindorf	16247
Lp	Florence, Laur. plut. 31.21*, 1450–1475	Flor. 21 Matthiae, Dindorf	16251
L	Florence, Laur. plut. 32.02*, 1300–1320		16268
Rf	Florence, Laur. plut. 32.33*, ca. 1290–1300	Flor. 33 Matthiae, Dindorf	16297
La	Florence, Laur. plut. 91sup.6*, ca. 1495	Fl. 6 Matthiae, Dindorf (who use same for Lb)	16866
Pl	Heidelberg, Palat. gr. 18*, 14th c.		32452
H	Jerusalem, Patriarchal Libr. Τάφου 36, ca. 1000	h P-W	35273
Lv	Leeuwarden, Provinciale Bibliotheek van Friesland 34, 16th c.		37614
Le	Leiden, Vossianus gr. Q 33, 1475–1500		38140
Zl	London, Additional 10057*, 1340–1350		38827
Za	London, Arundel 540*, 1450–1475		39291
U	London, Harley 5725*, ca. 1500	used by Diggle *Andr.* for Lw	39653
Q	London, Harley 5743*, ca. 1475	Q first half *Tro.*, q second half Diggle; H P-W	39671
Hl	London, Harley 6300*, 1500–1525	J Porson	39695
Lw	Louvain, Louaniensis deperditus, 6th–7th c.(?)	U Diggle *Andr.*	
Mt	Madrid, Bibl. Nacional 4677, ca. 1300		40164
Ry	Manchester, Rylands 1689, 14th c. (end)		
Xm	Milan, Ambros. B 97 sup., 1320–1330		42342
Aa	Milan, Ambros. C 44 sup., 14th c.		42409
Ab	Milan, Ambros. F 74 sup., ca.1300		42757
Xn	Milan, Ambros. G 43 sup., 1310–1320		42809
Zm	Milan, Ambros. I 47 sup., early 14th c. (perhaps 1310–1320)		42903
G	Milan, Ambros. L 39 sup., ca. 1320	Q Schwartz (*vita, hyp. Hec.*)	42949

SIGLA FOR MANUSCRIPTS OF EURIPIDES

Ao	Milan, Ambros. O 123 sup., 16th c.	Mb Merro	43074
Af	Milan, Ambros. S.P. 10/26c, (formerly Ambros. F 205 inf.), 13th c.	Af Diggle *Rhesus*, W Diggle *Andr.*; D P-W	42792
Me	Modena, Bibl. Estense α.Q.5.19, 15th c.		43381
Xe	Modena, Bibl. Estense α.U.9.19, 1310–1320		43486
Mo	Modena, Bibl. Estense α.U.9.22, 1450–1475	used by Diggle *Hec.* for Mq; used by Diggle *Or.* for Munich 510	43489
Es	Modena, Bibl. Estense γ.L.11.23, 15 c.		43557
Ms	Moscow, Gos. Istor. Muzei, Synod. Bibl. gr. 272 (Vlad. 508), 15th c.		43897
Mq	Moscow, Gos. Istor. Muzei, Synod. Bibl. gr. 501 (Vlad. 480), 1603?	Mo Diggle *Hec.*	44126
Dr	Moscow (formerly Dresden), Rossijskij Gosudarstvennyj Archiv Drevnich Aktov (RGADA), Ф.1607, Dresden Da 22, 15th c.		44398
Zs	Mt. Sinai, Sinaiticus gr. 1196, ca. 1330		59571
Mc	Munich, Cod. gr. 258, 1504–1525		44705
Mn	Munich, Cod. gr. 560*, 14th c. (early?)	C Matthiae, Dindorf	45008
Y	Naples, II.F.9, ca. 1320–1330	a Schwartz, N Cobet and P-W, Neap. Diggle	46177
Yn	Naples, II.F.37, ca. 1300		46206
N	Naples, II.F.41, 1504–1525		46210
Ne	Naples, Vindob. Gr. 17 (former Vienna Suppl. gr. 19), 1450–1500		45973
X	Oxford, Auct. F.3.25, ca. 1330–1340		47085
Ox	Oxford, Auct. T.4.10, 1326 / late 15th c.		47196
Xa	Oxford, Barocci 120*, ca. 1320–1330		47407
Do	Oxford, D'Orville 72, 1450/51		47835
Jo	Oxford, D'Orville 73, 15th c. (end)		47836
Xo	Oxford, Laud gr. 54, 14th c. (perhaps ca. 1330)		48275
Pg	Paris, Bibliothèque Sainte-Geneviève 3400, 14th c. (early)	G Schwartz (*vita*), old shelfmark S. Gen. 36	54060
Pc	Paris, grec 1087*, ca.1300		50683
Ua	Paris, grec 2598*, 1467		52233
A	Paris, grec 2712*, ca. 1300	Par. A Matthiae, E P-W	52347
B	Paris, grec 2713*, 11th c. (early)	Par. B Matthiae, b P-W	52348

Xg	Paris, grec 2794 + 2800*, ca. 1340		52431, 52437
Xd	Paris, grec 2795*, ca. 1340	Xe Diggle *Or.*; used by Diggle *Or.* for Paris Coislin 169	52432
Pa	Paris, grec 2801*, 1350–1400	Xf Diggle *Or.*	52438
Xy	Paris, grec 2802*, ca. 1320	Xg Diggle *Or.*	52439
Xh	Paris, grec 2803*, ca. 1450		52440
Ub	Paris, grec 2806*, ca. 1500		52443
Pb	Paris, grec 2810*, 15th c. (end)		52447
Pp	Paris, grec 2815*, 1400–1450		52453
Ph	Paris, grec 2818*, ca. 1500	Pr Cavarzeran	52456
Xf	Paris, grec 2820*, 1320–1330		52458
Jp	Paris, grec 2823*, ca. 1500		52461
Uc	Paris, Suppl. gr. 97*, ca. 1475		52867
Am	Paris, Suppl. gr. 212*, 15th c. (end)		52982
An	Paris, Suppl. gr. 393*, 15th c.		53141
Fp	Parma, Parmensis 154, 1350–1375	Tp Mastronarde and Bremer, Diggle	54164
Pr	Reims, Bibl. Municipale 1306 (J 733)*, ca. 1290–1300		55784
T	Rome, Bibl. Angelica, gr. 14, 1300–1325		55921
S	Salamanca, Bibl. Univ. 31, 1326		56451
Th	Thessalonica, Γυμνάσιον, unnumbered (lost in fire 1890), 16th c.	t P-W	
C	Turin, Bibl. Naz., B.IV.13, 1300–1350	T Matthiae, Dindorf, Schwartz	63719
Zu	Uppsala, Univ. Libr. gr. 15*, 1300–1350		64428
gB	Vatican, Barberin. gr. 4*, ca. 1300	Gb Matthiessen	64552
Vo	Vatican, Ottobon. gr. 339*, 16th c.	O Schwartz; Y Diggle *Andr.*	65582
Zo	Vatican, Ottobon. gr. 346*, 1475–1500		65589
Va	Vatican, Palat. gr. 98, 14th c.	Rom. B Matthiae	65831
Jb	Vatican, Palat. gr. 151, 1475–1500		65883
P	Vatican, Palat. gr. 287*, 1320–1325	Rom. C Matthiae	66019
Vq	Vatican, Palat. gr. 319*, 15th c. (end)		66051
Vr	Vatican, Palat. gr. 343*, ca. 1500	Pv Diggle *Hipp.*	66075
Xu	Vatican, Urbinas gr. 140*, ca. 1320–1330		66607
Ta	Vatican, Urbinas gr. 142*, 1325–1350 (perhaps 1340–1350)		66609
Xr	Vatican, Vatic. gr. 50, ca. 1350		66681
Zb	Vatican, Vatic. gr. 51, 1320–1330		66682
Vb	Vatican, Vatic. gr. 53, 15th c.		66684
Xs	Vatican, Vatic. gr. 56, 1300–1350		66687

V	Vatican, Vatic. gr. 909*, 1250–1280	A Dindorf, Schwartz, Rom. A Matthiae; R Cobet; B P-W	67540
Vn	Vatican, Vatic. gr. 910*, 14th c.	C Diggle *Med. Hipp.*	67541
R	Vatican, Vatic. gr. 1135*, late 13th c.		67766
Ra	Vatican, Vatic. gr. 1325, 15th c.		67956
Rv	Vatican, Vatic. gr. 1332, 14th c.		67963
Sa	Vatican, Vatic. gr. 1345*, ca. 1300	V Schwartz *vita*, hyp. Hec.	67976
Xp	Vatican, Vatic. gr. 1363, ca. 1340		67995
Vd	Vatican, Vatic. gr. 1824* (81r–87v *Or.*), 15th c.	Zv Diggle	68453
Zv	Vatican, Vatic. gr. 1824* (31–37v *Phoen.*), early 14th c. (perhaps ca. 1315)	used by Diggle for Vd	68453
F	Venice, Marc. gr. 468 (coll. 653), late 13th c.	Y Schwartz (*hyp. Hec.*)	69939
Yv	Venice, Marc. gr. 469 (coll. 799), 1413		69940
Mp	Venice, Marc. gr. 470 (coll.824), ca. 1465		69941
M	Venice, Marc. gr. 471 (coll. 765), 1000–1050	V Cobet; A P-W	69942
Xv	Venice, Marc. gr. 515 (coll. 772), ca. 1320–1330		69986
Mb	Venice, Marc. gr. 620 (coll. 890), 1420–1430	used by Merro for Ao	70091
Mu	Venice, Marc. gr. IX 10 (coll. 1160), 1494–1500		70462
Jv	Venice, Marc. gr. IX 15 (coll. 1372), 15th c. (end)		70467
Ml	Venice, Marc. lat. XIV 232 (coll. 4257), 1325–1350		70696
Rw	Vienna, phil. gr. 119, ca. 1300	W Schwartz (*vita*)	71233
Vp	Vienna, phil. gr. 161, 1412		71275
Wp	Vienna, phil. gr. 197, 1400–1450		71311
Gr	Wolfenbüttel, Gud. gr. 15 (first hand), 1320–1330		72059
Gu	Wolfenbüttel, Gud. gr. 15 (second hand), 1320–1330 (or later?)		72059
Arsenius	ed. princeps, 1534*	I Matthiae, Dindorf	
Al	editio Aldina, 1503*	so Matthiessen	

List 2: by siglum

siglum	location, library shelfmark, date	other sigla, or other uses of a siglum	numéro Diktyon
A	Paris, grec 2712*, ca. 1300	Par. A Matthiae, E P-W	52347
Aa	Milan, Ambros. C 44 sup., 14th c.		42409
Ab	Milan, Ambros. F 74 sup., ca.1300		42757
Ad	Athos, Dionysiou 334, 15th c.		20302
Ae	El Escorial, Ω.I.9, 16th c.		15059
Af	Milan, Ambros. S.P. 10/26c, (formerly Ambros. F 205 inf.), 13th c.	Af Diggle *Rhesus*, W Diggle *Andr.*; D P-W	42792
Al	editio Aldina, 1503*	so Matthiessen	
Am	Paris, Suppl. gr. 212*, 15th c. (end)		52982
An	Paris, Suppl. gr. 393*, 15th c.		53141
Ao	Milan, Ambros. O 123 sup., 16th c.	Mb Merro	43074
Arsenius	ed. princeps, 1534*	I Matthiae, Dindorf	
At	Athos, Vatopediou 671 (Arkadios-Eustratiades), 1420–1443		18815
B	Paris, grec 2713*, 11th c. (early)	Par. B Matthiae; b P-W	52348
C	Turin, Bibl. Naz., B.IV.13, 1300–1350	T Matthiae, Dindorf, Schwartz	63719
Co	Cambridge, Univ. Libr. Dd.11.70, 16th c.		12149
Cr	Cremona, Bibl. Gov. 130, ca. 1350 (or 1330–1340)		13187
D	Florence, Laur. plut. 31.15*, 14th c.	d P-W	16245
Do	Oxford, D'Orville 72, 1450/51		47835
Dr	Moscow (formerly Dresden), Rossijskij Gosudarstvennyj Archiv Drevnich Aktov (RGADA), Φ.1607, Dresden Da 22 , 15th c.		44398
Es	Modena, Bibl. Estense γ.L.11.23, 15 c.		43557
F	Venice, Marc. gr. 468 (coll. 653), late 13th c.	Y Schwartz (*hyp. Hec.*)	69939
Fp	Parma, Parmensis 154, 1350–1375	Tp Mastronarde and Bremer, Diggle	54164
G	Milan, Ambros. L 39 sup., ca. 1320	Q Schwartz (*vita, hyp. Hec.*)	42949
gB	Vatican, Barberin. gr. 4*, ca. 1300	Gb Matthiessen	64552
gE	El Escorial, X.I.13, early 14th c.	Ge Matthiessen	14971
Gr	Wolfenbüttel, Gud. gr. 15 (first hand), 1320–1330		72059
Gu	Wolfenbüttel, Gud. gr. 15 (second hand), 1320–1330 (or later?)		72059
gV	Athos, Vatopediou 36 (Lamberz), (early?) 12th c.	Ga Matthiessen	18183

H	Jerusalem, Patriarchal Libr. Τάφου 36, ca. 1000	h P-W	35273
Hl	London, Harley 6300*, 1500–1525	J Porson	39695
Hn	Copenhagen, GKS 417, ca. 1475	Haun Diggle; C P-W	37158
J	Cambridge, Univ. Libr. Nn.3.13, ca. 1480		12243
Ja	Athens, Ethn. Bibl. 1057, late 15th c.		3353
Jb	Vatican, Palat. gr. 151, 1475–1500		65883
Jo	Oxford, D'Orville 73, 15th c. (end)		47836
Jp	Paris, grec 2823*, ca. 1500		52461
Jv	Venice, Marc. gr. IX 15 (coll. 1372), 15th c. (end)		70467
K	Florence, Laur. conv. sopp. 66, ca. 1291	used by P-W, Diggle *Hipp.* for codex P. Berol. 5005	15814
L	Florence, Laur. plut. 32.02*, 1300–1320		16268
La	Florence, Laur. plut. 91sup.6*, ca. 1495	Fl. 6 Matthiae, Dindorf (who use same for Lb)	16866
Lb	Florence, Laur. plut. 31.06*, 15th c. (end)	Fl. 6 Matthiae, Dindorf (who use same for La)	16237
Le	Leiden, Vossianus gr. Q 33, 1475–1500		38140
Lp	Florence, Laur. plut. 31.21*, 1450–1475	Flor. 21 Matthiae, Dindorf	16251
Lr	Florence, Laur. plut. 31.17*, 1431		16247
Lv	Leeuwarden, Provinciale Bibliotheek van Friesland 34, 16th c.		37614
Lw	Louvain, Louaniensis deperditus, 6th–7th c.(?)	U Diggle *Andr.*	
M	Venice, Marc. gr. 471 (coll. 765), 1000–1050	V Cobet, A P-W	69942
Mb	Venice, Marc. gr. 620 (coll. 890), 1420–1430	used by Merro for Ao	70091
Mc	Munich, Cod. gr. 258, 1504–1525		44705
Me	Modena, Bibl. Estense α.Q.5.19, 15th c.		43381
Ml	Venice, Marc. lat. XIV 232 (coll. 4257), 1325–1350		70696
Mn	Munich, Cod. gr. 560*, 14th c. (early?)	C Matthiae, Dindorf	45008
Mo	Modena, Bibl. Estense α.U.9.22, 1450–1475	used by Diggle *Hec.* for Mq; used by Diggle *Or.* for Munich 510	43489
Mp	Venice, Marc. gr. 470 (coll.824), ca. 1465		69941

Mq	Moscow, Gos. Istor. Muzei, Synod. Bibl. gr. 501 (Vlad. 480), 1603?	Mo Diggle *Hec.*	44126
Ms	Moscow, Gos. Istor. Muzei, Synod. Bibl. gr. 272 (Vlad. 508), 15th c.		43897
Mt	Madrid, Bibl. Nacional 4677, ca. 1300		40164
Mu	Venice, Marc. gr. IX 10 (coll. 1160), 1494–1500		70462
N	Naples, II.F.41, 1504–1525		46210
Ne	Naples, Vindob. Gr. 17 (former Vienna Suppl. gr. 19), 1450–1500		45973
O	Florence, Laur. plut. 31.10*, ca. 1175 (or earlier?)	Flor. 10 Matthiae, Dindorf, c P-W	16241
Ox	Oxford, Auct. T.4.10, 1326 / late 15th c.		47196
P	Florence, Laur. conv. sopp. 172, 1320–1325	G P-W	15874
P	Vatican, Palat. gr. 287*, 1320–1325	Rom. C Matthiae	66019
Pa	Paris, grec 2801*, 1350–1400	Xf Diggle *Or.*	52438
Pb	Paris, grec 2810*, 15th c. (end)		52447
Pc	Paris, grec 1087*, ca.1300		50683
Pg	Paris, Bibliothèque Sainte-Geneviève 3400, 14th c. (early)	G Schwartz (*vita*), old shelfmark S. Gen. 36	54060
Ph	Paris, grec 2818*, ca. 1500	Pr Cavarzeran	52456
Pk	Cambridge, Corpus Christi College 403*, 15th c. (end)	Xc Diggle; C.C.C. Matthiae, C Porson	11831
Pl	Heidelberg, Palat. gr. 18*, 14th c.		32452
Pp	Paris, grec 2815*, 1400–1450		52453
Pr	Reims, Bibl. Municipale 1306 (J 733)*, ca. 1290–1300		55784
Q	London, Harley 5743*, ca. 1475	Q first half *Tro.*, q second half Diggle; H P=W	39671
R	Vatican, Vatic. gr. 1135*, late 13th c.		67766
Ra	Vatican, Vatic. gr. 1325, 15th c.		67956
Rf	Florence, Laur. plut. 32.33*, ca. 1290–1300	Flor. 33 Matthiae, Dindorf	16297
Rv	Vatican, Vatic. gr. 1332, 14th c.		67963
Rw	Vienna, phil. gr. 119, ca. 1300	W Schwartz (*vita*)	71233
Ry	Manchester, Rylands 1689, 14th c. (end)		
S	Salamanca, Bibl. Univ. 31, 1326		56451
Sa	Vatican, Vatic. gr. 1345*, ca. 1300	V Schwartz *vita*, hyp. *Hec.*	67976
Sb	Florence, Laur. plut. 31.03*, 1287		16234
Si	Athos, Iviron (Iberorum) 185 (Lambros = Monastery shelf no. 438), 15th c.		23782

T	Rome, Bibl. Angelica, gr. 14, 1300–1325		55921
Ta	Vatican, Urbinas gr. 142*, 1325–1350 (perhaps 1340–1350)		66609
Th	Thessalonica, Γυμνάσιον, unnumbered (lost in fire 1890), 16th c.	t P-W	
U	London, Harley 5725*, ca. 1500	used by Diggle *Andr.* for Lw	39653
Ua	Paris, grec 2598*, 1467		52233
Ub	Paris, grec 2806*, ca. 1500		52443
Uc	Paris, Suppl. gr. 97*, ca. 1475		52867
V	Vatican, Vatic. gr. 909*, 1250–1280	A Dindorf, Schwartz, Rom. A Matthiae; R Cobet; B P-W	67540
Va	Vatican, Palat. gr. 98, 14th c.	Rom. B Matthiae	65831
Vb	Vatican, Vatic. gr. 53, 15th c.		66684
Vd	Vatican, Vatic. gr. 1824* (81r–87v *Or.*), 15th c.	Zv Diggle	68453
Vn	Vatican, Vatic. gr. 910*, 14th c.	C Diggle *Med. Hipp.*	67541
Vo	Vatican, Ottobon. gr. 339*, 16th c.	O Schwartz; Y Diggle *Andr.*	65582
Vp	Vienna, phil. gr. 161, 1412		71275
Vq	Vatican, Palat. gr. 319*, 15th c. (end)		66051
Vr	Vatican, Palat. gr. 343*, ca. 1500	Pv Diggle *Hipp.*	66075
W	Athos, Iviron (Iberorum) 161 (Lambros = Monastery shelf no. 209), ca. 1300	E Diggle; used by P-W for Π^2 of *Rhesus*	23758
Wp	Vienna, phil. gr. 197, 1400–1450		71311
X	Oxford, Auct. F.3.25, ca. 1330–1340		47085
Xa	Oxford, Barocci 120*, ca. 1320–1330		47407
Xb	Florence, Laur. conv. sopp. 71, early 14th c. (perhaps 1310–1320)	Flor. 76 Matthiae, Dindorf	15817
Xc	Florence, Laur. conv. sopp. 11, 1320–1330	Flor. 56 Matthiae, Dindorf	15785
Xd	Paris, grec 2795*, ca. 1340	Xe Diggle *Or.*; used by Diggle *Or.* for Paris Coislin 169	52432
Xe	Modena, Bibl. Estense α.U.9.19, 1310–1320		43486
Xf	Paris, grec 2820*, 1320–1330		52458
Xg	Paris, grec 2794 + 2800*, ca. 1340		52431, 52437
Xh	Paris, grec 2803*, ca. 1450		52440
Xm	Milan, Ambros. B 97 sup., 1320–1330		42342

Xn	Milan, Ambros. G 43 sup., 1310–1320		42809
Xo	Oxford, Laud gr. 54, 14th c. (perhaps ca. 1330)		48275
Xp	Vatican, Vatic. gr. 1363, ca. 1340		67995
Xr	Vatican, Vatic. gr. 50, ca. 1350		66681
Xs	Vatican, Vatic. gr. 56, 1300–1350		66687
Xu	Vatican, Urbinas gr. 140*, ca. 1320–1330		66607
Xv	Venice, Marc. gr. 515 (coll. 772), ca. 1320–1330		69986
Xy	Paris, grec 2802*, ca. 1320	Xg Diggle *Or.*	52439
Y	Naples, II.F.9, ca. 1320–1330	a Schwartz, N Cobet and P-W, Neap. Diggle	46177
Yf	Florence, Laur. conv. sopp. 98, 14th c.	Flor. 59 Matthiae, Dindorf	15830
Yn	Naples, II.F.37, ca. 1300		46206
Yv	Venice, Marc. gr. 469 (coll. 799), 1413		69940
Z	Cambridge, Univ. Libr. Nn.3.14, 1320–1330	fol. 1–121 only	12244
Za	London, Arundel 540*, 1450–1475		39291
Zb	Vatican, Vatic. gr. 51, 1320–1330		66682
Zc	Copenhagen, GKS 3549, early 14th c.	H Schwartz (*vita*)	37215
Zd	Cambridge, Univ. Libr. Nn.3.14, 1450–1500	fol. 122–207 only	12244
Zl	London, Additional 10057*, 1340–1350		38827
Zm	Milan, Ambros. I 47 sup., early 14th c. (perhaps 1310–1320)		42903
Zo	Vatican, Ottobon. gr. 346*, 1475–1500		65589
Zs	Mt. Sinai, Sinaiticus gr. 1196, ca. 1330		59571
Zu	Uppsala, Univ. Libr. gr. 15*, 1300–1350		64428
Zv	Vatican, Vatic. gr. 1824* (31–37v *Phoen.*), early 14th c. (perhaps ca. 1315)		68453
Zx	Cambridge, Univ. Libr. Mm.1.11, ca. 1330–1340	Cant. Porson, Matthiae; Mm Mastronarde and Bremer, Diggle	12225

Other manuscripts with previous sigla, not adopted:

Florence	Laur. plut. 31.01*	apogr. Flor. Diggle *Hel.* (copy of L)
Florence	Riccardianus 77	apogr. Flor. Diggle, vol. 2 (copy of L)
London	Additional 4952*	L Porson
London	Arundel 522*	K Porson
Munich	graecus 510	Mo Diggle *Or.*
Paris	Coislon 169	Xd Diggle *Or.*
Paris	grec 2813*	Z Schwartz, *hyp. Hec.*
Paris	grec 2817*	apogr. Par. Diggle (copy of L)
Paris	grec 2887*	apogr. Par. Diggle (copy of L)

URLs for online images in the relevant collections:

Cambridge, Corpus Christi College: parker.stanford.edu/parker/ (by subscription)
Florence, Biblioteca Medicea Laurenziana: teca.bmlonline.it (new version at mss.bmlonline.it, but inoperable as of late 2017)
Heidelberg: digi.ub.uni-heidelberg.de/diglit/cpgraec18/
London: www.bl.uk/manuscripts/Default.aspx
Munich: www.digitale-sammlungen.de/index.html (for Mn search "cod.graec. 560")
Oxford: digital.bodleian.ox.ac.uk
Paris: gallica.bnf.fr
Reims: (interim access) bvmm.irht.cnrs.fr/resultRecherche/resultRecherche.php?COMPOSITION_ID=16215 (new presentation at www.bm-reims.fr is planned for 2018)
Vatican: digi.vatlib.it
Arsenius: books.google.com (https://books.google.com/books?id=6vlPAAAAcAAJ)
Aldine edition: hathitrust.org (https://hdl.handle.net/2027/ucm.5316862907)

LIST OF PLATES

1. Abbreviations in M
2. Letter Forms in M
3. Letter Forms and Abbreviations in M
4. Abbreviations and *hermēneia* Notations in M
5. Truncation in V and Hands of V
6. Ligatures in V
7. Letter Forms in V

Preliminary Studies on the Scholia to Euripides

CHAPTER 1

The Scholia and the Ancient and Medieval Tradition of Commenting on Euripides

1. EDITING THE SCHOLIA

Scholia have survived in the medieval tradition of a selection of nine plays of Euripides.[1] As with Aeschylus, Sophocles, and Aristophanes, a triad of his plays received the most attention from readers, teachers, scholars, and copyists during the middle and late Byzantine periods: *Hecuba*, *Orestes*, and *Phoenissae* (to which I will frequently refer as "the triad" or "the triad plays"). The other select plays (which may be termed "non-triad") that have annotations are *Hippolytus*, *Medea*, *Andromache*, *Alcestis*, *Rhesus*, *Troades*: the first two have substantial corpora of notes, the second pair somewhat less, and the annotation that survives on *Rhesus* and *Troades* is rather sparse.[2]

A large collection of scholia on seven of the plays of Euripides (*Rhesus* and *Troades* were not yet included) was first compiled for publication in the 16th century by Aristobulus Apostolis (or Apostolius), an emigré scholar from Crete who often worked in Venice. Aristobulus is also known as Arsenius of Monemvasia (a small island just off the coast of southeastern Laconia), where he was archbishop for a time, and the latter is the name used on the title page of his

---

[1] The origin of the selection is uncertain. Before the accumulation of the evidence of ancient bookrolls and codices provided by papyri (and parchments) from Egypt, it was held to have come about by a deliberate process as early as the 2nd century CE. If the selection was deliberate, it probably arose at least two or three centuries later than that. It cannot be excluded, however, that there were multiple smaller collections that eventually fed into what we find in the Byzantine manuscripts. See Mastronarde 2017a for further discussion and references.
[2] *Bacchae* was the tenth play in the selection, and has barely survived in the manuscript tradition as the text only, without annotation.

edition, which was published in Venice in 1534, the year before his death.[3] This collection of scholia was reprinted frequently into the 17th and 18th centuries, with minor changes in the wording and in the order of the notes.[4] Even in the 19th century, in the edition of August Matthiae the scholia that are not followed by a manuscript siglum are carried over from the Arsenian tradition, while in the edition of Wilhelm Dindorf the items from Arsenius are given the siglum I, on a par with the sigla for the manuscripts he used. Arsenius drew upon more than one source for his collection, and it is likely that he sometimes produced his own combinations of pre-existing material or added phrases of his own to them. Many scholia have variants proving dependency on B and/or its apographs.[5] Some of the long continuous paraphrasing scholia for *Hecuba* and *Orestes* attested only in Arsenius were evidently created by minor modifications (mostly by subtraction of the words that already appear in the poetic text) of the paraphrases that survive in the manuscript Yv. On the other hand, the long paraphrases for *Phoenissae*, as well as many of the Arsenian paraphrases of single lines or of couplets for all the triad plays, differ considerably from the paraphrases in Yv on the same passages. For such divergent paraphrases, no source has yet been identified in extant copies, and they may have been created by Arsenius himself by a process of stitching together glosses he found in the manuscripts.[6]

Serious attention to the manuscript sources and to the emendation of the scholia began with Valckenaer's *Phoenissae* in 1755.[7] In a separately paginated appendix, he edited the scholia on *Phoenissae* only, distinguishing between those from the vulgate printed tradition (Arsenius), those added by Barnes, Piers, and King from copies in Oxford and Cambridge, those he transcribed himself from a Leiden codex, and those transcribed from Mn a few generations earlier by G. F.

---

[3] Arsenius 1534. For a discussion of Arsenius' life and activities see Geanakoplos 1962: 167–200; Bietenholz and Deutscher 1985: 68–69; Flamand 2017 (with further references).

[4] Thus wherever there is a need to be certain what Arsenius himself printed, it is necessary to check the original printing rather than rely on any of the reprints. The first reprint with some corrections was that of Hervagius in Basel: Arsenius 1544. Among the later complete editions of Euripides that included the Arsenian collection were those of Paulus Stephanus 1602 and of Joshua Barnes 1694.

[5] See Cavarzeran 2016: 57–63 for discussion and examples from Sch. Hipp. For a detailed demonstration of how Arsenius drew on multiple sources, surviving and lost, when he gathered and "edited" scholia on the *Odyssey* (also making changes of phrasing and apparently correcting some corrupt passages by conjecture) see Pontani 2011: 486–502.

[6] For some examples showing the similarities and differences between Yv and the Arsenian notes, see the Appendix to this chapter. I defer a fuller analysis of Arsenius' sources to a later date, when I will have a much more complete inventory of scholia on *Hecuba*, *Orestes*, and *Phoenissae*.

[7] See also Cavarzeran 2016: 66–69 for a commented bibliography of the editions of scholia to *Hippolytus* from Arsenius to Schwartz.

Tryllitsch.⁸ Compilation of this kind was extended further by the work of August Matthiae, who edited the scholia on the usual seven plays in 1817–1818 as part of his multi-volume edition of Euripides.⁹ The scholia on *Rhesus* and *Troades*, as transcribed imperfectly (because of the poor condition of the codex at that time) from V (Vat. gr. 909) by Hieronymus Amatius (Girolamo Amati, 1768–1834), were first printed in 1821,¹⁰ and improved in 1837 by the editorial attention of two scholars, C. F. Kampmann and (*Rhesus* only) F. Vater.¹¹ In the middle of the 19th century, when Adolf Kirchhoff and August Nauck produced the first editions of Euripides' plays based on the older manuscripts, eschewing the "Byzantine" (that is, Palaeologan) witnesses, Wilhelm Dindorf's scholia edition of 1863¹² was able to include a larger proportion of the scholia in the older manuscripts than previously, but he still incorporated many from younger witnesses, and his work can be thought of as the last flowering of the polymathic textual scholarship that antedated modern editorial method. One can get some idea of the work of the Palaeologan scholars Moschopulus, Thomas, and Triclinius from Dindorf, but his sources were almost always at several removes from the earliest available evidence, and the material that he did include is distorted by omissions and additions.¹³ In contrast, the edition of the old scholia by Eduard Schwartz

---

⁸ Valckenaer 1755. For Tryllitsch (1688–1715), see pp. vi–vii of Valckenaer's preface. The Oxford manuscript is Bodleian Library, Barocci 74, early 16th century, a transcription of most of the annotation, but no text, from a Triclinian witness (Turyn 1957: 197). The Cambridge manuscript is Corpus Christi College 403 (Pk), 15th century, with Moschopulean and other scholia (Turyn 1957: 123). The Leiden codex is Bibliothek der Rijks-Universiteit, Vossianus graecus Q 33, ca. 1500, with various scholia from a Triclinian source and from elsewhere (Turyn 1957: 339).

⁹ Matthiae 1813–1837. His vol. 4 (1817) contains scholia on *Hecuba* and *Orestes*; vol. 5 (1818) contains scholia on *Phoenissae*, *Hippolytus*, *Medea*, *Alcestis*, *Andromache*, and a few scholia (Triclinius') on the alphabetic plays from L.

¹⁰ In the Glasgow ed. 5:581–610. Amati's transcription also appeared, with a few notes supplying emendations, in (Ludwig) Dindorf 1825: 445–483.

¹¹ Kampmann in Matthiae, vol. 10: 119–162; Vater 1837. Using M as well as V, C. G. Cobet edited a small selection of emended or previously unpublished scholia on all nine plays in Geel 1846: 249–310.

¹² Dindorf vol. 1 contains preface, versions of the *Life of Euripides*, scholia on *Rhesus*, *Troades*, *Hippolytus*, *Hecuba*; vol. 2 contains scholia on *Orestes*; vol. 3 contains scholia on *Phoenissae*; vol. 4 contains scholia on *Medea*, *Alcestis*, *Andromache*, addenda and index.

¹³ A full assessment of the gains for knowledge of the Palaeologan scholars' scholia must await the completion of fuller collations of the whole triad in at least a dozen manuscripts. From current samples (very complete for *Orestes* 1–500, sporadic for scattered passages elsewhere in the triad), it is clear that the main defects in Dindorf are the use of an incomplete and sometimes corrupt source for the Triclinian material and the unreliability of the distinction between Gr and Gu (Gr is usually writing Mochopulean notes, but sometimes Thoman ones, and Gu is usually writing Thoman notes, but sometimes Moschopulean ones); moreover, Gu at times alters wording, or adds notes from other sources or his own composition.

(1887–1891)[14] may be regarded, so far as I know, as the first scientifically rigorous edition of scholia on Greek poetry.[15]

In a way that is often typical of the 19th-century approach to manuscript sources, Schwartz exercised a degree of selectivity that sometimes creates a misleading impression or that suppresses material that other scholars would consider important. This is most apparent in the scholia on the triad, since the paucity of sources for the other plays somewhat reduced any tendency to be selective, but has recently been made clear for *Hippolytus* as well in Cavarzeran's new edition. Schwartz believed that his edition could present an assumed single and uniform recension of the scholia that existed in manuscripts earlier than the 11th century.[16] It seems to me far more likely that there were always variant collections of annotation, with different notes included, with shorter and longer versions of what were essentially the same note, and with more or less polished versions of the same note. Editors of Euripides have observed that Schwartz did not have a sound principle for informing his readers about the lemmata: in vol. I he simply gives the lemma in M, if it has one, and elsewhere he occasionally identifies the source of a lemma he prints, but without indication of variant lemma readings in other witnesses. He inspected a number of manuscripts of the Palaeologan period or later (some of those now called *recentiores* for the text of the triad), but cited them only when he judged that they correctly filled a lacuna in his main manuscripts or offered correct names in mythological or genealogical notes. His collations of M, B, and V were extremely detailed and of admirable accuracy in view of the fact that he did not have access to an ultraviolet lamp or digital images to enlarge. But even for these three manuscripts, he did not report everything. Some of the M-scholia for *Hippolytus* are shorter versions of scholia found in the other witnesses, and Schwartz did not always record these (some, but not all, of these neglected scholia are very damaged and can now be partially read only under ultraviolet light). Schwartz believed that B was of the 13th century, whereas experts now place it in the 11th, and thus as old as or older than

---

[14] Vol. I contains the scholia on the triad plays, vol. II those on the other select plays, along with a detailed index.

[15] See Wilamowitz 1887, a review of volume I, for the approval of reducing the mass of scholia on the triad to one third of the length in Dindorf, and for the hope that when a new edition is prepared in a few generations the future editor will exclude even more scholia than Schwartz. On the difficulties and history of editing scholiastic corpora see Pontani 2016: 313–318; at 315 n. 10 he cites Schwartz's edition along with the Pindar scholia of Drachmann 1903–1927 as exceptional examples earlier than the massive edition of the Aristophanes scholia (Koster, Holwerda et al. 1960–2007) and the acclaimed edition of some important *Iliad* scholia, Erbse 1969–1988.

[16] Schwartz I.ix: *eam igitur philologis praebuisse recensionem mihi videor quae cum codicibus saeculo XI antiquioribus tradita esset, per quattuor illos supra indicatos* [scil. our MBCV] *quamvis mutata et varia tamen si omnia spectaveris una eademque conservata est.*

M.[17] This misdating may have contributed to his policy of reporting some of B's unique versions of scholia only in his apparatus[18] as well as to his decision not to report B for *Andromache*.[19] Schwartz's collation of the Turin manuscript C was, as he himself noted, much more hurried and suffers from omissions and from more frequent inaccuracies than for MBV.

The unfortunate effects of Schwartz's selectivity are most severe if one is pursuing the goal of understanding the circulation and reuse of annotations on Euripides throughout the Byzantine period, rather than the supposedly original 9th- or 10th-century version of a corpus of scholia. Every annotated manuscript of Euripides (as of other classical authors) has something to tell us about the resources, the interests, and the skill-level of a particular scribe or scriptorium at a particular time. This is as true of the older surviving manuscripts as it is of the more recent ones. But Schwartz's edition is not complete even in the treatment of the glosses in M, and is far more selective for BV, and especially incomplete in regard to C.[20] Thus it is impossible to make a sound judgment of what the collaborating (early Palaeologan, or even Nicaean?) scribes of V[21] were doing when they transcribed a generous set of discursive scholia from an older and partially damaged exemplar and also entered supralinear notes of various types, unless one obtains a complete picture of what is present in the extant earlier witnesses, M, B, O (where annotated), and H (where extant and legible). The same is true of the annotations of the famous Palaeologan scholars Manuel Moschopulus, Thomas Magister, and Demetrius Triclinius. With the guidance provided by Triclinius' autograph annotations in T and with the evidence of a number of manuscripts (identified by Turyn and Günther)[22] containing fairly uniform sets of the annotations, it is indeed possible to identify most of the Palaeologan scholia compiled by these named scholars. But in order to understand how these

---

[17] The 11th-century date of B was favored by Omont, Vitelli, and T. W. Allen (as noted by Turyn 1957: 87 n. 140), has been accepted by most editors of Euripides for a couple of generations, and is endorsed in the recent online description at gallica.fr. A 12-century date of B was accepted in an earlier work by Omont and by Turyn in 1957, and has been revived without adequate justification by Tuilier 2010. Schwartz assumed M was of the 12th century, but it should be dated to the 11th: see Chapter 4.

[18] With the consequence that they are not present in the corpus digitized by the TLG.

[19] Schwartz II.iv: *codicem Parisinum 2713 in Andromachae scholiis prorsus abiciendum esse intellexi postquam eum totum contuli; adeo brevem et in peius mutatum recensionem praebet.* Moreover, for *Andromache* V contains, entered above many lines by the original hand, a number of sentence-length paraphrasing scholia not reported by Schwartz (and usually not in Dindorf either), omitted apparently on the same principle by which he omitted a large number of V's glosses.

[20] Schwartz I.viii: *in codice Taurinensi haec genera* [scil. supralinear glosses, intermarginal notes, marked distinctively in reporting MBV] *non distinxi quoniam temporis inopia pressus scholia intermarginalia et glossas non omnes contuli.*

[21] For fuller discussion of V and its two scribes see Chapter 5.

[22] Günther 1995.

scholars worked, one needs the full context of previous annotations, especially of the glosses and shorter versions that were important in the earlier teaching tradition. That context includes not only HMBOV (and C), but several *recentiores* (e.g., MnPrRRfRwRvSSa). As Kjeld Matthiessen pointed out,[23] some conclusions reached in Hans-Christian Günther's important study of the circulation of scholia in the Moschopulean and Thoman traditions are insecure and subject to revision upon adequate treatment of the annotations in the *recentiores*. Furthermore, even if we gain a thorough coverage of Euripidean annotation, many questions about sources and circulation of knowledge will remain open until the corpora of scholia on other authors read and annotated in the 11th to 14th centuries have become equally accessible and until more Byzantine grammatial treatises and teaching materials are published according to modern standards.

What is needed, then, is a more comprehensive approach to the annotations in medieval manuscripts of classical texts. There are of course several reasons why comprehensiveness has not usually been a goal in the past. In a printed edition there is usually some limit on coverage or detail conditioned by economic concerns, such as the cost of production and the cost to the potential purchasers, or by concerns about the physical format. The print format is not really well suited to editions of scholia. A digital edition or digital corpus suffers from no such constraints, and is in fact superior to a printed edition if there is useful searching and also a way to filter the information so that those with particular interests need not be overwhelmed by the sheer volume of disparate material. Another obstacle to comprehensiveness in the past, however, lay in traditional biases of classical studies. When you can study Aeschylus and Pindar and other brilliant authors, why spend time on jejune and belated ancillary material like scholiastic commentary? Or if scholia are to be edited and studied, it has usually been assumed that only "old scholia," in which there are some potential traces of Alexandrian scholarship, are worthy of serious effort, while younger scholia may be ignored, and that those interested in them may be left to consult old and deficient editions or to look at the manuscripts themselves. Nowadays, when there is a greater interest in the postclassical, the non-canonical, and the paraliterary, this prejudice has decreased, but is far from absent.

In addition, there should now also be a more realistic view of what most of our collections of tragic scholia actually represent. In the old scholia on Euripides as defined by Eduard Schwartz, only a very small proportion reflects identifiable views of Alexandrian scholars or refers to variant readings; most of the annotations reflect the interests and needs of the educational system of the Roman period and late antiquity (or even the middle Byzantine period). Therefore, the scholia have a great deal to tell us about reception, about the changing

---

[23] Matthiessen 2001.

society of the recipients, about their interests in and assumptions about rhetorical and literary theory, about the fashion for mythography exhibited throughout antiquity and the Byzantine period, about educational practices and levels of cultural literacy, and about the development of the Greek language. And in some of these respects, the value of younger scholia may not be so sharply different from that of many of the older scholia. In addition, we must be aware that better and more comprehensive editions of such material are a great benefit to the advance of Byzantine studies.

A second aspect of comprehensiveness in connection with a digital format is also important. Much of classical scholarship is built from the amassing of data: each datum may be by itself rather banal or uninteresting, but the accumulation of many such pieces is essential and those who collect the pieces never know what new and useful things will be done with them later. One of the great potentials of our digital age is to test new questions and new answers, by more efficient querying and manipulation of data collections in digital form. This notion is well recognized in connection with papyri and inscriptions and archaeological data, but scholia as well surely offer a type of data that are likely to be more effectively queried and analyzed when we have accurate and large-scale knowledge of more corpora without severe prefiltering by the scholars who are reading the manuscripts, and without the inconvenience of a myriad of separate printed volumes or the obstacles to research posed by traditional copyright.[24]

2. THE DEVELOPMENT OF ANNOTATION ON EURIPIDES IN ANTIQUITY

It is not the purpose of this section to review in detail the development of ancient scholarship on Euripides or on tragedy in general,[25] but to indicate briefly how much (or how little, in most cases) we know for certain about the streams of scholarship that fed into the corpus of scholia we now have. The works of the great tragedians were read and analyzed by the sophists, Aristotle and his Peripatetic followers, and by scholars of many kinds in Hellenistic and Roman Alexandria and other centers of learning. Aristotelian research into the history

---

[24] It should be clear that my project is quite different from that of, e.g., G. Xenis, who is interested in presenting "the oldest *recoverable* version and corpus" (his italics) of Sophoclean scholia (Xenis 2010a: 19, 21, 97). One might well attempt to do that for the Euripidean corpus, but in my view such a project should follow after the full medieval tradition is explored *and* made known (rather than suppressed). There is of course room for both approaches, as the inclusion of Cavarzeran 2016 in the same series as Xenis 2010a and Xenis 2010b makes clear.

[25] For overviews and detailed discussions, see Wilamowitz 1895, Pfeiffer 1968, Dickey 2007, Novokhatko 2015, Montana 2015, Matthaios 2015. For a collection of texts see Bagordo 1998.

of dramatic competitons in the main Attic festivals helped to establish a chronology and list of plays, which fed not only into Aristotle's own works on poets and poetics, but also into the inscriptional records, the cataloguing done by Callimachus in the Alexandrian library, the didaskalic notices apparently included in Aristophanes of Byzantium's short factual hypotheses to the plays he edited, and the few surviving scholia that show a scholar deploying chronological data to solve a problem.[26] Antiquarian scholars, local historians, biographers, and scholars dealing with variations of mythic stories, gods and their epithets or cults, or amazing phenomena (*paradoxa*) sifted through the plays for material. Philological scholars could address problems in the tragedies in treatises (*sungrammata*) on particular topics and in lexical studies as well as (from the 2nd century BCE on) in commentaries devoted to a particular play (*hypomnēmata*).

Although papyri from Egypt have given us scraps of commentaries on Homer, Pindar, comedy, and lyric poets and some prose authors, the discoveries so far have been less generous for tragedy.[27] Perhaps the explanation is that the well-educated persons located in the areas from which our papyri usually come acquired and used commentaries especially for the texts that had the densest incidence of puzzling words and expressions. The language and customs in Homer, the high-style vocabulary, dialects, intricate syntax, and allusive narrative technique of lyric, and the many persons and references to historical events and *realia* in comedy may well have inspired a more frequent need to consult erudite references for help, whereas at least the iambics of tragedy, especially in the case of Euripides, could more easily be handled by an experienced reader. Another potential problem with our evidence for ancient commentaries is the possibility that the dominance of Homeric scholarship is misleading, in as much as the special linguistic problems and the extraordinary cultural prestige of the Homeric epics attracted enormous and variegated scholarly effort over almost two millenia,[28] and so it may be unsafe to infer that other commentaries necessarily followed the same model. How, in fact, are we to imagine the contours and

---

[26] References to relative chronology or archon-year chronology are more common in the scholia on Aristophanes because of the topical references (but Sch. Arist. Ran. 53 deals with allusion to a recent tragedy); for an example from tragedy see Sch. Or. 371, which interprets the portrayal of Menelaus as a hostile allusion to contemporary Spartans as untrustworthy in the eyes of the Athenians.

[27] For an overview of the variety of formats and contents of *hypomnēmata*, see Del Fabbro 1979; for some updates to her inventory and consideration of how material from commentaries entered the margins of papyrus rolls and early codices of literary texts, see Messeri Savorelli and Pintaudi 2002; for commented editions see the ongoing publications in the series *Commentaria et Lexica Graeca in Papyris Reperta* (2004–). For a Homer commentary of great interest published in 2012, see P.Oxy 76.5095 (ed. F. Montanari) and Montana 2013. The marginalia are mostly available for study in the invaluable collection by McNamee 2007.

[28] For an overview of this tradition of scholarship in regard to the *Odyssey*, see Pontani 2011.

density of an ancient commentary on a tragedy by a high-level scholar like Callistratus[29] or Didymus?[30] Did such a commentary try to address the whole play virtually line by line, or work through selected problems associated with passages at irregular intervals and address the textual problems denoted by critical signs? Were all commentaries discursive, like the Derveni Papyrus commentary on an Orphic Theogony, Hipparchus on Aratus' *Phaenomena*, or philosophical commentaries (e.g., Alexander of Aphrodisias on Aristotle)? Or were some a series of lemmata followed by notes of a telegraphic brevity, the sort of notes we find in the margins of literary papyri and in some surviving fragments of commentaries? Or were they generally a mixture of the two styles? Given that there were more than 200 plays of the three great tragedians extant in the Alexandrian Library and thus presumably edited by Aristophanes of Byzantium, did Callistratus or Didymus write *hypomnēmata* for all of them, and on the same scale for all that they did treat? For Didymus we have an extensive papyrus with commentary on some speeches of Demosthenes,[31] but it is debated whether the papyrus provides us only with excerpts from a longer work or is evidence that Didymus could indeed be very selective. In any case, the nature of the prose orations is so different from the nature of a dramatic text that one should not assume that this commentary and one on a play of Euripides were very similar. On the other hand, Didymus' fondness for quotation of erudite historical and antiquarian sources and passages of poetry and for expressing disagreement with earlier commentators is confirmed by many of the passages in the Pindaric scholia that can be considered fragments of Didymus.[32] Much more is known, of course, of Didymus' comments on Homer,[33] but even there his work has been sliced up and excerpted in the scholiastic tradition, and, as just mentioned, Homeric scholarship was in some ways *sui generis* and does not necessarily offer a reliable parallel for commentating on other authors.

We do not yet have any fragment of a *hypomnēma* on a play of Euripides. Papyri of Euripides' plays have given us occasional glosses, some of which are comparable to those in the medieval tradition.[34] Two more extensive fragments of annotations written separately from a text of a play (both probably from the 6th century CE) are of different kinds. P. Würzburg 1[35] provides on both sides of

---

[29] On Callistratus, see below at note 78.
[30] On Didymus of Alexandria, active in the age of Augustus, see Pfeiffer 1968: 274–279; Montana 2015: 172–178 (with additional references).
[31] See the edition of Pearson and Stephens 1983 and the discussions of Gibson 2002 and Harding 2006.
[32] See the brief assessment of selected examples in Braswell 2011.
[33] For an assessment of Didymus' sources and working methods in his commentaries on Homer, see West 2001: 46–85.
[34] These are gathered in McNamee 2007: 253–257.
[35] See Essler et al. 2013, and McNamee forthcoming.

a single preserved sheet a collection of miscellaneous scholia on *Phoenissae*: these were probably recorded for private use by a mid-level schoolteacher or a student aiming to become a teacher. The wording in some cases is similar to that in the old scholia, but never shows an exact match for a long stretch of words. P. Oslo inv. 1662[36] appears to be a fuller and more scholarly version of our present Sch. Tro. 9 (Schwartz II.347, 7-15). The first overlap, concerning sacred wars over Delphi, is between line 1 of the papyrus note and lines 13-15 of the scholion, but the papyrus then quotes Thucydides at length while the scholion has only ὡς Θουκυδίδης φησί. After that quotation, line 8 of the papyrus proceeds to a different issue (Epeius termed a Parnassian), which occurs at the beginning of the scholion (line 9). We can see, then, that the different remarks have ended up in the opposite order in the papyrus and in the scholion. But the original extent and context of the annotation in the papyrus is quite uncertain, and it may be a note written for some reason on a loose sheet of papyrus (the back is blank). The material is presumably drawn from a commentary, but in its present state shows the continuity of our tradition rather than the contours of the larger commentary.

In the high-level commentaries of Alexandrian scholars, it was customary to cite other scholars by name and, at least by the time of Didymus, to include quotations (sometimes extensive ones) from poetry and prose texts that were cited for comparison or to establish historical context or allusions (or to make criticisms of the scholarship of others). Little of such quotation survives in the Euripidean scholia. Because the original scholarship was repurposed over time for the broader audience of educated readers and for school learners (from the elementary schoolroom up to the rhetorician's class), such scholarly detail could often be considered unnecessary or pedantic. Thus the vast majority of extant notes became anonymous, the names of specific scholars were replaced with τινές ("some") or ἄλλοι ("others") or οἱ ὑπομνηματισάμενοι ("those who have commented" or "the commentators"),[37] and verbatim quotations of sources and comparanda were shortened or completely omitted. This process of adaptation

---

[36] See the discussion of McNamee forthcoming; also Stroppa 2008: 60-61, Stroppa 2009: 302. The first edition is Eitrem and Amundsen 1957. This piece is dated to the 5th century by Eitrem and Amundsen, but to the 6th by Stroppa 2008 and by McNamee.

[37] The TLG offers 240 hits for ὑπομνηματίζομαι, but that total is inflated by double entries (both in editions of fragments and in the source texts). In scholia on various authors, the plural οἱ ὑπομνηματισάμενοι occurs only 14 times (one of these is Sch. Andr. 32), and the singular once (Sch. Or. 1384). The plural may be conventional and thus conceal a reference to a single scholar: e.g., Wilamowitz 1895: 160 n. 179 understood οἱ φαύλως ὑπομνηματισάμενοι in Sch. Andr. 32 as referring to Didymus. Since later teachers and commentators knew that one commentary had routinely borrowed from another, they could consider a view to have been held by the transmitters as well as the original exponent, and thus the plural was natural.

(which we as professional scholars might consider "dumbing down") affected more severely the plays that were popular among teachers and readers. Thus although the extant scholia on *Troades* and *Rhesus* (the last plays in the commentated selection) are sparse, they include some items full of quotations of scholars, historians, and poets. For the triad plays and some other select plays there is a much larger accretion of simple glosses and paraphrases and short identifications of places and persons, as well as short mythological summaries, and proportionally not so many named sources or quotations.

Whenever we do find a note that cites, or even quotes verbatim, authors of τραγῳδούμενα[38] (principally concerned with comparing versions of myth in tragedy to those in Homer and other sources), general mythographers, chroniclers of local history, monuments, and rituals, it has reasonably been inferred (at least so far as concerns the sources going back to the 1st century BCE and earlier) that the content has been handed down from Didymus, since he is known to have consulted countless books now lost and to have quoted them extensively. Didymus himself may have had the practice of recycling material from his philological predecessors, like Aristophanes and Callistratus, without naming them.[39] And he himself apparently suffered the same fate at the hands of his successors: although his name appears more often than any other scholar in the Euripides scholia (19 times: 8 on the triad plays, 10 on *Medea* and *Andromache*, and 1 on *Troades*), this is a small number of attestations relative to the total of many thousands of notes and relative to the number that modern scholars have been inclined to attribute to his commentaries.[40]

Didymus is named in one of the two subscriptions to the Euripides scholia

---

[38] Among such authors and works, Asclepiades of Tragilus is one of those named most frequently. The title is present only in Sch. Alc. 1 (*FGrHist* 12 F 9, on Apollo's servitude in Admetus' house); but it is given by Athenaeus 456B in a passage verbally close to Sch. Phoen. 50 (*FGrHist* 12 F 7a, riddle of the Sphinx), whence the mention in Sch. Phoen. 45 (*FGrHist* 12 F 7b, about the Thebans trying to answer the Sphinx) is similarly secured; the damaged Sch. Rh. 916a Merro (*FGrHist* 12 F 10, on Thamyris and the Muses) appears to have a reference to Book 2 of the work. No title or book number is present in Sch. Or. 1645 (*FGrHist* 12 F 26, on the death of Orestes—location, manner, and age), but the ascription seems inevitable. Two other mentions of an Asclepiades are more likely to refer to the Samian poet, as Schwartz suggested, and are included but termed doubtful by Jacoby: Sch. BPr Hec. 1273 (*FGrHist* 12 F 24, περὶ τοῦ κυνὸς σήματος καὶ Ἀσκληπιάδης φησὶν ὅτι κυνὸς καλοῦσι δυσμόρου σῆμα [similar phrase also in Sch. V Hec. 1271]), Sch. Andr. 32 (*FGrHist* 12 F 23, Σωσιφάνης δὲ καὶ Ἀσκληπιάδης φασὶν ἐξ αὐτῆς Νεοπτολέμῳ Ἀγχίαλον γενέσθαι). In general see *FGrHist* 12 Jacoby and Pagani 2004; the article of Wentzel 1896 is outdated.

[39] As remarked, e.g., by Gudeman 1919: 1743.

[40] For a selection of these, see for example Wilamowitz 1895: 160–162 nn. 79–83; Elsperger 1907: 108–122 with the table on 158–166. At some later stage in my work on the scholia I hope to assess the various claims of Didymean origin for notes that are now anonymous, but in the present context that problem would take us too far afield.

that have survived.⁴¹ These subscriptions appear at the end of *Orestes* in several manuscripts and at the end of *Medea* in one. The *Orestes* subscription exists in both B and M (both of the 11th century), our two oldest witnesses with substantial corpora of scholia. It is to be noted that the corpora in B and M represent slightly different recensions, so the subscription apparently derives from a source earlier than these two. This subscription has also been transmitted in some copies of *Orestes* that do not in fact contain the old scholia, because it had become attached to a note about tragedy and comedy and the "happy ending" of *Orestes*, a note which was sometimes part of the prefatory items before *Orestes* and sometimes placed after the last scholion. These circumstances of survival should make us pause to wonder how accurately the subscription actually applies to our corpus of old scholia, since it could have been handed on even as the corpus itself was modified in large or small ways. One would suspect that the subscriptions and the compilation they reflect occurred either in the early Byzantine period (4th to 7th centuries CE) or else in the 10th century (possibly even the 9th, but it appears that most of the revived scholarly attention to pagan literature at that time was directed to prose authors).⁴² The choice between these two periods cannot be resolved on current evidence concerning the tradition of Euripides, and this is not the place to go over again the evidence for the broader debate about the origins of large corpora of marginal annotation in codices (as opposed to the occasional, brief notes that are already found in papyrus rolls as well as in early codices).⁴³ The issue was studied with great subtlety by Günther

---

⁴¹ Subscriptions referring to the sources of annotations also exist for 22 books of the *Iliad* in Marcianus graecus 454 (A of Homer), for three plays of Aristophanes in Marcianus graecus 474 (V of Aristophanes), and for the scholia on Apollonius Rhodius in Laurentianus plut. 32.09. See Cavallo 1992: 99–104, Montana 2014b: 35; and the study of the Homeric ones in Pagani 2014.

⁴² Wilamowitz 1895: 200 tried to be more precise about the date of compilation, judging the compiler to be a man of the same stamp, and more or less of the same time period, as Niketas (or Niketes) of Serrha ("ein Mann vom Schlage und ziemlich auch der Zeit des Niketes von Serrha": a scribe who copied Marcianus gr. 476 of Lycophron in the 11th cent.; note that the identification of this scribe Niketas with Niketes of Serrha is rejected by Cavallo 1992: 107 n. 32). Wilamowitz conceded, however, that the Euripidean compiler might have found a notice in similar language already present in some manuscripts he drew on; and the current estimate of the dates of M and B make the 11th century too late for the compilation referred to in the subscription.

⁴³ Two minor points I would nevertheless like to make: (1) the transition of commentaries to the margin need not have been the same for all authors (Homer exegesis, being so massive, might have been more of a challenge and happened later than others); (2) the argument that only minuscule script allows the marginal space to be adequate is dubious, since majuscule (and cursive) of very small format existed in antiquity, as did abbreviation by signs and truncation, and small majuscule script was in fact used for some dense marginal commentaries in minuscule manuscripts of the 10th century and later: on size of writing see McNamee 2007: 86–90, and on small majuscule see below Chapter 4 at note 47.

Zuntz,[44] who argued that composite commentaries incorporating learned material from Didymus and others, along with different kinds of information and help developed in and important to the teaching tradition, reached by late antiquity a form that contained most of what we have in most scholia corpora, but that such complete composite commentaries continued to be transmitted separately from the commented texts until the adoption, in the 9th century, of a new format in which the extensive commentary is written in substantial marginal regions on three (or sometimes four) sides of the text. Subsequently, some scholars, in particular Wilson and McNamee, have given arguments in favor of the format having begun already in late antiquity, and in recent years Montana has reasserted the arguments for the later period.[45]

Here are the Euripidean subscriptions:

Sch. Or. subscription: πρὸς διάφορα ἀντίγραφα παραγέγραπται ἐκ τοῦ Διονυσίου ὑπομνήματος ὁλοσχερῶς καὶ τῶν μικτῶν. MBCNeRRw, CrGuLbPk XaZc[46]

By reference to various copies, <these annotations> have been written in the margin [*or* cited *or* extracted?] from the commentary of Dionysius entirely [*or* in general?] and from the mixed commentaries.

Sch. Med. subscription: πρὸς διάφορα ἀντίγραφα Διονυσίου ὁλοσχερὲς καί τινα τῶν Διδύμου. B

By reference to various copies <of annotations> of Dionysius entirely [*or* in general?] and some of those of Didymus.

The translations are not certain. ὁλοσχερῶς/ὁλοσχερὲς can have either meaning indicated above, but the contrast in the *Medea* subscription between ὁλοσχερὲς and τινα seems to me to favor "entirely."[47] There is also a current debate whether in subscriptions like this παραγέγραπται (used also in the Aristophanes scholia) or παράκειται (used in subscriptions to the *Iliad* and to the scholia on Apollonius Rhodius) originally meant "are written in the margin" or should rather be rendered as "are cited" or "are extracted."[48] I need not pursue that issue here. The essential point for my purposes is the fact of compilation from multiple sources, including from previous compilations (τὰ μικτά), rather

---

[44] Zuntz 1939; cf. Zuntz 1965: 272–275.
[45] Wilson 1967, 1983b; McNamee 2007: 79–92; Montana 2011, 2014b (with additional references).
[46] The manuscripts of the first group carry the old scholia (but each in somewhat different form and extent), while none of the second group contains a large set of old scholia.
[47] In the second subscription, now truncated but presumably originally a fuller sentence, τινα is better taken as "some annotations" (that is, not the whole commentary) rather than "some copies" (ἀντίγραφα). In the subscriptions in Venetus A of Homer (παράκειται τὰ Ἀριστονίκου σημεῖα καὶ τὰ Διδύμου Περὶ τῆς Ἀριστάρχειου διορθώσεως, τινὰ δὲ καὶ ἐκ τῆς Ἰλιακῆς προσῳδίας Ἡρωδιανοῦ καὶ ἐκ τῶν Νικάνορος Περὶ στιγμῆς), τινα means "some annotations."
[48] In favor of the latter see the recent discussions of Montana 2014a and 2014b and Pagani 2014.

than at what date the compilation was written in the margin.

After Didymus, various unknown scholars will have pillaged his commentary while adding their own material, others may have copied only selections from Didymus and still entitled it as Didymus' *hypomnēma*, and some commentaries (τὰ μικτά) will have been formed by combining notes from multiple sources, including no doubt notes descended from Didymus. We cannot identify or date with any certainty the Dionysius referred to in the subscriptions. Cohn noted that this Dionysius may be the same as the Dionysius always named in conjunction with a Crates and a Eucleides as a trio of sources by Tzetzes in various connections with drama. Although some scholars find this not improbable, it remains just a possibility, since the reliability of this kind of source claim in Tzetzes is itself uncertain.[49] Likewise, we cannot know whether Dionysius wrote a high-level commentary or compiled learned notes with the paraphrases and other material of more interest in the teaching tradition of the Roman period and early Byzantium.[50]

Given the processes of filtering, reuse, and repurposing of notes for educational needs or for those of the cultured reader who was not a philological scholar, one should not expect the surviving corpus to give us good access to ancient *hypomnēmata* and other scholarly works from the Hellenistic and early Roman period. It is indeed sobering to see how rarely the names of the philological experts earlier than Didymus appear in the extant scholia. The following rapid survey is not intended to be a presentation of the nature and extent of ancient studies on tragedy, but is offered simply to indicate how little secure information is attached to the names that do survive in the scholia.[51]

Aristotle is never named in connection with any literary-critical observation about a passage, though one can frequently see the influence of his theories and

---

[49] Cohn 1903; Matthaios 2015: 248–249; Tuilier 1968: 215–223; Pagani 2013 (with further references, and mention of the problem of how reliable Tzetzes' citation is, on which see also Broggiato 2001: xxv–xxvii). In Sch. Arist. Plut. [rec. 2] 253a and in a scholion on his own work, Tzetzes says his Dionysius is from Halicarnassus, and this led Tuilier to identify the Dionysius of the subscription with the grammarian Aelius Dionysius of Halicarnassus of the 2nd century CE; but again it is doubtful whether we can trust that Tzetzes was justified in locating his Dionysius in this way.

[50] Wilamowitz 1895: 201 conjectured that Dionysius was the source of the "trivial exegesis very close to paraphrase" in our scholia, while the learned material came from Didymus and other sources, but did not believe the date of Dionysius could be fixed any more precisely than the period from the 2nd century CE (the too-early date at which Wilamowitz placed the tragic selections in which he believed) to the 5th century (*terminus ante quem* because of a relation he suspected between elements of the glossary of Cyrillus and the "trivial paraphrases" of the ten select plays).

[51] See the surveys cited in note 25 above and the collection of texts in Bagordo 1998. Thus I do not mention scholars reported to have commented on Euripides whose names do not survive in the extant scholia (e.g., Soteridas of Epidaurus: Matthaios 2015: 227; Bagordo 1998: 65, 165–166).

terminology.⁵² A work called *Hypomnemata* of Aristotle (but elsewhere ascribed to "Aristotle or Theophrastus" and probably a Peripatetic collection of items of mixed origin) is cited in the hypothesis to *Medea* for the assertion that Euripides borrowed from a *Medea* by Neophron.⁵³ The two remaining mentions in the scholia are quite late.⁵⁴

Aristotle's student Dicaearchus⁵⁵ likewise appears in two hypotheses for matters of literary history: Euripides' borrowing from Neophron in *Medea* (fr. 53 Wehrli = fr. 62 Mirhady, citing the work *Life of Greece*), and citation of a first iambic trimeter of *Rhesus* (fr. 81 Wehrli = fr. 114 Mirhady). Dicaearchus' name is also associated in antiquity with summaries (hypotheses) of dramatic plots of Sophocles and Euripides (fr. 78 Wehrli = fr. 112 Mirhady), and Demetrius Triclinius added the narrative hypothesis of *Alcestis* on fol. 176v of L and (uniquely among the medieval witnesses of this or any other hypothesis) entitled it ὑπόθεσις Ἀλκήστιδος Δικαιάρχου, "Dicaearchus' hypothesis of *Alcestis*." Thus in modern times some have believed the narrative hypotheses or epitomes found before most plays in our medieval witnesses derive from Dicaearchus, and with the discovery of alphabetic collections of similar hypotheses in papyri from the 1st century CE onward, some ascribe that collection to him. The vocabulary and prose style and other factors (such as alphabetization) suggest, however, that these narratives were written later than Dicaearchus. Dicaearchus presumably did write about the versions of myths used by the tragedians, but it is probable that the ascription of these hypotheses to him is false, similar to the misascription of later iambic hypotheses of Sophocles and Menander to Aristophanes of Byzantium.⁵⁶ Outside of the hypotheses, there is just one citation of Dicaearchus

---

⁵² See especially Meijering 1987 and Nünlist 2009.

⁵³ Aristotle, fr. 635 Rose. For the basic issues about this claim, see Mastronarde 2002: 57–64; for more recent bibliography see the discussion of Lucarini 2013.

⁵⁴ Sch. Hipp. 191 cites Aristotle in an irrelevant discussion of whether the sun's light is material or not, but the language of the note (e.g., τὴν φωτιστικὴν αὐτοῦ δύναμιν) is late antique or Byzantine and the reference may be to a commentary; Schwartz noted *caveas ne hoc in ipsis Aristotelis libris quaeras*, but for φῶς mentioned in connection with σῶμα see *Top.* 146a13–20; and see now Cavarzeran at Sch. Hipp. 196a. Sch. Hipp. 656 (656b Cavarzeran) is first attested around 1300 (the hand I call V³) and at least part of it is related to Ioannes Tzetzes (see Chapter 2 at note 55).

⁵⁵ See Novokhatko 2015: 57 and the edition of fragments by Mirhady 2001.

⁵⁶ On the narrative hypotheses in general see Meccariello 2014 and van Rossum-Steenbeck 1988. On the problem of the ascription to Dicaearchus see Meccariello 2014: 67–82, who suggests (80–82) as an alternative to a false attribution (argued by Rusten 1982) that the name may be correct, but refer to a later Dicaearchus, perhaps the one mentioned in *Suda* δ 1063 as from Sparta and a student of Aristarchus. On the misascribed metrical hypotheses see Meccariello 2014: 11–12. After Meccariello the evidence has also been examined in detail by Verhasselt 2015, who comes to the same conclusion that the summaries have been incorrectly attributed to the Messenian Dicaearchus, and does not exclude entirely the idea that there was a homonymous Dicaearchus, noting the suggestion of Fuhr 1841: 70 n. 59 that one might emend Δικαιάρχου τινὰς ὑποθέσεις in Sextus Empiricus' testimony to Δικαιάρχου τινὸς ὑποθέσεις.

in the scholia (Sch. Andr. 1) for a mythographic/historical detail (fr. 53 Wehrli = fr. 66 Mirhady).

Zenodotus' name survives once, amidst the mass of citations for the parentage of Europa in Sch. Rh. 29.[57] We cannot be sure where he addressed the issue.

Fragments of Callimachus' poetry are cited about a dozen times, but the only certain scholarly reference is in Sch. Andr. 445 (on that play's having the name Democrates attached, scil. in the production records?).[58] The opinion about Europa in Sch. Rh. 29 might also be from a scholarly work, since Zenodotus is said to have adopted an opinion from Callimachus.

Crates[59] is named in connection with three *problēmata* on which he expressed opinions, and these notices probably survive because they attracted the disagreement of commentators of the Alexandrian school.[60] In Sch. Phoen. 208 (fr. 87 Broggiato), regarding the much debated question of the route taken by the Phoenician maidens from Tyre to Thebes, Crates argued that the reference to Zephyrus indicates that the season is spring rather than that the Phoenician ship was propelled by the west wind. The issue in Sch. Rh. 5 (fr. 88 Broggiato) concerns the divisions responsible for the five night watches assumed by the playwright in lines 538–545: Crates, separating Coroebus from the Paionians, made an implausible claim that the Cilicians and Mysians in *Rh.* 540–541 are treated as the same group by the poet. This view is reported and refuted at some length in a discussion that is plausibly attributed to Didymus.[61] In Sch. Rh. 528 (fr. 88 Broggiato) he claimed that Euripides got his astronomy wrong because he was young when he wrote the play. Finally, a more elementary observation about genealogy, how Strophius and Pylades are related to Agamemnon and Orestes, is also ascribed to Crates in Sch. Or. 1233 (fr. 86 Broggiato).[62]

Aristophanes of Byzantium[63] is of course named in the heading of several terse, fact-filled *hypotheseis* that presumably descend from his scholarly work, though they have suffered losses and probably in some cases additions over the

---

[57] *FGrHist* 19 F 3. For Zenodotus in general, mostly known for his Homeric scholarship, see Montana 2015: 102–106.

[58] For discussion see Allan 2000: 149–52.

[59] See Broggiato 2001, Pagani 2007–2009 (with further references), Montana 2015: 148–153.

[60] It must be remembered that commentators are more likely to name a predecessor when expressing disagreement than when repeating a generally accepted view, and thus our sources may give us a skewed picture of scholarly polemics.

[61] Most recently by Merro 2008.

[62] Because this seems to be a simple genealogical point, Schwartz suspected the name Crates is corrupt and thought Pherecydes more likely, while Jacoby in *FGrHist* 376 F 6 offered ⟨Νικό⟩κρατης (a corruption found elsewhere: see Broggiato).

[63] See Montana 2015: 118–126; fragments in Slater 1986.

centuries of transmission.⁶⁴ He is also very important because the textual authority of his editions of the tragedians for subsequent scholars may be compared to the position held by Aristarchus for Homer, and his editions also influenced the book trade in that his division of the lyric passages into short cola dominated the textual tradition after his time. In addition, Aristophanes' lexical works contributed to the traditions of later commentary and lexicography. Some of his fragments⁶⁵ cite Euripidean passages as illustrations, but no gloss in the surviving scholia is ever ascribed to him explicitly. This is not surprising given the long tradition of transmission, which probably included movement of an explanation back and forth between specific commentaries and lexicographic works.

In his editions Aristophanes apparently used critical signs to mark passages worthy of note for textual or other issues, but did not write commentaries himself.⁶⁶ In our scholia we have three attestations of readings accepted by Aristophanes, all related to *Orestes*, probably all reported by his student Callistratus, though he is named in only one of them.⁶⁷ He is also cited three times for matters of interpretation. In one case, Sch. Or. 488, it is not clear whether his opinion has been lost in a lacuna or somewhat obscured during transmission.⁶⁸ Sch. Tro. 47 (fr. 391 Slater) says that he cited Euripides in connection with a possible athetesis in Homer:

σεσημείωται ὡς [Wilamowitz; καὶ V] μηκέτι αὐτῆς οἰκουμένης· ὑπώπτευκε γὰρ Ἀριστοφάνης ἐκ τούτου ⟨τὸ⟩ [add. Nauck] [*Il.* 20.307] 'νῦν δὲ δὴ Αἰνείαο βίη Τρώεσσιν ἀνάξει'

The line has attracted scholarly notice (*or* been marked with a sign) because it (the city Troy) is no longer inhabited; for Aristophanes suspected on the basis of this

---

⁶⁴ For doubt about the Aristophanic origins of "critical assessments" in some *hypotheseis* see Mastronarde 1994: 168 n. 2. For discussion and fuller bibliography, see Meccariello 2014: 7–11.
⁶⁵ See fragments 4, 15, 31, 32, 48, 202–203, 264–268, 313, 338, 378, dub. 417 Slater.
⁶⁶ For an alternative view that credits the early Alexandrian scholars with more intensive work (e.g., a *diorthōsis* of the tragic texts by Alexander of Aetolia) and does not exclude that Aristophanes may have written commentaries, see Carrara 2007.
⁶⁷ Sch. Or. 714, 1038, 1287 (= frr. 387–389 Slater). In the first, Aristophanes' reading is clearly the better one (Ἄργους γαῖαν rather than Ἄργου γαῖαν in 714); at 1038 his δόμον seems to me, as to Diggle, superior to γόνον, though the latter can be defended; at 1287 the singular verb with ξίφη as subject is bolder (the swords personified to feel awe at Helen's beauty) and probably to be accepted instead of the plural with Orestes and Pylades as subject accepted by Aristophanes (it must remain unclear whether the second omega in ἐκκεκώφωνται for ἐκκεκώφηνται in the scholia really represents Aristophanes' preference or is a banalization introduced in transmission).
⁶⁸ Fr. 386 Slater. Schwartz correctly believed the syntax of transmitted ὁ δὲ Ἀριστοφάνης φησὶ πᾶν τὸ ἐξ ἀνάγκης γινόμενον δουλοῖ, οἷον ταπεινοῖ, κατὰ τὴν τῶν σοφῶν κρίσιν is defective. Either it should have been, e.g., ⟨ἢ οὕτως, ὡς⟩ {ὁ δὲ} Ἀριστοφάνης φησί, or there is something missing after φησι, which could be either something like ⟨ὅτι τὸ δοῦλον τίθεται ἀντὶ τοῦ ταπεινόν, ἵν᾽ ᾖ⟩ or a completely different lost opinion, with the following phrase being an unrelated part of this conflated scholion.

(line) the verse [*Iliad* 20.307] 'and now indeed mighty Aeneas will rule over the Trojans.'"[69]

Slater suggested that this cannot be an accurate representation of Aristophanes' athetesis on the grounds that this scholar well knew how to differentiate between the treatment of something in Homer and the versions of later poets. On the other hand, the speaker here is the god Poseidon, so it might have occurred to a scholar promoting proper omniscience in literary divinities to reason that if the god does not show awareness of a renewed Troy under Aeneas, that version is incompatible with the claim about Aeneas.

The most intriguing reference is in Sch. Hipp. 171 τήνδε κομίζουσ' ἔξω (fr. 390a–b Slater), on whether or not the eccyclema[70] was used, or ought to have been used, but there is an unfortunate corruption that leaves us with two different paths of emendation that would ascribe opposite opinions to Aristophanes.

> τοῦτο σεσημείωται τῷ Ἀριστοφάνει ὅτι καίτοι τῷ ἐκκυκλήματι χρώμενος τὸ ἐκκομίζουσα προσέθηκε περισσῶς. MV
>
> This passage was marked as noteworthy by Aristophanes because although using the eccyclema he added the word "bringing out" superfluously.
>
> τοῦτο σεσημείωκεν Ἀριστοφάνης, ὅτι κατὰ τὸ ἀκριβὲς τὸ ἐκκύκλημα †τοιοῦτόν ἐστι† τῇ ὑποθέσει. ²ἐπὶ γὰρ τῆς σκηνῆς δείκνυται τὰ ἔνδον πραττόμενα, ὁ δὲ ἔξω προϊοῦσαν αὐτὴν ὑποτίθεται. B
>
> Aristophanes marked this passage as noteworthy because in exact terms the eccyclema †is such†[71] to/by the assumed situation: for (with that machine) events happening indoors are shown on stage, but Euripides presents her (Phaedra) as proceeding outside.[72]

Some scholars think that Aristophanes was criticizing his contemporary theater practitioners for using the eccyclema, on the ground that the platform is properly used to show something indoors, whereas κομίζουσα in Euripides' text (corrupted to ἐκκομίζουσα in the scholion as we have it now) indicates Phaedra

---

[69] The assignment of this unanchored note to line 47 is somewhat arbitrary. It is continued from the note on *Tro.* 44 γαμεῖ βιαίως (on fol. 262v containing *Tro.* 26–44; line 47 is on 263r), but notes that have been conflated with other notes are not always in sequence. It may originally have belonged to 26 ἐρημία γὰρ πόλιν ὅταν λάβῃ κακή (or less likely 15 ἔρημα δ' ἄλση), rather than to 47 ἦσθ' ἂν ἐν βάθροις ἔτι.

[70] For the latest in the long series of discussions of the eccyclema see Lucarini 2016.

[71] Emendations for τοιοῦτόν ἐστι include οὐκ οἰκεῖόν ἐστι (Trendelenburg), ἀνοίκειόν ἐστι (Elsperger); ἐπιτήδειόν ἐστι (Malzan), οἰκεῖόν ἐστι (Holwerda), ἀκόλουθόν ἐστι (Holwerda), ἐναντιοῦται (Slater).

[72] Cf. the discussions in Belardinelli 2000: 245–249 (with further references); Slater 1986: 150–151; Csapo and Slater 1995: 271; and now Cavarzeran 2016:148. Note that the longer version, in B, is oddly marked by Schwartz with an obelus to indicate it is "recent."

is being brought out of the house and Euripides correctly did not use it.⁷³ Others think Aristophanes believed that Euripides himself used the eccyclema and is criticizing him for putting κομίζουσα in his text and for using a device that he judged ought to be used only for revealing indoor scenes.⁷⁴ Others think he was criticizing Euripides for not using the eccyclema, agreeing with the directors who later used the platform because they judged it unrealistic for a sick person to be brought outdoors rather than revealed within,⁷⁵ or that he was simply commenting that one might expect it to be used but that Euripides did not do so.⁷⁶ Apart from the probable corruption in the second version, one must often, when reading in scholia an explanation of a sign or a reading credited to a famous scholar, entertain the question whether the transmitter of this information had accurate knowledge of the motivations of that scholar or rather inferred on his own (and possibly misleadingly) what the motivation was. Therefore, it is impossible here to be sure what Aristophanes said and why. Some modern scholars⁷⁷ have been inclined to ascribe most references to theater practice and actors' gestures to Aristophanes, but there can be no certainty about such ascriptions.

Callistratus,⁷⁸ pupil of Aristophanes, is credited with writing commentaries. His name survives only in the scholia on *Orestes*. He is cited once as reporting Aristophanes' reading (Sch. Or. 1028) and, as noted above, may have been the ultimate source when the few other such readings are reported; also once as the exponent of reading third-person verbs (νόση, δοξάζη) instead of second-person forms (Sch. Or. 314); and lastly for a rather laconic exegesis of the debated phrase διὰ τριῶν (Sch. Or. 434):

πρῶτον τῶν πολιτῶν, δεύτερον Οἴακος. διὸ ἐπάγει "'τίς ἄλλος," ἵνα

---

⁷³ Meijering 1987: 131–132.
⁷⁴ Schrader 1864: 47–48, Trendelenburg 1867: 49–53, who (following Lachmann) compares Sch. Alc. 233 (on the choral announcement of Alcestis' emergence) οὐκ εὖ· κατὰ γὰρ τὴν ὑπόθεσιν ὡς ἔσω πραττόμενα δεῖ ταῦτα θεωρεῖσθαι ("not well done, for according to the assumed scenario one must view these actions as taking place indoors") and takes this view to be that of Aristophanes.
⁷⁵ Wilamowitz 1895: 154 n. 64; Elsperger 1907: 70–71; Holwerda 1976: 177, 195–198, approved by Lucarini 2016: 152–153. If this interpretation were true, it would not speak well of Aristophanes' judgment: could a man with the experience of having read several hundred tragedies be so insensitive to the conventions of the genre (in particular the need for characters to speak in public, contrary to a fully realistic adherence to proprieties), and was he so unappreciative of the effects of the references to the outdoors (hunting, horse-training, pure water) enabled by Euripides' decision to bring Phaedra outside?
⁷⁶ Malzan 1908: 10. Other possibilities are also to be found in the literature on this problem, including the notion (which I would reject) that Aristophanes based his opinion that the eccyclema was used here on a stage direction carried in the textual tradition since the time of first production: e.g., Weissmann 1896: 26.
⁷⁷ E.g., Wilamowitz 1895: 153–155, with nn. 60–64.
⁷⁸ See Montana 2007–2008 and Montana 2015: 127–128.

πληρώση τοὺς τρεῖς. τινὲς δὲ τριῶν φασι τῶν Ἐρινύων. προεῖπε γὰρ [408] "ἔδοξ' ἰδεῖν τρεῖς νυκτὶ προσφερεῖς κόρας." τινὲς δέ φασι τῆς συνέσεως, τῆς λύπης καὶ τῆς μανίας. ἐν δὲ τοῖς Καλλιστράτου γέγραπται· ἐπιζητήσειεν ἄν τις πῶς διὰ τριῶν εἴρηκεν, εἰ μὴ διὰ τὸ Ἀγαμέμνονα καὶ Διομήδην καὶ Ὀδυσσέα μετασχεῖν τοῦ φόνου Παλαμήδους. MCVBR^{b}Sa^{79}

First the citizens, secondly Oeax. Therefore he (Menelaus) follows on with "who else?" so that he may fill out the three. Some say by three he means the Erinyes, because he said previously "I thought I saw three maidens similar to night." Some others say the three are awareness (of guilt), pain, and madness. And in the commentaries of Callistratus is written: one might seek (in vain) an answer to the problem in what sense he has said "through three," unless (it is) because Agamemnon, Diomedes, and Odysseus participated in the murder of Palamedes.

The great Homeric scholar Aristarchus[80] is named a single time in Sch. Rh. 540, which very briefly alludes to the *problēma* concerning the night watches. From this we can infer that in refuting Crates in Sch. Rh. 5 (the longer discussion of the same *problēma*), Didymus was adopting and supporting Aristarchus' view. Possibly Didymus was doing so without naming him; but we cannot rely on our scholia to preserve the exact wording of Didymus' commentary.

Parmeniscus,[81] probably active in the second half of the 2nd century BCE, is another scholar who certainly handled problems in Euripides, and his name appears in the scholia of three plays. It cannot be determined whether the reported opinions were contained in commentaries or in a work containing miscellaneous *problēmata* on Euripides.[82] In Sch. Med. 9[83] and 264 (on the killing of Medea's children) he is cited for a mythographic problem; in Sch. Tro. 228 for a geographic one (two rivers named Krathis); in Sch. Rhes. 528 for an astronomical one (on πρῶτα σημεῖα). Other citations indicate exegesis of particular phrases: Sch. Rhes. 523 (about προταινί being Boeotian), Sch. Tro. 221 (on Φοινίκας ἀντήρη).

Apollodorus of Tarsus[84] is quoted in Sch. Med. 148 and 169 for discussion of

---

[79] A truncated version, lacking the last lines about Callistratus, is in VMnPr^{s}R^a and twice in S.
[80] See Montana 2015: 130–143, with many references.
[81] See Ippolito 2005 and the edition of Breithaupt 1915, both with further references.
[82] Breithaupt 1915: 22–37 argued that he wrote commentaries on some plays: he gives references to earlier discussions and himself suggests additional scholia on *Rhesus* that might be derived from Parmeniscus. Wendel 1949 and Ippolito 2005 consider the evidence insufficient to decide what kind of works provided these opinions of Parmeniscus.
[83] The tidbit of supposed literary history in Sch. Med. 9 (that Euripides was paid by the Corinthians to have Medea kill her sons instead of representing them as responsible) probably comes from the same discussion as that quoted in Sch. Med. 264.
[84] Wentzel 1894b. Nothing more is known of this scholar, who is attested elsewhere only in Sch. vet. Arist. Ran. 320f, Sch. Tz. Arist. Ran. 320a. (The doctrine of the Aristophanes scholion is also transmitted in Hesychius δ 975 s.v. Διαγόρας, where the name is transmitted as Diodorus instead.) A

a problem of speaker assignment and addressee. He impossibly assigns *Medea* 148 (first line of a lyric strophe) to Medea, making it the last line of her utterance from indoors, in order to explain the Nurse's reference in 169 to her calling on Zeus. He blames actors for messing up the text (τοὺς δ' ὑποκριτὰς συγχέειν; αἰτίους εἶναι τοὺς ὑποκριτάς, συγχέοντας τὰ χορικά). In both cases Didymus is cited for the opposing view. Again we cannot judge whether Apollodorus wrote a commentary on *Medea* or handled the problem in a treatise of some kind.

Apollodorus of Cyrene[85] is cited only in Sch. Or. 1384, where his suggestion that ἁρμάτειον μέλος is a stage direction (παρεπιγραφή) is reported and rejected. He may have been early enough to be known to Didymus, who also discussed this vexed phrase, but the reports of different views are now jumbled and the compilation in our scholion is later than Didymus, so we cannot be sure that Didymus was refuting Apollodorus here.[86]

Timachidas of Rhodes is another possible commentator from the first half of the 1st century BCE, if it is correct to connect the author of glosses and of comments on Euripides, Aristophanes, and others with the author (or co-author) of the Lindian register of dedications.[87] If the identification is rejected, then he may still be of about this date, if Didymus is the source of the criticisms of his opinions that survive in our scholia.[88] His identification of a *husteron proteron* in the opening lines of *Medea* was criticized (ἀγνοήσας) by a later commentator who preferred to see a rhetorical heightening effect (ἐπεξεργασία) or poetic trope (ὑπέρθεσις) when the nurse transitions to wishing away even the cutting of the pine tree for wood for the Argo (hyp. Med. (a) 30–33 Diggle; Sch. B Med. 1 = fr.

---

different Apollodorus of Tarsus wrote tragedies in the first half of the 4th century BCE (*TrGF* 64, cf. *Suda* α 3406). Schwartz plausibly suspected that the Apollodorus mentioned as attesting a version of Hermione's demise (Sch. Andr. 32) may be the tragic poet.

[85] Wentzel 1894a; Dyck 1981. He is elsewhere known for lexicographic items that have survived in later lexica; he was already used by Pamphilus (as reported by Athenaeus 11.74), who is dated to the second half of the first century CE (on the dating see Matthaios 2015: 227).

[86] Wilamowitz 1895: 162 n. 63.

[87] New edition of the fragments in Matijašić 2014b, earlier one in Blinkenberg 1915, esp. 41–47 for fragments of the hexameter poem Δεῖπνον (= *SupplHell* 366-367) and comments that have survived on Aristophanes' *Frogs*, on Menander's *Kolax*, and on *Medea*. See also *FGrHist* 532 Jacoby; Ziegler 1936; Montana 2006. Ziegler acknowledges that the identification of the commentator with the author of the Lindian Chronicle is not certain, and doubts about the identification are expressed by Matijašić 2014a. It is also to be noted that the name has been restored in several places in the ascribed fragments (Matijašić 2014b: 121).

[88] So Wilamowitz 1895: 156 n. 71, who compares Didymus' criticism of Parmeniscus (τούτῳ δὲ ἐναντιοῦται) in Sch. Med. 264 and the disagreement with Apollodorus of Tarsus mentioned above. On the basis of other references and possible references, Matijašić 2014b: 114–118 places him more loosely between about 150 BCE and 50 CE; but later (138) he postulates that Didymus had access to Timachidas' commentary on *Medea*.

30a–b Matijašić). He is again scorned as unsophisticated by the commentator in Sch. Med. 167 (fr. 31 Matijašić), who says that Timachidas was "carried along toward the obvious" (ἐπὶ τὰ πρόχειρα πᾶσιν ἐνεχθείς)[89] when he identified the slain brother as Apsyrtus, since Euripides never used an explicit name for this brother in *Medea* or *Aegeus*. The tone of these reports perhaps reflects an Alexandrian scholar's comfort with castigating a scholar from another setting, and possibly these remarks go back to Didymus.

For Didymus himself, it has already been noted that his name survives 19 times in the Euripidean scholia. Several of these notes deal with *problēmata*. We have already seen his disagreement with Parmeniscus about the Corinthian history of Medea and her children (Sch. Med. 264) and with Apollodous of Tarsus about whether or how Medea invokes Zeus (Sch. Med. 148, 167). Didymus proposes a non-mythological solution to the vexed question of the sense of ἁρμάτειον μέλος (Sch. Or. 1384), and comments on the equally puzzling expression τὰς ἀνάγκας οἱ νόμοι διώρισαν (Sch. Hec. 847, saying it expresses the opposite of the meaning needed in the passage). Criticisms of the poet or his characters are exemplified in four different remarks on *Andromache*: Sch. Andr. 330 and 362 declare Andromache's statements to Menelaus to be contrary to the requirements of the situation and not appropriate to her as a non-Greek woman; Sch. Andr. 885 indicates that Orestes' initial story to the chorus (and Hermione) is "false" (either it is contrary to the traditional version of the myth, or the character is lying); Sch. Andr. 1077 finds fault with the use of a conventional motif of grief-stricken speechlessness. In Sch. Med. 356 and 380 he accuses the actors of being responsible for the interpolation of line 380 after 356.[90] He makes a valid point of intertextual comparison in Sch. Phoen. 751 when he says Euripides avoids naming the Theban champions because Aeschylus had already done this in *Septem*. The details that Didymus supplies about Lemnian myth in Sch. Hec. 887, however, go far beyond what is relevant to the passage. Matters of more routine grammatical interpretation occur in other passages. His explanations are not very convincing in those passages where modern editors assume the reading he explains is corrupt (Sch. Hec. 729, Sch. Med. 737) or spurious (Sch. Phoen. 1747); nor is his idea that a vocative in *Hecuba* is directed to Polydorus, not a self-address (Sch. Hec. 736). The terse report in Sch. Tro. 1079 ὁ Δίδυμος τὸν ἐμπυρισμόν, ἀπὸ τοῦ αἴθεσθαι perhaps means "Didymus (interprets *aithera*) as

---

[89] Criticism is implied by the use of ἐνεχθείς, which is not neutral, but implies lack of control, and by the very inclusion of the participial phrase, whereas a neutral report would be simply "Timachidas says the speaker/poet means Apsyrtus."

[90] The iterated line is not found after 356 in our manuscript tradition. Either Didymus himself saw it in a copy or copies known to him, or he knew of it from the report of an earlier scholar, possibly Aristophanes or Callistratus.

'the burning,' by its derivation from *aithesthai*"; if so, he apparently misconstrues αἰθέρα τε as coordinated with τάδε as object of φρονεῖς rather than with ἕδρανον as object of ἐπιβεβώς. On the other hand, accurate linguistic knowledge lies behind his comment on the old Attic first-person form ἦ ("I was") in Sch. Hec. 13. From these scholia in which Didymus is actually named, one may be inclined to conclude that, all in all, the generally negative assessment of his judgment is closer to the truth than attempts to rehabilitate his reputation.[91]

Those who wrote commentaries or who added or reconfigured annotations on Euripides in the centuries after Didymus are mostly unknown to us. Apart from the mysterious Dionysius of the subscriptions cited above, we find three individuals engaged in exegesis such as might come from a commentary. Irenaeus will be discussed below. The other two, Aeschines and Aeschrio, are otherwise unknown and could could even be late antique or Byzantine *grammatici*. Aeschines' two contributions confine themselves to verbal exegesis:

> Sch. Or. 12 τὸν τῆς ἀρχῆς στέφανον. Αἰσχίνης γὰρ στέμματα τὰ ἔριά φησιν ἀπὸ τοῦ στέφειν τὰς ἠλακάτας· ἐξ ὧν γίνονται οἱ στέφανοι τῶν βασιλέων.
>
> The crown of rule. For Aeschines says that *stemmata* refers to the wool threads (by derivation from their wreathing (*stephein*) the distaff), out of which the crowns of kings are made.
>
> Sch. Or. 1371 Αἰσχίνης δὲ τὴν ὑπέρ ἀντὶ τῆς πρό φησίν, ἵν' ᾖ ἀντὶ τοῦ πρὸ τεράμνων.
>
> Aeschines says that the preposition *huper* is used in the sense of the preposition *pro*, so that the sense is "in front of the beams."

The first of these notes continues with further exegesis and paraphrase, but that continuation is probably the work of the commentator quoting Aeschines. Aeschines' contribution is perhaps the etymological explanation, since the notion that στέμματα and ἔρια are synonyms is also found in Sch. Soph. OC 475, *Suda* κ 792, *Et. Magn.* s.v. εἰρεσιώνη.

Aeschrio's remarks about the rivers named Krathis are quoted in a note that cites Parmeniscus. It is not impossible that this comes from something other than a commentary on the play (compare the uncertainty about what kind of work of Parmeniscus was used here).

> Sch. Tro. 228 ... ὁ δὲ Αἰσχρίων φησὶν ὅτι ἐν Πελοποννήσῳ ἦν Κρᾶθις καλούμενος ποταμός, ὃς ἐποίει τὰς κόμας ξανθὰς τῶν λουομένων· οἱ δὲ ἀπὸ Πελοποννήσου ἀποικίαν στειλάμενοι καὶ κτίσαντες Σύβαριν τὸν ἐκεῖ ποταμὸν ὠνόμασαν Κρᾶθιν. ἀπὸ οὖν τοῦ ἐν Πελοποννήσῳ ὁ Εὐριπίδης τοῦ ἐν Ἰταλίᾳ μέμνηται ὡς οὐ μόνον τὸ {αὐτὸ} ὄνομα ἔχοντος τοῦ ἐν Ἀχαΐᾳ ποταμοῦ, ἀλλὰ καὶ τὴν δύναμιν.

---

[91] On divergent judgments of Didymus see Montana 2015: 178 n. 558.

But Aeschrio says that in the Peloponnesus there was a river called Krathis, which turned blond the hair of those who washed in it. Those who went on a colonizing expedition from the Peloponnesus and founded Sybaris named the river there Krathis. So then, from the one in the Peloponnesus Euripides has mentioned the one in Italy as not only having the {same} name of the river in Achaea, but also its special power.

Irenaeus has sometimes been identified with the grammarian of the 1st century CE also known by the Latin name Minucius Pacatus,[92] but it is more plausible that the Irenaeus quoted in scholia on Apollonius Rhodius and Euripides and cited once as author of a commentary on Herodotus is a different individual, active in the second half of the 2nd century.[93] At any rate, the surviving notes on Euripides are extended paraphrases that seem suited to mid-level teaching or the earliest level of rhetorical training.

> Sch. Med. 214 ὦ Κορίνθιαι γυναῖκες, ἐξῆλθον ἐκ τῶν δόμων, ἵνα μὴ μέμψησθέ μοι, καίτοι ἐπίσταμαι πολλοὺς τῶν ἀνθρώπων σεμνοὺς γεγῶτας, τοὺς μὲν ὀμμάτων ἄπο, τοὺς δ' ἐν θυραίοις, οἷον ὑπερηφάνους νομιζομένους τοὺς μὲν ἀπὸ τοῦ χωρίζεσθαι καὶ ἄποθεν τῶν ὀμμάτων εἶναι, τοὺς δὲ διὰ τὸ προέρχεσθαι καὶ συνεχῶς ἐπιφαίνεσθαι· ἐξ οὗ τὸ ἀπανταχόθεν ἐπίφθονον καὶ εὐδιάβολον τῶν ἀνθρώπων συνάγει, ὅτι εἰς μηδὲν ἀρέσκονται. εἶτα πάλιν κατὰ τούτων ἐπιφέρει ὅτι καὶ οἱ ἀφ' ἡσύχου ποδὸς καὶ ἐν ἐρημίᾳ τὰ ἑαυτῶν πράττοντες δύσκλειαν κτῶνται καὶ ἀργίαν, οἷον καὶ οὗτοι διαβάλλονται ὑπὲρ τούτου. οὕτως ὁ Εἰρηναῖος.

O women of Corinth, I have come out of the house in order that you not reproach me; yet I know that many among mortals are proud, some away from the eyes, others among those outside, that is to say, the ones considered to be haughty because of their separating themselves and being far from people's eyes, the others because they go forth and are constantly conspicuous. From this, she infers the universal human trait of envy and readiness to accept aspersions, the fact that people are not satisfied in any respect. Then in addition she adds the charge against these people that even those who act from quiet foot, that is, minding their own business in isolation, earn ill repute and the charge of laziness, that is to say, these too are criticized for this behavior. Thus explains Irenaeus.

> Sch. Med. 219 δίκη γὰρ οὐκ ἔνεστ' ἐν ὀφθαλμοῖς βροτῶν: φησὶν ὅτι διὰ τοῦτο προῆλθον πρὸς ὑμᾶς, καίτοι ἐπισταμένη ὅτι καὶ τὸ ἐπιφοιτᾶν ἐπικίνδυνόν ἐστιν, ὅμως δ' οὖν, ἵνα {μὴ} δι' ἔργων καὶ ἀπ' αὐτῆς τῆς διανοίας γνωρίσητέ

---

[92] See Regali 2007.

[93] The identification of the commentator with the grammarian is espoused by Haupt 1876a and Cohn 1905, but for the separation of the two (and the estimated date of the commentator) see Wendel 1932: 106–107 (citing earlier proponents of the separation), Matthaios 2015: 240. The fragments are collected in Haupt 1876a: 439–440, who did not include Sch. Med. 214 because the phrase ascribing it to Irenaeus was not present in editions earlier than Schwartz.

με ἥτις εἰμί. οὐ γὰρ, φησὶν, ἐν ὀφθαλμοῖς ἀνδρῶν καὶ ἐν τῇ ὄψει μόνῃ περί τινος δίκη καὶ κρίσις ἐστίν, ἤτοι τὸ δίκαιον οὐκ ἀπὸ μόνης τῆς ὄψεως εὑρίσκεται. τὸ δὲ κατάλληλον οὕτως μᾶλλον σαφὲς γίνεται· ὅτι ἡ δίκη οὐκ ἔστιν ἐν ὀφθαλμοῖς βροτῶν, οὐδὲ δίκαιος οὗτος ὃς πρὶν τὸ σπλάγχνον σαφῶς ἐκμαθεῖν τοῦ πέλας, στυγεῖ ἀπὸ τῆς ὄψεώς τινα οὐδὲν ἠδικημένος ὑπ' αὐτοῦ. οὕτως Εἰρηναῖος.

For there is no justice in the eyes of mortals: she is saying that I came forth to you for this reason, even though I know that simply to come out is risky, but all the same I do so in order that through my actions and from my very cast of mind you may know who I am. For, she says, there is not in the eyes of men, that is, in their sight alone, justice and (true) judgment concerning a person, in other words, what is just is not discovered from sight alone. The sequence of ideas becomes clearer in this way: that justice is not present in the eyes of mortals, nor is that man just who, before he clearly learns in full about the inward being, hates someone on sight, though not having been in any way wronged by him. Thus explains Irenaeus.

There are only a few other sources named in the scholia that date from after the time of Didymus.[94] Plutarch's *Homeric Meletai* is cited in Sch. Alc. 1128 (= Plutarch fr. 126 Sandbach). The extant scholia infrequently cite a few major grammatical authorities of the Imperial period, Apion (once) and Herodian (four times), as well as (from the late 4th–early 5th cent.) Theodosius (once).[95] The Atticist lexicographer Phrynichus[96] (2nd cent. CE) is cited in Sch. Med. 1027. Helladius' *Chrestomathia* (4th cent. CE) may be the source the quotation about *symbola* in Sch. Med. 613 or it may come from a different Helladius active in the late 4th and early 5th centuries.[97]

---

[94] Apart from the instances to be mentioned in this paragraph, Wilamowitz 1895: 197 n. 151 also suggests other scholia that he would date to the period after Didymus: Sch. Med. 687, because it makes use of pseudo-Apollodorus; Sch. Andr. 229, because he believes that the citation of Lycophron must reflect the later popularity of this author; Sch. Or. 225, because of its citation of Apollonius Rhodius, since he assumes that the *Argonautica* was not excerpted in earlier glossaries.
[95] On these grammarians see Matthaios 2015: 221–223, 261–264, 267–268.
[96] See Regali 2008.
[97] Ascription to the first Helladius (early 4th cent., son of Besantinous, from Antinoopolis: Photius, *Bibliotheca* codex 279; Gudeman 1912; Kaster 1988: 411–412; Alpers 2001: 199), as proposed by Haupt 1876b and accepted by Wilamowitz 1895: 197 n. 151, seems to me preferable. The second is the Alexandrian grammarian Helladius (Kaster 1988: 289; Matthaios 2015: 268) who compiled a lexicon (Λέξεως παντοίας χρῆσις κατὰ στοιχεῖον) read by Photius and used as a source by later lexicographers: Photius, *Bibliotheca* codex 145; *Suda* ε 732. Heimannsfeld 1911: 14 judges that the Alexandrian has as much claim to the observation about *symbola* as the Antinoopolite (see also Meliadò 2005). This same Alexandrian Helladius, after his flight to Constantinople, was probably the teacher of the ecclesiastical historian Socrates (Photius, *Bibliotheca* codex 28), presumably shortly before 400, although in the index to Henry 1959–1977 prepared by J. Schamp this teacher is listed as a third Helladius.

It appears, then, that the bulk of the erudite material to which names are still attached in the scholia to Euripides comes from the period up to and including Didymus, and that commentators after Didymus probably knew of such sources only through Didymus or those who copied from Didymus, and not from direct consultation of the sources. We have no idea, however, how many stages of anonymous adaptation, filtering, and compilation our corpus went through between the 2nd century CE and what we find in the minuscule manuscripts over 800 years later.

3. THE SCHOLIA IN THE MIDDLE AGES

The earliest more or less complete manuscripts that carry a substantial corpus of old scholia are M and B, both of the 11th century.[98] These represent very ambitious efforts to include in one codex several of the select plays of Euripides along with annotation: M, in its current state, contains the triad plus *Andromache* and most of *Hippolytus*, while B contains the triad (now absent the first 522 lines of *Hec.*) plus *Hippolytus*, *Medea*, *Alcestis*, and *Andromache* (with a few pages of *Andr.* lost). The annotation, except in the case of M's limited set for *Hippolytus*, is overall a generous collection occupying the ample outer margins, and sometimes other spaces are used as well. Both manuscripts use the format known as annotation "en couronne" or, more accurately, "a cornice."[99] The writing is mostly confined to a large bounding rectangle that leaves some margin on all sides, and within that rectangle the poetic text is confined to a smaller rectangle in the central inner portion of the pages (in M the text rectangle normally accommodates 28 lines; in B, generally between 27 and 32 lines). The principal locations for the commentary, which is visually marked by the use of a smaller script, are what I like to refer to as the top block, the side or margin block, and the bottom block. The top and bottom blocks extend the full width of the large rectangle and occupy the spaces above and below the text rectangle: the number of lines accommodated in the top and bottom blocks may vary considerably in B, while in M the top block is usually 9 lines and the bottom block more variable. The side block spans the narrower outer rectangle that matches the text rectangle in height. In both, on full pages, the scholia generally flow continuously from

---

[98] On the date of M see Chapter 4.
[99] On the formats used to combine text and comments, see the older survey in Irigoin 1984 and the important considerations in the more recent works of Maniaci 2002 and 2006.

top block to side block and from side block to bottom block.[100] There is clearly a general preference for keeping scholia on the same page as the lemma to which they refer, but in both cases the scribe occasionally found it necessary to complete the sequence belonging on one page on the next page. When pages are very full, glosses or short notes may also be placed between the lines, crowded in the intermarginal space (by which I mean the space between the text block and the side block, much more rarely between text block and top or bottom block), or even in the very narrow inner margin between text block and binding.[101] When the collection of scholia for the lines on a page is less abundant, the bottom block may be unused, and sometimes part of the lower end of the side block is also blank. If scholia are especially sparse, scholia may be located at intervals in the side block matching the level of the relevant lemmata. On the fuller pages, one usually finds both lemmata and reference symbols[102] to relate the note to the relevant line or phrase in the text, but in both M and B the practice is quite inconsistent, in that after a stretch of constantly using lemmata the scribe may omit them for another stretch, or after using one system of reference markers, such as letters as numerals, the scribe may switch to symbols.[103] When the intermarginal space is used, it may be a matter of adding material from a different source, but it may also be due to the need to fit too many notes on the same page with the verses they apply to, and the intermarginal positioning may at times have arisen in an ancestor and been imitated in subsequent copies. It must have been no easy task to arrange scholia for most efficient consultation, and it is not surprising that sometimes the scribes were unable to keep annotation on the same page as the relevant line.[104] When the annotation is sparse enough and the scribe chooses to place notes so that each begins at the level of the line to which it applies, a reference symbol is not needed and the lemma as well is usually omitted. The scribe of M, however, often seeks a balance on the page, and may distribute notes so that one block in the upper margin and extending a few lines into the upper side block area is counterbalanced by a block beginning with a few lines toward the bottom of the side block and continuing into the bottom

---

[100] Maniaci 2006, studying two laboriously prepared Homer manuscripts, detects an effort in them to avoid flowing from one scholia block to the next. I do not find it odd that very few scribes would have expended the time and effort to adhere to the refinements of positioning that she posits as the goals of the particular scribes whose habits she scrutinizes.

[101] Later hands sometimes add annotations in the top, outer, or bottom margin, outside the area originally reserved for writing.

[102] For some general considerations about "signes de renvoi" applied to annotation in papyri and manuscripts, see Atsalos 1991.

[103] For an example of this, see the discussion of symbols used in M in Chapter 4.

[104] See Appendix to Chapter 4 for the mismatch between lemmata in the text and the position of the notes on fol. 95r–105r of *Phoenissae* in M. See again Maniaci 2006 for a pair of Homeric manuscripts of Homer in which the scribes worked very hard to avoid carryover from one page to the next.

margin area. In this case the side margin has a large blank area.[105]

One supposes that M and B come from high-level sources: perhaps a major center of learning, but the very existence of these is quite uncertain; or, alternatively, a circle of learned (and wealthy) individuals who collectively collect, recopy, and read classical literature.[106] These codices perhaps served as reference copies for advanced readers, teachers, and students. M in particular shows relatively little additional annotation by later users, although the text has been collated and corrected in places, and the use of the manuscript in teaching at a later date may be reflected in the marginal markings of the type β ἑρμηνεία added by a crude later hand.[107] B shows much more evidence of prolonged use, with multiple scribes, probably dating from close to the time of the original scribe to the Palaeologan period and later, adding glosses or short notes, recording textual variants or making corrections of the text, and rewriting faded words. But not all copies of the plays of Euripides will have been as ambitious as M and B. In the twelfth century, Ioannikios' manuscript O is ambitious in the sense that it contains seven full plays and almost three quarters of *Rhesus* (as well as the seven extant plays of Sophocles), and it is now known that Ioannikios was part of a circle that dealt with advanced topics and copied learned prose works.[108] But in the Euripides portion of the manuscript only the first three plays, *Hecuba*, *Orestes*, and *Medea*, are provided with a very limited selection of annotation based on the old scholia, often shortened in an idiosyncratic way, and even in these plays annotation is absent for long stretches of the text.[109] Ioannikios' circle apparently did not aspire to very advanced and thorough study or teaching of the tragedians, at least not in this copy. Something similar can perhaps be said of H, which is generally thought to be a little earlier than M and B. This codex was in use over a long period of time. Daitz identified eight hands for the annotation, ranging in date over three centuries, with the majority of the scholia by the first hand, ca. 1000, and by the third, for which he suggests the range 1050–1150. Even the

---

[105] For us, an unfortunate effect of this aesthetic choice in M is that many scholia that could easily have fit in the undamaged side margin of a page if the sequence had continued unbroken from the top of the page have been severely damaged or made largely illegible because the bottoms of M's pages have suffered the most from water damage and abrasion.

[106] On the phenomenon of erudite circles and their role in transmission of pagan literature, see Cavallo 2008.

[107] See Chapter 4 after note 71.

[108] Wilson 1983a and 1991, Degni 2008a, Baldi 2011, Nesseris forthcoming. Ioannikios is the scribe of the text of O, but as with several other codices he wrote, the annotation is added by a collaborator of his (called scribe B by Degni 2008a). On the sparse, truncated, and idiosyncratic annotation of the same manuscript for Sophocles (siglum K), see Xenis 2010a: 34–37.

[109] The situation is not much better in the Sophocles part: there are sporadic notes, usually fairly short, on *Ajax*, *Electra*, and *Antigone*, a few on the beginning of *Trachiniae*, and one or two on *Oedipus Tyrannus*.

latest hand can be no later than ca. 1300, when the Euripides book was dismantled and its pages reused for the uppermost text. The later users were not afraid to make casual additions, and thus this copy was probably intended for the everyday use of less advanced readers, whether students or teachers. The difference in purpose and audience is reflected in the way H very often truncates a scholion,[110] usually providing the first sentence or so and omitting the remaining two-thirds or one half. The omitted part often includes a quotation of a parallel passage or an alternative interpretation or additional paraphrase.[111] Here are a few examples from Sch. Or., without an apparatus of variants:

Or. 108 ἕρπειν] τὸ ἕρπειν κυρίως ἐπὶ ὄφεως. Mˢ

τὸ δὲ ἕρπειν κυρίως ἐπὶ ὄφεως λέγεται. C

κυρίως ἐπὶ τῆς ὄφεως. Hˢ

herpein] the verb *herpein* (is used) properly of (the movement of) a serpent. Mˢ

And the verb *herpein* is used properly of (the movement of) a serpent. O

Properly applied to the serpent. Hˢ

Or. 115 οἰνωπόν τ' ἄχνην] ἐμφαντικῶς τὴν δαψιλῆ τοῦ οἴνου ῥύσιν διὰ [γὰρ added in most mss] τῆς ἄχνης ἐσήμανε. τοῦτο δὲ ἐπὶ τῶν κυμάτων εἴρηται [*Il.* 4.426]· "ἀποπτύει δ' ἁλὸς ἄχνην." οἱ δὲ ἀκύρως τὴν οἰνόχροα τρίχα φασί. λάχνη γὰρ ἡ θρὶξ, ἀλλ' ἄχνη τὸ λεπτὸν μέρος, ὃ κατέχειν τις οὐ δύναται, οἱονεὶ ἀέχη τις οὖσα. MBCVMnPrRRwS

ἐμφαντικῶς τὴν τοῦ οἴνου δαψιλῆ ῥύσιν. ἄχνη δὲ ἐπὶ τῶν κυμάτων. Ο

δαψιλῆ τοῦ οἴνου ῥύσιν, διὰ γὰρ τῆς ἄχνης τοῦτο ἐσήμανεν. οἱ δὲ οἰνόχροα τρίχα φασί. Η

The poet indicated the abundant flow of wine vividly by using the word *achnē*. And this word has been used of waves (in Homer): "the sea spits forth a foam of salt water." Some say it is used in a transferred sense to mean wine-colored hair. For hair is called *lachnē*, but *achnē* is used of the fine portion of hair that one is not able to grasp/control, as if being some unheld thing (*aechē*). MBCV etc.

Vividly (he expresses) the abundant flow of wine. And *achnē* in application to waves. O

Abundant flow of wine, for this is what he expressed by *achnē*. Others say (it means) wine-colored hair. H

---

[110] A reader points out to me that the truncation of scholia may be due to a lack of space or the aesthetic preferences of the scribe. Even in those cases, it would be significant that the scribe did not choose a format that would accommodate fuller annotation.

[111] In the first 500 lines of Or., note Sch. 108, 109, 115, 116, 121, 127, 128, 131, 142, 144, 147, 149, 174, 191, 335, 340, 356, 411. More definitive analysis of the H-scholia awaits the publication of the new enhanced images created for the Palamedes Project (palamedes.uni-goettingen.de; see Albrecht 2012) and the associated discussion by the project's collaborators.

Or. 121 τοῖν τ' ἀθλίοιν] καὶ αὐτῶν μέμνηται, ἵνα μὴ δόξῃ παντελῶς λιθοκάρδιος εἶναι, ὅμως μετὰ ἀρᾶς. τὸ γὰρ "οὓς ἀπώλεσεν θεός" δοκεῖ μὲν συναχθομένη λέγειν, πανούργως δὲ ἐμφαίνει ὅτι θεοῖς ἀπηχθημένοι εἰσίν. οὐ γὰρ ἀπολλύει εἶπεν, ἀλλ' ἀπώλεσεν, ὡς ἐγνωσμένης ἤδη τῆς παρὰ θεῶν δυσμενείας. MBCVPrRw

μέμνηται καὶ αὐτῶν, ἵνα μὴ δόξῃ παντελῶς λιθοκάρδιος εἶναι. Η

She also mentions them (Orestes and Electra), in order not to seem completely stone-hearted, but even so she does so with a curse. For she seems to utter the phrase "whom god destroyed" sharing their distress, but maliciously she indirectly suggests that they are hated by the gods. For she doesn't say "is destroying" but "has destroyed," as if the hostility on the part of the gods is already decided. MBCVPrRw

She also mentions them, in order not to seem completely stone-hearted. H

Or. 128 εἴδετε παρ' ἄκρας] τὸ εἴδετε ἀντὶ τοῦ ἴδοι τις ἄν, ὡς τὸ [Il. 3.220] "φαίης κε ζάκοτον" καὶ [Il. 4.223] "ἔνθ' οὐκ ἂν βρίζοντα ἴδοις." ἔνιοι δέ φασι ταῖς δμωσὶ ταῦτα λέγειν. οἱ δὲ πρὸς τὸ θέατρον, ὃ καὶ ἄμεινον. ἐφελκυστικὸς γάρ ἐστιν ἀεὶ μᾶλλον τῶν θεατῶν ὁ ποιητής, οὐ φροντίζων τῶν ἀκριβολογούντων. MBVCMnPrRSSa

ἴδοι τις. ἔνιοι δέ φασι ταῖς δμώαισι ταῦτα λέγειν· ὃ ἄμεινον. H[s]

did you see along the tips] The word "did you see" is equivalent to "one might see," as (in Homer) "you might say (he was) mightily angry" and "you would not see him dozing." Some say that she addresses this to servant-women, others say it is directed to the audience, which is better. For the poet is always rather inclined to draw in the audience, showing no regard for those who are fussy about details. MBVC etc.

One might see. Some say she says this to servant-women, which is better. H

All these show how H abbreviates to the minimum possible length. In Sch. Or. 108 the other two witnesses have what we might call the run-on version of this note: in ancient commentaries a paragraph of explanations might discuss a phrase or sentence or several lines of text, and the typical transition to the next point of explanation within the paragraph is by quoting the word from the text—the word that would serve as a lemma if the annotations were separated and not run together. So here in M τὸ ἕρπειν is incorporated, even though the note is written above the line over the word to which it applies, and in C the phrase is continued, with τὸ δὲ ἕρπειν, from a comment about παρθένοισιν in the same verse. Sch. Or. 121 shows O also drastically shortening the note, in a different way, but characteristically both H and O omit the quoted example. In Sch. Or. 128 one cannot be certain whether the shortening has unintentionally related ὃ ἄμεινον ("which is better") to the only view retained from the longer form (that the imperative is addressed to servants), or whether the abridger has consciously decided to reject the view involving audience address preferred by the author of the longer note.

Such shortened versions are much less common in M and B, but examples can be found even in those manuscripts. For whatever reason, M's source for *Hippolytus* had a reduced set of annotations with many short versions. As mentioned earlier,[112] Schwartz sometimes failed to report these short versions, printing the fuller version from BVN and only rarely mentioning in the apparatus that M too had part of the note. One example of a shortened version in B is Sch. Or. 234, which will be quoted later in this discussion. The implication of our already finding shortened versions in HMB from around 1000 and the half century or so after is that these less ambitious alternatives already existed from early in the minuscule tradition: they either arose not long after the fuller annotations entered into the minuscule tradition (around or soon after 900?), or they already existed in the commentary or annotation tradition surviving from late antiquity.

The exact wording of scholia is generally subject to minor modifications, since the scribes do not treat the paratext with the same fidelity as the commentated text. Some such modifications are in the direction of simpler words or words more typical of Byzantine Greek, and rarely one even finds Byzantine morphology adopted (e.g., νὰ for ἵνα; ὄψις from Latin *obses*, hostage). In several places one can observe H substituting a simpler or more obvious word for the word that is found in the other witnesses,[113] as in the following from Sch. Or.:

Or. 157 τί φῄς ὦ τάλας] οἰκειούμενος τὰς συμφορὰς ὁ χορὸς καὶ συναχθόμενος γεγωνότερον ἀνέκραγε [ἐξεβόησε H] τὸ ὦ τάλας· διό φησιν ὀλεῖς, εἰ βλέφαρα κινήσεις.

what are you saying? oh wretched one!] Making the misfortunes their own and sharing in the grief the chorus cried out [shouted out H] more loudly the words "oh wretched one." Therefore she (Electra) says "you'll destroy (him), if you stir his eyelids."

Or. 162 ἄδικος ἄδικα] ... ἢ τὸ ἄδικα ἐδίκασεν ἐμφαίνει ὅτι δικαίως μὲν ἐμαντεύσατο [ἐψηφίσατο H] τὸν φόνον τῆς μητρός, ἀδικεῖ δὲ τῷ δράσαντι μὴ ἐπικουρῶν. ...

unjust (one) unjust (things)] ... or the phrase "he gave unjust judgments" means that although he justly gave an oracular command for [decreed H] the murder of the mother, he acts unjustly in not giving aid to the one who acted.

Or. 211 ὕπνου θέλγητρον] τὸ βαθύτατον τοῦ ὕπνου, τὸ μάλιστα θέλγειν δυνάμενον τοὺς ἀσθενοῦντας [ἀρρώστους H]· ὁ γὰρ ἐλαφρὸς φαντασίαις ἀναμέμικται.

---
[112] See above after note 16.
[113] For a similar phenomenon in what he calls "minority scholia" of Sophocles see Xenis 2010a: 15–16.

charm of sleep] the deepest form of sleep, the one most able to soothe/enchant those who are weak with illness [the sick H]. For light sleep is mixed with (disturbing) visions.

Or. 331 ἵνα μεσόμφαλοι λέγονται] ... ὅθεν ὀμφαλὸς ἐκλήθη. ἀνακεῖσθαί τε χρυσοῦς ἀετούς φασι τῶν μυθευομένων ἀετῶν ὑπομνήματα [μνημεῖα H].
where are said to be (the hollows) located at the navel marking the middle] ... wherefore it was called navel. And they say golden eagles have been dedicated as reminders [memorials H] of the eagles in the mythical story.

We may note that in Sch. Or. 162 ἐψηφίσατο reflects a late usage, of a god or king decreeing or commanding an action,[114] as used for instance of Zeus in Sch. D Il. 1.400, while in Sch. Or. 331 μνημεῖα is a more obvious word for "'memorial, visible reminder" than ὑπομνήματα, which is common in scholiastic language for the commentaries that were the ultimate source of many scholia.

Along with the shortening of notes and adjustment of vocabulary, another feature of H's annotation pointing to the context of teaching at a fairly basic level, or of ordinary readers as opposed to philological experts, is the inclusion of notes explaining deictics or the style of delivery. Here are three examples:

Or. 199 τέκνα τε τάδε] δεικτικῶς φησιν ἑαυτὴν καὶ Ὀρέστην. H^margB^iC^i
By using the deictic she refers to herself and Orestes.

201 σύ] τοῦτο πρὸς ὀρέστην λέγει. H^marg
She says this to Orestes.

Or. 211 νῦν οὐ τραγῳδεῖ, ἀλλ' ἐν τῇ μανίᾳ. HB^iC^i
He does not speak tragically now, but during his madness.

Line 211 is the first spoken by Orestes as he awakens from his diseased slumber, and the note on 211 seems to mean "at this point Orestes does not speak in a tragic (exaggerated, passionate, ranting) fashion, but <he does so later> during his madness."[115] Schwartz, who did not yet have knowledge of H's readings, re-

---

[114] Cf. the version in V: ἄδικος ὁ λοξίας ἔδοξεν ἄδικα δικάσας, ἢ δικαίως ἐψηφίσατο τὸν φόνον ἀδίκως δὲ οὐ βοηθεῖ.

[115] Note, however, that the sense of τραγῳδεῖν in the scholia is not always obvious, as the action implied by the word sometimes is contrasted with singing and sometimes seems to be identified with singing. (The confusion stems in part from the development of the meanings of the verb: the meaning "declaim" or "express in exaggerated, pompous, overemotional style" developed as early as Plato and Demosthenes, while the meaning "sing" arose later and is reflected in modern Greek τραγουδῶ and τραγούδι.) A note positioned near Or. 1506 in MC (Schwartz assigned the note to 1505, but it probably comments on 1506 οὗτος ὃς πέφευγεν ἐκ δόμων) says ἐτραγῴδει ὁ Φρύξ, which could be "the Phrygian was singing" or "the Phrygian was delivering a highly stylized speech"; at Phoen. 690 τραγῳδεῖ Ἐτεοκλῆς must be just "Eteocles is speaking" (similarly at Hipp. 1257 τραγῳδεῖ

ported the annotations on 199 and 201 from B only (which he misdated by two centuries), since his reports of C were not complete. He marked both these notes with an obelus, damning them as "more recent." He never clearly states what "more recent" means in chronological terms, but he says in his preface (I.viii) that he uses this mark of "recentness" when two types of condemning evidence are both present: (1) the language or subject matter (*ex sermone vel argumento*); (2) the character of the witnesses (*ex codicum indole*). What we are dealing with, however, is not an issue of chronology, but one of purpose. Such notes provide help for the reader, whether they arose in private reading notes or from the practice of the schoolroom, where tradition maintained many of the same practices of paraphrase and explanation from antiquity through the whole Byzantine period. Dramatic texts that are being read will always require some recuperation of the speech situation by the reader or teacher.

At *Orestes* 201 σύ τε γὰρ ἐν νεκροῖς, modern scholars have also been puzzled by the transmitted second person pronoun, since immediately before this (195–199) Clytemnestra has been apostrophized with a vocative and been the subject of the second-person verbs, and there is no clear signal of a transition to a new addressee.[116] Concern for identifying the addressee is reflected also in O (ὀρέστα as gloss on σύ), in Xo (ὦ μῆτερ as gloss on σύ), and in the open-minded Thoman gloss ὦ μῆτερ ἢ ὦ ὀρέστα. We probably have a survival of an attempt to explain the transition to addressing Orestes in the first sentences of the discursive Sch. Or. 200 transmitted in VPrRRw (again marked with an obelus by Schwartz):

> ἐπειδὴ εἶπεν ἰσονέκυες, κατασκευάζει πῶς εἰσιν ἰσονέκυες, λέγουσα πρὸς τὸν Ὀρέστην· σὺ γὰρ, Ὀρέστα, ἐν νεκροῖς τό τε πλεῖον μέρος τῆς ἐμῆς ζωῆς οἴχεται ἐν δάκρυσι συνεχέσι καὶ στεναγμοῖς.
>
> Since she has said "as good as dead," she elaborates on how they are like the dead, saying to Orestes: "for you, Orestes, are among the dead, and the greater part of my life is gone in continual tears and lamentations."

The commentator perhaps considered the first-person plural in 200 ὀλόμεθ' ἰσονέκυες ὀλόμεθα as entailing "Orestes and I" and thus sufficiently suggestive of Orestes that in the elaboration or constructed proof (κατασκευάζει) Orestes

---

Θησεύς); at *Phoen.* 1485 Ἀντιγόνη τραγῳδεῖ could be a simple identification of the speaker or a comment on the style of her song or a comment that she is singing; in Sch. Andr. 103 Andromache's prologue rhesis is denied the status of μονῳδία with the explanation τραγῳδεῖ ("speaks tragic trimeters"?) γὰρ καὶ οὐκ ᾄδει. In Sch. Aesch. Prom. 555a (from the A-commentary) τραγῳδεῖν appears to mean "sing." The verb does not occur in the published scholia on Sophocles.

[116] Weil 1904 emended to ὅδε γὰρ ἐν νεκροῖς (accepted by Willink 1986, Diggle, and Kovacs). But very few ancient scholars proposed emendations of this sort, and it is usual for the commentators to struggle instead with multiple, often dubious, interpretations when confronted with a text that modern critics such as these judge corrupt.

can be understood as the second person meant by σύ.[117]

As is clear from the gloss on 201 in Xo and the Thoman gloss on the same line, the Palaeologan commentaries are very often aimed at a similar level of practical use. They may represent a somewhat new phenomenon in their abandonment of the anonymity that had characterized the scholiastic tradition for so long and in their effort to cover a substantial amount of text (compare, however, Tzetzes and Eustathius in the 12th century), but the educational practices Moschopulus and Thomas were serving had existed before, and there is no reason not to believe that notes identifying addressees go very far back in the tradition of annotation as well as in oral teaching.

The annotations found in the so-called codices *recentiores* of Euripides show a good deal of variation among themselves, but share certain characteristics. The selection of notes is often very unevenly distributed, usually with many notes on the beginning of a play and fewer or none after a certain point. Some *recentiores* contain additional scholia from the teaching tradition (a subject to be discussed in the next two chapters). Many of these manuscripts have no pretensions to aesthetic appeal in their script or their layout and seem to be informal products for personal use in an intellectually less ambitious milieu. PrSSa, in particular, lack a regular format for layout of the annotation and text: the format varies from page to page, and the demarcation between text blocks and annotation is often not well defined by spacing or by distinct contrast in the sizes of script used. Although notes occurring out of order and repeated notes are found from time to time even in M and B, some *recentiores* show more frequent displacements and at times share the same displacement, indicating a shared source. Although the scribes of some of the *recentiores* made an effort to use lemmata or rubrication or reference symbols to make it easier to find where each note begins and to what it applies, this is not always the case. The pages are thus not the product of careful planning, and in the cramped and disorganized format scholia are often located a page or two after the sheet on which the lemma appears.

As Schwartz knew, the *recentiores* sometimes provide words that have been lost in the transmission of the versions in MBCV[118] or feature correct proper names where the main manuscripts have corrupted forms. On the other hand, the *recentiores* are also prone to accidental omissions, substitution of late words,

---

[117] This is essentially how Medda 2001 views the passage in defending σύ τε γάρ.

[118] For example, in Sch. Or. 57 (οὐκ ὀρθῶς νῦν ποιοῦσί τινες τῶν ὑποκριτῶν πρῴ εἰσπορευομένην τὴν Ἑλένην καὶ τὰ λάφυρα. ῥητῶς γὰρ αὐτὴν φησὶ νυκτὸς ἀπεστάλθαι, τὰ δὲ κατὰ τὸ δρᾶμα ἡμέρᾳ συντελεῖται), the separation of πρὸ from εἰσπορευομένην in RS is close to Schwartz's correction πρῴ εἰσπορ., the words τὴν ἑλένην are in RRfSSa but omitted by other witnesses, and ῥητῶς (RRfRwSSa) has been corrupted to ἀρρήτω(ς) in MBCVPr; Sch. Or. 73, which alludes to an alphabetic play (*Heracles* 1219) and the lost *Ixion*, survives in VRRwSSa, but not in MBC.

and various forms of corruption, including implausible simplification of a longer corrupt text that made no sense. And they tend to exhibit the kind of shortening illustrated above for H and O. A few examples from Sch. Or. are set out here (without recording all the variant readings and emendations).

Or. 30 πρὸς οὐχ ἅπαντας] ¹οἱ μὲν γὰρ ἐπήνουν αὐτόν, οἱ δὲ οὔ. ²διὸ τὸ πρὸς οὐχ ἅπαντας εἶπεν.

not in everyone's eyes] ¹For some people praised him, others did not. ²Therefore she used the phrase "not in everyone's eyes."

Whole note in MCVPr(second version), with sentence 2 omitted in OAbPr(first version)RSSa

Or. 37 ὀνομάζειν γὰρ αἰδοῦμαι θεάς] ¹τὰς Ἐρινῦς. ²οὐκ ὀνομάζουσι δὲ, ἀλλ' εὐφημιζόμενοι Σεμνὰς θεὰς ἢ Εὐμενίδας καλοῦσιν. ³ὀνόματα δὲ τῶν Ἐρινύων Τισιφόνη Μέγαιρα Ἀλληκτώ.

out of respect I refrain from naming the goddesses] ¹the Erinyes. ²People do not use their name, but euphemistically they call them Revered goddesses or Eumenides. ³And the names of the Erinyes are Tisiphone, Megaera, Allecto.

Whole note in MCVBCrR(in block at end of play)RfRw, only sentences 1–2 in Pr(twice)R(in margin)S, only sentence 1 in Ab, only sentence 3 (added above the line) in MnS

Or. 81 ¹τί χρεὼν εἰπεῖν ἅτινα ὁρᾷς; ²τί δὲ ὁρᾷς; ³[81] "ἐν συμφοραῖσι τὸν Ἀγαμέμνονος γόνον." ⁴δῆλον δὲ ὅτι οὐ τὸν Ὀρέστην μόνον λέγει ἀλλὰ καὶ ἑαυτὴν Ἀγαμέμνονος γόνον. ⁵περὶ τῶν δύο γὰρ ἡ Ἑλένη ἐπύθετο λέγουσα [73] "πῶς, ὦ τάλαινα, σύ τε κασίγνητός τε σός." ⁶εἰκότως οὖν καὶ αὐτὴ ἐπάγει τὴν ἑαυτῆς ἄυπνον κηδεμονίαν καὶ τὴν Ὀρέστου νόσον.

BCVPrRfRw

What need is there to speak of the things that you see? And what do you see? "The offpsring of Agamemnon in severe distress." It is clear that she refers not just to Orestes but also to herself as the offspring of Agamemnon. For Helen asked about the two when she said "how (are you faring), poor girl, you and your brother." Suitably therefore she herself follows up with her own sleepless attendance (on her sick brother) and Orestes' sickness.

Or. 81 ¹τί ἔχω εἰπεῖν ἅτινα εἰσορᾷς καὶ παροῦσα; ²τί δὲ ὁρᾷς; ³ἐν συμφοραῖς ὄντα τὸν Ἀγαμέμνονος γόνον. ⁴ἐπάγει δὲ ἡ Ἠλέκτρα καὶ τὴν ἐπὶ τὸν Ὀρέστην ἄυπνον δυσδαιμονίαν καὶ τὴν τῆς νόσου καὶ τὴν ἐπ' αὐτοῦ αὐτῆς κακοπάθειαν. ⁵λέγει γὰρ ἐγὼ μὲν θάσσω, ὅ ἐστι κάθημαι παρεδρεύων, αὐτὸς δὲ τῇ νόσῳ τήκεται.

¹Why do I need to mention things that you see before your own eyes? ²And what do you see? ³The offspring of Agamemnon being in severe distress. ⁴And Electra follows up with her sleepless wretchedness (in attending) upon Orestes and the suffering of his sickness and her suffering over him. ⁵For she says "I am sitting here"—meaning "I sit in attendance—and he himself is wasting away from the disease."

R(twice)Sa, with sentences 2–4 om. S

Or. 162 ἄδικος ἄδικα] ¹τοῦτ' ἐστὶ τὸ ἀλλαχοῦ [Hipp. 701] εἰρημένον· ²"πρὸς τὰς τύχας γὰρ τὰς φρένας κεκτήμεθα." ³ἐπεὶ γὰρ ἔδοξεν ἀτυχῶς τῷ Ὀρέστῃ πεπτωκέναι τῆς μητρὸς ὁ φόνος, ἄδικος ὁ Λοξίας νενόμισται. ⁴ἢ τὸ ἄδικα ἐδίκασεν ἐμφαίνει ὅτι δικαίως μὲν ἐμαντεύσατο τὸν φόνον τῆς μητρός, ἀδικεῖ δὲ τῷ δράσαντι μὴ ἐπικουρῶν. ⁵τὸ δὲ ἑξῆς οὕτως· ⁶ὁ ἄδικος Λοξίας ἄδικα τότε ἐδίκασεν, ὅτε ἐπὶ τρίποδι Θέμιδος τὸν ἀπόφονον φόνον ἔλακεν ἐμῆς μητρός.

unjust (person) unjust (things)] ¹This is the situation spoken of elsewhere (*Hipp.* 701): ²"For we posssess our (reputation for) intelligence in accordance with our success or failure." ³For since the matricide seemed to have resulted in misfortune for Orestes, Loxias has been deemed unjust. ⁴Or the phrase "he gave unjust judgments" means/suggests that although he justly gave an oracular command for the murder of the mother, he acts unjustly in not giving aid to the one who acted. ⁵The run of the sense is as follows: ⁶The unjust Loxias gave unjust judgments at that time, when upon the tripod of Themis he proclaimed the unholy murder of my mother.

Full version HMBCPr(second version); 1-5 om. O, 1-4 om. Pr(first version), 1-3 ὁ φόνος om. MnRSSa, 1-2 om. Rw

It should be recalled, however, that such truncation occurs at times in M and B, and for B the instance in Sch. Or. 234 is especially revealing, since the quotation, which has suffered multiple corruptions, is reduced to its essential sense:

Or. 234 μεταβολὴ πάντων γλυκύ] ¹προσυπακουστέον τὸ κακῶν. ²κεκωμῴδηται δὲ ὁ στίχος. ³τὸ γὰρ ἐξ ὑγείας εἰς νόσον μεταβάλλειν οὐκ ἔστιν ἡδύ. ⁴φησὶ γοῦν ὁ κωμικός [adesp. 859 K-A, 115 Kock]·
⁵ὁ πρῶτος εἰπὼν "μεταβολὴ πάντων γλυκύ"
⁶οὐχ ὑγίαινε, δέσποτ'· ἐκ μὲν γὰρ κόπου
⁷γλυκεῖ' ἀνάπαυσις, ἐξ ἀλουσίας δ' ὕδωρ
⁸καὶ τὰ τοιαῦτα·
⁹ἢν δ' ἐκ πλουσίου
¹⁰πτωχὸν γενέσθαι, μεταβολὴ μὲν, ἡδὺ δ' οὔ.
¹¹ὥστ' οὐχὶ πάντων ἐστὶ μεταβολὴ γλυκύ.

MCVMnRᵃRᵇRwSSa

Change of all things is sweet] One must supply in addition the word "of evils." The verse has been ridiculed in comedy. For the change from health to sickness is not sweet. At any rate, the comic poet says: "The first person who said 'change of all things is a sweet thing' was not in his right mind, master. For after heavy toil cessation is sweet, and water after lack of bathing" and (the passage continued with) such examples. "But if (it comes about) that one becomes impoverished instead of wealthy, it is, to be sure, a change, but not sweet! So not of all things is change sweet."

Or. 234 μεταβολὴ πάντων γλυκύ] ¹προσυπακουστέον τὸ κακῶν. ²κεκωμῴδηται δὲ ὁ στίχος. ³τὸ γὰρ ἐξ ὑγείας εἰς νόσον μεταβαλεῖν οὐκ ἔστιν ἡδύ.

⁴φήσει γάρ τις ὡς ἐκ μὲν κόπου γλυκύτατον ἡ ἀνάπαυσις καὶ ἕτερα τοιαῦτα, ⁵ἐκ δὲ πλουσίου πτωχὸν γενέσθαι μεταβολὴ μέν, ἡδὺ δ' οὔ, ⁶ὥστε οὐχὶ πάντων ἡ μεταβολὴ γλυκύ.
BPr

Change of all things is sweet] One must supply in addition the word "of evils." The verse has been ridiculed in comedy. For the change from health to sickness is not sweet. For someone will say that cessation from heavy toil is very sweet, and other such examples, but to become impoverished instead of wealthy is, to be sure, a change, but not pleasant! So not of all things is change sweet.

This example illustrates two approaches to the difficulties posed by the quotation, in particular the apparent solecism of ἦν δ' ἐκ πλουσίου πτωχὸν γενέσθαι. The *recentiores* MnRSSa have the whole scholion along with MCVRw, but read πτωχὸς γένηται for πτωχὸν γενέσθαι, giving the subjunctive expected with ἤν. This is more likely an ameliorating correction than a survival of the truth. Kassel and Austin accordingly follow Schwartz in acknowledging that the preceding words, not quoted in our scholion, may have supplied the construction for γενέσθαι, as reflected in "it comes about" (*exempli gratia*) in the translation offered above. The shorter version in BPr also suggests that πτωχὸν γενέσθαι is the transmitted reading, for this version not only reduces the note by paraphrasing the quotation in briefer terms, but takes the opportunity to "correct" the syntax by removing ἤν and letting the infinitive be the subject with "is" understood. This is one piece of evidence that B carries at times a different recension of the scholia in which someone has tried to smooth out some of the difficulties and stylistic defects of some notes.[119]

4. GLOSSATION

The other characteristic that distinguishes the annotation in the *recentiores* is the much greater accumulation of supralinear annotation, mostly one- or two-word glosses, but also sometimes a paraphrase or short explanation that extends over most or all of a verse.[120] There are, to be sure, interlinear notes and short glosses in M and B, and indeed more of them by the original hands than one would gather from Schwartz's reports, since particularly in the triad he considered the

---

[119] I plan to treat this topic in more detail at a later date, when I have full evidence from all the plays carried by B. In the interim, see Cavarzeran's discussion (and proposed stemma) regarding *Hippolytus* (2016: 23–65).
[120] Sometimes, but not very often, a relatively short scholion that is in the margin in other witnesses will be placed above the line in one witness. This happens even in the older manuscripts, but more commonly in *recentiores* like Sa and Pr.

glosses that merely excerpted a word or phrase from the marginal scholia to be unworthy of recording. Nevertheless, the *recentiores* are different, once again because these are copies intended for a less advanced group of users. For quick reference, a supralinear note (or a gloss in the margin right beside the verse) is far easier to use than a longer discursive note, whether this is within a block of marginal scholia, located in another section of the codex (as in R, where most of the scholia on *Hecuba* precede the play and most of those on *Orestes* follow the play), or in an entirely separate commentary (as in N, and of course in the original ancient *hypomnēmata*). This technology for quick self-help has been the natural choice of readers and students from the bookrolls of Hellenistic times to modern printed books.

A thorough inventory of the glosses in many manuscripts reveals different styles and degrees of glossation and gives evidence of the prevalence of many standard traditional glosses and the probable circulation of some of the more unusual items. If we consider the triad plays, for which the glossation is naturally most abundant, there is a limited group of glosses that are shared by three or four of the main scholia witnesses MBCV. From the *recentiores* one can collect a larger (and in some ways more elementary) set of glosses, among which are items that are shared by several witnesses, including ones written in Southern Italy. Thus it seems likely that there was a kind of vulgate set of glosses, already in existence in the 12th century and earlier. These may be viewed as part of the apparatus of assistance for ordinary readers and mid-level teachers and students, along with the less ambitious exegeses and paraphrases intended for a lower level of readership. The scribes of the *recentiores* in the late 13th century and early 14th century could draw upon this stock, although it was of course possible for a scribe who wanted his copy to be even more useful to basic teaching to add his own further teachers' glosses of the type to be illustrated in more detail in the next chapter. Part of Moschopulus' project with the Euripidean triad may have been to provide a less haphazard, more consistent glossation for teaching purposes,[121] and he seems to have drawn freely on existing glosses, which we may find in manuscripts earlier than and more or less contemporary with him. A similar collection of glosses was created in the Thomano-Triclinian circle, and it is impossible to establish whether Thomas and his associates were initially aware of the Moschopulean annotation. The frequent differences between Thoman and Moschopulean glossation might be a sign that Thomas deliberately sought to offer an alternative, or simply the effect of his not having Moschopulus' work at hand. The overlaps might indicate either that he occasionally was content to reuse Moschopulean glosses or that both circles were independently using obvi-

---

[121] For viewing Moschopulus' project as one of curricular improvement and reform, see Gaul 2008: 184–190.

ous glosses or traditional glosses familiar in oral teaching or written in older manuscripts. For the most part, there was evidently not a strong sense of ownership of glosses, and they were a kind of common property of teachers. Just as Moschopulus took over passages from traditional schedographic sources in his *Schedographiae*,[122] or Thomas drew on earlier sources such as Phrynichus and Ammonius in his *Ecloge*,[123] so their glosses freely reused existing material. The more original parts of the exegetic content offered by Moschopulus and Thomas were the discursive scholia, even though some of those are obviously adapted from the old scholia.[124] Thus, these are the most reliable criterion by which to decide whether the scribe of a *recentior* may have had access to the Moschopulean or Thoman exegesis,[125] and it turns out that there is almost no sign of such access in the *recentiores* AaAbFMnPrRRfRwSSa. Occasional shared glosses are not probative, except in a few cases in which the pattern of agreement is striking, as for instance in many of the glosses added by the hand F² in the manuscript F, where we have no way to tell how much time passed between the writing of the manuscript by the original scribe and the work done by F². On the other hand, one can suspect that in some Palaeologan manuscripts a scribe or scholar has made a real effort to avoid borrowing glosses from elsewhere or using a familiar and obvious gloss. There are so many different glosses on some words that one may deduce that glossation (like etymologizing) could be a matter of competitive display whereby one teacher tried to outdo another and demonstrate his creativity and the extent of his learned vocabulary. This would account for instances in which the word in the text is not really so difficult, but the gloss provided appears to us to be very rarely attested and more abstruse than the lemma.[126]

---

[122] On this work see Keaney 1971, Gaul 2008: 175–176.

[123] On this work see Gaul 2007: 296–326, 2008: 184–190, and 2011: 141–144, 401–402.

[124] Note the heading at the beginning of *Hecuba* on fol. 74r of Zm: αὗται αἱ περὶ τὰς συντάξεις τῶν ἀποριῶν λύσεις καὶ πᾶσαι ἄλλαι ἐξηγήσεις εἰσὶ τοῦ σοφωτάτου καὶ ῥητορικωτάτου κυροῦ Θωμᾶ τοῦ Μαγίστρου, which emphasizes the solution of difficulties in the syntax—a good description of many of Thomas' discursive scholia. See Gaul 2007: 272 and 2011: 235–236.

[125] We cannot fix precisely enough either the date of most *recentiores* or the date at which Moschopulus' and Thomas' exegeses were ready to circulate. Several *recentiores* may be earlier than 1300, according to more recent estimates of dates by K. Matthiessen and N. Wilson. Moschopulus probably worked on the triad between 1295 and 1305. See Gaul 2008: 166–177 for the latest reconstruction of Moschopulus' career: according to Gaul, Moschopulus' scholarly career ended with his imprisonment in 1305–1306, and it was due to the efforts of his associates that from 1305 onward his commentary received wider circulation. For Thomas' life and dating, see Gaul 2011: 213–251. Gaul 2011: 396 suggests that Thomas' commentary on Euripides has a *terminus ante quem* of 1315 or 1319, which seems to be when Triclinius began work on T, the earliest form of which had the Thoman exegesis with Triclinius' earlier rounded breathing signs. Thomas' work may actually have been completed in the first decade of the century. Gaul 2007: 276 suggests that Thomas worked on his commentaries on drama during the period 1305–1315.

[126] Some examples of this phenomenon in the manuscript Zu are given in Chapter 2 (at note 11).

To substantiate these observations, I offer a series of examples, all from *Orestes* 1–500, for a few categories of relationship. First, some glosses that are present in some or all of HMBO before 1200 and then appear in V or one or more of the *recentiores* as well as in Moschopulean and/or Thoman witnesses. Some of these have evidently been excerpted from a discursive note, and in some cases it is clear the gloss was present in the lexicographic tradition at a much earlier point. If a plus sign (+) appears at the end, it indicates that there are additional witnesses from the 14th or 15th century that may depend on Moschopulus or Thomas.

Or. 50 νώ] ἡμᾶς B²O, VAaAbFKMnPrSSa, Mosch., Thom.+

Or. 62 παραψυχήν] παραμυθίαν O, VAa, Mosch., Thom.+; cf. Hesych. π 769 παραψυχή· παραμυθία

Or. 90 τεκοῦσα] μελέα O, AaFKPr, Thom.; cf. μελέα in discursive note here.

Or. 152 χρόνια] βραδέως O, MnSSa, Mosch.+

Or. 178 κατάπτερος] ταχεῖα HMO, VFRSa, Thom.+

Or. 185 λέχεος] κοίτης O, VR, Thom.+; cf. Mosch. ἀπὸ τῆς κοίτης; cf. Hesych. λ 767, 773; Photius λ 231; *Et. gen.* λ 71.

Or. 186 παρέξεις] αὐτῷ O, Thom.+; cf. αὐτῷ παρέξεις in long paraphrase Sch. Or. 183–186.

Or. 187 θρόει] λέγε H, V, KMnRRfSSa, Mosch., Thom.+; cf. λέγε ποῖον τέλος κτλ in discursive note.

Or. 325–326 ἐκλαθέσθαι] ὥστε O, MnPr, Mosch.+

Or. 329 ἀπόφατιν] μαντείαν O, AaAbKMnRS, Thom.; cf. κακὴν μαντείαν Mosch.+; cf. μαντείαν in discursive Sch. Or. 327–328.

Or. 396 ἡ σύνεσις] ἡ συνείδησις H, FRf, Mosch., Thom.+; cf. ὑπὸ τῆς συνειδήσεως in discursive note.

Or. 452 ἀντιλάζου] ἀντιλαμβάνου MO, VAaAbFKMnRSSaRSa, Mosch., Thom.+; cf. Hesych. α 5428 ἀντιλάζυσθαι· ἀντιλαβέσθαι, and the use of ἀντελαμβάνετο in Sch. Med. 1216 to explain ἀντελάζετ'.

Or. 482 ἔκγονος] υἱὸς O, AaAbK, Mosch.+; cf. υἱός in discursive note.

The frequency of H and O in the previous listing is noteworthy, since we have seen above that these two witnesses do not aim to include a fuller corpus of annotation such as we find in MBV. They also provide a few examples of glosses that reappear in Moschopulus or Thomas without being present in V or any of the mentioned *recentiores*:

Or. 162 ἔλακεν] εἶπεν H, Thom.

Or. 329 ἔλακεν] εἶπεν O, Mosch.+

Or. 488 ἐν] παρὰ O, Mosch.+; cf. παρὰ τοῖς φρονίμοις in discursive note.

Next, some examples where the gloss first appears in V and/or *recentiores*, then in Moschopulus or Thomas:

Or. 25 ὑφάσματι] χιτῶνι VSa, Thom.+

Or. 32 μετέσχον] συνεκοινώνησα V, ἐκοινώσησα Rf, Mosch.+; cf. κεκοινώκηκε in the discursive note.

Or. 33 συγκατείργασται] ἀντὶ τοῦ συνέπραξεν V, συνέπραξε Mosch.+

Or. 36 αἷμα] ὁ φόνος AaKSSa, Mosch., Thom.+

Or. 36 νιν] αὐτὸν τὸν ὀρέστην V, αὐτὸν AbFMnRfS, Thom.? (only ZZa)

Or. 36 τροχηλατεῖ] ταράσσει V, Mosch.+

Or. 38 εὐμενίδας] τὰς ἐριν(ν)ύας AaAbMn (also, above 37 θεὰς, PrS), Mosch., Thom.+

Or. 41 διὰ δέρης] διὰ λαιμοῦ FPrS, λαιμοῦ AaAbR, τοῦ λαιμοῦ Mn, Mosch.+

Or. 41 ἐδέξατο] ὁ ὀρέστης PrMnRS, Thom.

Or. 42 χλανιδίων] ἱματίων AaAbMnPrS, Thom.+

Or. 44 ἔμφρων] γενόμενος AaAbKMnPrRSSa, Mosch.+

Or. 55 ὁρμεῖ] ἐλλιμενίζει τὴν ναῦν VPrSa, ἐλλιμενίζει Ab, Thom.+, cf. ἀντὶ τοῦ τῷ αἰγιαλῷ ἐνελιμένισεν Mosch.

Or. 58 στείχουσαν] πορευομένην V, Mosch.+; cf. προεισπορευομένην or similar in sch. vet.

Or. 59 εἰς πετρῶν ἔλθη βολάς] ἤγουν λιθοβολήσῃ αὐτὴν V, Thom.

Or. 59 τεθνᾶσιν] ἀπέθανον V, Mosch., Thom.+

Or. 60 προὔπεμψεν] προαπέστειλεν V, Thom.+

Or. 66 γέγηθε] χαίρει VR, Mosch.+, Photius γ 45, *Suda* γ 91

Or. 134 ἐκτήξουσ'] δαμάσουσι AaAbMnPrRSSa, Thom.+

Or. 149 ἄτρεμας] ἡσύχως AaAbMnRSSa, Mosch., Thom.+, Hesych. α 8144, *Et. gen.* α 1364, cf. Sch. Tz. Arist. Nub. 261

Or. 189 βορᾶς] τροφῆς AaAbMnRSSa, Mosch., Thom.+, Photius β 213, *Suda* β 390

Or. 219 ὄμορξον] ἀποσπόγγισον AaFMnPrRRfSSa, Mosch., Thom.+

Or. 328 ὀρεχθεὶς] ἐπιθυμήσας AaAbFKMnPrRS, Thom.+

Or. 382 πρωτόλεια] ἐπίρρημα ἀντὶ τοῦ πρώτως AbMnPrRS, πρώτως Rf, Mosch.+

Finally, Moschopulus and/or Thomas deriving a gloss from a discursive old scholion or sharing a gloss established in the lexicographic tradition, without evidence that previous scribes had done so already:

Or. 36 τροχηλατεῖ] ἐλαύνει Mosch., Hesych. τ 1526 (cf. Photius τ 607, *Suda* τ 1068, etc.), also in discursive sch. vet.

Or. 439 τί δρῶντες] οὐκ ἐῶσιν Thom., from the discursive note.

Sometimes a gloss is attested in only one *recentior* and also in Moschopulus or Thomas, and one may wonder whether the influence is from Moschopulus or Thomas instead. For example, at Or. 25 ἀπείρῳ is glossed with κυκλοτερεῖ in Sa as well as by Moschopulus. But κυκλοτερής is elsewhere a gloss in Hesychius (for δινωτοῖς, ὁλοιοτρόχος, περιηγές), and is used in Sch. Aesch. (for περίδρομον, and for κυκλωτῷ), and Sch. Hesiod (for ἐϋστεφάνῳ), so this may be a case of independently arriving at the same gloss, or, in line with what is implied by the above examples, Moschopulus has adopted a gloss he found in an earlier manuscript. To prove access to the Moschopulean or to the Thoman exegesis, one would want to see a discursive scholion adopted in one of the *recentiores*, or at least a supralinear gloss of several words in length. So far very few possible examples of this have been discovered. The most striking is the following:

> Sch. Or. 349 ἧ πατὴρ ἦν ἄναξ: ὅρα ὅπως ὁ ποιητὴς εἰς τὸν κανόνα τῆς ἠθοποιΐας τῷ μὲν παρεληλυθότι χρόνῳ χρᾶται ἐν τῷ λέγειν "ἧ πατὴρ ἦν ἄναξ," τῷ δὲ ἐνεστῶτι ἐν τῷ λέγειν [357] "νῦν δ' εἰμὶ δοῦλος," τῷ δὲ μέλλοντι ὅταν λέγῃ [359–360] "ἔπειτ' ἴσως ἂν δεσποτῶν ὠμῶν φρένας / τύχοιμι" καὶ τὰ λοιπά. Pr
>
> ὅρα ὅπως ὁ ποιητὴς εἰς τὸν κανόνα τῆς ἠθοποιΐας τῷ μὲν παρεληλυθότι χρόνῳ <u>χρῆται</u> ἐν τῷ λέγειν "ἧ πατὴρ μὲν ἦν ἄναξ," τῷ δέ <u>γε</u> ἐνεστῶτι ἐν τῷ [357] "νῦν δ' εἰμὶ δούλη," τῷ δὲ μέλλοντι ὅταν λέγῃ [359–360] "ἔπειτ' ἴσως ἂν δεσποτῶν <u>γ'</u> ὠμῶν φρένας / τύχοιμι" καὶ τὰ λοιπά. Thomas (ZZaZmTGu, minor variations ignored here)
>
> Observe how the poet in regard to the rule of ethopoeia uses the past tense in saying "whose father was a king," the present in saying "but now I am a slave," and the future when she says "furthermore, perhaps I would get cruel-minded masters" and the rest.

Here it seems more probable that Thomas has appropriated the observation of some previous teacher. First, Pr, as will be seen in the next two chapters, contains many anonymous teachers' notes from earlier sources. Second, the differences suggest the priority of Pr: Thomas was likely to change Koine χρᾶται (a form very common in scholia) to the more Attic χρῆται (cf. his *Eclog.* 391, 11 χρῆται, οὐ χρᾶται), to use the more expressive δέ γε, and to adjust the quotation of 359 to the reading with γ' added, which was known in the Thomano-Triclinian circle.[127] Third, this juncture of ἠθοποιΐα and κανών is attested in TLG elsewhere only in Eustathius, in didactic observations likewise beginning

---

[127] This erroneous reading is attested in LZcZm. ZZaGu have the γ' in the scholion, but not in the text. This γ' is omitted from the scholion by Triclinius, but in the text (here written by Triclinius himself) there is an erasure (the trace looks more like the top of tall tau, however).

with ὅρα.¹²⁸ The comment is probably that of a 12th-century teacher, either Eustathius himself or someone influenced by him. Teachers' notes from the 12th century and earlier are the subject of fuller investigation in the next two chapters.

---

¹²⁸ Eust. in Il. 22.56-59 (IV.570, 18-19) ἔνθα καὶ ὅρα τὰ ῥηθέντα συχνὰ κόμματα διά τε σπουδὴν ῥήτορος καὶ διὰ τὸν τῆς ἠθοποιίας κανόνα καὶ μάλιστα τῆς παθητικῆς; Eust. in Od. 13.215 (II.46, 34-36) ὅρα δὲ τὴν ῥηθεῖσαν ἠθοποιίαν ἀπολύτως τε κατὰ τὸ κομματικὸν προηγμένην καὶ ἀνθηρῶς ἔχουσαν, καὶ ὅλως ἐκτεθειμένην κατὰ τὸν ὕστερον παρατηρηθέντα ἐν ταῖς ἠθοποιίαις κανόνα.

APPENDIX TO CHAPTER 1

The Yv Paraphrast and the Periphrastic Scholia in Arsenius

The first printed edition of Euripidean scholia contains a number of annotations on the triad plays for which the source is uncertain. These are any items that meet both of the following conditions: (1) they have only the siglum I in Dindorf's edition; (2) they have not been carried over into Schwartz's edition with attestation from one of the manuscripts he used. Most of these are paraphrasing scholia, ranging from the rephrasing of a single line of a stichomythia to continous paraphrase of dozens of lines of a character's speech or a choral stanza.

Turyn correctly detected a connection between some long paraphrases in Arsenius and the unusually complete paraphrasing found in the surviving manuscript Yv, Venice Marcianus graecus 469 (Zanetti 799), dated 10 January 1413 by the scribe Stephanos Medeias (*RGK* I #366), although Turyn's belief that the paraphrase had something to do with Planudes is to be rejected.[1]

Glossing and paraphrasing were standard parts of the teaching process. A teacher could lead his less experienced students through a passage containing unusual words, stylized word order, and poetic or artful constructions by restating the passage with more straightforward vocabulary, word order, and syntax. Presumably, students could also be drilled or tested by being required to produce a similar paraphrase to demonstrate how they understood a passage. The longer continuous paraphrases in Yv should be regarded as a kind of virtuoso performance of a certain style of teaching. The exhaustiveness or obsessiveness of the process (Günther speaks of "a perverse perfection") in Yv is not dissimilar to what we see in the parsings and etymologies added for every word of an example passage used in schedography. In the most typical form the Yv-paraphrast

---

[1] Mastronarde and Bremer 1982: 27–28 (considering only the case of *Phoen.*); Günther 1995: 147 (who suggests that the paraphrast could even be Stephanos himself). To be fair, although Turyn 1957: 68–79 often spoke of the paraphrase as Planudean and even at one point claimed to infer Planudes' style of paraphrase from it, nevertheless at the very end (79) he reduced the claim somewhat: "The Venice paraphrases of Yv seem to be a special product of some ingenious scholar who used Planudean and Moschopulean scholia for his continuous renderings of longer passages of Euripides."

repeats the words of the poetic text itself, but follows each one with a gloss (many taken from the traditional Moschopulean collection) preceded by καί, ἤγουν, ἤτοι, or ἀντὶ τοῦ, and also supplies understood connectives or copulas and makes explicit the reference of most pronouns.

The following passages demonstrate the method of the Yv-paraphrast and the plausibility of the hypothesis that exactly this paraphrase was sometimes a source for Arsenius. Words that occur in the text of *Orestes* (even if in a different order or with elision or crasis in the play) are underlined, and words that are omitted in Arsenius' adaptation are enclosed in parentheses.

Orestes 1–14

¹ὡς ἐπέρχεται (με) δηλόνοτι εἰπεῖν ἔπος (ὧδε καὶ) οὕτως, ἤτοι ὡς ἐν συντόμῳ εἰπεῖν· ²οὐκ ἔστιν οὐδὲν (δεινὸν καὶ) χαλεπὸν οὐδὲ πάθος καὶ κάκωσις οὐδὲ συμφορὰ (καὶ πληγὴ θεήλατος καὶ) ἀπὸ θεῶν πεμφθεῖσα, ³ἧς οὐκ ἂν (ἄραιτο καὶ) βαστάσοι (καὶ λάβοι ἄχθος καὶ) βάρος φύσις ἀνθρώπου. ⁴ὁ γὰρ μακάριος Τάνταλος, καὶ οὐκ ὀνειδίζω τὰς τύχας, (πεφυκὼς καὶ) γεννηθεὶς, ὡς λέγουσιν, ἀπὸ τοῦ Διὸς, ⁵(δειμαίνων καὶ) φοβούμενος (τὸν πέτρον ἀντὶ τοῦ) τὴν πέτραν (τὸν ὑπερτέλλοντα καὶ) τὸν ὑπερκείμενον τῆς κορυφῆς, ⁶(ποτᾶται καὶ) κρέμαται (ἀέρι καὶ) κατὰ τὸν ἀέρα, ⁷καὶ (τίνει καὶ) δίδωσι ταύτην (τὴν δίκην καὶ) τὴν τιμωρίαν, ὡς μὲν λέγουσιν (ἀντὶ τοῦ ὡς λέγουσι μήν), ⁸ὅτι ἄνθρωπος ὤν, ἔχων ἀξίωμα κοινῆς τραπέζης ἴσον τοῖς θεοῖς, ἔσχε γλῶσσαν (ἀκόλαστον ἤτοι ἀπαίδευτον καὶ) ἀκράτητον, νόσον αἰσχίστην καὶ χαλεπωτάτην. ⁹οὗτος ὁ Τάνταλος (φυτεύει ἀντὶ τοῦ) ἐγέννησε Πέλοπα, (τοῦδε) καὶ ἀπὸ τοῦδε ἔφυ ὁ Ἀτρεὺς, ᾧ Ἀτρεῖ (ἡ θεὰ ἤτοι) ἡ Μοῖρα ἡ Κλωθὼ ξήνασα καὶ κατασκευάσασα, ἤτοι παρασχοῦσα, τὰ στέμματα καὶ τὴν βασιλείαν, ¹⁰ἐπέκλωσε, καὶ εἱμαρμένον ἐποίησε, θέσθαι καὶ ποιῆσαι ἔριν πόλεμόν τε τῷ Θυέστῃ, ὄντι συγγόνῳ καὶ ἀδελφῷ.

Yv (52r–v), Arsen. (1–3 with lemma οὐκ ἔστιν οὐδὲν δεινόν = p. 56v, 12-15; 4–10 with lemma ὁ γὰρ μακάριος = p. 57r, 3ff.)

3 βαστάσει Arsen. | ἡ add. before φύσις Arsen. | 5 τὸν ὑπερκείμενον] τὴν ὑπερκειμένην Arsen. | κορυφῆς] κεφαλῆς Arsen. | 6 κατὰ τὸν ἀέρα] ἐν τῷ ἀέρι Arsen.

As can be seen, Arsenius eliminates many of the words quoted from the text, making the paraphrase less elementary, and makes only a few other adjustments: an added article, κεφαλῆς for κορυφῆς (oddly unglossed in Yv), and choice of a different preposition. A more substantial choice is the elimination of the ἀντὶ τοῦ ὡς λέγουσι μήν: apparently, Arsenius considered it incorrect to view such a solitary μέν as equivalent to μήν.

Orestes 14–27

¹(τί δεῖ μετρήσασθαι) ἀντὶ τοῦ εἰς μέτρον θεῖναι ἐμὲ τὰ ἄρρητα, ἤτοι τὰ μὴ πρέποντα λέγεσθαι ὡς αἰσχρά. ²(ἔδαισε δ' οὖν καὶ) εὐώχησε (νιν καὶ) αὐτὸν τὸν Θυέστην ὁ Ἀτρεὺς, τὰ τέκνα αὐτοῦ δηλονότι ἀποκτείνας. ³ἀπὸ τοῦ Ἀτρέως δὲ, τὰς γὰρ ἐν μέσῳ (τύχας καὶ) δυστυχίας σιγῶ, ἔφυ ὁ κλεινὸς Ἀγαμέμνων, εἰ δὴ κλεινὸς, ὁ Μενέλεώς τε ἀπὸ μητρὸς (Κρήσσης καὶ) Κρητικῆς τῆς Ἀερόπης. ⁴(γαμεῖ δέ ἤτοι) εἰς γυναῖκα (λαμβάνει τουτέστιν) ἔλαβε ὁ μὲν

Μενέλεως τὴν Ἑλένην, (τὴν στυγουμένην καὶ) μισουμένην (τοῖς θεοῖς καὶ) ὑπὸ τῶν θεῶν, ⁵ὁ δὲ Ἀγαμέμνων ὁ ἄναξ τὸ λέχος τῆς Κλυταιμνήστρας, περιφραστικῶς ἀντὶ τοῦ τὴν Κλυταιμνήστραν, τὸ ἐπίσημον καὶ διάδηλον, διὰ τὸν φόνον δηλονότι, εἰς Ἕλληνας. ⁶ᾧ Ἀγαμέμνονι παρθένοι μὲν τρεῖς (ἔφυμεν καὶ) ἐγεννήθημεν ἐκ μιᾶς μητρὸς ἀνοσιωτάτης, (ἡ) Χρυσόθεμις, (ἡ) Ἰφιγένεια (τὲ) ἐγὼ τὲ ἡ Ἠλέκτρα, ἄρσην τὲ Ὀρέστης. ⁷(ἣ καὶ) ἥτις (ἤγουν) Κλυταιμνήστρα περιβαλοῦσα καὶ περικρύψασα (τὸν πόσιν καὶ) τὸν ἄνδρα ἐν (ὑφάσματι καὶ) ἱματίῳ (ἀπείρῳ καὶ) κυκλοτερεῖ, (τουτέστι) μὴ ἔχοντι διέξοδον, ἔκτεινεν. ⁸ὧν δὲ (ἕκατι καὶ) χάριν, ἔκτεινε δηλονότι, οὐ καλόν ἐστι παρθένῳ λέγειν, τουτέστιν ἐμοί. ⁹(ἐῶ καὶ) ἀφίημι τοῦτο ἀσαφὲς καὶ ἄρρητον (ὥστε σκοπεῖν ἀντὶ τοῦ) σκοπεῖσθαι (ἐν κοινῷ ἤτοι) ἐν τῷ δήμῳ.

Yv (52v-53r), Arsen. (1 with lemma τί τ' ἄρρητα = 58v, 16-18; 2-9 with lemma ἔδαισε δ' οὖν νιν = p. 59r, 3-22)

1 after ἐμὲ add. παρθένον οὖσαν Arsen. | 2 εὐώχησα Yv, εὐώχησεν Arsen. | 3 extra phrases added in Arsen. (see discussion below) | 4 δὲ add. after γυναῖκα Arsen. | ἔλαβεν Arsen. | μενέλαος Arsen. | 6 ἀνοσιωτάτης μητρὸς transp. Arsen. | ἐγὼ τὲ] καὶ ἐγὼ Arsen. | 7 περιβαλλοῦσα Yv | 8 after ἐμοὶ add. τῇ παρθένῳ Arsen.

In this paraphrase, Arsenius' changes are very minor, but the insertion of extra phrases in sentence 3 is a strong proof of descent from Yv. Just at the point where εἰ δὴ κλεινὸς ends a line in the margin block of the scholia in Yv, a two-line interlinear note in different ink begins in the intermarginal space to the left of text block and continues over the whole of line 17 (this is done, contrary to the usual placement of interlinear glossing, to make sure there is sufficient space for the longish note). This note combines and expands two Thoman glosses, the second including the addition καὶ ... μοιχείαν found in Gu and not in the other Thoman witnesses: κλεινὸς μὲν, ὡς ὑπὲρ τῆς Ἑλλάδος εἰς Τροίαν στρατεύσας· εἰ δὴ κλεινὸς ὡς ἀθλίως ἀποθανὼν καὶ τὴν τῆς γυναικὸς ὑποστὰς μοιχείαν. In Arsenius, κλεινὸς μὲν ... στρατεύσας is added after ἀγαμέμνων, and then in place of bare εἰ δὴ κλεινὸς as in Yv Arsenius prints all of εἰ δὴ κλεινὸς ... μοιχείαν. Here, perhaps, Arsenius recognized that the paraphrase was deficient in not explaining κλεινός, εἰ δὴ κλεινός, and his addition is not a transcription error, but a conscious effort to complete the paraphrast's job.

There is no need to record here the Yv paraphrast's notes covering *Orestes* 28-70.[2] There too Arsenius differs almost entirely by the sort of omission illustrated in the two examples above. One substantive change he makes is in the paraphrase applying to line 46, where he alters the opening words of Yv (ἔδοξε δὲ καὶ ἐκυρώθη τῷδε τῷ Ἄργει ἀντὶ τοῦ τοῖς Ἀργείοις) to ἐκυρώθη δὲ τοῖς Ἀργείοις, τὸ περιέχον ἀντὶ τοῦ περιεχομένου. Using the noun for the container in place of the noun for the contained is a common scholiastic explanation for a collective noun or for synecdoche. In the prologue of *Orestes* we find examples in the V scholiast's unique note on 41 διὰ δέρης: τουτέστι διὰ τοῦ λάρυγγος· δέρην ὠνόμασεν ἀπὸ τοῦ περιέχοντος δηλῶν τὸ περιεχόμενον, in the

---

[2] *Or.* 28-33: Yv (53r), Arsen. (p. 60v, 6-14, out of order); *Or.* 34-45: Yv (53r-v), Arsen. (p. 60v, 14-16 and 16-28); *Or.* 46-70: Yv (53v-54v), Arsen. (p. 60v, 28-p. 61r, 25).

gloss in S alone above 49 (ἀργείων πόλις) ἀπὸ τοῦ περιέχοντος τὸ περιεχόμενον, and here at 46 (and probably the source of Arsenius' addition) a gloss by a later hand in B ἀπὸ τοῦ περιέχοντος τὸ περιεχόμενον. Cavarzeran has shown that B or one of its apographs was available to Arsenius for the scholia on *Hippolytus*, and this coincidence suggests the same thing.³

Two extended paraphrases from the early scenes of *Hecuba*⁴ show similarly close affinities with Arsenius' versions, with Arsenius omitting words in an almost predictable way. It will not be clear without further tedious investigation of Yv (not a high priority at the moment) whether the same closeness of Yv and Arsenius applies equally to paraphrases for the later parts of *Hecuba* and *Orestes*, but the test samples collated for *Phoenissae* do present a rather different picture.⁵ At the start of that play, Arsenius ignores Yv's paraphrase of the prologue (lines 1–87), but for the next extended speech (88–102) he follows Yv closely. Later in the play, the correspondence between Arsenius' paraphrases and those of Yv is so weak that it is not useful to collate one against the other. The two versions must instead be shown in parallel columns to make clear how different Arsenius' choices are. Either he felt he needed to rework what he saw in Yv radically, with much more extensive alterations than for the other plays or even for *Phoenissae* 88–102; or he decided he could provide a better paraphrase on his own; or he followed another paraphrastic source, now lost. In some places his paraphrase does seem superior, so perhaps the second explanation is most likely.

Phoenissae 963–976

Yv (143r–v)

Arsen. (p. 178r, 28–p. 178v, 16), with lemma ἐγὼ γὰρ οὔ ποτ' εἰς τόδ' εἶμι

¹τί δ' ἂν εἴποι τις, δηλονότι πρᾶγμα, ἤτοι δῆλοι οἱ ἐμοὶ λόγοι·

²ἐγὼ γὰρ οὔποτε εἶμι καὶ ἐλεύσομαι εἰς τόδε τῆς συμφορᾶς, ἀντὶ τοῦ εἰς ταύτην τὴν συμφορὰν, ὥστε προθεῖναι ἤτοι ἔκδοτον ποιῆσαι τῇ πόλει τὸν παῖδα σφαγέντα, ἀντὶ τοῦ σφαγησόμενον.

³πᾶσι γὰρ ἀνθρώποις ὁ βίος δηλονότι καὶ ἡ ζωὴ φιλότεκνος, οὐδ' ἂν δοίη τις τὸν ἑαυτοῦ παῖδα εἰς τὸ κτανεῖν αὐτόν τινα δηλονότι.

¹ἐγὼ γὰρ οὐδέποτε εἰς τοῦτο τῆς συμφορᾶς, ἀντὶ τοῦ εἰς τοιαύτην συμφορὰν, ἀπελεύσομαι, ὥστε παραθεῖναι τῇ πόλει τοῦτον σφαγέντα, ἀντὶ τοῦ ὥστε σφαγιασθῆναι ὑπὲρ τῆς πόλεως.

²πᾶσι γὰρ ἀνθρώποις ὑπάρχει φιλότεκνος ὁ βίος, ἤγουν πάντες ἄνθρωποι τὰ ἑαυτῶν τέκνα φιλοῦσι, οὐδέ τις ἂν δοίη τὸν αὐτοῦ παῖδα, ὥστε φονευθῆναι.

---

³ Cavarzeran 2016: 58–61. I have not yet studied the apographs of B, Mu and Ph, which Cavarzeran finds share many errors with Arsenius in addition to the ones shared with B itself.
⁴ *Hec.* 59–100: Yv (8r–9r), Arsen. (p. 5v, 7–p. 6r, 25); *Hec.* 163–177: Yv (11v–12r), Arsen. (p. 9r, 3–14).
⁵ As already noted in Mastronarde and Bremer 1982: 28.

⁴μὴ εὐλογείτω καὶ μὴ ἐπαινείτω τις ἐμὲ, κτείνων τὰ ἐμὰ τέκνα.

⁵αὐτὸς δὲ καὶ ἐγὼ (καὶ γὰρ ἵσταμαι διὰ μέσου) ἐν βίῳ ὡραίῳ καὶ ἐγκαίρῳ, πρὸς τελευτὴν δηλονότι, ἕτοιμος θνήσκειν ἐκλυτήριον πατρίδος, ἤτοι εἰς ἐλευθερίαν καὶ εἰς λύτρωσιν.

⁶ἀλλ' ὦ τέκνον εἴα ἀντὶ τοῦ ἄγε, πρὶν καὶ πρὸ τοῦ μαθεῖν τοῦτο δηλονότι πᾶσαν τὴν πόλιν, ἐάσας τὰ θεσπίσματα καὶ τὰ μαντεύματα τοῦ μάντεως τὰ ἀκόλαστα ἤτοι τὰ ἀπαίδευτα καὶ χωρὶς συστολῆς εἰρημένα, φεῦγε ὡς καὶ λίαν τάχιστα, ἀπαλλαχθεὶς καὶ ἀποστὰς τῆσδε τῆς χθονός.

⁷λέξει γὰρ τάδε ταῖς ἀρχαῖς ἀντὶ τοῦ τοῖς ἄρχουσι καὶ τοῖς στρατηλάταις καὶ τοῖς ἡγεμόσι, μολὼν καὶ ἐλθὼν ἐπὶ τὰς ἑπτὰ πύλας καὶ ἐπὶ τοὺς λοχαγέτας ἤτοι τοὺς τῶν ταγμάτων ἡγεμόνας.

⁸κἂν μὲν φθάσωμεν καὶ προλάβωμεν, ἔστι σωτηρία σοί.

⁹ἐὰν δὲ ὑστερήσῃς καὶ ὕστερος φανείης, ἤγουν βραδύνῃς, οἰχόμεθα καὶ ἐφθάρημεν· κατθανῇ καὶ ἀποθανῇ.

³μὴ ἐπαινείτω μέ τις λόγους εὐλόγους λέγων, τἀμὰ τέκνα συμβουλεύων με κτείνειν.

⁴ἐγὼ δὲ θνήσκειν ὑπὲρ πατρίδος ἕτοιμός εἰμι, ἀπολυόμενος αὐτὴν τῶν περιεστώτων κακῶν. ⁵ἐν ζωῇ γὰρ ἐγκαίρῳ καθίσταμαι.

⁶ἀλλ' ἄγε, ὦ παῖ, πρὸ τοῦ τὴν πόλιν μαθεῖν, τὰ ἀπαίδευτα τοῦ μάντεως ἐάσας χρηστήρια, φεῦγε λίαν ταχέως τῆς χθονὸς ταύτης ἐλευθερωθείς.

⁷λέξει γὰρ τοῖς ἄρχουσι καὶ τοῖς στρατηγοῖς ταῦτα, ἐπὶ τὰς ἑπτὰ πύλας καὶ τοὺς λοχαγέτας παραγενόμενος.

⁸καὶ ἐὰν προφθάσωμεν, ὑπάρχει σοι σωτηρία.

⁹ἐὰν δὲ ὑστερηθῇς, ἀπωλόμεθα· ἀποθανῇ γάρ.

orthographica
2 τὸν αὑτοῦ Arsen.
3 με τὶς Arsen.
τὰ μὰ or τἀμὰ Arsen.
9 ἀπολόμεθα Arsen.

Phoenissae 991–1012

Yv (144r–v)

Arsen. (p. 179r, 12–p. 179v, 7), with lemma γυναῖκες

¹ὦ γυναῖκες, ὡς καὶ λίαν εὖ ἤτοι ἐπιτηδείως ἐξεῖλον τοῦ πατρός, ἤτοι ἀπὸ τοῦ ἐμοῦ πατρὸς ἐξέβαλον τὸν φόβον, κλέψας καὶ ἀπατήσας αὐτὸν δηλονότι λόγοις καὶ διὰ λόγων, ὥστε τυχεῖν ἐκείνων δηλονότι ἃ βούλομαι καὶ θέλω.

¹ὦ γυναῖκες, λίαν ἐπιτηδείως καὶ καλῶς ἐξέβαλον τὸν φόβον τοῦ πατρὸς, διὰ λόγων ἀπατήσας αὐτὸν, ὥστε τυχεῖν ὧν βούλομαι.

²ὅς, ἤγουν ὁ πατὴρ, κομίζει καὶ ἐκπέμπει ἐμὲ καὶ δίδωσι δειλίαν, ἀποστερῶν τὴν πόλιν τῆς τύχης καὶ τῆς εὐτυχίας.

²ὅστις ὁ πατὴρ φυγαδεύει καὶ ὑπεξάγει τῆς πόλεως, τῆς εὐτυχίας ἀποστερῶν με καὶ φόβῳ δίδωσιν ἐμέ.

³καὶ σύγγνωστα μὲν ἀντὶ τοῦ συγγνώμης ἄξιον τὸ πρᾶγμα τῷ γέροντι, τὸ ἐμὸν δὲ ἤτοι τὸ κατ' ἐμὲ οὐκ ἔχει συγγνώμην, γενέσθαι προδότην τῆς πατρίδος, ἣ ἐγείνατο ἐμέ.

³καὶ συγγνώμης ἄξιον τὸ πρᾶγμα τῷ πατρὶ, τὸ κατ' ἐμὲ δ' οὐδαμῶς συγγνώμην ἔχει, τὸ γενέσθαι προδότην τῆς πατρίδος, ἥτις ἐγέννησέ με.

⁴ὡς ἂν οὖν εἰδῆτε καὶ γνωρίσητε, εἶμι καὶ ἀπελεύσομαι, δώσω τε τὴν ψυχὴν καὶ τὴν ζωὴν ὥστε θανεῖν ὑπὲρ τῆσδε τῆς χθονός.

⁴ἵνα οὖν γνῶτε, ἀπελεύσομαι, καὶ σώσω τὴν πόλιν, τὴν δὲ ζωὴν δώσω, ὥστε ἀποθανεῖν ὑπὲρ τῆσδε τῆς χθονός.

⁵αἰσχρὸν γὰρ καὶ ἀπρεπὲς καὶ ἄσχημον εἰ οἱ μὲν ἐλεύθεροι θεσφάτων καὶ μαντευμάτων καὶ οὐκ ἀφιγμένοι εἰς ἀνάγκην δαιμόνων ἤτοι τῆς τύχης, στάντες παρὰ τὴν ἀσπίδα οὐκ ὀκνήσουσι καὶ δειλιάσουσι θανεῖν, μαχόμενοι πάροιθεν καὶ ἔμπροσθεν τῶν πύργων ὑπὲρ τῆς πάτρας καὶ τῆς πατρίδος,

⁵αἰσχύνης γὰρ ἄξιον (λείπει τὸ εἰ) ἐὰν οἱ τῶν μαντευμάτων ἐλεύθεροι καὶ ὑπὸ τῶν θεῶν μὴ ἀναγκαζόμενοι οὐκ ἀναβάλλονται ἀποθανεῖν παρὰ πόλεμον στάντες, καὶ ὑπὲρ τῆς πατρίδος ἔμπροσθεν τῶν πύργων μαχόμενοι,

⁶ἐγὼ δὲ προδοὺς καὶ καταλιπὼν τὸν πατέρα καὶ τὸν κασίγνητον καὶ τὸν ἀδελφὸν τὴν πόλιν τε ἐμαυτοῦ, ὡς καὶ καθὰ δειλὸς ἄπειμι καὶ ἀπελεύσομαι ἔξω τῆς χθονός, ὅπου δ' ἂν ζῶ, φανήσομαι κακὸς καὶ δειλός.

⁶ἐγὼ δὲ, πατέρα καὶ ἀδελφὸν προδοὺς καὶ πόλιν τὴν ἐμαυτοῦ, ὡς ἄνανδρος ἔξω τῆς χθονὸς ἀπελεύσομαι, καὶ ὅπου ἂν ζῶ, κακότροπος φανήσομαι.

⁷οὐ μὰ τὸν Ζῆνα καὶ τὸν Δία τὸν μετ' ἄστρων ἤτοι τὸν ἐν τῷ οὐρανῷ, καὶ τὸν Ἄρην τὸν φόνιον καὶ τὸν φονικόν, ὅς, Ἄρης, τοὺς σπαρτοὺς τοὺς ἀνατείλαντας καὶ ἀναδοθέντας ποτὲ ἐκ τῆς γαίας καὶ ἐκ τῆς γῆς ἱδρύσατο καὶ κατέστησεν ἄνακτας τῆσδε τῆς γῆς.

⁸ἀλλ' εἶμι καὶ ἀπελεύσομαι, καὶ στὰς ἐκ τῶν ἄκρων ἐπάλξεων σφάξας ἐμαυτὸν εἰς τὸν σηκὸν ἤτοι εἰς τὸν φωλεὸν τοῦ δράκοντος τὸν μελεμβαφῆ καὶ τὸν μέλανα καὶ σκοτεινόν, ἔνθα καὶ ὅπου ἐξηγήσατο καὶ εἶπεν ὁ μάντις, ἐλευθερώσω τὴν γαῖαν καὶ τὴν γῆν.

⁷οὐ ποιήσω τοῦτο, μὰ τὸν μετ' ἄστρων Ζῆνα· τὸν ἥλιον φησὶ τὸν αἴτιον τοῦ ἐμοῦ φόνου. ἄρη δὲ φόνιον· ἐπειδὴ οὗτος φονικὸς τῶν σπαρτῶν δράκοντα καταστήσας αὐτόθι φύλακα τῆς κρήνης, ἐξ οὗ τῶν ὀδόντων οἱ σπαρτοί· ὅστις τοὺς ἀναδοθέντας ποτὲ ἐκ τῆς γῆς σπαρτοὺς δεσπότας καὶ βασιλεῖς τῆσδε τῆς γῆς κατεστήσατο.

⁸ἀλλ' ἀπελεύσομαι, καὶ στὰς ἐκ τοῦ ἄκρου τῶν ἐπάλξεων, καὶ σφάξας ἐμαυτὸν εἰς τὴν θαλάμην τὴν σκοτεινὴν τοῦ δράκοντος, ὅπου ὁ Τειρεσίας διηγήσατο καὶ παρήνεσε φονευθῆναι, ἐλευθερώσω τὴν γῆν.

orthographica
2 δειλίαν] λίαν a.c. Yv
4 τὲ Yv
6 τὲ Yv

Phoenissae 1019–1042

Yv (145r-v)

Arsen. (p. 179v, 24–p. 180r, 5 and 11–21), with lemma ἔβας

¹ἔβης ἔβης ἤτοι ἦλθες, ὦ πτεροῦσ(σ)α καὶ ὦ πτερόε(σ)σα Σφὶγξ δηλονότι, λόχευμα καὶ γέννημα τῆς γῆς καὶ τῆς νερτέρου καὶ καταχθονίου Ἐχίδνης,

¹ἦλθες, ἦλθες, ὦ πτερόεσσα Σφὶγξ, γέννημα μὲν τῆς τῶν Θηβαίων γῆς (ἐνταῦθα γὰρ ἐγεννήθης), λόχευμα δὲ τοῦ Τυφῶνος καὶ τῆς καταχθονίου Ἐχίδνης,

²ἐπὶ ἁρπαγῇ τῶν Καδμείων, πολύστονος ἤτοι πολλῶν στεναγμῶν αἰτία, πολύμοχθος ἤτοι πολλῶν μόχθων αἰτία, μιξοπάρθενος ἤτοι ἐκ θηρίου καὶ γυναικὸς συντεθειμένον ζῶον,

²ἐπὶ ἁρπαγῇ τῶν Θηβαίων, πολλῶν στεναγμῶν αἰτία, πολύφθορε, μιξοπάρθενε (ἔχεις γὰρ τὰ μὲν παρθένου, τὰ δὲ θηρὸς),

³τέρας καὶ σημεῖον δάϊον καὶ πολεμικόν.

³ξένης καὶ παραδόξου φύσεως φονικὸν τέρας τοῖς τε φοιταλέοις καὶ μανικοῖς πτεροῖς καὶ τοῖς ὄνυξι τοῖς ὠμὰ τὰ κρέα ἁρπάζουσι πρὸς σίτησιν.

⁴ἃ καὶ ἥτις ποτὲ ἐκ τῶν τόπων τῆς Δίρκης τοὺς νέους πεδαίρουσα καὶ εἰς ὕψος αἴρουσα, ἐν πτεροῖς φοιτῶσι καὶ μεμηνόσι καὶ ἐν χηλαῖς καὶ ὄνυξιν ὠμοσίτοις καὶ θηριώδεσιν, ἐπέφερες ἐπέφερες μοῦσαν καὶ ᾠδὴν ἄλυρον καὶ κακόλυρον, ἐρινννύν τε καὶ φθορὰν οὐλομένην καὶ ἀξίαν ἀπωλείας, λέγω ἄχεα καὶ λύπας τῇ πατρίδι φόνια καὶ φονικά.

⁵φόνιος καὶ φονικὸς ἐκ τῶν θεῶν καὶ ἀπὸ τῶν θεῶν ὅς, ἀντὶ τοῦ ἐκεῖνος, ἦν ὁ πράξας τάδε.

⁶ἰάλεμοι δὲ καὶ θρῆνοι μητέρων, ἐπὶ τέκνοις δηλονότι, ἰάλεμοι δέ καὶ θρῆνοι παρθένων, ἐπὶ μητράσι δηλονότι, ἐστέναζον, ἀντὶ τοῦ μετὰ στεναγμῶν ἀνέπεμπον, ἐν τοῖς οἴκοις βοὴν ἰήϊον καὶ θρηνητικὴν, μέλος ἰήϊον καὶ θρηνητικὸν.

⁷ἄλλος ἄλλον ἐπωττότυζεν ἤτοι ἐσχετλίαζε καὶ ἔκλαιε ἐν διαδοχαῖς καὶ κατὰ διαδοχὴν ἀνὰ τὴν πτόλιν ἀντὶ τοῦ τὴν πόλιν.

⁸βροντῇ δὲ ἦν ὅμοιος ὁ στεναγμὸς καὶ ἡ ἰαχὴ καὶ ἡ βοή, ὁπότε ἡ πτεροῦσ(σ)α, ἀντὶ τοῦ ἡ πτερόεσσα, παρθένος ἤγουν ἡ Σφὶγξ ἀφανίσειε καὶ ἠφάνισέ τινα τῶν ἀνδρῶν τῆς πόλεως.

8 βροντὴ Yv

⁴ἥτις πεδαίρουσα τοὺς νέους, ἀπὸ τῆς γῆς εἰς ὕψος αἴρουσα ποτὲ ἐκ τῶν τόπων τῆς Δίρκης, ἤτοι ἐκ τῶν Θηβῶν, περιῆγες καὶ περιέφερες ἄναυλον καὶ ἀνήδονον ᾠδὴν, λέγω φόνους καὶ λύπας ταῖς Θήβαις. τινὲς δὲ τὸ φόνια πρὸς τὰ ἑξῆς· ὃς τάδε τὰ φόνια πράξας φόνιος ἦν θεός.

⁵ὁ ἐκ θεῶν ταῦτα πράξας αὐτὸς φόνιος ἦν.

⁶αἱ δὲ ἰάλεμοι τῶν παρθένων καὶ τῶν μητέρων ἐστέναζον ἐν τοῖς οἴκοις, πενθοῦσαι αἱ μὲν τὰ τέκνα, αἱ δὲ τοὺς ἀδελφούς.

⁷Ιὴν δὲ βοὰν: θρηνηντικὴν βοήν· διὸ ἐπὶ μὲν θρήνων ψιλοῦται, ἐπὶ δὲ παιώνων δασύνεται· ἐπωτότυζεν: ἄλλος ἄλλην ἐθρήνει.

⁸ὁ στεναγμὸς δὲ καὶ ἡ ἠχὴ βροντῇ ὑπῆρχεν ὅμοιος, ὅταν ἀναρπάσειεν ἡ Σφὶγξ ἀπὸ τῆς πόλεώς τινα τῶν ἀνδρῶν, θρῆνος καὶ βοὴ ἐγένετο.

4 between ᾠδὴν and λέγω, Arsen. inserts an exegetic scholion and then adds new lemma ἄχεα πατρίδι φόνια before λέγω
7 Ιὴν with enlarged initial and no breathing sign, as if a new lemma
8 πόλεως τινὰ Arsen.

Arsenius also departed more radically from Yv, or did not use Yv at all, in relation to the paraphrases of sections of stichomythia or short dialogue. Samples taken from all three plays show the same degree of strong divergence between Yv and Arsenius when Arsenius bothers to include a short paraphrase, for in many cases he apparently decided it was not worthwhile either to copy Yv or to provide any paraphrase for simple, short sentences. The following samples do not require detailed discussion, but it is noteworthy that Arsenius shows awareness of B-scholia and in a few places (*Hec.* 422, 426, *Or.* 743) followed a Triclinian copy (it is known that Arsenius used a Triclinian copy, since the *editio princeps* contains a few metrical scholia from Triclinius). There are only a few short paraphrases that seem to be versions of Yv created by elimination or substitution of some words (e.g., *Hec.* 429, *Or.* 749, 752, *Phoen.* 984).

Hecuba 415–431

Yv (21r–v)   Arsen. (p. 17v, 5–p. 18r, 5)

415
ὦ θύγατερ, ἡμεῖς δὲ δουλεύσομεν ἐν   415
τῷ φάει καὶ ἐν τῷ φωτὶ ἀντὶ τοῦ ἐγὼ   ὦ θύγατερ, ἐγὼ δὲ δουλεύσω ἐν τῇ
δούλη ἔσομαι ἐν τῷ φωτὶ ἤγουν ἐν τῷ   παρούσῃ ζωῇ.
βίῳ.

416   (414 & 416)
ἄπειμι κατὰ κοινοῦ, ἄνυμφος ἀντὶ τοῦ   ὦ μῆτερ ὦ τεκοῦσα, ἀπέρχομαι εἰς τὸν
ἀνυμφεύτος, ἀνυμέναιος ἤτοι χωρὶς   ἅδην ἀνύμφευτος καὶ ἄμοιρος ὑμεναίων
ὑμεναίων, ὧν νυμφευμάτων δηλονότι   ὧν ἔπρεπεν ἐμὲ λαχεῖν δηλονότι.
καὶ ὑμεναίων ἐχρῆν καὶ ἔπρεπε τυχεῖν
ἐμέ.

417
οἰκτρὰ καὶ ἐλεεινὴ σὺ ὦ τέκνον, ἀθλία
δὲ γυνὴ ἐγώ.

418
ἐκεῖ δὲ λέγω, ἐν τῷ τόπῳ τοῦ ἅδου
κείσομαι χωρὶς σέθεν καὶ σοῦ.

419   419 οἴμοι τί δράσω
οἴμοι τί ἵνα δράσω; πῆ καὶ πῶς   οἴμοι τί ποιήσω, εἰς ποίαν τύχην
τελευτήσω τὸν βίον καὶ τὴν ζωήν.   καταντήσω, ποῖον τέλος ἕξω τοῦ βίου,
                                                    ποῦ πληρώσω τὸν βίον.

420   420 δούλη θανοῦμαι
δούλη θανοῦμαι οὖσα πατρὸς   οὖσα πατρὸς ἐλευθέρου ἤτοι βασιλέως.
ἐλευθέρου ἤτοι βασιλέως.   ἐλεύθερος κατὰ ψυχὴν καὶ ἐλεύθερος
                                                    κατὰ σῶμα, ὁ καλῶς ἐκτραφείς, ἤτοι
                                                    εὐτυχῶς καὶ ἐλευθερίως. ὁμοίως καὶ
                                                    δοῦλος· καὶ ἐπὶ μὲν τοῦ σώματος ὁ
                                                    ἐωνημένος, ἐπὶ δὲ ψυχῆς ὁ κόλαξ.
                                                    ἀπελεύθερος δὲ ὁ ἀργυρώνητος μὲν
                                                    πρῶτον, εἶτα ἐλευθερωθείς, ὁ δὲ
                                                    ἐλευθερώσας αὐτὸν πάτρων, καὶ
                                                    κλίνεται πάτρωνος.

421
ἡμεῖς δὲ ἄμοιροι καὶ ἐστερημένοι τέκνων πεντήκοντα.

421 ἡμεῖς δὲ
ἡμεῖς δὲ ἄμοιροι καὶ ἐστερημένοι πεντήκοντα τέκνων. δεκαεννέα ἐγέννησεν αὕτη· αὔξουσα δὲ τὸ πάθος $\bar{\nu}$ λέγει, ἢ ὅτι συμπεριλαμβάνει καὶ τοὺς νόθους τοῦ Πριάμου παῖδας σὺν τοῖς παισὶν ἑαυτῆς διὰ τὴν διάθεσιν τοῦ ἀνδρός.
Gu, Arsen.

422
τί ἵνα εἴπω σοὶ καὶ περὶ σοῦ πρὸς τὸν ἕκτορα ἢ πρὸς τὸν πόσιν καὶ τὸν ἄνδρα τὸν γέροντα.

422 τί σοι πρὸς ἕκτορα
τί βούλει ἵνα ἕνεκα σοῦ εἴπω πρὸς τὸν Ἕκτορα, ἢ πρὸς τὸν γέροντα Πρίαμον τὸν σὸν πόσιν ἤγουν ἄνδρα.
Mosch., T, Arsen.
ἵνα om. Gr
πρίαμον T, Arsen., om. Mosch.
σὸν om. Gr
πόσιν ἤγουν om. Arsen.
ἤγουν ἄνδρα om. Gr

423
ἄγγελλε καὶ μήνυε καὶ λέγε ἐμὲ ἀθλιωτάτην πασῶν γυναικῶν δηλονότι.

423
μήνυε πασῶν γυναικῶν ἀθλιωτάτην.

424
ὦ στέρνα καὶ στήθη καὶ ὦ μαστοὶ οἳ καὶ οἵτινες ἐθρέψατε καὶ ἀνεθρέψατε ἐμὲ ἡδέως.

425
ὦ καὶ φεῦ, ὦ θύγατερ, ἕνεκα τῆς ἀθλίας τύχης καὶ δυστυχίας τῆς ἀώρου καὶ ταχυθανάτου.

425
ὦ τῆς πρὶν τοῦ προσήκοντος καιροῦ ἀθλίας τύχης.

426
χαῖρε ὦ τεκοῦσα, χαῖρε μοι τὲ ὦ Κασάνδρα.

426 χαῖρ' ὦ τεκοῦσα, χαῖρε Κασάνδρα τ' ἐμοί
τὸ ἐμοί οὐ πρὸς τὸ Κασάνδρα ἐστίν (εἰ γὰρ ἦν οὕτω, διὰ τοῦ η ὤφειλε γράφεσθαι), ἀλλὰ πρὸς τὸ χαῖρε. σύναπτε δὲ καὶ πρὸς ἀμφότερα, χαῖρέ μοι, ὦ τεκοῦσα, καὶ χαῖρέ μοι, ὦ Κασάνδρα.
T(Ta), Arsen.
συνάπτεται Ta (T washed out)

427
χαίρουσιν ἄλλοι, τουτέστιν οἱ
φονεύοντες Ἕλληνες, τῇ μητρὶ δὲ
τουτέστιν ἐμοὶ οὐκ ἔστι χαρά.

428
χαῖρε καὶ ὁ κάσις καὶ ὁ ἀδελφὸς, ὁ
πολύδωρος, ὁ ὢν δηλονότι ἐν τοῖς
θραξὶ τοῖς φιλίπποις καὶ τοῖς ἱππικοῖς.

429
εἰ ζῇ, χαιρήσεται δηλονότι. ἀπιστῶ δὲ
εἰ ζῇ. ὧδε καὶ οὕτω κατὰ πάντα
δυστυχῶ.

430
ζῇ, καὶ θανούσης σοῦ δηλονότι
συγκλείσει καὶ καλύψει τὸ σὸν ὄμμα
ἀντὶ τοῦ τοὺς σοὺς ὀφθαλμούς.

431
τέθνηκα ἔγωγε ὑπὸ τῶν κακῶν, πρὶν
θανεῖν τὸν φυσικὸν θάνατον δηλονότι.

427 χαίρουσιν ἄλλοι
μητρὶ δ' οὐκ ἔστι τὸ χαίρειν δηλονότι.

428
χαῖρε καὶ ὁ ἐμὸς ἀδελφὸς ὁ Πολύδωρος
ὁ ὑπάρχων ἐν τοῖς ἱππικοῖς Θραξίν
Mosch., Arsen.
ὁ (before πολύδ.) om. Arsen.

429 εἰ ζῇ γε
χαιρήσεται δηλονότι. ἀπιστῶ δὲ, ὅτι
οὕτω κατὰ πάντα δυστυχῶ.

Orestes 734–754

Yv (78r–v)

734
οἰχόμεθα ἀντὶ τοῦ ἀπολώλαμεν, ὡς
καὶ ἵνα δηλώσω σοι τὰ ἐμὰ κακὰ καὶ
τὰς ἐμὰς δυστυχίας ἐν βραχεῖ ἤτοι
συντόμως.

735
συγκατασκάπτοις ἂν ἀντὶ τοῦ
συγκαταβάλοις ἂν ἡμᾶς· κοινὰ γὰρ
τὰ τῶν φίλων.
ἡμᾶς] ἡμῶν Yv

736
ὁ μενέλαος κάκιστος ἐγένετο δηλονότι
εἰς ἐμὲ καὶ εἰς τὴν ἐμὴν κασιγνήτην.

Arsen. (p. 102r, 8–p. 102v, 4)

734
ἀπολώλαμεν, ὡς ἐν βραχεῖ σοι λόγῳ
τὰς ἐμὰς δυστυχίας δηλώσω.

735
συγκαταχωννύεις, συναναιρεῖς,
συνδιαφθείρεις καὶ ἡμᾶς.
B, Arsen.
καὶ om. B

736
ὁ Μενέλαος κάκιστος ἐφάνη εἰς ἐμὲ καὶ
τὴν ἐμὴν ἀδελφήν.

737
εἰκότως καὶ πρεπόντως ἔχει, τὸ
πρᾶγμα δηλονότι, ὥστε ἄνδρα κακῆς
γυναικὸς γίνεσθαι κακὸν.

738
μολὼν καὶ ἐλθὼν ἀπέδωκεν ἐμοὶ
ταυτὸν καὶ ὅμοιον ὥσπερ οὐκ ἐλθών.

738
οὕτως ἐμοὶ προσηνέχθη ὡς μὴ
παραγενόμενος.
MBC, Arsen.

739
ἢ γὰρ ἀντὶ τοῦ ἄρα ἔστιν ἀφιγμένος
ἀντὶ τοῦ ἀφῖκται ὡς ἀληθῶς καὶ κατὰ
ἀλήθειαν εἰς τήνδε τὴν χθόνα.

740
χρόνιος ἤτοι βραδέως ἦλθεν, ἀλλ'
ὅμως τάχιστα ἤτοι λίαν συντόμως
ἐφωράθη καὶ ἐφάνη τοῖς φίλοις καὶ
πρὸς τοὺς φίλους κακός.

740
χρόνιος ἀντὶ τοῦ μετὰ χρόνον πολύν·
ὅμως κἂν βραδὺ παρεγένετο, ἀλλὰ
τάχιστα τοῖς φίλοις ἐφωράθη κακός.
B, Arsen.

741
ἄρα δηλονότι κατὰ κοινοῦ ἐλήλυθε καὶ
ἦλθε ναυστολῶν καὶ διὰ νηὸς ἄγων
καὶ δάμαρτα τὴν κακίστην καὶ
κακοτροπωτάτην.

741
καὶ τὴν γυναῖκα τὴν κακοτροπωτάτην
διὰ νεὼς ἦλθεν ἄγων.

742
οὐκ ἐκεῖνος ἤγαγεν ἐκείνην δηλονότι,
ἀλλ' ἐκείνη ἤγαγεν ἐκεῖνον ἐνθάδε.

742
διαβάλλει ὡς γυναικοκρατούμενον
αὐτὸν καὶ ὡς οὐκ ἂν ἐληλυθότα, εἰ μὴ
παραγέγονεν ἡ Ἑλένη. κωμῳδεῖται δὲ
ὁ στίχος διὰ τὴν ταυτότητα.
MBCVR, Arsen.

743
ποῦ ἐστιν ἡ ἑλένη δηλονότι, ἡ γυνὴ
μία οὖσα ὤλεσε πλείστους τῶν
ἀχαιῶν.

743
τῷ ὑποτακτικῷ συνυπάγει τὸν λόγον.
ὀφείλων γὰρ εἰπεῖν, ποῦ ἐστιν ἡ γυνή, ἡ
πλείστους ὤλεσεν Ἀχαιῶν; ὁ δέ φησι,
ποῦ ἐστιν ἥτις γυνὴ πλείστους Ἀχαιῶν
ὤλεσεν;
Mosch., T, Arsen.
ὤλεσεν ἀχαιῶν T, Arsen., ἀχ. ὤλεσεν
Mosch.

744
ἐν τοῖς ἐμοῖς δόμοις ἐστὶ δηλονότι, εἰ
καὶ χρεὼν καὶ πρέπον καλεῖσθαι
τούσδε ἐμούς.

745
σὺ δὲ τίνας λόγους ἔλεξας τῷ κασιγνήτῳ τοῦ σοῦ πατρός.

746
ἔλεξα δηλονότι μὴ ἰδεῖν ἐμὲ θανόντα ὑπὸ τῶν ἀστῶν μηδὲ τὴν ἐμὴν κασιγνήτην καὶ ἀδελφὴν.

747
πρὸς τῶν θεῶν τί εἶπεν ὁ μενέλαος πρὸς τάδε. θέλω εἰδέναι τοῦτο.

748
εὐλαβεῖτο ἤτοι ἐδειλία καὶ ἐφοβεῖτο ὃ καὶ ὅπερ οἱ κακοὶ καὶ οἱ κακότροποι φίλοι δρῶσι τοῖς φίλοις καὶ πρὸς τοὺς φίλους.

748
ἐδειλία, ὅπερ λέγουσιν οἱ κακοὶ φίλοι μὴ θέλοντες τοῖς φίλοις βοηθεῖν, λέγοντες εὐλαβούμεθα, ἤτοι δειλιῶμεν καὶ φοβούμεθα. γνησίου γὰρ φίλου τὸ καὶ ὑπὲρ δύναμιν τολμᾶν, ὅπερ εὐλαβεῖσθαι αὐτὸς ἔλεγεν.
B, Arsen.
ἐδειλία om. B
ἤτοι ... φοβούμεθα om. B
καὶ om. Arsen.

749
εἰς ποίαν σκῆψιν καὶ πρόφασιν προβαίνων καὶ προχωρῶν. τοῦτο μαθὼν ἔχω πάντα.

749 σκῆψιν εἰς ποίαν
εἰς ποίαν πρόφασιν προχωρῶν; τοῦτο μαθὼν πάντ' ἔχω.

750
οὗτος ἦλθεν ὁ πατὴρ ὁ σπείρας τὰς ἀρίστας θυγατέρας, κατ' εἰρωνείαν.

751
τὸν τυνδάρ() λέγεις. ἴσως ἦλθε θυμούμενος καὶ ὀργιζόμενος σοὶ καὶ κατὰ σοῦ ἕνεκα τῆς θυγατρός.

752
αἰσθάνῃ ἤτοι νοεῖς. μᾶλλον εἵλετο καὶ προέκρινε τὸ τούτου κῆδος καὶ τὴν συγγένειαν ἢ καὶ παρὸ τοῦ πατρός.

752 αἰσθάνῃ
νοεῖς. τὴν τούτου συγγένειαν προέκρινε μᾶλλον ἢ τὴν τοῦ ἐμοῦ πατρός.

753
οὐκ ἐτόλμησεν ἤτοι οὐχ ὑπέμεινε καὶ οὐκ ἠθέλησεν ἀντιλάζυσθαι καὶ ἀντιλαμβάνεσθαι τῶν σῶν πόνων παρών.

754
οὐδαμῶς δηλονότι. οὐ γὰρ αἰχμητὴς καὶ πολεμιστὴς πέφυκε καὶ ὑπάρχει, ἐν γυναιξὶ δὲ ἄλκιμος καὶ ἰσχυρός.

753
καὶ οὐχ ὑπέμεινεν ἀντιλαμβάνεσθαι τῶν σῶν πόνων παραγενόμενος.

754
οὐδαμῶς· οὐ γὰρ πολεμιστὴς ὑπάρχει, γενναῖος δ' ἐν γυναιξί.

Phoenissae 977–989

Yv (143v–144r)

977
ποῖ δῆτα ἵνα φεύγω. εἰς τίνα πόλιν, εἰς τίνα τῶν ξένων καὶ ἀπὸ τῶν φίλων.

978
ἐκεῖσε λέγω ἄπελθε δηλονότι ὅπου μάλιστα ἔσῃ ἐκποδὼν καὶ μακρὰν τῆσδε τῆς χθονός.

979
οὐκοῦν εἰκὸς καὶ πρέπον φράζειν καὶ λέγειν σὲ ἐκπονεῖν δὲ καὶ ἐνεργεῖν ἐμέ.

980
Δελφοὺς περάσας καὶ διαβάς, φεῦγε.

Arsenius (p. 178v, 16–p. 179r, 9)

977 ποῦ δῆτα
ποῦ λοιπὸν φύγω, εἰς τίνα πόλιν, εἰς τίνα τῶν φίλων;

978 ὅπου
ποῦ; ὅπου μακρὰν μάλιστα τῆσδε τῆς γῆς γενήσῃ.

979 οὐκοῦν
πρέπον σε λοιπὸν ὅπου πορευθῶ λέγειν, ἐκπληροῦν δ' ἐμέ.

980 Δελφοὺς περάσας
ἐκ τῶν Δελφῶν περάσας δηλονότι. εἰς οὐδὲν δὲ χρήσιμον τοπογραφεῖ. μᾶλλον δὲ αὐτὸν ἐχρῆν σκοπεῖν ὅπως τῶν πολεμίων παρακαθιζομένων λήσῃ φεύγων ὁ Μενοικεύς.
MBCV, Arsen.
περάσας om. MCV
first δὲ om. MCV
παρακαθεζομένων MCV
λήσει B, λήσεται MCV
ὁ μεν. φεύγων transp. MC, φεύγων om. V

980
ποῖ χρὴ μολεῖν καὶ ἀπελθεῖν ἐμὲ τοὺς Δελφοὺς διαβάντα δηλονότι.

981
εἰς τὴν γῆν τὴν Αἰτωλίδα καὶ τὴν τῶν Αἰτωλῶν.

981
ἐκ δὲ τῆσδε ποῖ ἵνα περῶ καὶ περάσω καὶ ἀπέλθω.

982
εἰς τὸ οὖδας τὸ Θεσπρωτὸν ἤτοι εἰς τὴν γῆν τῶν Θεσπρωτῶν τὴν νῦν Μεθάνην καλουμένην.

982
εἰς τὰ σεμνὰ βάθρα τῆς Δωδώνης, τουτέστι ἔνθα ἵδρυται ἡ Δωδώνη.

982 σεμνὰ
τὰ σεβάσμια τῆς Δωδώνης θεμέλια
(continues into next)
B, Arsen.

983
ἔγνως.

983
τί δῆτα γενήσεταί μοι ἔρυμα ἤτοι ἀσφάλεια καὶ φυλακὴ κατὰ τὴν ὁδόν.

983 (continued from previous)
φύλαγμά μοι γενήσεται, ὅ ἐστι ποία πόλις δεξαμένη με σώσει.
MBCV, Arsen.
με transp. after ποία MCV

984
πόμπιμος ὁ δαίμων· ὁδηγὸς ὁ θεός, ὁ Ζεὺς δηλονότι διὰ τῶν αὐτοῦ χρησμῶν.

984 πόμπιμος ὁ δαίμων
ὁδηγήσει σε ἡ τύχη.
cf. Thom., T ἤγουν ἡ σὴ ὁδηγήσει σε τύχη

984
χρημάτων δὲ τίς πόρος καὶ ἀφορμή.

984 χρημάτων δὲ
τίς εὐπορία.
cf. gloss MCV εὐπορία for πόρος

985
ἐγὼ πορεύσω καὶ παρέξω χρυσόν.

985 ἐγὼ πορεύσω
ἀντὶ τοῦ πέμψω χρυσὸν.

985
εὖ λέγεις ὦ πάτερ.

985
καλῶς λέγεις, ὦ πάτερ.

986
χώρει νυν καὶ ἀπέρχου δή.

986
ἀπέρχου δή.

986–989
πρὸς τὴν σὴν κασιγνήτην καὶ ἀδελφὴν, τὴν Ἰοκάστην λέγω, μολὼν καὶ ἀπελθών, ἧς πρῶτον εἵλκυσα τὸν μαστὸν στερηθεὶς μητρὸς τῆς ἐμῆς δηλονότι καὶ ὀρφανὸς γενόμενος, ἀποζυγεὶς καὶ στερηθεὶς ἐκείνης. ὡς προσηγορήσων καὶ προσαγορεύσων, τὸ κοινῶς ἀποχαιρετίσων, εἶμι καὶ ἀπελεύσομαι καὶ σώσω τὴν βίον ἤγουν τὴν ζωὴν τὴν ἐμαυτοῦ.
after βίον began to write αὐ(τῆς?), but deleted

986 ὡς σὴν πρὸς
ἐκ παραλλήλου, ἢ ἡ εἰς περιττή.

πρὸς τὴν σὴν κασιγνήτην Ἰοκάστην ἐλθών, ἧστινος καταρχὰς τὸν μαστὸν ἐθήλασα, τῆς μητρὸς στερηθεὶς καὶ ὀρφανὸς γενόμενος, προσαγορεύ(σ)ων ἐκείνην καὶ συνταξόμενος ἀπελεύσομαι διατηρήσων τὴν ἐμαυτοῦ ζωήν.

Chapter 2

Teachers' Scholia, Tzetzes, and Planudes

1. "GRAMMATICAL" SCHOLIA OR TEACHERS' NOTES

In the previous chapter I argued that classification of the Euripidean scholia as *vetera* vs. *recentiora* is in many cases problematic and misleading. While no system of stratification (or tagging in an XML structure for the online edition) will be without its imperfections or disadvantages, it does seem to me important to recognize that the difference between scholarly treatment at an advanced level, on the one hand, and less ambitious treatment emphasizing paraphrase and help with rare words and sophisticated syntax, on the other, is as much a matter of intended audience as of chronology. Of course, if we could go as far back into antiquity as the commentaries of the generations before Didymus and of Didymus himself, we would probably find a very high proportion of what we would consider advanced scholarly discussion. But what we actually have access to in the extant tradition of Euripidean scholia was first consolidated some centuries after Didymus and was created, and handed on and modified, in order to meet the needs of less ambitious users. Some of the elementary or mid-level help in the scholia goes back to the Roman Imperial period, if not earlier; and, given the conservative nature of the educational system and the apprenticeship-style conveyance of professional teaching skills from one generation to the next, even an explanation first recorded in our developing corpus in, say, the 6th century CE may have been current for many generations before that. Therefore, a classification into *scholia vetera* and *scholia recentiora* should not be understood as claiming that we can establish on a sound and consistent basis the relative chronology of various notes. It is hard, however, to abandon these terms, despite the uncertainties, and the current XML structure (in the type attribute for each scholion element) uses these terms in the following way. The type "vet" is used when there is a high probability that the note existed (allowing for minor variations) before about 1000 (with no claim as to how much earlier any single note originated). For the triad plays this means, in essence, recorded by the first hand in a manuscript earlier than 1100 (HMB) or the first hand(s) in the later witnesses V and C, which, despite being of the 13th and 14th centuries respectively, are copied from sources for the most part as old as HMB. The type "rec" is used, in contrast, for notes that are first attested in the late 13th century and early 14th century in the manuscripts known as the *recentiores* of Euripides (in particular, MnPrRRfRvRwSSa); again this designation makes no claim about how much earlier than, say, 1280 these notes may have originated. Scholia associated with Maximus Planudes, Manuel Moschopulus, Thomas Magister, and Demetrius Triclinius are each given a type of their own based on the presumed author's name. Finally, additional simple anonymous notes that first appear in manuscripts from ca. 1300 on, that is, contemporary with or later than the work of Moschopulus and Thomas but not securely associated with them, are given the type "pllgn" (for Palaeologan).

The *scholia recentiora* include some shortened versions of the *scholia vetera*, or barely shortened but reworded versions, in both cases adjusted for less ambitious readers and earlier stages of the educational system. Examples were given in Chapter 1, where we saw that similar shortened versions existed already in H, and also in M (for *Hippolytus*) and in B (especially for *Andromache*).[1] In addition, some *scholia recentiora* evince their educational role at a less ambitious level by the greater prominence of what can be called grammatical elements in the notes.[2] "Grammatical" here refers to the activities of the *grammaticus*, a teacher who is using the ancient texts to expand his students' vocabulary and morphology, their awareness of distinctions of meaning among uses of a single word or between words of similar reference, their knowledge of syntax and of rhetorical tropes, and their exposure to etymologies. Ole L. Smith pointed out the frequent appearance of these in the manuscripts of classical authors.[3] Ruth

---

[1] On B see Chapter 1, note 19. Not all the scholia in B are shortened; many are the same or virtually the same as notes Schwartz edited from the later manuscripts VVo..

[2] Another index of this middling context is the greater frequency of misguided interpretations. There are already some ill-considered interpretations of syntax and sense in the older scholia (some ascribed to named scholars), but more mistakes can be found in Palaeologan-era manuscripts. Teachers and students treated the text before them extremely atomistically (compare the word-by-word parsing and etymologizing in schedography) and sometimes one finds an erroneous gloss that shows the reader was not looking forward to the next line or even to the rest of the current line, but looking at one word in isolation and trying to give it a sense or construction based only on what had been read so far.

[3] Smith 1996. He is one of the few scholars specializing in tragic scholia who mentions just how elementary some glossing is, and this article as a whole is an excellent statement of the need to recognize the variety of audiences served by the annotations, although he does not recognize the importance of a competitive spirit between (at least some) teachers, similar to what existed among Hellenistic scholars and late antique educators. Nevertheless, in his own otherwise very inclusive

Webb and others have illuminated how classical texts were used for teaching of orthography, grammar, and vocabulary, showing that teachers and students, in certain contexts at least, treated the texts not as ones to be appreciated on a literary level, but as a storehouse of examples and prompts for mastering details of the artificial language they needed in order to acquire or maintain elite status in Byzantine society.[4]

A glance at the explanations on *Iliad* 1 by Ioannes Tzetzes gives an indication of several kinds of grammatical scholia. Within the short range of notes on *Il.* 1.98–100,[5] we find a paraphrase clarifying a verbal tmesis, with the addition "hyperbaton, in the Ionic manner"; a gloss with a simple etymology; an overdrawn distinction between prepositions (εἰς is used with inanimate objects, πρός with animate objects); explanation of three poetic pronoun forms attached to the occurrence of one of them in the text; parsing, principal parts, and derivation of two verb forms. Homer was such a fundamental text in teaching from the earliest stage that we have much more of this grammatical material surviving, particularly as compiled in the *Epimerismi Homerici*. Notes of this kind occur sporadically among the old scholia on Euripides, but in greater number in the scholia that I classify among the *scholia recentiora*.

In such annotation, the actual meaning of the ancient text is sometimes of little importance, as a word in the text is seen rather as a jumping-off point for a lesson in grammar or vocabulary. These concerns leave less room for more scholarly questions directly related to the text and its literary interpretation. We can recognize some of this same educational bias in the annotations on the triad associated with Manuel Moschopulus (or in a few cases Planudes) and Thomas Magister, although they seem to be engaged in a more disciplined project, which I think might be viewed as a reaction against, or at least refinement of, the teaching tradition reflected in the manuscripts in circulation in previous generations.

Before considering some categories of discursive teachers' scholia, it will be useful to show that already at the level of the interlinear glosses we can identify some characteristic features of manuscripts whose annotation is aimed at a lower

---

edition of the scholia on *Septem*, he excludes this kind of annotation (Smith 1982: xxii). Xenis 2010a: 17 also mentions this type of scholia, again excluding them from his edition.

[4] See esp. Webb 1994 and 1997, Nünlist 2012, and Gaul 2011 (with many additional references). Similarly, it has been noted by Dyck 1986 that Michael Psellus' appreciation of Euripides in comparison with George of Pisidia seems to reflect that Psellus' interest lay mainly in the usefulness of the tragedies as rhetorical examples.

[5] These are among the first in the edition of Lolos 1981, covering the notes on *Iliad* 1.97–609: specifically, on *Il.* 1.98 (nos. 31, 32), 1.100 (nos. 34, 36, 37, 38). The newer edition of Papathomopoulos 2007 has not been available to me and is not currently present in TLG, nor does the TLG include the obsolete editions of the scholia on *Iliad* 1.1–96 published by Hermann 1812 and Bachmann 1832, who believed these were the only ones surviving.

or middle level of educational practice. These features may not be known to many casual users of editions of scholia because editors usually have excluded them from what they publish as the corpus of scholia.

1. Article glosses: Annotation for a higher level will usually have none of these, but for the lower levels one can find manuscripts that provide some of the nouns in the text with a gloss consisting of the article in the appropriate gender, number, and case. Some scribes obsessively place an article above almost every noun that does not already have one in the text. It is not always entirely clear what information is being conveyed: in some cases it may be showing that the anarthrous noun in the poetic text needs to be understood as definite (the article would be present in prose); in other cases, it may be identifying the word as a noun rather than an adjective (but sometimes the article is above an adjective along with another above its governing noun); and in others it may provide an indication or a confirmation of the gender and case of the noun or adjective (for vocabulary practice or a reminder of the case appropriate with a particular verb). Thus the gloss may be related to correct paraphrase or to correct parsing, skills expected of the teacher and perhaps also tested by interrogation of the students. Examples from *Orestes* 1–10: 1 ἔπος] τὸ R; 3 ἄχθος] τὸ PrSZu; 3 ἀνθρώπου] τοῦ S; 3 φύσις] ἡ PcS; 4 τύχας] τὰς F²MnS; 5 Διός] τοῦ AbS; 5 Τάνταλος] ὁ F²Ox; 6 πέτρον] τὸν ZZaZmTZbGu (Thom.); 7 δίκην] τὴν XXaXbTYYfGrZc (Mosch.); 10 γλῶσσαν] τὴν F²; 10 αἰσχίστην] τὴν O. Note the presence of such a gloss in O, the attestation in the *recentiores* AbFMnPrSR, and the occasional use of the article gloss in Moschopulus and Thomas. In various stretches of the text one may find a scribe being particularly thorough in the use of such glosses: e.g., F², S, and Ox offer examples of this behavior.

2. There are various disambiguating glosses found in manuscripts intended to provide more basic help. For homophone words, these may go back to texts that had no or very few diacritics and no word division, but they persist in manuscripts that have abundant diacritics and even in those with word division (although in the more crowded and informally written copies of the Palaeologan era, it is often difficult to detect word division visually).[6] For other words, they help identify which meaning applies when a word has a large number of alternative uses.

2a. Disambiguating gloss on ὡς: The best example of the disambiguating gloss is the treatment of the conjunction/particle ὡς. Even the major manuscripts of old scholia will have a few instances where the word is glossed, but a sure sign of mid-level teachers' annotation is the tendency to supply every instance of ὡς with a gloss from among a group of choices. The choices (with

---

[6] This persistence may be due to conservatism in the teaching tradition, but in some cases it may also reflect the fact that students did not then understand or pay attention to distinctions in accentuation, just as many modern students do not, even when they are explicitly taught.

examples again from *Orestes*) are ὅτι for noun-clauses (91 Ab²; 93 V³RSGu; 128 AbFMnRRfSSa), καθά (καθάπερ, κάθως) for similes (8 Thom.; 45 MnZbZcZlGCrOx; 341 Aa³GP²Y²; 343 Aa³AbKMnG), λίαν for exclamatory uses (93 Aa²Gu; 125 B³Aa³AbKSZmGuGCr; 126 AbPrMn, Mosch., Thom.; 212 AaAbK, Mosch., Thom.+; 213 AbKR, Mosch., Thom.+) or sometimes instead ὄντως (126 AaZu, 213 AaZu, 217 and 226 F²), ἐπεί for temporal uses (90 Thom.+), ἵνα for purpose (265 FPRSa, Mosch., Thom.+), πῶς (or ὅπως) for manner-clauses (90 K, Mosch.+; 128 AaKMnSa, Mosch., Thom.+; 265 AaAbMnRSSa).

2b. Disambiguating gloss on ἤ: The form with circumflex and smooth breathing may have ἆρα to indicate a question (233 AaAbFMnPrSSa, Mosch., Thom.; 435 AaAbMnRSaCrOx, Mosch.) or ὄντως (435 Thom.) to indicate affirmative "indeed." The form with circumflex and rough breathing may be glossed with ᾗτινι (ᾗτινι) to indicate the feminine dative of the relative pronoun (49 Ab²SCrOx; 402 CrOx) as opposed to an adverbial use.

2c. Disambiguating gloss on the relative pronoun: Forms of ὅς, ἥ, ὅ that can be mistaken for an article or a demonstrative (or possessive adjective as in Homer) are shown to be the relative pronoun by the use of the indefinite relative form as a gloss (29 ἥτις AaAbF²MnPcSCrOxYf²Zl; 49 ᾗτινι Ab²SCrOx; 78 ἥντινα Ox; 33 ὅς] ὅστις SCrOx), and the Doric feminine ἅ is similarly distinguished from a neuter plural ἅ (81 ἅ γε] ἥτις AbPrRRwSCrOx, ἥτις ἢ ἅτινα Thom.; 206 ἅτε] ἥτις V¹CAaKMnS, Thom.+ vs. ἅτε] καθὰ AbFMnSaCrOx, Tricl.).

3. Prepositional glosses: Poetic case usages without preposition are often clarified by glossing with the standard preposition, such as εἰς above an accusative of direction or goal (303 σῖτον] εἰς F; 1094 γῆν δελφίδ'] εἰς Mosch.; 1490 δόμοις] εἰς Mosch.), or ἐν with a locative dative (103 ἄργει] ἐν F²GB³; 315 βροτοῖσιν] ἐν R).[7] Middle to late Byzantine glosses also feature the frequent use of ἐν to explain an instrumental dative, a usage one can also find, for instance, in the verse of Ioannes Tzetzes: (54 πλάτῃ] ἐν F; 282 νόσοις] ἐν AaSOx, Thom.; 304 προσεδρείᾳ] ἐν F; 305 πολλῇ δ' ἁβροσύνῃ] ἐν F, Thom.).[8] Plain genitives with verbs of being born often have a gloss of ἀπό (5 διός] ἀπό KMnRw, Mosch.+; 11 τοῦ] ἀπό PcS, Mosch.+; 16 ἀτρέως] ἀπό AaAb²MnPrSSa, Mosch.+) or ἐκ (5 διός] ἐκ F²Gu; 16 ἀτρέως] ἐκ F), and other expressions with a plain genitive of separation are treated similarly (251 κακῶν] ἀπό ZuCrOx). A related form of explanation occurs with partitive genitives, which may be distin-

---

[7] Explanation of these inherited usages as due to omission of a preposition goes back to antiquity, since it was used by Aristarchus: Matthaios 1999: 176–179 (fr. 195–204), 597–602.
[8] Note, however, that an even more common way to treat instrumental datives is by glossing with διά plus genitive of the same noun.

guished from other independent genitives by use of the gloss ἀπό (264 τῶν ἐμῶν ἐρινύων] ἀπό Aa², Mosch.+; 385 νερτέρων] ἀπό B³). Comparable too is the frequent use of the gloss ἕνεκα/ἕνεκεν for genitives of cause, especially after the φεῦ or οἴμοι (327 μόχθων] ἕνεκεν AbMnRSCrOx, ἕνεκα Mosch.+; 412 διωγμῶν] ἕνεκα AbF²KMn, Mosch., Thom.+) or with ἄθλιος, μέλεος, and the like (160 ἐχθίστων θεόθεν ἐργμάτων] ἕνεκα (Aa²FMnPrRSSa, Thom.+, cf. Mosch. ἕνεκα τῶν θεοστυγεστάτων πράξεων).

4. Help with pronouns: The poetic pronoun νιν is frequently glossed with αὐτόν or αὐτήν (15 νιν] αὐτὸν τὸν Θυέστην VS, Mosch.+, τὸν Θυέστην AaAb KMnPcPrRRfSa, CrOx, Thom.; 36 νιν] αὐτὸν AbF²GMnRfS, ZZa (Thom.?), αὐτὸν τὸν Ὀρέστην VYf²; 119 νιν] αὐτήν V¹AaF²GMnRRfSSa, ZZlGu (Thom.?)). The demonstratives and the oblique cases of αὐτός, or again νιν, are frequently glossed with the precise identification of the antecedent of the pronoun (11 οὗτος] ὁ Τάνταλος V¹AaAbFMnPcPrRS, Thom.+; 69 κείνου] τοῦ Μενελάου AaAnRSa; 38 τόνδ'] τὸν Ὀρέστην Zb²; 500 αὐτὸν] τὸν Ὀρέστην V¹AaMnPrRS, Mosch.+). In some manuscripts this process is almost obsessive, with the same antecedent being supplied more than once within a few lines. The demonstrative ὅδε in some copies is routinely glossed with the corresponding form of οὗτος (33 τάδε/τόδε] ταῦτα/τοῦτο R/Mn; 38 τόνδ'] τοῦτον F²S; 91 τάδ'] ταῦτα F²), because otherwise the letter-sequence might be read as the article followed by δέ.[9]

5. In a few manuscripts most forms of "to be" are glossed with the corresponding form of ὑπάρχω. For some forms it may have arisen from the need to disambiguate forms of "to be" from other words that looked the same except for the diacritics (such as εἶμι, εἶσι, ὤν, ἤν, ἥν), but the gloss is not confined to forms that actually involve ambiguous spelling. Perhaps this standard gloss owes something to the fact that the verb εἰμί is irregular and its conjugation had changed by Byzantine times. For example: 1 οὐκ ἔστιν] οὐχ ὑπάρχει F²CrOx; 8 ὤν] καὶ ὑπάρχων F²Mn; 13 ὄντι] καὶ ὑπάχοντι MnF²CrOx; 86 εἶ] ὑπάρχεις CrOxZl; 126 εἶ] ὑπάρχεις AbF²RfSCrOx; 228 εἰμί] ὑπάρχω Ox; 264 οὖσα] ὑπάρχουσα CrOx.

6. It is not common, but occasionally τε will be glossed with καί: 71 R, 120 Zu, 282 Zu, 315 Zu.

7. Unnecessary or abstruse glosses: in some manuscripts there is such enthusiasm for glossing several words per line that one finds glosses that seem rarer or

---

[9] This is partly a matter of guarding against inattention to diacritics, but note that some medieval scribes treat δε as an enclitic like τε (and even more often δ' in the same way as τ'), and thus when they write ὅδε (ὅδ'), with the gap between letters too tight to detect a space before delta if one was intended, one can be uncertain whether they intended what we present as ὅδε or what we present as ὁ δέ (or for pronominal ὁ in some editions ὃ δέ). The gloss could resolve the ambiguity for the medieval reader. Somewhat related is the habit of glossing ὧδε with οὕτως.

more obscure than the word being glossed. Such glossing may have a vocabulary-building benefit,[10] but it seems that some teachers viewed provision of glossing as a competitive activity. Even if perfectly adequate glosses were already available in the tradition, to be seen in manuscripts as old as 1000 or in the abundant Moschopulean copies, such a teacher insists on coming up with an alternative. So for ἀπείρηκ' in *Or.* 91, where we find ἀπεῖπον in PrRfZu and ἀπέκαμον in AbS, and where Moschopulus supplied ἐξητόνησα, adjusted to ἐξητόνηκα in G (possibly Georgius Phrancopulus),[11] and Thomas glossed with ἀπηγόρευσα (adjusted to ἀπηγόρευσεν by Triclinius), Zu comes up with an exquisite ἀπεμηχάνησα.[12] At *Or.* 125 μέμνησ' did not attract any glosses in the *recentiores* or Moschopulus or Thomas, but Zu presents καὶ μνείαν ποίησον.[13] At *Or.* 128 ἀπέθρισε(ν) or ἀπέθριξε(ν) is given the obvious glosses ἔκοψε (V¹MnPrSCrOx), ἀπέκοψε (Aa²F²RRfSa, Mosch.+), and ἀπέτεμε (Ab, Thom.), but Zu supplies ἀντὶ τοῦ ἀπομερίσασα. At *Or.* 200 ὀλόμεθ' did not attract any glosses before 1300, but Thomas used the standard gloss for destruction or killing, φθειρόμεθα (cf. ἐφθάρμεθα in Xo²), and in F² we find another standard gloss of verbs of destruction, ἠφανίσμεθα: here Zu presents καὶ ὀλέθριον (read ὀλέθριοι) ἐγενόμεθα.

If we turn now to telltale signs of teachers' notes in the discursive scholia usually placed in the margin (but occasionally in interlinear position in some manuscripts), we may begin with the question-and-answer type of explanation of a syntactic phenomenon.[14] A few of these are found in the old scholia. For

---

[10] Webb 1994: 101 n. 49 remarks: "It should be noted, however, that interlinear glosses are not necessarily simpler terms than the words in the text and seem to have functioned also to widen students' vocabulary." See also Webb 1997: 9–10: "The same word may be both glossed and used as a gloss on another within the same passage, suggesting that the purpose of some of these interlinear glosses was to extend the pupils' vocabulary by providing synonyms."

[11] *PLP* 30135, *RGK* 3A, #242. Following Turyn 1964: 108–109, Gaul 2008: 178–182 argues that Phrancopulus was the scribe of the large etymological dictionary in Vat. gr. 7, not just the author of the dictionary; the scribe of Vat. gr. 7 is the same as the scribe of G.

[12] There is one instance of the middle ἀπομηχανῶμαι in a 12th-century Byzantine text cited in *LBG* (*sich ausdenken, zu gewinnen suchen*) and present in TLG, but the Zu gloss appears to mean "I have used up all my means, I have become helpless."

[13] Zl, however, glossed the whole phrase τῆς πάλιν μέμνησ' ὁδοῦ with ἐνθυμοῦ ὑποστρέψαι.

[14] The question-and-answer format is, of course, not confined to such grammatical notes. It was the standard form of the ancient *problēma*, often beginning with a question, or with ζητοῦσι or διαπορεῖται followed by an indirect question. For a *problēma* that attracted many solutions and survived in a long scholion, see Sch. Phoen. 208 διαπορεῖται πῶς λέγουσιν αἱ κατὰ τὸν χορὸν κτλ on the problem of the references to the Ionian Sea, Sicily, Zephyrus, and "by oar" (ἐλάτᾳ); for a shorter note of this type, see Sch. Phoen. 21 ("how is it that the woman [Jocasta], having previous knowledge of the oracle, did not dissuade Laius from intercourse?"). In the latter example, it is relevant to note that the alternative reworded version found only in V (using διὰ τί) is marked with an

example, in *Orestes* 1-2 there are multiple potential antecedents for the genitive relative pronoun that begins line 3. A modern grammarian would be inclined to say that in such a situation in Greek there are always two options available, using a plural relative pronoun to incorporate all the earlier nouns or making the relative pronoun agree in gender and number with the closest noun only. The scholion that survives in MCV and a few *recentiores* (PrRRfRw) and with abbreviation in O and other *recentiores* (MnSSa) explains the usage as follows:[15]

> *Or.* 2 οὐδὲ πάθος οὐδὲ συμφοράν: διὰ τί εἰρηκὼς ἔπος καὶ πάθος πρὸς τὸ θηλυκὸν τὰ ἑξῆς συνέταξε φάσκων "ἧς οὐκ ἂν ἄραιτ' ἄχθος"; φαμὲν οὖν ὅτι προτιμᾶται τοῦ οὐδετέρου τὸ θηλυκόν, καὶ διὰ τοῦτο πρὸς αὐτὸ ἐποίησε τὴν σύνταξιν.
>
> Why, having said *epos* and *pathos* [neuter nouns], did he (the poet) make the following phrase agree with the feminine in saying "of which [fem.] it would not take upon itself the burden"? We say, then, that the feminine receives preference over the neuter, and therefore he made the agreement with it.

The use of "we say, then" mimics the oral teaching in a classroom or lecture hall. Another stylistic feature to note is the introduction of the final phrase by "and for this reason" and in particular the sort of "ring composition" echo with variation: πρὸς αὐτὸ ~ πρὸς τὸ θηλυκόν, ἐποίησε τὴν σύνταξιν ~ συνέταξε.[16]

Scholia of this type are more frequent for *Hecuba* than for *Orestes* or *Phoenissae*, because it was probably the first tragedy studied by students, if it is legitimate to assume that late antique and medieval teachers introduced their students to tragedy with a Euripidean play rather than a Sophoclean one. While Dindorf's edition by chance included a few scholia of this type, the extent to which such notes have survived emerges only through study of the neglected *recentiores* and other manuscripts from about 1300 onward, and the examples cited here and in the next chapter are drawn from what are so far only partial collations of the relevant witnesses. The following are from the first 500 lines of *Hecuba*, where several, but not all, of the *recentiores* have been sampled. In several cases one can see a straining to draw implausible distinctions—one of the features that shows the potential competitive aspect of performing as a grammarian before a class and of recording one's explanations for others.

> *Hec.* 1 ἥκω: ¹καὶ διὰ τί εἶπεν ἥκω οἱονεὶ ἔρχομαι. ²τὸ γὰρ ἥκον ἐπὶ συνισταμένου τινὸς δηλοῦται πράγματος, καθὼς λέγομεν "ἐγὼ κατελθὼν εἰς

---

obelus by Schwartz as "more recent," but whatever its date of composition it represents, I suggest, a teacher's simplification of the thought and language.

[15] Four different shorter and reworded versions of this explanation are found in B (εἰς θηλυκὸν δὲ ἐξ οὐδετέρου τὸν λόγον ἀπέδωκεν ἐπειδὴ προτιμᾶται τοῦ οὐδετέρου τὸ θηλυκόν) and the later manuscripts Pc, Y, and Gu.

[16] For another example of the type surviving in M as well as V and a few *recentiores*, see Sch. Hec. 9.

τὸν αἰγιαλὸν καὶ ἀποστραφεὶς ἥκον, ἰδοὺ πάρειμι." ³τὸ δὲ ἥκω ἐπὶ κινομένου καὶ οὐκ ὄντος οὐδὲ συνισταμένου πράγματος σημαίνεται, καθὼς καὶ ἐνταῦθα λέλεκται. ⁴σφαγεὶς γὰρ ὁ πολύδωρος λέγει ἥκω ἀντὶ τοῦ ἔρχομαι, τὸ δὲ ἥκω οὐ δηλοῖ συνιστάμενόν τι καὶ οὐσιωδῶς ἔχον τὴν οἰκείαν σύστασιν. 1-2 SSa, 3-4 Sa

And why did he say *hēkō* in the sense of *erchomai*? For the (imperfect form) *hēkon* is indicated when applying to something formed into a body, just as we say "After going down to the shore and turning back I have arrived, and here I am." But the (present form) *hēkō* is indicated when applying to a thing in motion and not existing, nor formed into a body, just as in fact it has been used here. Because he was murdered, Polydorus says *hēkō* instead of *erchomai*, and *hēkō* does not indicate something formed into a body and really having its proper constitution.

Hec. 8-9 διὰ τί εἶπεν "ὃς τὴν ἀρίστην χερρονησίαν πλάκα σπείρει"; καλῶς εἶπεν διότι ὡς ὢν βασιλεὺς συνῆγεν ἀπὸ τοῦ λαοῦ ὥσπερ καρπὸν ἐσπαρμένον τὸ χρυσίον. RSSa

Why did he say "who sows the excellent plain of the Chersonese"? He said this well because as king he used to gather money from his people just like a crop that had been sown.

Hec. 9 ¹διὰ τί εἶπε "λαὸν εὐθύνων δορί"; ²οὐκ ἀλόγως· βαρβάρους γὰρ ὄντας αὐτοὺς τῇ διὰ ξίφους ἀπειλῇ ὑπέτασσεν. 1-2 SSa, 2 M[17]

Why did he say "steering the people with his spear"? (He phrased it) not unreasonably, for since they were barbarians he kept them subdued by the threat of armed force.

Hec. 14 διὰ τί εἶπεν ὅπλα καὶ ἔγχος; διὰ τὸ εἶναι πολλὰ ὅπλα τῶν τεχνῶν εἶπε καὶ ἔγχος ἵνα δείξῃ ὅτι ἅρματα λέγει. Sa

Why did he say *hopla* and *engchos*? Because of the fact that there are many *hopla* (gear) belonging to the crafts, he said *engchos* (sword) as well, in order to show that he means military gear.[18]

---

[17] This example illustrates how the teacher's scholia could simply expand a transmitted scholion by preposing the question, if the shorter form in M is actually the basis of the SSa version. But can we be completely sure that M does not carry a more concise form adapted from the longer version? Another example of a preposed question occurs in Sch. Hec. 175 μετάληψις αἰσθήσεως καλεῖται τὸ σχῆμα κτλ (Schw. I.28, 16-19, from V), where SSa prepose διατί οὐκ εἶπεν ὅτι νὰ ἀκούσῃς, ἀλλὰ νὰ ἴδῃς. ἀλλὰ, and R preposes πῶς εἶπεν ἵνα ἴδῃς οἵαν φάμεν (read φάμαν) ἀκούω περὶ τῆς σῆς ψυχῆς.

[18] Sa applies a rough breathing to ἅρματα under the influence of ἅρμα = "chariot." ἅρμα (usually pl. ἅρματα) in Byzantine Greek (άρμα in modern Greek) is "arms" (borrowed from Latin). The gloss ἅρματα (again, with rough breathing) appears above *Hec.* 14 ὅπλα in RSSaXo² among the manuscripts collated so far for this passage.

Hec. 39 εὐθύνοντας: διὰ τί εἶπεν εὐθύνοντας καὶ οὐκ εἶπεν εὐθῦνον; τοῦτο τὸ σχῆμα ἔστι (sic) καινοπρεπές. οὐκ ἀπέβλεψε γὰρ πρὸς τὴν σύνταξιν ἀλλὰ πρὸς τὸ σημαινόμενον τῆς λέξεως. SSa

Why did he say (masculine plural accusative) *euthunontas* and not say (neuter singular accusative) *euthunon*? This figure of speech is novel/unusual (as opposed to common/ordinary usage). He did not look toward the syntax (for the agreement) but toward the meaning of the term.

Hec. 39 εἰναλίαν πλάτην: διὰ τί εἶπεν εἰναλίαν πλάτην; διὰ τὸ εἶναι καὶ χερσαίαν ἤγουν τὸ πτύον. SSa

Why did he say "oar of the sea"? Because there also exists an oar of the land, that is to say, the winnowing fan.

Hec. 143 ὁρμήσων: διὰ τί ὥσπερ τὸ πλουτῶ ἐγώ, πλουτίζω δὲ ἕτερον οὐ λέγεται καὶ τὸ ὁρμῶ ἐγώ, ὁρμίζω δὲ ἕτερον; ἵνα μὴ συνεμπέσῃ τὸ ὁρμίζω τὸ ἐλλιμενίζω, διὸ λέγεται καὶ ὁρμῶ ἐγὼ καὶ ὁρμῶ ἕτερον. Pr

Why does one not say also "I rest at mooring" (*hormō*), but "I cause someone/something else to be moored" (*hormizō*), just as one says "I am wealthy" (*ploutō*), but "I make someone else wealthy" (*ploutizō*)? In order that there not be confusion with *hormizō*, meaning "arrive/stay in a harbor," for which reason one says both "I move" (*hormō egō*) and "I cause another to be move" (*hormō heteron*).

148 ὀρφανόν: διὰ τί εἶπεν ὀρφανὸν καὶ οὐκ εἶπεν ὀρφανήν; ἢ διὰ τὸ δεῖξαι τὸ ἀνδρεῖον τοῦ φρονήματος τῆς γυναικός, ἢ ἐχρήσατο τῷ λόγῳ ὡς πολλοὶ λέγοντες ὁ ἄνθρωπος καὶ ἡ ἄνθρωπος, ὁ κάλλιστος καὶ ἡ κάλλιστος καὶ ἄλλα πλείονα. οὕτως οὖν ὡς οἶμαι ἐχρήσατο τῷ λόγῳ ὁ παρὼν ποιητὴς εἰπὼν ὀρφανόν. R

Why did he say *orphanon* (form that is masculine or unmarked common masculine/feminine gender) and not say *orphanēn* (form that is marked as feminine gender)? Either in order to show the manliness of the woman's spirit, or he used the word as many do when they say *anthrōpos* with both a masculine and a feminine article, *kallistos* with both a masculine and a feminine article,[19] and several others. So, I believe, the present poet used the word in this way when he said *orphanon*.[20]

---

[19] TLG provides a few examples: ἡ κάλλιστος/τὴν κάλλιστον four times in Ioannes Camaterus, *Introductio in astronomian* (12th cent.); also Michael Psellus, *Oratoria minora* 25, 57 τὴν κάλλιστον προαιρεῖσθαι καὶ τεχνικώτατον λόγου δημιουργίαν (11th cent.).

[20] The feminine (in -αν or -ην) is a variant or gloss here in several manuscripts. Note also Triclinius' note, with a more learned and less fanciful explanation: ἡμέτερον· τὸ ὀρφανὸν ἀντὶ τοῦ ὀρφανήν, ἀττικῶς, ὡς καὶ Ἀριστοφάνης [*Nub.* 53] "οὐ μὴν ἐρῶ γ' ὡς ἀργὸς ἦν" ἀντὶ τοῦ ἀργή. οὐ χρὴ τοίνυν ὀρφανὰν γράφειν ὡς ἔν τισιν εὔρηται· οὐ γὰρ ἁρμόζει τῷ μέτρῳ. ("My own annotation: the form with masculine ending instead of the form with feminine ending, in the Attic [= literary] manner, just as Aristophanes also says 'I will not say, however, that she was idle' with *argos* for *argē*. So one should not write *ophanan* as is found in some copies; for that does not fit the meter.")

A second pedagogical interest that could be served by grammatical scholia is the improvement of the student's vocabulary and of the "Attic" purity of his writing style. Some teachers' scholia point out the fine distinctions in meaning between nearly synonymous words. The formula seen in such notes takes the form διαφέρει/διαφέρουσι X καὶ Y (καὶ Z ...), or διαφέρει (τὸ) X τοῦ Y, or some slight variation on these. Distinctions of this type were already taught by the sophists in the 5th century BCE, and in the early second century CE, at the height of the Atticist movement, an important lexicon of synonymous or similar words was compiled (probably by Herennius Philo), and epitomized versions survive under the name Ammonius (*De adfinium vocabulorum differentia*).[21] Typical short examples are Ammonius 4 Nickau ἄγειν καὶ φέρειν διαφέρει. ἄγεται μὲν γὰρ τὰ ἔμψυχα· φέρεται δὲ τὰ ἄψυχα. Ὅμηρος [*Od.* 4.622]· "οἱ δ' ἦγον ⟨μὲν μῆλα⟩, φέρον δ' εὐήνορα οἶνον" ("the verbs *agein* and *pherein* [both meaning bring/carry] differ in sense: For animate beings are brought (*agetai*), while inanimate things are brought (*pheretai*). Homer: 'and they brought/led along the sheep and brought/carried the excellent wine'"); 7 Nickau ἄγριος καὶ ἀγρεῖος διαφέρει. ἄγριος μὲν γάρ ἐστιν ὁ ὠμός, ἀγρεῖος δὲ ὁ ἀγροῖκος ("*agrios* and *agreios* differ in sense: *agrios* refers to one who is savage, *agreios* to a rustic/bumpkin"). Notes of this type can be found in the Homeric scholia and scholia on other authors, in lexicographers, and in the *Epimerismi Homerici*. In the Euripidean scholia, διαφέρει notes of this type are attested a few times in MB:

> *Phoen.* 1010 σηκόν: διαφέρει σηκὸς καὶ ἄδυτον. ὁ μὲν γὰρ σηκὸς ἐπὶ [τάφου add. B] ἀνθρώπου, τὸ δὲ ἄδυτον ἐπὶ θεοῦ. MBCV
>
> *Sēkos* and *aduton* differ in meaning. For *sēkos* is used in reference to a human [human's tomb B], while *aduton* is used in reference to a god.
>
> *Phoen.* 1116 ἐπιτολαῖσιν: ἐπιτολὴ δὲ καὶ ἀνατολὴ διαφέρει· ἀνατολὴ μέν ἐστι τῶν μεγίστων ἄστρων τῶν προαναβαινόντων, ἐπιτολὴ δὲ τῶν ἐλαττόνων τῶν μετ' ἐκεῖνα. MC
>
> *Epitolē* and *anatolē* differ in meaning. *Anatolē* is the rising of the greatest stars that mount the heavens first, *epitolē* is the rising of the lesser stars that follow them.[22]

---

[21] Nickau 1966; Alpers 2001: 200–201; Dickey 2007: 94–96, with further references; Matthaios 2015: 234–235, 286–287.

[22] Ancient astronomical texts, lexicographic sources, and other scholia explain the distinction in more than one way (e.g., *anatolē* is any rising of a star and *epitolē* is the rising of a star along with the sun; or *anatolē* is the rising of a star with the sun, *epitolē* the rising a little before the sun; or *anatolē* of the sun vs. *epitolē* of stars). The distinction here bears most similarity in sense, but not in exact words, to Sch. Arat. 247 ἄλλο δὲ ἐπιτολὴ καὶ ἄλλο ἀνατολή. ἀνατολὴ μὲν γάρ ἐστιν ἡ τοῦ ζῳδίου παντός, καθό ἐστιν ἡ τοῦ ἡλίου, ἐπιφάνεια, ἐπιτολὴ δὲ τὸ ὑπὸ τὸ ζῴδιον, and *Anonymi Miscellanea Philosophica (Codex Baroccianus Graecus 131)* 18 (61, 15) ἄλλο ἀνατολὴ καὶ ἄλλο

Somewhat more discursive notes showing the same interest in distinctions of meaning are the following:[23]

Med. 469 θράσος: οὐ θράσος ἐστὶ κακῶς φίλους δράσαντα ἐναντίον βλέπειν ἀλλὰ μᾶλλον ἀναίδεια. τινὲς δὲ ἐπιλαμβάνονται Εὐριπίδου, ὡς κακῶς εἰρηκότος· τὸ γὰρ θράσος ἔδει μᾶλλον εἰπεῖν θάρσος. διαφέρει γὰρ ὡς ἀρετὴ κακίας· τὸ μὲν γὰρ ἐπὶ κακοῦ καὶ ῥιψοκινδύνου τάσσεται, τὸ δὲ ἐπὶ ἀγαθοῦ. ὅθεν οἱ παλαιοὶ αὐτὸ διώρισαν οὕτως, ὅτι θάρσος μὲν τὸ τῆς ψυχῆς παράστημα μετὰ λογισμοῦ, θράσος δὲ ἡ ἀλόγιστος ὁρμή. BV[3]

It is not boldness to treat your friends badly and then look them in the face, but rather shamelessness. Some criticize Euripides, saying he spoke badly. For the word *thrasos* here he ought to have said *tharsos*. For they differ from each other as a virtue from a vice. For the one is applied to something bad and reckless, the other to something good. Whence the ancients made the distinction about it in this way, that *tharsos* is the inspired condition of the soul accompanied by reasoning, but *thrasos* is the soul's irrational impulse.[24]

Andr. 616 τρωθεὶς: (σημειωτέον ὅτι prep. V) τρωθεὶς εἶπεν, οὐ βληθείς· καὶ γὰρ ἐβλήθη ὑπὸ Πανδάρου. διαφέρει δὲ τὸ βληθῆναι τοῦ τρωθῆναι. Ὅμηρος [*Il.* 11.660–661] "βέβληται μὲν ὁ Τυδείδης ... οὔτασται δ' Ὀδυσσεύς." MNVVo

(One should remark that) he said *trōtheis* (wounded) and not *blētheis* (stricken by an arrow). For in fact Menelaus was stricken by an arrow by Pandarus. And *blēthēnai* (be stricken) differs in meaning from *trōthēnai* (be wounded). Homer: "The son of Tydeus has been stricken ... and Odysseus has been pierced by a spear."[25]

Of the διαφέρει-notes collated so far, the vast majority (more than 40) are from the *recentiores* (mainly PrRSSa) and V and absent from MBC, and these are concentrated in the scholia on *Hecuba* (for which the *recentiores* have been only partially collated so far). Some examples will be discussed in the next chapter in

---

ἐπιτολή. ἀνατολὴ μὲν γὰρ ἡ τοῦ ζῳδίου παντὸς ἐπιφάνεια, ἐπιτολὴ δὲ τὸ ὑπ' αὐτὸ ζῳδίον ὅταν συνανατείλῃ.

[23] Other examples: Sch. Hec. 288 on φθόνος and νέμεσις (MVPrSa); Sch. Hec. 567 on ἀρτηρία and φλέψ (MBVGu); Sch. Phoen. 271 on ἐσχάρα and βωμός (B).

[24] This distinction goes back to Homeric scholarship (and was in the lexicographic tradition, Ammonius 233 Nickau θράσος καὶ θάρσος διαφέρει. θράσος μὲν γάρ ἐστιν ἄλογος ὁρμή, θάρσος δὲ ἔλλογος ὁρμή, etc.) and was indeed a fact of classical Attic prose usage. The accusation that Euripides erred is found in *Et. Gud.* 255, 27–32 Sturz, and in item 17 in the collection περὶ ἀκυρολογίας edited in Nickau 1966, where the distinction is expressed in almost the same language and is followed by ὅθεν Εὐριπίδης ἁμαρτάνει λέγων ... . The occasional poetic use of θράσος in a "good" sense was, however, not confined to Euripides, and the criticism in the scholion is captious.

[25] The quotation of these Homeric lines shows that the commentator is familiar with the traditional discussion of βέβληται vs. οὔτασται in Homeric scholarship on those lines, and with Aristonicus' habit of commenting when βάλλω denotes actual wounding as opposed to simply hitting (e.g., Sch. Il. 3.80b, 82b, 4.157a Erbse). But nothing quite like this is found in TLG.

connection with a set of teachers' notes on *Hecuba*, and we will also observe there the tendency of some such notes to draw dubious distinctions. The low number discovered so far for the other two plays of the triad is probably genuinely indicative, despite the current incompleteness of the collations for *Orestes* and *Phoenissae*: in *Orestes* 1–500, where all the major *recentiores* have been collated, only Pr, F, and Yf have provided διαφέρει-notes (one each), and the select passages from *Orestes* 501–1693 and from *Phoenissae* that have been fairly thoroughly collated for other reasons have produced single examples from the late hand in V and from Yf.

Another vocabulary-building technique that has roots in antiquity and appears in a number of teachers' scholia is the note of the σημαίνει-type. The formulaic phrase associated with this type is τὸ X σημαίνει δύο (or τρία or another number[26]). It can be found in the exegetic and grammatical tradition of early Roman Imperial times (instances can be found in Erotian and Apollonius Sophista), and it was perhaps already in use in Hellenistic times. There are many examples in the scholiastic tradition,[27] the lexica, and the *Epimerismi Homerici*. This type is not found in MB, but in V and some *recentiores*, and perhaps much earlier in H, although in a variant form lacking the formula with a number.

> *Andr.* 167 τευχέων: σημαίνει καὶ τὸ πολεμικὸν ὅπλον, σημαίνει δὲ καὶ τὸ ἀγγεῖον. V(perhaps H)[28]
>
> *Teuchos* means the gear (armor) for war, and it also means the vessel (urn).[29]
>
> *Hec.* 168 βίος: βίος δὲ σημαίν[ει ϛ̄· τὸν] παρόντα κόσμον, τὸν χρόνον τῆς [ἑκάστου] ζωῆς, τὴν τέχνην, τὴν κατάστα[σιν, τὴν περι]ουσίαν καὶ τὰ πρὸς τὸ ζῆν. V
>
> *Bios* has six meanings: the present world, the time of each man's life, the craft (one lives by), one's condition, survival, and the means for living.[30]

---

[26] The highest number I have found is σημαίνει ὀκτώ for eight meanings of the prefix α in Sch. PrSa Hec. 612 (going beyond the seven in the version in V that is in Schwartz).

[27] For instance, almost a dozen in scholia on the Aristophanic triad (plus seven more in Tzetzes' scholia on those plays); Sch. Aesch. Septem 370g, 534f, 534l, 1025g; at least eleven examples in Tzetzes' scholia on *Iliad* 1.

[28] What can be seen on the facsimile (Daitz 1970: Plate 43) is the compendium for the first καὶ and αἱ of the second σημαίνει, and Daitz 1979: 74 suggests that the rest, using the same words as in V, would fit the lost space. We await the public availability of the new images of H (see Albrecht 2012) to see whether this reconstruction can be more cogently verified or refuted.

[29] This doctrine is not in other sources; instead we find the contrast between the meanings "vessel" and "book-volume": Moeris τ 25 τεῦχος τὸ ἀγγεῖον Ἀττικοί· τὸ δὲ βιβλίον λέγουσιν Ἕλληνες, cf. Photius τ 224 τεῦχος· οὐ μόνον τὸ βιβλίον, ἀλλὰ πᾶν ἀγγεῖον, Thomas Mag. *Eclog.* 349, 9 τεῦχος ἐπὶ ἀγγείου Ἀττικοὶ, ἐπὶ δὲ βιβλίου Ἕλληνες.

[30] The parallel that is closest is Sch. Tzetz. Arist. Plut. 500b βίος ϛ' σημαίνει· τὸν παρόντα κόσμον, τὸν χρόνον τῆς ἑκάστου ζωῆς, τὴν ζωὴν αὐτήν ἤτοι τὰ πρὸς τὸ ζῆν χρήσιμα, τὴν περιουσίαν

Hec. 304 ἀνδρί: τὸ ἀνήρ σημαίνει ε̄· τὸν ἁπλῶς ἄνθρωπον, τὸν ἀντιδια-
στελλόμενον πρὸς τὴν γυναῖκα, τὸν ἀνδρὸς ἡλικίαν φθάσαντα, τὸν ἀνδρεῖον,
καὶ τὸν γυναικὶ συναφθέντα. V³PrSa

Anēr has five meanings: a human being; man as distinguished from woman; one who has reached the mature stage of life of a male; one who is manly; and one who is wed to a wife.[31]

So far, σημαίνει-type scholia have been found about 20 times for words in *Hecuba*, but apart from the note on *Andr.* 167 (quoted above), the only items from other plays are notes on *Or.* 117 δωρεῖται and 220 πέλανος transmitted only in Gu (14th cent.).

By far the most common type of teachers' scholia is that which offers an etymology. The belief that words were formed by some rational process from meaningful smaller elements that explained the sense of the composite words was strongly rooted in the Greek tradition.[32] Etymological play with proper names to reveal a deeper meaning was an element of traditional poetic wisdom, as illustrated by Hesiod's connection of Titans (Τιτῆνες), retribution (τίσις), and overstraining (τιταίνω) in *Theogony* 207–210 or by Aeschylus' connection of Zeus to causation in *Agamemnon* 1485–1486 (διαὶ Διὸς παναιτίου πανεργέτα). From the age of the sophists onward this etymological method was applied more and more broadly, and Plato's *Cratylus* was an authoritative text exemplifying the method, for later readers overlooked Plato's own intention to show that the method could not yield true knowledge. Etymological explanations entered into the philology and grammatical studies of the Hellenistic and Roman Impe-

---

ἑκάστου, τὴν τέχνην, καὶ τὸ ἐπιτήδευμα, ὡς τὸ "σεμνοῦ ἢ ἀσέμνου βίου ἄνθρωπος." For only five meanings see *Et. Magn.* s.v. βίος (198, 14–18) ποσαχῶς ὁ βίος; πενταχῶς. βίος, ὁ χρόνος τῆς ζωῆς· βίος καὶ ἡ ἐντεῦθεν τῆς ψυχῆς μετάστασις· βίος καὶ ἐν ᾧ τις διατρίβει· βίος καὶ τὸ ἐπιτήδευμα, εἴτε ἰατρός ἐστιν, ἢ μηχανικός, ἢ τεκτονικός, καὶ τὰ ὅμοια· βίος καὶ τὸ εἶδος τῆς ζωῆς, καθὸ λέγομεν τὸν μὲν σεμνὸν καὶ κόσμιον ἐλέσθαι βίον, τὸν δὲ ἄσεμνον καὶ ἄμουσον.

[31] Again the closest parallel is with Tzetzes, Sch. Il. 1.151 (no. 29) πέντε σημαίνει τὸ ἀνήρ· τὸν τῇ φύσει ἄνδρα πρὸς ἀντιδιαστολὴν γυναικός· τὸν σύζυγον· τὸν ἡλικίαν ἄνδρος ἔχοντα· τὸν ἀνδρεῖον· καὶ τὸν ἁπλῶς ἄνθρωπον, ὡς νῦν, ὥσπερ ἐστὶ καὶ τὸ μακάριος ἀνήρ· cf. Sch. Tzetz. Hes. Op. 3 τὸ ἀνήρ σημαίνει πέντε· τὸν ἀνδρεῖον, τὸν γήμαντα, τὸν φύσει, τὸν ἀνδρὸς ἡλικίαν λαβόντα, καὶ τὸν ἄνθρωπον. But the doctrine of five meanings is also in Apion(?) (Ludwich 1917: 220, 10–16) ἀνήρ σημαίνει ε΄· τὸν ἀνδρεῖον, ὡς "ἄνδρά μοι ἔννεπε, Μοῦσα" (*Od.* 1.1) καὶ "ἄνερες ἔστε, φίλοι" (*Il.* 8.174). καὶ τὸν γεγαμηκότα, οἷον "ἀνὴρ ἠδὲ γυνή" (*Od.* 6.184). καὶ τὸν ἀνδρὸς ἡλικίαν ἔχοντα· "καί μιν ἔφην ἔσεσθαι ἐν ἀνδράσιν οὔ τι χερείω" (*Od.* 14.176). καὶ τὸν ἄνθρωπον κοινῶς· "Αἰθίοπας, τοὶ διχθὰ δεδαίαται, ἔσχατοι ἀνδρῶν" (*Od.* 1.23). καὶ τὸν ἄρρενα· "ἄνδρες κίκλησκον καλλίζωνοί τε γυναῖκες" (*Il.* 7.139). In other sources there are only four meanings (omitting "human being"): Sch. Hom. Od. 1d1, 1d2 Pontani (with other parallels in his apparatus); Choeroboscus, *Epimerismi in Psalmos* 6, 24–32.

[32] See the overview of the practice and its history and significance in Sluiter 2015, with further references.

rial periods.³³ The more remote the language of literature became from the vernacular, the more prestige, it appears, accrued to the ability to etymologize in this traditional manner. The Byzantines collected such etymological information in the *Epimerismi Homerici* and the massive etymological dictionaries, and the teachers' scholia on various authors show that scholars and teachers were sometimes not simply repeating an etymology they found in a lexicon, but creating a variation or a completely new one on their own. They and their students must have been convinced that having a word etymologically explained contributed to proper acquisition of vocabulary and proper understanding of distinctions between different words. Alternative derivations might be offered as equally possible since any of them might serve the mnemonic function. Fluency in offering etymologies must indeed have been one weapon in the arsenal of skills a teacher used to impress his students, compete with rivals, and gain prestige among men of literary culture.³⁴

So far almost 200 short etymological notes have been found during collations. Most of these are for the triad plays, with *Hecuba* offering many more examples than *Orestes* and *Phoenissae*, and those notes are transmitted especially in the *recentiores* and other Palaeologan manuscripts, with only about 30 instances found in MB (a couple even on non-triad plays). An even more skewed distribution in favor of later manuscripts is evident for the Aeschylean and Sophoclean triad plays for which there exist adequate editions of more than just the scholia in the oldest manuscript (Laur. plut. 32.09): that is, for *Septem*, *Prometheus*, and *Ajax*, one can find dozens of instances by searching for the formulaic παρὰ τὸ or ἀπὸ τοῦ, and only a handful of these are in the scholia of the Medicean/Laurentian manuscript.³⁵ For Euripides, the etymologies attested in the earlier witnesses seem often to be well integrated into a larger discussion, whereas in the teachers' annotations the etymology is usually offered for its own sake. Here are some examples, to which I have added parallels or sources identified so far:³⁶

Or. 331 μεσόμφαλοι: ὀμφαλὸς κέκληται ἡ Πυθὼ παρὰ τὰς ὀμφὰς τὰς ὑπὸ τοῦ θεοῦ χρηστηριαζομένας. ἢ παρὰ τὸ εἶναι ἐν μέσῳ τῆς οἰκουμένης τὴν Πυθώ. λέγεται γὰρ τὸν Δία μαθεῖν βουλόμενον τὸ μέσον τῆς γῆς δύο ἀετοὺς

---

³³ See Matthaios 2015: 198 and 204–205 on ἐτυμολογίας εὕρεσις as a standard part of the grammarian's discipline; on Orion and other compilations, 287–288 (with further references). On lexicography in general see also Alpers 2001, especially 203–204 on the tradition of the Byzantine etymological dictionaries.

³⁴ Sluiter 2015: 902–903, 918, 921–922.

³⁵ For Aristophanes, the distribution for cases of the formulas παρὰ τὸ and ἀπὸ τοῦ is more nearly equal between the old scholia on the one side and the Tzetzean and Palaeologan on the other side. There are many more unusual words (comic coinages and actual words) in Aristophanes that invite analysis of derivation.

³⁶ Additional examples are discussed in the next chapter.

ἰσοταχεῖς ἀφεῖναι, τὸν μὲν ἀπὸ δύσεως, τὸν δὲ ἀπὸ ἀνατολῆς, καὶ ἐκεῖσε αὐτοὺς ἀπαντῆσαι, ὅθεν ὀμφαλὸς ἐκλήθη. ἀνακεῖσθαί τε χρυσοῦς ἀετούς φασι τῶν μυθευομένων ἀετῶν ὑπομνήματα. MBCOPrRw (small traces survive in H)
Pytho is called navel by derivation from the utterances (*omphai*) pronounced in prophecy by the god. Or from the fact that Pytho is in the middle of the inhabited world. The story goes that when Zeus wanted to find the position of the middle of the earth he released two equally swift eagles, one from the west and one from the east, and they met there, wherefore it was called navel. And they say that eagles made of gold are dedicated as memorials of the eagles in the myth.

The derivation from ὀμφή is not attested elsewhere.

Hec. 609 λάτρι: ἡ μετὰ φόβου δουλεύουσα, παρὰ τὸ λα̅ ἐπιτατικὸν καὶ τὸ τρεῖν ὃ σημαίνει τὸ φοβεῖσθαι. MB(twice)VPr
latri: A woman serving as slave with fear, derived from the intensifer *la* and the verb *trein* which means to be afraid.

This etymology is attested also in *Et. Gen.* λ 41 (cf. s.v. λάτρις *Et. Magn.* 557, 36–38, Ps.-Zonaras 1282, 11–12): λάτρις· ὁ μισθῷ δουλεύων. λάτρον γὰρ ὁ μισθός. ἢ παρὰ τὸ ΛΑ ἐπιτατικὸν καὶ τὸ τρεῖν, ὅ ἐστιν τὸ φοβεῖσθαι. ζήτει εἰς τὸ Ὀνοματικὸν Γεωργίου ⟨τοῦ⟩ Χοιροβοσκοῦ. The reference to Choeroboscus survives only in *Et. Gen.*

Phoen. 1296 φεῦ δᾶ: οἱ μὲν ὡς ἓν μέρος λόγου ἀνέγνωσαν τὸ φεῦδα ὡς ἐν παρολκῇ τοῦ δᾶ· ἔνιοι δὲ ἀντὶ τοῦ φεῦ δή· τινὲς δὲ ἀντὶ τοῦ φεῦ γῆ, κατὰ πάθος μεταβληθέντος τοῦ γ̅ εἰς δ, ὡς ἐν τῷ Δημήτηρ, πηγή πηδή, παρὰ τὸ τὸ ὕδωρ πηδᾶν ἄνω. MBV
Pheu da: some have interpreted this as a single unit of speech, *pheuda*, assuming that the *da* is a superfluous addition. Some interpret it as equivalent to *pheu dē* (*pheu* indeed). And some as equivalent to *pheu gē* (*pheu*, earth), the gamma having been changed to delta by linguistic modification, as is also seen in Demeter and in *pēgē* (spring) from original *pēdē*, derived from the fact that the water leaps (*pēdan*) up.

A similar etymological connection of δᾶ with γᾶ/γῆ is attested in Sch. Opp. Hal. 1.234, which reads in part οὐτιδανοῖο· ἀπὸ τοῦ οὔτι τὸ οὐδαμῶς καὶ τοῦ γάνος ἡ χαρά, καὶ τροπῇ τοῦ γ εἰς δ δανός, ὡς τὸ ὦ γᾶ καὶ ὦ γῆ ὦ δᾶ παρ' Αἰσχύλῳ; but the view that Δημήτηρ is from Γῆ μήτηρ is traditional. The etymology of πηγή from πηδάω is common; cf. Orion 137, 17–18 Sturz: πηγή· παρὰ τὸ πηδῶ ῥῆμα. πηδή καὶ πηγή. Ἡρωδιανὸς ἐν Ἐπιμερισμοῖς.

Med. 399 λυγροὺς: χαλεποὺς παρὰ τὸ λίαν ὑγροὺς εἶναι. V
lugrous: harsh/difficult, derived from being exceedingly moist.

This etymology is closest to that in Sch. vet. Hes. Op. 524-526, 12-13 Pertusi: παρὰ τὸ λυγρὸν τοῦ λευγαλέου ῥηθέντος ὥσπερ καὶ τὸ λυγρὸν αὐτὸ πεποίηται λίαν ὑγρὸν ὄν. The connection of λυγρός with ὑγρός, however, was also assumed in the interpretation of λευγαλέῳ in *Il.* 21.281, as is clear from Sch. A and Sch. T on that line. The latter begins λευγαλέῳ: χαλεπῷ, οὐ διύγρῳ, ὡς Ἡσίοδος.

> *Hec.* 31 ἐρημώσας: ἔρημος ἀπὸ τοῦ ἔραν μόνην ἤτοι γῆν εἶναι. SSa
> *Erēmos* derived from the fact that it is only (*monos*) *era*, that is, earth.

This derivation is found in Sch. vet. Arist. Plut. 447 alpha, Choeroboscus, *Epimerismi in Psalmos* 183, 3, and some of the *Etymologica*.

> *Hec.* 121 βάκχης: ἀπὸ τοῦ βοὴν ἐκχέειν. PrSa
> *bakchē*: derived from pouring out (*ekcheein*) a loud cry (*boē*).

This derivation is attested earlier in Sch. Tzetz. Lycophr. 28 (βακχεῖον): ἐτυμολογεῖται δὲ παρὰ τὸ ἐκχέειν τὴν βοήν, and later in Sch. Hec. 121 (βάκχης) in Gu: ἡ ἐκκεχυμένη τὴν βάσιν ἢ τὴν βοήν.

> *Hec.* 213 λώβην: λώβη γὰρ ἡ ὕβρις, γίνεται δὲ ἀπὸ τοῦ διὰ λαοῦ βαίνειν, τουτέστι πομπεύεσθαι. ἐπὶ ὕβρει δὲ εἶπε καθόσον ἔμελλε στῆναι ἐνώπιον τοῦ λαοῦ οἳ ποτὲ ταύτην οὐκ ἐθεῶντο κατὰ συνέχειαν, ἐπὶ λύμῃ δὲ εἶπε καθόσον ἔμελλε σφαγιασθῆναι. RSa
> For *lōbē* means outrage, and it is formed from walking (*bainein*) amidst the people (*laos*), that is, being paraded ostentatiously. He/she used the phrase "for outrage" because she was about to stand in front of the crowd of people who previously did not look upon her continuously, and he/she said "for ruin" because she was about to be sacrificed.

A brief parallel is provided by Sch. Opp. Hal. 2.613: λώβην· λώβη ἀπὸ τοῦ λαὸς καὶ τοῦ βαίνω, λαόβη τις οὖσα, καὶ κράσει τοῦ αο εἰς ω μέγα λώβη. The scholia on Oppian have not been edited and studied sufficiently for us to determine whether this is likely to share a source with or be borrowed from Eustathius' etymology, which is somewhat closer to our version: *in Il.* 1.232 (I.144, 2-5) οὕτω καὶ ὧδε τὸ "ἦ γὰρ ἂν νῦν ὕστατα λωβήσαιο" ἀντὶ τοῦ τὰ ὕστερα ἂν ἐλωβήσω ἤγουν ὕβρισας. λώβη γὰρ ἡ εἰς τὸ φανερὸν ὕβρις καὶ ὡς εἰπεῖν ἐν μέσῳ λαοῦ βαίνουσα εἴς τινα, οἱονεὶ λαόβη καὶ κατὰ κρᾶσιν λώβη.

Hec. 1061 μάρψαι: κρατῆσαι, ἀπὸ τοῦ μὰρ ἡ χείρ. Pr
Marpsai: to seize/grasp, from the word *mar* meaning hand.

The doctrine goes back to Homeric commentaries: Sch. T Il.15.137a1 τὸ δὲ μάρψει κυρίως τὸ χερσὶ συλλήψεται· μάρη γὰρ αἱ χεῖρες, ἔνθεν καὶ εὐμαρής; Sch. b Il. 15.137a2 κυρίως χερσὶ συλλήψεται· μάρη γὰρ ἡ χεὶρ κατὰ Πίνδαρον, ὅθεν καὶ εὐμαρές; Orion s.v. μάρψαι: κυρίως τὸ ἐν ταῖς χερσὶ συλλαβεῖν. μάρη γὰρ ἔλεγον τὰς χεῖρας. ἔνθεν τὸ εὐχερές, εὐμαρές. οὕτως εὗρον ἐν Ὑπομνήματι Ἰλιάδος. Note, however, that κρατέω as glossing verb is paralleled in Sch. Opp. Hal. 2.175 μεμαρπώς· λαβών, κρατήσας, συλλαβών· ἀπὸ τοῦ μαρπῶ τὸ λαμβάνω, τροπὴ δ' ἀπὸ τοῦ μὰρ ἡ χείρ.

It would be a mistake to consider the traits of teachers' scholia described above to be a development of the Palaeologan era. While the *recentiores* carrying such scholia are from that era, the number of such scholia in V as opposed to MB points to an alternative tradition that the collaborating scribes of V drew upon when they compiled the codex and its original annotation in the period 1250–1280 (probably), drawing on a damaged exemplar of older date (or else that older exemplar already contained them). That alternative tradition exploited other scholia and *Etymologica* and had some relation to Ioannes Tzetzes and Eustathius, and it will be possible to deduce more about it at a later date, when the scholia on the triad are more fully collated. It is also significant that the set of teachers' notes discussed in the next chapter was copied in 1287 from an older source that included material ascribed to Isaac Tzetzes, and the existence of the same notes in R from South Italy[37] and in SSa from the East (Constantinople, one assumes) is most easily explained if the common source goes back a century or more before the Palaeologan era. This conclusion fits with the 12th-century dating proposed by Herington and Smith for what has been called the A-commentary or Φ-commentary on Aeschylus, where knowledge of Ioannes Tzetzes and Eustathius has also been detected.

2. TZETZES AND THE TEACHING TRADITION

Before moving on in the next chapter to the investigation of the set of notes just referred to, it will be useful to review what we know so far about the traces of annotations by Ioannes Tzetzes and Maximus Planudes on Euripides, starting in this section with the former. Ioannes Tzetzes[38] taught, read, and commented on

---

[37] See Arnesano 2008: 37 and 79, with further references.
[38] For general discussions of Tzetzes see Wendel 1948, Wilson 1996: 190–196, Pontani 2015: 378–385.

classical texts over several decades of the 12th century: his birth is placed around 1110, while the date of his death has been variously estimated. There are no letters of Tzetzes that can be dated after 1166, at which date he complains of poor health. The received opinion[39] has been that he lived until at least 1180, since a poem ascribed to him in a manuscript was considered to refer to the death of Manuel Comnenus in that year; but some scholars deny the ascription and others that the allusion is to Manuel Comnenus. An even later *terminus post quem* of 1185 would apply if an anonymous poem referring to the end of the dynasty of the Comneni is accepted as Tzetzes' work, but that is doubtful.[40] The traditional date receives some support if the scribe of Ambrosianus C 222 inf. was indeed a student of Tzetzes and was born between 1150 and 1160.[41] A recent attempt to find a terminus in the period 1174–1178 is based on the belief that in a poem praising Michael Psellus' paraphrase of Aristotle's *De interpretatione*[42] Tzetzes borrowed an image from a work of Eustathius.[43] But it has been shown that the imitation is more likely to be in the other direction.[44] So there remains some uncertainty as to the true length of Tzetzes' scholarly career, but even on the shortest estimate it must have extended over a period of at least about 35 years.

We know that Tzetzes created Prolegomena to comedy (and drama in general) and commented extensively on several plays of Aristophanes, and revised his scholia on those comedies over the course of his career. He adapted old scholia, sometimes expressing disagreement with them, and added information derived from his extensive reading. His annotations on Hesiod's *Works and Days* reused or adapted parts of the commentary that went under the name of Proclus (though it contained a mixture of material), added more discursive notes based on his extensive reading of other texts and other corpora of scholia, and also provided the more elementary help of interlinear glosses. He prefaced this work with an extensive *Life of Hesiod* and Prolegomena. He did similar adaptation and supplementation of older material with the scholia on Lycophron, and the Oppian scholia are also believed to contain Tzetzean material. At a less advanced level, as already mentioned, he compiled annotations on Book 1 of the

---

[39] Wendel 1948: 1961 (cf. 2001–2002); Wilson 1996: 190 accepts ca. 1180 as the date of his death.

[40] Wendel 1948: 2002 (on work #32 in his list).

[41] This is the conclusion of the study of C 222 inf. by Mazzucchi 2003 and 2004 (see 2004: 437), since he places the writing of this codex in the period 1180 to 1186.

[42] Duffy 1998.

[43] *Oration* 6, Wirth 2000: 89–90, lines 15–21. Agiotis 2013 notes the similarity and argues for Tzetzes' borrowing from Eustathius.

[44] Cullhed 2015. Cullhed identifies a probable source for Tzetzes' use of the image and also points out the poem's use of the standard Byzantine dodecasyllable instead of the ἴαμβοι τεχνικοί that Tzetzes preferred by the 1160s.

Iliad. An example of sporadic notation upon a text occurs in a manuscript of Thucydides that he read carefully and equipped with about 50 scattered notes.[45]

If we turn to tragedy, it is well known, on the one hand, that Tzetzes was an avid reader of scholia in older manuscripts, including those on tragedy, and he may have had access to versions less corrupt or more complete than our surviving witnesses. He drew on this material for his own erudite commentaries, and many of his quotations of lost poets and other kinds of learned matter come from scholia.[46] On the other hand, the evidence for annotation on tragedy is much slimmer. In analyzing the scholia on *Prometheus*, Herington speculated that what he calls the A-commentary was compiled in the 12th century by someone influenced by Tzetzes, but not by Tzetzes himself, recognizing that there is a lack of evidence in this commentary for Tzetzes' characteristic combative and boastful tone.[47] In an article, Smith argued, on the other hand, for the Tzetzean authorship of the A-commentary and for Tzetzes' borrowing of some notes from Eusthathius' commentary on the *Iliad*.[48] In his edition, however, he expresses himself more cautiously and does not state clearly what Tzetzes' contribution is and to which form of the A-commentary it applied.[49] The issue remains doubtful, but there is at least one note that someone later (in Athos Iviron 161 (209), I of Aeschylus, W of Euripides) ascribed to Tzetzes, suggesting at a minimum that Tzetzes left behind (or some student copied down from his oral teaching) scattered annotations on Aeschylus. In addition, Smith pointed to Sch. Aesch. Prom. 36c, which repeats the Tzetzean Sch. Arist. Nub. 176a, but this could as easily be someone else borrowing verbatim from the Aristophanes commentary.[50] There is also a small group of notes in metrical form analyzed by Allegrini: these confirm that Tzetzes made sporadic comments on Aeschylus, but this again does

---

[45] Luzzatto 1999.
[46] See Pontani 2015: 380–384; Pace 2011: 12–18 on the sources of his verse treatise περὶ τραγικῆς ποιήσεως.
[47] Herington 1972: 43–44. Compare West 1998: xx: *Compositus* [scil. *commentarius*] *esse videtur saeculo fere duodecimo, et in cod. I ad Sept. 374 ascribitur Tzetzae, quod tamen nemini persuadebit qui scurrae istius vaniloquentiam novit.*
[48] Smith 1980.
[49] Smith 1982: xv–xx recognizes a purer original form of recension A (or, as other call it, Φ) and an impure one that is interpolated with elements from Psellus, Eustathius, Tzetzes, and the *Etymologicum Magnum*; he states that "there is reason to believe that Ioannes Tzetzes was the author or propagator of recension A" without making clear whether he means the original form or the expanded version.
[50] There is the further tantalizing evidence of a 16th-century codex at El Escorial destroyed in the fire of 1671, for which the handwritten catalogue entry of the late 16th century claims the presence of *Ioannis Tzetzae scholia in 5 libros Halieuticon Oppiani, in Promethea, in Septem ad Thebas, in Persas* (it also included Eustathius' commentary on Dionysius Periegetes and scholia on epigrams collected by Arsenius). But in a codex of this date the ascription could easily be falsification. See Andres 1968: 128 (no. 286 = E. I. 17).

not suggest a sustained effort of commentary.⁵¹ For Sophocles as well it is possible to find a few notes explicitly assigned to Tzetzes (including one written in verse, a characteristic of some of his occasional annotations) and to speculate about his authorship of a few more, but there is no way to prove a large commentary on any of the triad plays,⁵² for we know only of some scattered notes that contain his name or are labeled as "of Tzetzes."

The evidence for Tzetzes' commenting on Euripides available in Dindorf and Schwartz is no more abundant than the evidence for Aeschylus and Sophocles. Dindorf had reported one scholion in V mentioning Tzetzes, and in Schwartz's edition there are two more. The presence of the notes in V is in accord with the hypothesis that V carries a set of old scholia augmented with teachers' notes from an earlier generation. Let us first consider the two scholia written by the original hand of V.

> *Hec.* 1220 πενομένοις: Τζέτζης νῦν ἀντὶ τοῦ ἐνδεέσι· πένης γὰρ ὁ χειρῶναξ. V
>
> *penomenois*: Tzetzes says it is used here instead of *endeesi*; for poor (*penēs*) is (normally) used of the handicraftsman (*or* of one who works with his hands).

No comment on this word survives in MB, but some readers or teachers wanted to make clear the reference of the dative plural, since the noun it agrees with occurs two lines earlier (1218 Ἀχαιοῖσιν): thus Pr glosses with ἤγουν τοῖς Ἀχαιοῖς, and V has τοῖς Ἕλλησιν ἐνδεέσι, the latter combining the identification of the reference with the same gloss used by Tzetzes. The second half of Tzetzes' comment is apparently about the normal meaning of the root *pen-*, as if he had explicitly said the application to the Greek army is a transferred use, or as if he had included the adverb κυρίως ("properly") in the second clause. There are two other late Greek passages that associate the words πένης and χειρῶναξ.⁵³ The other example from V shows Tzetzes reacting to an interpretation he found in the old scholia, quoted first here.

> *Med.* 1201 γναθμοῖς ἀδήλοις: αἱ δὲ σάρκες, φησί, τῶν γνάθων κατέρρεον ὑπὸ τῶν ἀδηλοποιῶν φαρμάκων. δοτικὴ δὲ ἀντὶ τῆς γενικῆς γράφεται. BV¹
>
> unseen jaws: the flesh (the poet means) of the jaws was dissolved by the potion that made them indistinct; dative is used in place of genitive.

---

⁵¹ Allegrini 1971–1972.

⁵² Bevilacqua 1973–1974, with references to earlier discussions. The stylistic criteria by which Bevilacqua claims for Tzetzes some notes not explicitly ascribed to him are not reliable. Some are just formulae shared by teachers (such as asking διὰ τί and then answering).

⁵³ Basilius, *De vita et miraculis sanctae Theclae* 1.23 εἰ γὰρ καὶ εἰς πένητας καὶ χειρώνακτας τετέλεκεν ὁ ἄνθρωπος οὗτος; Ioannes Zonaras, *Homilia de Hypapante* 7 πένης γὰρ ὁ Ἰωσὴφ ἦν καὶ βίον μεταδιώκων χειρώνακτα.

τοῦ Τζέτζου: ἐν τοῖς σιαγόσι καὶ τοῖς στόμασι· τίνων; τῶν φαρμάκων. τὸ σχόλιον δὲ φλυαρεῖ· ὡσανεὶ γὰρ τὰ φάρμακα ὀδόντας εἶχον. —V¹

note of Tzetzes: by means of the jaws and mouths. Of what? Of the potion. The (old) scholion (on this line) speaks nonsense. For it is as if the potion had teeth.

The interpretation transmitted in the old scholion is indeed a stupid one, resorting to the notion of *antiptōsis* (use of one case for another), a favorite scholiastic device to deal with an obscurity or corruption. Here "jaws" is made to depend on "flesh" as if the dative were genitive, but Tzetzes rejects this and correctly explains the metaphorical usage. Here we may note the question-and-answer form, and we also see the critical tone often associated with Tzetzes. For the verb φλυαρεῖν compare Tzetzes' scholion on his own *Chiliades* 3.363 οἱ δὲ μικρὰ ταῦτα γράφοντες ἄλλως φλυαροῦσιν, Sch. Tzetz. Arist. Nub. 6a ἔα δὲ σχολιογραφούντων τὰς ἐκ γαστρὸς αὐτῶν συγγραφὰς τὰς ἀργιννούσας καὶ φλυαρούσας, and the discussion below of Sch. Hipp. 1013–1015, where the verb is applied to the author of the lines rather than to the interpreters. Elsewhere alternative terms like παραληρεῖν (Sch. Nub. 713, of Hermogenes) and ληρεῖν appear (e.g., *Chil.* 10.323, 276; 12.397, 11; 12.399, 209, of other interpreters). It is interesting to note that critical terms such as these, along with ἀμαθής, are used in some notes by Thomas Magister and less often, in reference to matters of scansion, by Triclinius. On the other hand, such abuse is not found in Moschopulus, and manuscripts in the Thoman-Triclinian group often reveal that someone in that circle toned down the language by using a milder alternative for ληροῦσι.[54]

At *Hippolytus* 656, a note is added by the later, very cursive and sloppy hand called in my analysis V³ (probably a generation or two later than the original hands V and V¹; on these hands and dating, see Chapter 5).

Hipp. 656 εὐσεβές: Ἀριστοτέλης φησὶν δίκαιον καὶ ὅσιον διαφέρειν· δίκαιον ἔλεγον[55] τὸ εἰς ἀνθρώπους, ὅσιον δὲ τὸ εἰς θεούς. Τζέτζης δέ φησιν διαφέρειν ὅσιον δίκαιον εὐσεβές, δίκαιον εἰς ζῶντας ἀνθρώπους, εὐσεβὲς εἰς θεούς, ὅσιον εἰς νεκρούς· ὅθεν καὶ ⟨ὁσία⟩ [suppl. Schwartz] ἡ ταφή. V³

Aristotle says that *dikaion* and *hosion* differ in sense: people used to call *dikaion* what is directed toward humans and *hosion* what is directed toward gods. But

---

[54] A full list of such changes must wait for the completion of collation of all Thoman scholia for the triad plays, but as an example Sch. Thom. Or. 162 may be offered: οἱ λαμβάνοντες εἰς τὸ ἄδικος ἔξωθεν τὸ ὑπάρχει καὶ στίζοντες ἐνταῦθα ληροῦσι κτλ. (for ληροῦσι, attested in ZZaZbZlZm, Triclinius substitutes ἀμαθεῖς and Gu gives οὐ καλῶς ποιοῦσι).

[55] Thus V³, but Schwartz does not punctuate after διαφέρειν and tacitly corrects to λέγων (which is supported by λέγοντες in the comparandum about to be quoted). This is Sch. Hipp. 656b Cavarzeran: he does not report ἔλεγον and records in his apparatus that the scribe wrote εὐσεβὲς after the first φησὶν but not that the scribe also lined it out, nor that καὶ is added above the line after being omitted between δίκαιον and ὅσιον. See the recent online image of fol. 175v.

Tzetzes says that *hosion*, *dikaion*, and *eusebes* differ in sense: *dikaion* applies to living human beings, *eusebes* to gods, and *hosion* to the dead. Wherefore burial-rites are in fact *hosia*.

This note is of the grammatical sort, specifically the διαφέρει-type mentioned earlier. As Cavarzeran has pointed out, the closest parallel to this is a scholion of Tzetzes on Aristophanes, *Plutus* 682 (second recension):

> ἰστέον δὲ ὡς διαφέρει εὐσεβὲς καὶ δίκαιον καὶ ὅσιον κατὰ κυριολογίαν· τὸ εὐσεβὲς γὰρ πρὸς θεὸν λέγεται, τὸ δὲ δίκαιον πρὸς ζῶντας ἀνθρώπους, πρὸς τοὺς τεθνηκότας δὲ ὅσιον· ὅθε καὶ ὁσίας φαμὲν τὰς ταφὰς καὶ τοὺς ἐνταφιασμούς. νῦν δὲ ὁσίαν παραχρηστικῶς ἀλλ' οὐ καταχρηστικῶς. ... αὕτη διαφορά ἐστιν εὐσεβοῦς, δικαίου καὶ ὁσίου, κἄνπερ ὁ Πλάτων, ἔτι δὲ καὶ ὁ πολὺς Ἀριστοτέλης διαφορὰν ὁσίου μόνου φασὶ καὶ δικαίου, τὸ ὅσιον ἐπὶ θεῶν λέγοντες, τὸ δὲ δίκαιον ἐπ' ἀνθρώπων.

One must know that *eusebes* and *dikaion* and *hosion* differ in sense in proper usage. The term *eusebes* applies to a god, *dikaion* to living men, and *hosion* to the dead. Therefore we call burials and layings out for burial *hosion*. But in this passage it is used in a secondary sense, but not improperly. ... This is the distinction in sense of *eusebes*, *dikaion*, and *hosion*, even though Plato, and even the great Aristotle, speak of a distinction only of *hosion* and *dikaion*, saying *hosion* applies to gods, *dikaion* to men.

Tzetzes has taken the threefold distinction from Menander Rhetor,[56] and in the fuller scholion on *Plutus* goes out of his way to complain about the twofold distinction of Plato,[57] and though he cites Aristotle too, there is no obvious passage of Aristotle to identify for the distinction, so this detail is an error or self-aggrandizement. The version of V³ on *Hippolytus* seems to be a somewhat careless condensation of the note on *Plutus*. This hand often adds teachers' notes, some found in V uniquely, some shared with various *recentiores*, and some

---

[56] 361, 17–20 ἔστι δὲ δικαιοσύνης μὲν μέρη εὐσέβεια, δικαιοπραγία καὶ ὁσιότης. εὐσέβεια μὲν περὶ τοὺς θεούς, δικαιοπραγία δὲ περὶ τοὺς ἀνθρώπους, ὁσιότης δὲ περὶ τοὺς κατοιχομένους. Compare the language of a passage of ps.-Aristotle, *de virtutibus et vitiis* 1250⁹b19–24 ἔστι δὲ πρώτη τῶν δικαιοσυνῶν πρὸς τοὺς θεούς, εἶτα πρὸς δαίμονας, εἶτα πρὸς πατρίδα καὶ γονεῖς, εἶτα πρὸς τοὺς κατοιχομένους· ἐν οἷς ἐστιν ἡ εὐσέβεια, ἤτοι μέρος οὖσα δικαιοσύνης ἢ παρακολουθοῦσα. ἀκολουθεῖ δὲ τῇ δικαιοσύνῃ καὶ ὁσιότης καὶ ἀλήθεια καὶ ἡ πίστις καὶ ἡ μισοπονηρία.

[57] *Euthyphro* 12e and the surrounding passage; cf. ps.-Plato, *Definitiones* 415a9 for ὅσιον directed to the gods. Some commentators on Hermogenes also ascribe to Plato a diaeresis of δίκαιον as genus into ὅσιον (related to gods) and δίκαιον as homonymous species (*Rhetores Graeci* 4.400, 26–28, 4.731, 16–19 Walz), and this latter is taken up in the Thoman note on *Hecuba* 788 ὅσιον λέγεται τὸ δίκαιον. διαφέρει δὲ τοῦτο, ὅτι τὸ δίκαιον, ὥσπερ γένος ὄν, διαιρεῖται εἰς ὅσιον καὶ δίκαιον· καὶ τὸ μὲν πρὸς θεὸν ἐξ ἀνθρώπων γενόμενον ὅσιον καλοῦμεν, τὸ δὲ πρὸς ἀνθρώπους, δίκαιον. ἐνταῦθα δὲ καταχρηστικῶς ἡ Ἑκάβη τὸ ὅσιον λέγει (ZZaZmTGu).

found in the set of notes on *Hecuba* to be discussed in the next chapter.

Several other hints of connection to Tzetzes may be detected in the scholia on *Hippolytus* written by V³, as Cavarzeran recently noted.[58] A very short note on *Hipp.* 337 says that Pasiphae fell in love with a general named Taurus ("Bull"), an idea that derives from a common ancient rationalization of the myth of the monstrous Minotaur born of her love for an actual bull.[59] The intercourse of this general Taurus with Pasiphae is mentioned, however, in two stories in Tzetzes' *Chiliades* (1.19, 528–529; 12.409, 399–400). At *Hipp.* 384 the note in V³ provides an etymology of λέσχη that is closely related to Tzetzes' version of a scholion on Hesiod:

> *Hipp.* 384: λέσχαι κυρίως[60] λέγονται τὰ τῶν βαναύσων ἐργαστήρια παρὰ τὸ τοὺς λαοὺς ἴσχειν. πρώην γὰρ ἀνεῳγμένα ἦσαν καὶ οἱ βουλόμενοι πάντες τὸν χειμῶνα εἰσήρχοντο ἐκεῖσε θέλοντες θερμανθῆναι καὶ καθήμενοι αἰσχροὺς λόγους πρὸς ἀλλήλους ἀνέπεμπον, ὅθεν καὶ ἐκλήθη λέσχη ἡ ὕβρις. V³
>
> *Leschai* is used in its proper sense of the workshops of humble craftsmen, derived from containing the people. For in the early days the shops were open and all the craftsmen during the winter went in there wanting to be warmed, and as they sat there they addressed shameful stories/words to each other. For which reason, in fact, wanton speech (*hubris*) was called *leschē*.
>
> Sch. Tzetz. Hes. Op. 491 πὰρ δ' ἴθι χάλκειον θῶκον: ἐν δὲ τῇ ἀροσίμῳ ὥρᾳ, κἂν εἴη χειμέριος, παράδραμε τὸν χάλκειον θῶκον, ἤγουν τὴν ἐν τοῖς χαλκείοις καθέδραν, καὶ τὴν λέσχην καὶ συντυχίαν καὶ φλυαρίαν τὴν ἐπὶ τῇ ἀλέᾳ καὶ θέρμῃ γινομένην. τὸ γὰρ παλαιὸν τὰ χαλκεῖα καὶ πάντα τὰ ἐργαστήρια τὰ πῦρ ἔχοντα ἄθυρα ἦν· ἃ καὶ λέσχας ἐκάλουν, ὅτι οἱ πένητες εἰσερχόμενοι καὶ μᾶλλον ἐν χειμῶνι ἐν τῷ θερμαίνεσθαι λέσχας καὶ φλυαρίας λόγων συνέπλεκον. ἐν τῷ ἀροσίμῳ οὖν καιρῷ, παράδραμε, φησί, τὴν ἐν τοῖς χαλκείοις καθέδραν, ἢ τὸ καθῆσθαι ἐν τῷ σῷ οἴκῳ, καὶ θερμαίνεσθαι κατὰ τὴν ἐν τοῖς χαλκείοις τῶν πενεστέρων καθέδραν.
>
> And pass by the seat of the bronzeworking smithy: and in the season for sowing, even if it is wintry, pass by the seat in the smithy, that is, the sitting-place in the smithy, and the chatting and meeting together and drivel that occurs in the heat and warmth. For in the old days the smithies and all the workshops that had fire were without doors. And they used to call them *leschai*, because poor men, coming in even more in the winter, while warming themselves, wove together chats

---

[58] Cavarzeran 2016: 40. My discussion had mostly been written before his edition appeared, but I owe to him recognition of similarities to Tzetzes in the scholia on lines 337, 820, and 887.

[59] E.g., Plut. *Theseus* 19, Palaephatus 2, Georgius Syncellus, *Ecloga chronographica* 199, 21–27.

[60] Cavarzeran reads οὕτως, but this very confusingly written sequence of strokes is rather κυρίως. In five places V³ writes out the full κυρί with suspended sign for ως, but here and in two other places he gives his version of a standard truncated abbreviation: see the online images for this note (168r), Sch. Or. 795 κυρίως κῆδος ἡ ἐπιγαμβρεία (47r), and Sch. Phoen. 40 ἐνστάτης κυρίως ἂν κληθείη οἰδίπους (68r).

(*leschai*) and nonsensical sorts of talk. In the season of sowing, then, he says, pass by the seat in the smithies, or sitting in your house, and bypass warming yourself amid the seating of the poor men in the smithies.

Although similar details can be found in other scholia on this line (both anonymous and ascribed to Proclus), Tzetzes' version is the only one that contains the combination of the word ἐργαστήριον and the detail about openness or lack of doors. What is additional in the note in V³ is the simple etymology, a unique one, as often with such teachers' scholia: the usual etymologies of λέσχη are from λέγω or from λέχος with inserted sigma.

The word ἀλαστόρων in *Hipp*. 820 is the occasion of the following note written by V³:

ἀλάστορες λέγονται οἱ Τελχῖνες. καὶ γὰρ λέγεται· ἐν ταῖς Ἀθήναις ἔρ(ρ)αινον τὸ ὕδωρ τὸ θαλάσσιον διὰ τὸ μὴ φύεσθαι τὸ σῖτον. ὀνόματα δὲ αὐτῶν Ἑκαταῖος Μεγαλήσιος Μίμων. ἀπὸ τότε δὲ ἐκλήθησαν καὶ πάντες οἱ κακοὶ καὶ βλάπτοντες τοὺς ἄλλους ἀλάστορες παρὰ τὸ τηρεῖν τὰς ἅλας.[61]

The Telchines are called *alastores*. In fact the story is told: in Athens they (the *alastores*) used to sprinkle sea water in order that the grain not grow. Their names were Hecataeus, Megalesius, Mimon. And from that time indeed all those who are evil and harm others have been called *alastores*, derived from keeping watch (*tērein*) on the salt waters (*halas*).

This is an abbreviated and altered (or misunderstood) version of information from Tzetzes' *Chiliades* again (7.113, 119–128; 12.447, 826–831). The proper names of the Telchines in our note are three of the six given by Tzetzes (and Tzetzes is the only source extant for the set of names), but Tzetzes' Ἀκταῖος has been corrupted to Ἑκαταῖος. In addition, the derivation of the word ἀλάστορες is similar, but not the same. The author of the note in V³ has introduced the notion of salty sea water,[62] where Tzetzes, following Strabo 14.2.7 and other earlier sources, says these demons used the water of the Styx to poison the land for agriculture; and V³ writes and intends ἅλας[63] ("salty waters, sea waters") while Tzetzes' derivation is from ἄλας (ἄλη taken as a recondite word for βλάβη), an

---

[61] This is Sch. Hipp. 820d in Cavarzeran, but he wrongly gives Ἑκάτη for Ἑκαταῖος and τοῦδε for τότε.

[62] Sch. Soph. Aj. 373 is printed from Laurentianus Conv. Soppr. 152 (G of Sophocles, dated 1282) by Christodoulou in a corrupt form ἀλάστορες δαίμονες φανεροὶ περὶ τὰς ἅλας †ἐπιτηρεῖν τοῖς θεμένοις†, which should be emended at least to φθονεροὶ παρὰ τὸ, but it remains an open question how to correct the remainder and whether the original form had ἅλας or ἄλας.

[63] Cavarzeran prints ἄλας without any note in the apparatus.

attempt to improve one of the etymologies in *Et. Gen.* α 400 ἢ ὁ τὰ ἄλαστα τηρῶν.[64]

Another notion without extant parallel except in Tzetzes is that those given to passionate anger are "sons of Poseidon" (the sea god being allegorically understood in typical Tzetzean fashion). This is taken up in a note by V³ apparently belonging to *Hipp.* 887 ὦ πάτερ Πόσειδον and inspired by Theseus' angry behavior:

> πάντας μὲν τοὺς θυμικοὺς, πλὴν τοὺς λελογισμένον ἔχοντας θυμὸν, λέγουσιν εἶναι υἱοὺς Ποσειδῶνος, τοὺς δὲ ἀλόγιστον ἔχοντας υἱοὺς Ἄρεος.
>
> They say that all passionate men, except those who have a reasoned passion, are sons of Poseidon, while those who have an irrational passion are sons of Ares.

The first claim is found in Tzetzes' note on Lycophron's *Alexandra* 157 τοὺς γὰρ θυμικοὺς καὶ ἀνδρείους καλοῦσι παῖδας καὶ ἐραστὰς Ποσειδῶνος and in similar terms in his Sch. Il. 1.350 (no. 18) and in *Chiliades* 2.51, 745–747. The second claim seems not to be connected to Tzetzes, although at one place in his *Allegories of the Iliad* he equates Ares with θυμός (16.186). It is related, however, to a familiar allegorical interpretation: Eustathius repeatedly connects Ares with ἀλόγιστος or ἀλόγιστος θυμός, following ps.-Plutarch, *de Homero* 1056–1057 (ἀντιτάσσει ...) τὴν δὲ Ἀθηνᾶν τῷ Ἄρει, τὸ λογικὸν τῷ ἀλογίστῳ.

The final example is quite uncertain, and the connection is suggested only by the presence of the note in V, added once again by V³, and the fact that the poet is berated with the term φλυαρεῖ ("speaks nonsense"), which Tzetzes uses several times of Aristophanes.[65]

> *Hipp.* 1013–1015 (ἀλλ' ὡς τυραννεῖν ἡδὺ τοῖσι σώφροσιν κτλ): φλυαρεῖ Εὐριπίδης· πάντες γὰρ ἐπιθυμοῦσι τῆς βασιλείας δι' ἣν καὶ πόλεμοι καὶ μάχαι. V³
>
> Euripides speaks nonsense here; for all men desire kingship, on account of which there are wars and battles.

Apart from the cases just listed, we may also refer back to the two anonymous σημαίνει-notes on *Hec.* 168 and 304[66] and the etymological note on *Hec.* 121 quoted in the previous section, for which the nearest parallels came from Tzetzes. Most of the examples considered above point toward people applying tidbits of erudition from Tzetzes' works to relevant passage in Euripides (sometimes, of course, this could have been Tzetzes himself) rather than providing

---

[64] In *Chiliades* 12.447, 826–828 Tzetzes gives first ἄλας + τηρεῖν, but then recommends ἐν ἄλαις + τείρειν, with the learned observation τείρω τόρος τὸ δάμασμα, ὡς ἐκ τοῦ φέρω φόρος, that is, his second suggestion better accounts for the o-vowel.

[65] Sch. Tz. Ran. 358a, Sch. Tz. (Ambr. C 222 inf.) Ran. 1144a, 1225, arg. Tz. Equ.

[66] See notes 30 and 31 above.

evidence for any sustained effort to comment thoroughly on a Euripidean tragedy.

In considering Tzetzes' reading and possibly commenting on Euripides, we must also take into consideration how he talks about his scholarly attention to Euripides in a long note on Aristophanes, *Frogs* 1328 [*TrGF* T 151a + 217 Kannicht]. He refers here to a lost work of his entitled *Logismoi*, which is also mentioned in his *Chiliades* 11.369, 246-249 (in a section finding fault with some of Hermogenes' teachings on rhetoric):

Ἀλλ' ἤδη σε συνέχεεν ὁ ἀμαθὴς ἐπάρχῳ,
ὁ λογιστὴς τῶν παλαιῶν, οὗ δι' ἰάμβων βίβλος[67]
τῶν λογισμῶν, γραμματικῶν, ῥητόρων, φιλοσόφων,
τῶν μετρικῶν, ἱστορικῶν, μηχανικῶν, τῶν ἄλλων.

But already the "ignorant one" [Tzetzes] used to confound you [Hermogenes] in the eyes of the eparch,
[Tzetzes,] the auditor/inspector of the ancients, of whom there is a book in iambics of critiques, (auditor/inspector) of grammarians, orators, philosophers,
of the experts on meter, historians, writers on mechanics, and the others.

The scholion on *Frogs* begins with a rant against the old scholiasts (οἱ σχολιογράφοι οὗτοι οἱ παλαιοί) for failing to comment on interesting matters in the preceding text but rather here accepting Aristophanes' criticism of Euripides (at the end of the old scholion, Tzetzes read the comment δείκνυσιν αὐτὸν πάνυ φαυλότατον, "he shows Euripides to be truly most vile"). As elsewhere, Tzetzes judges that Aristophanes displays effrontery in mocking what he is mocking. From this point it will be useful to quote extensively:

Sch. Tzetz. (cod. Ambros. C 222 inf.) Arist. Ran. 1328 [= Eur. T 151a + 217 Kannicht]: ὦ πλεῖστα μῶροι καὶ φρενῶν τητώμενοι, ἀλιτηρίῳ ἀνθρώπῳ εἰκαῖα ληροῦντι πείθεσθε καὶ συμπεριφέρεσθε; νὴ τὴν ἀλήθειαν, εἰ μέλη παρεθέμην θρηνώδη τινὰ Εὐριπίδου, εἰς δάκρυα ἂν ὑμᾶς παρεκίνησα. καὶ τῆς σαφηνείας ὁ ἄνθρωπος καὶ τῆς δεξιωτάτης ἑνὸς ἑκάστου δράματος ἀφηγήσεως καὶ προοιμίων καὶ τῶν λοιπῶν μερῶν οὐ μόνον ἐστὶν οὐ κατάμομφος, ἀλλὰ καὶ ἀξιεπαίνετος· ὁ Αἰσχύλος δὲ καὶ ὑπέρευγε, πλὴν μέντοι τοῦ κρημνολεκτεῖν καὶ χαίρειν ἄγαν τῇ ἀσαφείᾳ. ὁ δ' Εὐριπίδης τὸ ἀνοικειοπρόσωπον ἔχει ἐπίληπτον καὶ τὸ ἐναντιοῦσθαι αὐτὸς ἑαυτῷ ἐν πολλοῖς καὶ ἄλλα ἄττα βραχέα, ἅπερ εἰ θέλοι τις ἀκριβῶς γνῶναι, ἀναλεξάσθω βίβλον ἐμήν, ἐν ᾗ παντοίων σοφῶν πραγματείας ὑπέβαλον λογισμοῖς, <u>Εὐριπίδου μὲν δράματα πεντή-κοντα δύο, καὶ ἑτέρων παντοίας τέχνης σοφῶν βίβλους ἑκατὸν ἐννεακαίδεκα·</u> ὧν πασῶν λογισμοὺς βίβλος μία ἐμοῦ περιέχει στίχοις ἰάμβοις τοῖς πλείοσιν,

---

[67] With Wendel 1948: 2004 I do not place a comma after βίβλος, but Leone 1968 places one there (and hence TLG).

οὐκ ὀλίγοις δὲ καὶ μέτρων ἑτέρων· ...⁶⁸ ταύτην ἐμοῦ τὴν βίβλον ἀναλεξάμενος, ὅστις ἄν γε βούλοιτο, Αἰσχύλου τε εὕροι καὶ Εὐριπίδου καὶ ἄλλων πολλῶν αἰτιάματα, πλημμελείᾳ τῇ περὶ τὴν τέχνην καὶ τὴν ἀλήθειαν ὑποπεπτωκότας τοῖς λογισμοῖς, οὐ μέντοι διὰ ψευδοῦς γελοιάζουσαν κωμῳδίαν οὐδὲ δυσμένειαν.

O (old scholiasts) utterly foolish and devoid of wits, do you trust and associate yourself with (Aristophanes) a wicked man spouting random nonsense? In the name of truth, if I set before you some mournful songs of Euripides, I would have stirred you to tears. And the man is not only not blameworthy but indeed deserving of praise for his clarity and for the very skilful narration offered by every single play and for his proems and the rest of the parts. And Aeschylus is likewise amazingly praiseworthy—except, however, for his use of craggy language and his excessive delight in obscurity. Euripides can be criticized for unsuitability of character-portrayal and for contradicting himself in many details and for some other minor points. If anyone wants to discover these in exact detail, let him read through my book, in which I have subjected the treatments of all kinds of learned authors to critical scrutiny: <u>(I have subjected) 52 dramas of Euripides (to such scrutiny) and 119 books of other experts in all sorts of craft</u>. [or <u>(I have subjected) Euripides' dramas (to) 52 (investigations), and the books of other experts in all sorts of craft (to) 119 (investigations)</u>?]. Of all these books a single book of mine contains critical examinations, mostly in iambics, but also in not a few other meters. ... Having read through this book of mine, whoever would want to, let him find criticisms of both Aeschylus and Euripides, and of many others, as ones who have fallen under exact scrutiny because of erroneous performance in relation of their craft or the truth, but he will not find, however, a comedy that stirs up laughter with lies, nor a spirit of hostility.

The key passage here is in the words underlined. From the contrast in the following sentence between "all these books" and Tzetzes' one book, it seems that the preceding number 119 ought to be the number of the books of other authors and 52 the number of Euripides' plays. But it is preposterous to believe that Tzetzes actually has access to 52 plays in the 12th century, and one would have to believe that Tzetzes is lying about the number in a boastful way (which many scholars would believe of him) or that he came to this total by including mythographic epitomes of plays as well as actual dramas.⁶⁹ To avoid such a claim, Wendel proposed an alternative interpretation, that 52 is the number of critical notes on Euripides' plays, not the number of plays.⁷⁰ Inconsistently, however, Wendel paraphrased the accompanying clause as if the number 119 went with

---

⁶⁸ Omitted here are some lines in which Tzetzes says that there exist other books of his having scattered critiques (λογισμοί) of other wise authors—critiques that are justified and not done in hostility or without reason.
⁶⁹ Magnelli 2003: 194 n. 10 for references to some views on this claim by Tzetzes. See also Koster's remarks in the apparatus at *SchArist* 4.3:1076–1077.
⁷⁰ Wendel 1948: 2004.

the books of the other authors, whereas one would readily assume it to be parallel to the phrase about Euripides and thus refer to 119 points of criticism, as in the alternative translation in brackets above. Fortunately, we do not have to decide about Tzetzes' veracity or mendacity, or about the accuracy or carelessness of his style, in order to conclude that Tzetzes commented on various things about Euripides, and to infer that these were most likely scattershot observations, not continuous annotations on any one drama, as we would also assume for the 119 other books (or notes?). That would accord with the way he commented on Thucydides and apparently on Aeschylus and Sophocles. We will have occasion to speculate in the next chapter whether we have other random notes with some connection to Tzetzes.

There is additional evidence of Tzetzes' views on Euripides in a scholion on Lycophron, where we again see him essentially adopting the ancient criticism of the characters and the commentators' or grammarians' preoccupation with self-contradiction. Also noteworthy, however, is the claim that a former king in actuality would never beg, which is reminiscent of the claim that everyone in fact desires kingship in the note on *Hipp.* 1013–1015, quoted above as a possible Tzetzean observation on Euripides.

> Sch. Lycophr. Alex. 14: δεῖ γὰρ τὸν ῥήτορα καὶ ποιητὴν ἀπομιμεῖσθαι τὰ ἤθη τῶν προκειμένων προσώπων καὶ μὴ ἀνηθίκευτον εἶναι καθάπερ ὁ Εὐριπίδης φιλοσοφούσας ἐπάγων ἐνίοτε βαρβάρους γυναῖκας καὶ δούλους δεσπόταις τραχυτάτως ἀντιλέγοντας καὶ βασιλεῖς προσαιτοῦντας μετὰ σπυρίδων ἢ πήρας, ὅπερ οὐκ ἂν γένοιτο· τίς γὰρ οὐκ αἰδεσθήσεται βασιλεὺς μετὰ τὴν τῆς βασιλείας καθαίρεσιν σπυρίδα κατέχειν καὶ ἄρτον ζητεῖν; ἢ τίς αὐτὸν καὶ οὕτως ἐκστάντα οὐκ ἂν πάλιν ἐτίμησε τὴν προτέραν ἐκείνου τύχην σκοπῶν; τοιαῦτα γοῦν πολλά φησιν Εὐριπίδης διὸ καὶ μεμπτός ἐστιν ἐν τούτοις ὡς μὴ τηρῶν ἠθῶν τὴν κατάστασιν. τὸ δὲ μεῖζον ὅτι καὶ ἐναντία πολλάκις ἑαυτῷ λέγει.

> The orator and the poet must imitate the character traits of the persons being represented, and the depicted person should not be unprovided with (appropriate) character, in the way that Euripides does it when he brings on at times barbarian women philosophizing and slaves very sharply speaking back to masters and kings begging with (beggar's) basket or pouch—something that would never occur. For what king, after being deprived of kingship, will not be ashamed to hold a beggar's basket and ask for bread? And who would fail in turn to honor him, even when he has thus abandoned his stature, in view of his previous fortune? At any rate Euripides says many such things, wherefore he is to be criticized in these points for not preserving the established configuration of character traits. And the more important point is that he also often contradicts himself.

Although Tzetzes could be basing his criticism about the begging king on Aristophanes and on the biographical/critical tradition, one must wonder whether the objection that no one would fail to honor a former king is a reaction to the scene in *Helen* where Menelaus is turned away at the door by an old woman servant. If so, this would be another piece of evidence for Tzetzes' having had access to a copy of the alphabetic plays.[71]

3. PLANUDES AND THE TEACHING TRADITION

Another notable teacher, Maximus Planudes, a century later than Tzetzes, can also be credited with scattered observations attached to some of the plays of Euripides, but again there seems to be no evidence of a sustained commentary.[72] Manuel Moschopulus was a younger associate of Planudes and probably the *grammaticus* providing most of the more elementary instruction in the Planudean circle, while Planudes tended to concentrate on more advanced topics. Along with other work of an educational and curricular nature, Moschopulus wrote basic commentaries on a selection of texts, among which were the triads of Sophocles and Euripides.[73] It is an unanswerable question whether or in what proportion the annotations most securely recognized as Moschopulean, through their presence in the key manuscripts XXaXbXo and their being marked as such by Triclinius in T, may incorporate material that Planudes taught orally within his circle. But we do have some explicit evidence in the manuscript Y, as Turyn pointed out long ago.[74]

Y is a rather ambitious copy of the triad, with the unusual addition of text and scholia of *Troades*.[75] Annotation has been added in several stages. The scribe who wrote the text of Euripides in Y also entered a substantial set of marginal

---

[71] See Magnelli 2003 on evidence in authors other than Eustathius that might suggest knowledge of the alphabetic plays before the time of Triclinius and the creation of L and P, and specifically 194–195 on Tzetzes (without mention of the scholion on Lycophron).

[72] On Planudes see Wendel 1950, Wilson 1996: 230–241, *PLP* #23308, and the additional bibliography in Günther 1995: 25 n. 1, as well as Pontani 2015: 409–415. For the question whether the manuscript V shows the influence of a new "Planudean" philology as once argued by Di Benedetto, see Chapter 5, section 1. Against Turyn's notion that the paraphrase in Yv is Planudean, see Chapter 1 (at note 6) and the Appendix to Chapter 1.

[73] For a good recent summary of Moschopulus' activities see Gaul 2008: 166–177 (171 on his role as *grammaticus*, 172–176 on his curricular efforts).

[74] See Turyn 1957, Chapter III, and in particular 54–56 on Y. I have not yet inspected Y in person, but I have excellent recent color TIFF images supplied by the Biblioteca Nazionale di Napoli, which have made it possible to read the small cursive script of some annotation impossible to decipher accurately on older images.

[75] Although I have not so far made more than a cursory examination of a few pages of *Troades* in this manuscript, I can confirm that Y copies *Troades* from V, and thereby incidentally gives proof that the hand known as V³ had made his additions before the date at which Y copied the glosses from V. From watermarks, Günther 1995: 26 estimated that this part of Y was written around 1320–1330.

scholia and supralinear glosses in the same ink as the text, and these are mostly Moschopulean. On a very few pages there are additions in red ink, which is a brighter red than that used by the rubricator for the display characters and the initial set of *personarum notae*; this brighter red is also used to add some *personarum notae* that were omitted in the initial rubrication. Probably both the darker and the brighter red elements are by the main scribe. There are also additions in black ink (sometimes in a disciplined script similar or identical to the original, sometimes in a more cursive form), and some of these are Moschopulean (as marked by Triclinius). This seems to me to be the main scribe adding notes at a subsequent stage.[76] A later stage of annotation (which I call Y²) is carried out in a light brown ink in markedly more cursive form, and these notes are usually versions of old scholia or close to or the same as teachers' scholia (of the types described earlier in the chapter) that are also found in a few other witnesses.

In the Euripides part of Y there are a number of instances where scholia are labeled (mostly in black ink) with μαξ or sometimes τοῦ αὐτοῦ (where the preceding note has μαξ), and fewer where the scribe used the label μαν. These latter are fewer, as Turyn and Günther noted, because the scribe apparently expected readers to realize that the scholia he was entering in the side column[77] were to be taken, by default, as Moschopulean. The label μαν was therefore needed only where he needed to inform the user that he was returning to the Moschopulean commentary in close proximity to something labeled as Planudean. There is an exception to this routine on fol. 100v, where the cursive hand Y² has added, in the upper left corner and across the top margin above the left column of verses, a long mythographic note about Aegyptus and Danaus in the Thoman form, which is an adaptation and expansion of the old scholion on *Hec.* 852. Above the right column of verses a Moschopulean note had been written in black ink. There is a μαν label above and to the left of this latter note; it is perhaps written by Y² rather than Y.[78] Sometimes the labels are very close to the present edge of the paper, and in one case the mu of μαν has been lost to trimming of the left margin. Therefore, unfortunately, we are left uncertain whether some labels may have been completely lost to trimming or wear of the outer margin.

---

[76] For more on this question see a few paragraphs below.

[77] The layout in Y is normally two columns of poetic text (read horizontally) and a narrower column of scholia in the outer margin; in entering the original set of annotation, the scribe used a bottom block, or less often a top block, only when the amount of scholia required it.

[78] Since the digital image I have does not show the entire left margin of this folio, I wondered whether there was a label for the Thoman note in the unshown margin; but Giambattita D'Alessio has kindly checked the original and there is no label present. I do not have images of the pages of Y outside the Euripides part, but according to the report of Gallavotti 1934: 310, there are some Thoman notes on the Sophoclean triad labeled μαγίστρ or θωμ μαγίστ.

Sometimes the Planudean notes have a cross prefixed. Prefixed crosses are used elsewhere, however, in this manuscript and sporadically in other manuscripts with no apparent consistency of purpose. The great exception is Triclinius' very scrupulous (but still not completely consistent) use of crosses in T to label Moschopulean scholia and glosses, either prefixed if the Moschopulean element is entirely new (in comparison to the Thoman that he entered earlier), or placed above the first letters of a gloss if all or part of it was already present as a Thoman annotation. I am therefore sceptical of the notion that crosses in Y might be reliable clues to Planudean origin in the absence of a label like μαξ. If one does choose to make such an assumption about prefixed crosses in Y, one must then wonder why just a few of these are also given the label μαξ.

The label appears on the prefatory matter for all three plays. On fol. 93r it is in the margin just above the first line of the page, which is the beginning of the *Life of Euripides*. Apparently, this is meant to apply to the following hypothesis to *Hecuba* as well, since for *Orestes* (104r) and *Phoenissae* (118r) the hypotheses have the label.[79] It is not clear exactly what the label means in this case. Are these versions of the *Life* and hypotheses that were located in an older source by Planudes or reviewed by Planudes? For *Phoenissae* a few of the distinctive readings of the Planudean/Moschopulean version of the hypothesis match those discovered in papyri, suggesting their survival in an alternative stream of tradition from antiquity.[80]

Günther, who has studied the whole manuscript Y in more detail, suggested that the μαξ labels are all by the same hand, which he calls Y[a], and further suggests that Y[a] is the same scribe who wrote what he calls the B part of the codex, which he believes was a replacement for the original pages of much of the Sophoclean portion (made, he believes, only ten years after its production, in order to make room for more scholia). He admitted, however, that the sample of this hand in the Euripides part is very small. Tuyrn has asserted that one scribe was responsible for the various scripts seen in Y, and Formentin, in the catalogue that appeared the same year as Günther's study, also recorded that the whole manuscript is by a single scribe.[81] Without having seen the Sophocles part of the manuscript, I cannot speak definitively on this issue.[82] But I note that on 93r, the *Life* and the hypothesis to *Hecuba* are written in black ink and with somewhat expanded horizontal spacing, in contrast to the brown-ink script of the play itself

---

[79] Günther 1995: 32 reached this conclusion as well.
[80] As noted by Barrett 1965; see also the apparatus for Arg. 1 to *Phoenissae* in Mastronarde 1988: 1, and Meccariello 2014: 342–357.
[81] Turyn 1972: I.39 (noting that in Venice XI, 1, the same scribe also exhibits these variations of script); Formentin 1995: 125 (citing Turyn). Ferroni 2011: 334 (who does not cite Günther in his study) accepts Formentin's description.
[82] I hope to inspect the manuscript in person at a later date, when the collation of Y is complete for the entire triad.

on 93v, but both seem to me to be by the original scribe Y, and the μαξ note on 93r seems to me to be in exactly the same black ink and exactly the same ductus as the the page's main text, different only slightly in the flourish at the end of ξ licensed by the open space. The label at the top of 93v is very similar to that on 93r, but smaller, while the label at the bottom of 93v is much more rapidly or cursively written. The same occurs on 94r, where the first two labels are more cursive and rapid (with the alpha extremely reduced), like the second one on 93v, while the third is written with more care and resembles the first on 93v, and all are in the same ink and appear to have been added at the same time. On 99v the Moschopulean scholia and glosses are in black ink, and the Planudean items are entered at the same time, not added later: the μαξ label and the τοῦ αὐτοῦ label are cursive again, but the nearby μαν label, clearly added at the same time, is neater. On the facing page, 100r, 6 lines of scholia in the middle of the page are in the brown ink of the poetic text, but a group higher up is in black ink, so clearly written separately, but they are, in my view, by the same scribe. In the Euripides' portion, the only labeled scholion that in my judgment may be by a different scribe is the last one detected, on *Or.* 1287, in the bottom margin of 114v, which seems different in ink and somewhat more cursive than the the note on *Or.* 1284 a little above it, which was part of the initial entry. Even here I am not sure it is not the same scribe, perhaps working with an awkward arm position and a pen tip that is in need of smoothing and sharpening. Thus, I hesitate to assert that the black-ink additions are anything other than the additions made by the original scribe Y, working at different times, with some variation occasioned by less effort to be disciplined and by the need to fit scholia into available open spaces.[83]

No Planudean scholia on *Phoenissae* have been detected in Y, and for *Orestes* there are only eight, compared to thirteen for *Hecuba*, a shorter play. This matches the bias observed earlier in connection with teachers' notes in V and certain *recentiores*: *Hecuba* was read first and by the greatest number of students and thus attracted more of this kind of note. Shortly, I will present the whole group[84] in a preliminary form: that is, the list of witnesses is based on what has been checked so far and it may need to be supplemented later,[85] and the remarks

---

[83] One must also bear in mind that if a scribe added corrections or additional glosses after the pages had been bound together, there will be some difference in ductus because writing in a bound volume is not the same as writing on an unbound sheet laid flat on the desk.

[84] Turyn 1957: 55–56 had printed fourteen of these, but one would have expected from his discussion that there were more to be found throughout the triad, which has proved not to be true. The seven notes in my list not already in Turyn are the those on *Hec.* 85, 973, *Or.* 221, 223, 919, 1284, 1287.

[85] Note that Gr/Gu is not cited for *Hec.* 1–89 because these are later replacement pages in the manuscript (written ca. 1450–1475). Dindorf misleadingly reports readings from the replacement pages using both Gr and Gu. (It is possible that the replacement was copied from damaged pages of the

on sources or parallels are also tentative. I have marked with an asterisk the nine notes that are only in Y, with a double asterisk the three that are in Y and Xo; the nine unmarked notes are found in the standard Moschopulean annotation, and Triclinius considered them Moschopulean and marked them accordingly with a cross in T. It is noticeable that only three of the thirteen notes on *Hecuba* are in this last subgroup, whereas for *Orestes* six out of eight are transmitted widely elsewhere as Moschopulean. Turyn wondered whether such situations of divergent identifications were due to a mistaken application of the μαξ label in Y or to the fact that Moschopulus was accustomed to take over Planudean material.[86] Such labeling was done, however, sporadically throughout the manuscript Y for other authors as well,[87] and it seems likely that most users of the Moschopulean commentaries did not know or care about the distinction between any Planudean substrate and the full commentary. Therefore, I believe the default assumption should be that the person adding the marks in Y acted with some care and with some kind of evidence. Whether we would consider that evidence fully trustworthy or not is a separate question. If the labels are trusted, however, we should also conclude that Moschopulus was freely reusing teachings of his teacher and senior colleague.

*Hec. 1 (κευθμῶνα): κευθμὼν ἀπὸ τοῦ κεύθω τὸ κρύπτω, ὁ κεκρυμμένος καὶ κατώτατος τόπος. Y

Keuthmōn from *keuthō* meaning "conceal," that is, the hidden and lowest place.

93v, black ink addition in top margin, with label and cross. Derivation from κεύθω and glossing with κρύπτω are commonplace: e.g., Apollon. Soph. *Lex. Hom.* 98, 20 κευθμῶνες αἱ καταδύσεις, παρὰ τὸ κεύθειν, ὅ ἐστι κρύπτειν; Hesych. κ 2393 κευθμῶνες· καταδύσεις· ἀπὸ τοῦ κεύθειν, ὅ ἐστιν κρύπτειν; Photius κ 633 κευθμώνων· κρυπτῶν τόπων, ἐνδοτάτων. Of the *recentiores*, R has the gloss κεκρυμμένον τόπον, while the Moschopulean gloss is ἤγουν τὸν ἀπόκρυφον τόπον. See also Chapter 3, section 2, on item 1 in the Miscellany of teachers' notes.

*Hec. 2a: ᾤκισται· τουτέστιν ὑπὸ τοῦ κλήρου ὃν μετὰ τὴν τοῦ Κρόνου τῆς βασιλείας ἔκπτωσιν ἐποίησεν ὁ Ζεὺς καὶ οἱ μετ' αὐτοῦ. Y

Has been settled: that is, by the lottery that Zeus and those with him conducted after Cronus' fall from the kingship.

---

original, but that is very hard to prove.) Similarly, Dindorf cites B for some of these notes, but for *Hecuba* 1–522 we have only late replacement pages in B.

[86] Turyn 1957: 55, discussing the first case, the note on *Hec.* 71.
[87] See Gallavotti 1934: 308–310 for some general remarks and for the Theocritean part; Pertusi 1951 for the Hesiod part; Turyn 1949: 114–119 for the Sophocles part.

93v, black ink addition, continued on same line as previous.[88] The juncture of Cronus (Saturn) with the word ἔκπτωσις is elsewhere attested in TLG only in astrological texts, with which Planudes, like most educated Byzantines, would have been familiar.

> *Hec. 2b: θεῶν· ἤγουν τῶν ἄστρων παρὰ τὸ θέω τὸ τρέχω. ὁ γὰρ Ἅιδης ὑποκάτω τῆς γῆς ὢν οὐκ ἄστρασι κεκόσμηται. Υ
>
> From the gods: in other words, from the stars; (*theos*) derived from *theō* meaning "run"; for Hades, being beneath the earth, is not adorned with stars.

93v, black ink addition on the line after the previous. The etymology from θέω based on reference to the stars goes back to Plato, *Cratylus* 397d2-4 ἅτε οὖν αὐτὰ ὁρῶντες πάντα ἀεὶ ἰόντα δρόμῳ καὶ θέοντα, ἀπὸ ταύτης τῆς φύσεως τῆς τοῦ θεῖν "θεοὺς" αὐτοὺς ἐπονομάσαι, and is cited in Church fathers (e.g., Euseb. *Praep. Evang.* 1.9.14, 6-8 μόνα δὲ τὰ φαινόμενα τῶν οὐρανίων ἄστρων, παρὰ τὸ θέειν, ὅπερ ἐστὶ τρέχειν, θεῶν δὴ προσηγορίας, ὡς αὐτοί φασιν, ἐτύγχανον, ps.-Anastas. *Quaestiones aliae, PG* 28: 773, 38) and reflected in *Epimerismi Hom.* on *Il.* 1.483a1, Choeroboscus, *Epimerismi in Psalmos* 99, 6.

> *Hec. 3: ἑκάβης παῖς γεγώς· τοῦτο ἐντελές· τὸ δὲ πριάμου τε πατρὸς οὐκ ἔστιν. ὅμως δὲ καὶ οὕτως κρεῖττον. ἐπεὶ πατὴρ ἄνευ υἱοῦ οὐ δύναται κληθῆναι. Υ
>
> Born the son of Hecuba: this phrase is complete in itself (i.e. it implies that Hecuba is mother), but the phrase "of Priam as father" is not (i.e. it adds "father" redundantly). Nevertheless even this way (with the redundancy) it is better, since one cannot be called a father without a son.

93v, black ink addition after last note of bottom block, with label and cross. No close parallel identified.

> *Hec. 12: βίου· τῆς πρὸς τὸ ζῆν ἐπιτηδείας τροφῆς νῦν. σημαίνει δὲ πολλὰ ὁ βίος· ἔνι γὰρ καὶ ἡ ζωὴ καὶ ἡ πρὸς τὸ καλὸν καὶ χεῖρον τῶν ἀνθρώπων διαγωγή. Υ
>
> Of life: here meaning the nourishment necessary for being alive. Life has many senses. For it can be both being alive and the conduct of life of humans with respect to the noble and the worse.

---

[88] This and the next are Planudean if we assume (in agreement with Günther 1995: 32) that the label and cross apply to the set of three notes (1, 2a, 2b) grouped together. Similarly the scholia on 3 and 12 are grouped with one label.

93v, black ink addition on the same line as the end of the previous.[89] For parallels attesting multiple meanings of βίος, see the discussion above of Sch. Hec. 168.[90]

Hec. 71 (μῆτερ[91] ὀνείρων): μητέρα τῶν ὀνείρων εἶπε τὴν γῆν, ἢ ὅτι ἐξ ἀντιφράξεως [ἀντιφράσεως YXaXb] τῆς σκιᾶς αὐτῆς ἡ νὺξ γίνεται, καθ' ἣν καθεύδοντες οἱ ἄνθρωποι τοὺς ὀνείρους βλέπουσιν, ἢ καθ' ἑτέρους, ὅτι ἐκ μὲν τῆς γῆς αἱ τροφαί, ἐκ δὲ τῶν τροφῶν οἱ ὕπνοι, ἐκ δὲ τῶν ὕπνων οἱ ὄνειροι. [ἐκ τῆς γῆς ἄρα οἱ ὄνειροι add. all except Y] Y, XXaXbXoT(with cross)YfZx

The poet called the earth the mother of dreams either because as a result of the interposition of the earth's shadow night occurs, during which men see dreams while sleeping; or according to others, because nourishment comes from the earth, and sleep results from our nourishment, and dreams come from sleep. (*added in other witnesses*: Therefore, dreams come from the earth.)

94r, part of original annotation of right margin block, following Sch. Mosch. Hec. 66, with label. The first explanation is taken from the old scholia, the second from an earlier teacher, probably of the 12th century. For further discussion, see Chapter 3, section 2, on item 9 in the Miscellany of notes.

Hec. 80 (μόνος οἴκων ἄγκυρ'): τουτέστι τελευταία ἄγκυρα, ἀπὸ μεταφορᾶς τῶν ναυτιλλομένων, οἳ τὰς ἄλλας ῥίψαντες ἀγκύρας, ἂν μηδὲν δι' αὐτῶν ἀνύσωσιν, ἐπὶ τῇ τελευταίᾳ [τὴν τελευταίαν YXa] τὰς ἐλπίδας ἔχουσιν. Y, XaXbXoT(with cross)

That is, last anchor; a metaphorical usage from those who travel by ship, who, after having cast off the other anchors, if they fail to accomplish anything using them, place their hopes on the last one.

94r, part of original annotation of right margin block, following the previous after a small blank interval, with label, but no cross. τελευταία ἄγκυρα was a proverbial expression, though it is first attested in Heliodorus, *Aethiop.* 8.6.9 τελευταίαν οὖν, εἰ δοκεῖ, τὸ τοῦ λόγου, ῥίψωμεν ἄγκυραν καὶ τὴν ἐμποδὼν γινομένην ἐκποδὼν ποιησώμεθα; it was a development of the proverbial ἱερὰ ἄγκυρα, which is attested as early as Plutarch and Galen. "Last anchor" is used by various Byzantine authors, including Psellus, Eustathius, and Planudes himself (*Epist.* 12, lines 19–80, τοῦτο γὰρ αὐτοῖς τελευταία λείπεται ἄγκυρα, ἐπεὶ τὰς ἄλλας πάσας οὗτος ἀφεῖλεν ἐνεχυράσας). For the explanation in this note compare the one found earlier in a scholion on ἱερὰν ἄγκυραν in Lucian,

---

[89] In the case of this and the preceding scholion, in the left margin there are also two reference symbols (matched at lines 3 and 12 of the text), one for each note at the level of the line in which it begins, and μαξ is placed a little to the left of these symbols at a level between the two.
[90] Above in this chapter at n. 30.
[91] μῆτερ is in the poetic text of all the listed witnesses except T, which has μᾶτηρ.

Juppiter tragoedus (21) 51 (ἄγκυρά ἐστιν ἐν τῇ νηὶ ἡ μεγίστη, ἣν καλοῦσιν ἱεράν. αὕτη δέ, ὅτε μέγας καταλάβῃ κίνδυνος, τελευταία βάλλεται. εἶπεν οὖν τοῦτο ὡς μέλλων τελευταῖον εἰπεῖν ἐπιχειρημάτων τὸ πάντων μέγιστον) and later in Michael Apostol. *Paroem.* cent. 9, 1 (ἱερὰ ἄγκυρα: ἡ μεγάλη βοήθεια. ἄγκυρά ἐστιν ἐν τῇ νηῒ ἱερὰ καλουμένη, καὶ ὅτε μέγας καταλαμβάνει κίνδυνος τελευταία βάλλεται).

Hec. 84 (γοερὸν): τὸ γοερὸν καὶ ὁ [ὁ om. XbY] γόος καὶ τὸ κωκύειν ποιαὶ φωναί εἰσιν, καὶ ταυτόν εἰσι [ἐστι T] τῇ τε ἐννοίᾳ καὶ τῇ προφορᾷ. συγγενῆ γάρ ἐστι [εἰσι a.c. Y] τὸ [τό τε XbXoT] $\bar{γ}$ καὶ $\bar{κ}$. μέσον γάρ ἐστι τὸ $\bar{γ}$ τοῦ $\bar{κ}$ καὶ $\bar{χ}$. Y, XaXbXoT(with cross)

Goeron (mournful) and goos (mourning cry) and kōkuein (to cry out koku) are onomatopoetic[92] words, and they are the same in their meaning and delivery. For the gamma and kappa are akin to each other, since gamma is in the middle between kappa and chi.

94r, part of original annotation of the right margin block, following the previous with no label and no cross.[93] No parallel for this is found in TLG.

***Hec.* 85 (οὔποτ' ἐμὰ φρὴν ἀλίαστος φρίσσει): οὐδέποτε γὰρ ὃ φοβοῦμαι διαδιδράσκω, ἀλλ' ἀεὶ τοῦτο πάσχω. Y, Xo

For I never escape from what I fear, but I always suffer this.

94r, black ink addition above the line, with a label, but no cross. The explanation is a shorter version of the final paraphrase given in the old scholion on this line (οἷον εἴ τι φοβοῦμαι καὶ ὑπονοῶ, τοῦτο καὶ γίνεται), and the same interpretation is featured in the separate Moschopulean note here, οὔποτε, φησίν, ἡ ἐμὴ φρὴν οὕτω φρίσσει. εἶτα ἐπάγει ἀλίαστος, ἤγουν ἄφυκτος φρίσσει [φρίσσει del. Arsenius], τουτέστιν, ὃ φοβεῖται ἡ ἐμὴ φρήν, οὐ δύναται τοῦτο φυγεῖν ("Never, she says, does my mind tremble so much with fear. Then she adds *aliastos*, that is, tremble without escape: that is, what my mind fears, it cannot escape this").

***Hec.* 87 (Ἑλένου ψυχάν): τουτέστι τὸν Ἕλενον· ἀπὸ τοῦ κρείττονος μέρους αὐτὸν ὀνομάζει, ὥσπερ καὶ ἡμεῖς ἀντὶ τοῦ τὸν δεῖνα εἰπεῖν τὴν ἱερὰν λέγομεν κεφαλήν. Y, Xo

---

[92] I owe to F. Pontani the recognition of this special sense of ποιὴ φωνή in the grammatical tradition.

[93] The label on the preceding note applies to this one as well, and Planudean origin is further implied by the presence of the label μαν on the next scholion in the margin block, with the Moschopulean note on 85 (quoted in discussion of the next item).

That is, Helenus. He names him from the more important part, just as we, instead of saying so and so, say the holy head.

94r, black ink addition at end of margin block, with a label and cross. The Moschopulean supralinear note on this phrase is τουτέστιν τὸν Ἕλενον. ἔζη γὰρ ("that is, Helenus. For he was alive"). The juncture ἱερὰ κεφαλή has a long history, and the vocative is repeatedly used in Gregorius Nazianzenus, Libanius, and Synesius. For ἀπὸ τοῦ κρείττονος μέρους in connection with ψυχή cf. Ioann. Philoponus, *de opificio mundi* (p. 224 Reichert), the heading ὅτι τὸ "ψυχὴν ζῶσαν" ἀπὸ τοῦ κρείττονος μέρους τὸ ὅλον ζῷον ἐδήλωσε.

> *Hec.* 752: ἱκετεύω· ἤγουν δέομαί σου, ἱκέτις γίνομαι τῶν σῶν γονάτων, ἤγουν ἅπτομαί σου. Y
>
> I supplicate: that is, I beg of you, I make myself a suppliant of your knees, or I cling to you.

99v, black ink (like almost all the marginal annotation on this page), with label and cross.

> *Hec.* 759 (οὐδέν τι τούτων ὧν σὺ δοξάζεις, ἄναξ): εἰς οὐδέν τι τούτων καλῶ σε ὦ ἄναξ ὧν ὑπονοεῖς. "ὃ" δὲ ἔμελλεν εἰπεῖν, διὰ δὲ τὴν προηγησαμένην πτῶσιν εἶπεν "ὧν." Y
>
> Lord, I do not call you to any of these things that you suspect. She was about to say "which" (accusative singular neuter from), but because of the preceding case ("of these things") she says "which things" (genitive plural neuter form).

99v, black ink (like almost all the marginal annotation on this page), with label τοῦ αὐτοῦ, no cross. The following note (on 762), also in black ink, is labeled with μαν. The juncture προηγηαμένη πτῶσις is attested only once elsewhere in TLG, in another explanation of shifting of case: Lesbonax, *de figuris* 13b, 23–25 τῶν αὐτῶν δὲ καὶ τὸ δοτικῆς πτώσεως προηγησαμένης εἰς γενικὴν ἀποδιδόναι· φασὶ γὰρ "οὐκ ἂν ἡμῖν συνέβη τοῦτο παθεῖν εὐσεβῶν ὄντων."

> *Hec.* 973 (μὴ δύσνοιαν ἡγήσῃ): τὸ μὴ ἐν μὲν τοῖς ἀορίστοις ὑποτακτικὸν, ἐν δὲ τοῖς ἐνεστῶσιν †ὑποτακτικόν† [read προστακτικόν]. Y
>
> The negative *mē* (of negative commands) is used with subjunctive in the aorist forms, but †with subjunctive† [read "with imperative"] in the present forms.

101r, in bottom margin, black ink (as used also for all the interlinear glosses on this page),[94] with label but no cross. Just below this note, the same hand adds in

---

[94] The only scholia in the margin block on 101r are two written by Y².

the same ink the paraphrasing Moschopulean scholion on 973 and labels it with μαν. With the necessary correction, the doctrine is paralleled by other grammarians' statements about μὴ ἀπαγορευτικόν: cf. *Excerpta e Herodiano* [Sp.] (e codd. Paris. gr. 2650 + 2662 + Paris. suppl. 70), fr. 93 Dain: τὸ μὴ ἀπαγορευτικὸν οὐ συντάσσεται σὺν τῷ ὑποτακτικῷ ἐνεστῶτι, ἀορίστῳ δέ· οἷον μὴ ποιῇς οὐκ εἴποις, μὴ ποιήσῃς δέ; Thom. Mag. *Eclog*. 233, 12 τὸ μή ἀπαγορευτικόν ἐστι, καὶ ἐπὶ μὲν ἐνεστῶτος προστακτικῷ συντάσσεται, ἐπὶ δὲ ἀορίστου καὶ τῶν ἄλλων ὑποτακτικῷ. οὐκ ἐρεῖς ἐπὶ ἐνεστῶτος μὴ τύπτῃς, ἀλλὰ μὴ τύπτε· μὴ τύψῃς δὲ ἐπὶ ἀορίστου καὶ τῶν ἄλλων χρόνων. The sense of ὑποτακτικός assumed in the translation above is, however, very odd.[95] This passage may be corrupt (one would expect ὑποτακτικῷ συντάσσεται);[96] or we have a teacher using a very compressed (non-standard) form of expression.

> *Or*. 220 (πέλανον): κυρίως πέλανος [XoY, πέλανον the rest] τὸ λεπτὸν πέμμα ᾧ χρῶνται πρὸς τὰς θυσίας. ἔνιοι δέ φασι καὶ πᾶν ἐξ ὑγροῦ πεπηγμένον. παρὰ τὸ παλῦναι, ὅ ἐστι λευκᾶναι. πέλανον ἐνταῦθα τὸν πεπηγότα ῥύπον ὑπὸ τοῦ ἀφροῦ. Y, XXaXbXoT(with cross)Yf(with cross)GGrAa
>
> Properly speaking, *pelanos* is the light cake/batter that people use for sacrifices. And some say it is also everything that is congealed from something liquid. Derived from *palunai*, which means "whiten." Here *pelanon* is the dirty crust congealed from the foam (of drool or of tears).

106r, part of the initial writing of margin block scholia, with label (but ξ almost entirely lost to damage at right edge of the folio), no cross. The label apparently applies to the whole subgroup of notes 220, 221, 223 (the latter two were identified as Planudean by Günther 1995: 227). On this occasion there is no label μαν to indicate when the commentary returns to Moschopulus, but there is a gap between the subgroup of three notes and the next item, which is the paraphrasing Moschopulean note on 235 (carried by the same witnesses, except Aa; T and Yf again have a cross). This note on πέλανος (the mss treat the word as proparoxytone rather than oxytone) is, except for the last sentence, merely a condensation of the old scholion on the word (this quotation ignores variants): κυρίως πέλανος τὸ λεπτὸν πέμμα ᾧ χρῶνται πρὸς τὰς θυσίας, παρὰ τὸ

---

[95] μή is included among subordinating conjunctions/particles (as it would be in fear-clauses and purpose clauses), but that is not the same: ps.-Herodian, *Partitiones* 277, 8–9 Boissonade τὰ ὑποτακτικὰ μόρια, ὡς ἐμάθομεν, ὑποτάσσουσι, πλὴν τοῦ μὴ ἀντὶ τοῦ οὐχὶ, καὶ ὅπως ἀντὶ τοῦ πῶς. ("The subordinating particles, as we learned, create subordination, except for μή when used for οὐχί, or ὅπως used for πῶς.")

[96] F. Pontani suggests to me that ⟨θέλει⟩ or the like might be supplied at the end.

πεπλατύνθαι. οἱ δέ φασι καὶ πᾶν ἐξ ὑγροῦ πεπηγός. ἔνιοι παρὰ τὴν παιπάλην· ἐκ γὰρ ταύτης ὡς ἐπὶ τὸ πλεῖστον γίνεται. ἢ παρὰ τὸ παλῦναι, ὅ ἐστι λευκᾶναι· Ὅμηρος [Il. 10.7]· "ἐπάλυνεν ἀρούρας." λευκὸν γὰρ τὸ πέμμα. οἱ δὲ ἀπὸ τοῦ πελάζειν καὶ ἱκετεύειν τοὺς θεοὺς δι' αὐτῶν (MCVB PrRw).

Or. 221 (κοὐκ ἀναίνομαι): συναινῶ τὸ συμφωνῶ καὶ ἐπινεύω, ᾧ ἐναντίον τὸ ἀναίνομαι. παραινῶ τὸ συμβουλεύω, ἐπαινῶ τὸ εὖ λέγω. Y, XXaXbXoT(with cross)Yf(with cross)GrG

Sunainō means "I agree" and "I consent," the opposite of which is *anainomai*. *Parainō* means "I advise," *epainō* means "I speak well of."

106r, second in the same subgroup just discussed, with no label and no cross. For the idea of συναινῶ and ἀναίνομαι as opposites, cf. Eust. *in Il.* 9.116 (II.671, 6-7) τὸ δὲ "ἀναίνεσθαι" ταὐτόν ἐστι τῷ μὴ αἰνεῖν, ἤγουν συναινεῖν καὶ συγκατατίθεσθαι.

Or. 223 (καὐχμώδη): ἐπομβρία, ὅταν ἐπάλληλοι ὄμβροι ὦσιν, ᾧ ἐναντίον ἡ ἀνομβρία. αὐχμὸς δὲ ἡ ἀπὸ τῆς ἀνομβρίας ξηρότης, ἀφ' οὗ αὐχμηρὸς καὶ αὐχμώδης, ἁπλῶς ὁ ξηρότητος μετέχων. Y, XXaXbXoT(with cross)YfGrG

A downpour (*epombria*) is when rains are continuous; the opposite of this is absence of rain (*anombria*). Drought (*auchmos*) is the dryness resulting from absence of rain, and derived from it are the adjectives *auchmēros* and *auchmōdēs*, meaning simply that which partakes of dryness.

106r, last in the same subgroup just discussed, with no label and no cross. The two terms are used as opposites in a few Byzantine authors (e.g., Oribasius, *Collectiones medicae* 5.3.10, 4-5 καὶ ὅλως αἱ μὲν ἐπομβρίαι γλυκύτερα παρέχουσιν [scil. τὰ ὕδατα], αἱ δ' ἀνομβρίαι καὶ οἱ αὐχμοὶ νιτρωδέστερα), and the first sentence is closely similar to Sch. rec. Arist. Nub. 1120f ἐπομβρία λέγεται, ὅταν ἐπάλληλοι ὄμβροι γίνωνται· οὗ/ἧς ἐναντίον ἡ ἀνομβρία. In Hesych. α 8322 and 8323 and elsewhere αὐχμοί and αὐχμός are glossed with ἀμομβρίαι and ἀμομβρία. The juncture ξηρότηρος μετέχειν is common in medical and astrological writers and also occurs in a Thoman scholion on *Prometheus* 366: μυδροκτυπεῖ ἤτοι χαλκεύει μύδρον καὶ πεπυρακτωμένον σίδηρον· μύδρος δὲ γίνεται ἀπὸ τοῦ μὴ ἔχειν ὕδωρ. ἐξικμάζεται γὰρ ὁ τοιοῦτος καὶ οὐδόλως μετέχει ὑγρότητος, ἀλλὰ μόνης ξηρότητος· ὁ δὲ μὴ τοιοῦτος ὑγρότητα ἔχων ποιεῖ καὶ ἰόν.[97]

---

[97] From Neapol. II F 31: Smyth 1921: 28-29.

**Or. 291 (εἰς σφαγὰς ὦσαι ξίφος): σφαγὴ καὶ ὁ τόπος ἐν ᾧ σφάζεταί τις καὶ ἡ ἐνέργεια αὐτή [Xo, αὐτῆς Y]. Y, Xo

Sphagē is both the place (of the body) at which someone is slaughtered and the activity itself (*or* the activity of it [slaughtering]).

106v, black ink addition, with label but no cross. For the not entirely obvious rendering of τόπος ἐν ᾧ (required by the sense of the passage), compare Hesych. σ 2826 σφαγή· ὁ κατὰ τὴν κατακλεῖδα τόπος; Sch. Aesch. Prom. 863 Herington σφαγαῖσι] τοῖς τόποις τοῦ σώματος ἐν αἷς [*sic*] καίριαι καὶ θανάσιμοι πληγαὶ γίνονται.

Or. 919 (κἀγορᾶς χραίνων κύκλον): οἱ γὰρ περὶ τὴν ἀγορὰν πορευόμενοι μεμολυσμένοι ἦσαν. Y, XXbXoT(with cross)YfGrG

For those who walk around the marketplace were tainted with filth.

111v, black ink addition in bottom margin, with label, but no cross. For the odd phrase with χραίνων, the surviving old scholia offer only the paraphrase ἐκκλησίας οὐ περιερχόμενος, οὐδὲ πλησιάζων, so it is not surprising that a comment was added by Planudes/Moschopulus. In some of the witnesses (XXo, and in supralinear position XbG) this follows on the Moschopulean gloss διατρίβων (making better sense of γάρ), but in YTYfGr the two are separate, with the gloss above the word and the other phrase in the margin.

Or. 1065 (τοῦ φόνου γενοῦ βραβεύς): κυρίως ὁ ἀγωνοθέτης λέγεται [ὁ add. Y] βραβεύς. Y, XXaXbXoTa(with cross)[98]YfGr

In the proper sense, the one who manages contests is called *brabeus*.

113r, in brown ink, with label, but no cross. Byzantine authors commonly pair for rhetorical effect ἀγωνοθέτης and βραβευτής (the later term for βραβεύς), and this pair is also used in defining αἰσυμνῆται, as in Sch. Hom. Od. 8.258. There is no parallel in TLG for this claim of its κυρίως sense, and a different claim is made for βραβευτής in *Et. Gen.* α 234: βραβευταί· διοικηταί, κριταί, ὁρισταί. κυρίως δὲ βραβευταὶ λέγονται οἱ τὴν ῥάβδον ἀπὸ φοίνικος ἤ τινος ἄλλου διδόντες σύμβολα τῆς νίκης, ῥαβδευταί τινες ὄντες· καὶ καθ' ὑπέρθεσιν τοῦ ρ̄ βραβευταί.

---

[98] Ta is cited because this note is now entirely washed out in T.

Or. 1284 (τί μέλλεθ' οἱ κατ' οἶκον ἐν ἡσυχίᾳ σφάγια φοινίσσειν;): τί βραδύνετε οἱ κατὰ τὸν οἶκον ὄντες, ἐν ἡσυχίᾳ ἤγουν ἐν ἀταραξίᾳ, ἐν ὅσῳ οὐδεὶς ὀχλεῖ, ὥστε σφάγια φοινίσσειν. ὥστε τὴν σφαγὴν ποιεῖν ὤφειλεν, ἐπεὶ δὲ τὸ ἀπὸ τῆς σφαγῆς αἷμα φοινίσσει, φησὶ σφάγια φοινίσσειν, ἀντὶ τοῦ αἷμα χεῖν διὰ σφαγῆς. Υ, XXaXbXoT(with cross)YfGrG
Why do you delay, you who are in the house, in peace, that is, without disturbance, as long as no one interferes, to redden the victim. He should have said "to perform the slaughter," but since the blood for the sacrificial slaughter reddens, he says redden the victim as equivalent to cause blood to be shed by means of slaughter.

114v, written by first hand, with a possible trace of a label in the water-damaged margin (its presence is also implied by τοῦ αὐτοῦ prefixed to the next scholion), but no cross. This is a more expansive rendering of the explanation that is found in MBC (διὰ τί ἀναβάλλεσθε, πρὸ τοῦ ἐπιστῆναι τινὰ, σφάγια φοινίσσειν· ἀντὶ τοῦ τὰ ξίφη μολύνειν· τουτέστι τὴν Ἑλένην φονεύειν).

Or. 1287 (ἐκκεκώφηται): ἀπὸ τοῦ κωφὸς κωφεύω, ἀφ' οὗ ἐκώφευον παρατατικὸς καὶ κωφεύσω μέλλων. μέσος[99] δὲ ὑπερσυντέλικος ἐκκεκώφειν ἑτεροκλίτως καὶ προσθήκη τῆς ἐκ, ἀπὸ τοῦ κωφέω κωφῶ ἀχρήστου, κατὰ τὴν ἀκολουθίαν τοῦ λέληκα. Συνέσ(ιος)· "ἀλλ' ἐκκεκώφει τὸ κάθαρμα," παρακείμενος ἐκκεκώφημαι, ὡς καὶ ἐνταῦθα ὁ Εὐριπίδης· "ἆρ' εἰς τὸ κάλλος ἐκεκώφητο ξίφη;" λέγεται δὲ ἐκκεκώφωμαι καὶ ἐκκεκώφωνται, καὶ ἔτι κεκώφωνται χωρὶς τῆς ἐκ, ἀφ' οὗ καὶ ἀόριστος ἐκωφώθην, ἀπὸ ἑτέρου πάλιν αὐτὰ θέματος ἀχρήστου τοῦ κωφόω κωφῶ. τὸ δὲ πρᾶγμα κωφότης λέγεται ὡς χωλότης καὶ τυφλότης. λέγεται καὶ κώφωσις. Υ[2]
From adjective *kōphos* (mute/deaf) is derived the verb *kōpheuō* (be mute), from which the imperfect is *ekōpheuon* and *kōpheusō* is the future. And the middle pluperfect is *ekkekōphein* with an irregular inflection and with addition of the prepositional prefix *ek*, from the unused base-form *kōpheō kōphō*, in accordance with the conjugational pattern of *leleka*. (Example:) Synesius [*Epist.* 5, p. 14, 16 Garzya = *Epist.* 4, p. 640 Hercher] "but the filthy creature had become deaf," perfect tense *ekkekōphēmai*, as also here Euripides: "Have the swords fallen dumb at the sight of her beauty?" And the word is found as *ekkekōphōmai* and *ekkekōphōntai*, and also *kekōphōntai* without the *ek*, from which also the aorist *ekōphōthēn*, these being again in turn from another unused base-form *kōphoō kōphō*. The thing produced is called *kōphotēs*, formed like *cholotēs* and *tuphlotēs*. The noun *kōphōsis* is also used.

---

[99] Y[2] has μέσως here, which must be a phonetic error. First, nominative μέσος is attested in the closely similar annotation about to be discussed. Second, an adverbial meaning μέσως "in a middle (i.e., intransitive) sense" does not make sense. ὑπερσυντέλικος is clear in the cited annotation as well, but in Y[2] it is rather sloppily written and apparently drastically abbreviated, and one may wonder whether the scribe did not really understand the abbreviation in the source.

114v, added in cursive hand in lighter brown ink, with label τοῦ αὐτοῦ (damaged, but also apparently in the same ink) and no cross. This is the most detailed and learned note of the group. Apart from the abundance of grammatical detail, it quotes a famous letter of Synesius, *Epist.* 5 Garzya (= *Epist.* 4 Hercher) about a terrifying voyage, an often-cited text well known to Byzantine readers. In Garzya's edition of Synesius ἐξεκεκώφει is printed and the variants reported from some manuscripts are ἐξεκώφει and ἐκεκώφει (which is clearly related to the ἐκκεκώφει in Y²). In the entry for ἐκκωφέω in the *Thesaurus Graecae Linguae* Ludwig Dindorf proposed regularizing the reading in Synesius to ἐξεκεκώφητο, and that is possibly what Synesius wrote in the early 5th century (the final -το having been lost by haplography before τὸ κάθαρμα), since the perfect middle-passive forms of this verb were quite popular in late antique and Byzantine authors. But Byzantine authors believed in and used the active perfect and pluperfect as intransitive, as Planudes is doing here by calling it "middle." The TLG offers four instances in Michael Psellus and Ioannes Zonaras, and there are also three instances of the apparent imperfect form ἐξεκώφει in Psellus and Theodorus Continuatus (which could be either a corruption or a pluperfect with reduplication omitted in the Byzantine fashion). It is noteworthy that the same rare piece of erudition is found in a work ascribed to Manuel Moschopulus, περὶ τῶν παθημάτων τῶν λέξεων.[100]

> ἀφαίρεσις δὲ τὸ ἐναντίον ὅταν ἀπὸ τῆς ἀρχῆς ἀφαιρεθῇ γράμμα φωνῆεν, συλλαβὴν δηλονότι ποιοῦν, ὃ γίνεται ἐν τῷ κείνος καὶ τῷ στράπτειν, δηλονότι ἀντὶ τοῦ ἀστράπτειν, καὶ τῷ θῆκεν ἀντὶ τοῦ ἔθηκεν, καὶ τῷ δεδώκει καὶ τῷ ἐκκεκώφει.[101]

[following discussing of *prosthesis*, addition of a syllable such as augment or reduplication at the start of a word] Aphairesis, on the contrary, is when a vowel is taken off the beginning of the word, that is, a vowel that forms a syllable; this occurs in *keinos* (for standard *ekeinos*), in *straptein*, I mean in place of *astraptein*, and *thēken* instead of *ethēken*, and in *dedōkei* (for *ededōkei* with augment) and *ekkekōphei* (for *exekekōphei* with augment).

The Planudean teaching of Sch. Or. 1287 is also found in an annotation on this Moschopulean passage in a Darmstadt codex, as reported by Bast. This version is longer, and to show the differences the shared wording is underlined in the Greek and the added words are underlined in the English:[102]

---

[100] The work is published in Schaefer 1811: 675ff., and see Bast's note in Schaefer 1811: 906–907 for the identification of the ascription in a Darmstadt manuscript.
[101] Schaefer 1811: 675–676.
[102] Schaefer 1811: 908–909.

ὡς ἀπὸ τοῦ χωλὸς γίνεται χωλεύω, οὕτως ἀπὸ τοῦ κωφὸς κωφεύω, ἀφ' οὗ ἐκώφευον παρατατικὸς καὶ κωφεύσω μέλλων. μέσος δὲ ὑπερσυντέλικος ἐκκεκώφειν ἑτεροκλίτως καὶ προσθέσει τῆς εκ, ἀπὸ τοῦ κωφέω κωφῶ ἀχρήστου, κατὰ τὴν ἀκολουθίαν τοῦ λέλακα. Συνέσιος· "ἀλλ' ἐκκεκώφει τὸ κάθαρμα." παρακείμενος ἐκκεκώφημαι, Εὐριπίδης· "ἆρ' εἰς τὸ κάλλος ἐκεκώφηται ξίφη;" λέγεται δὲ καὶ ἐκκεκώφωμαι καὶ ἐκκεκώφωκεν ἐνεργητικῶς ἀντὶ τοῦ κωφεύειν ἐποίησεν. "ἡμῶν οὖν, ὦ Σώκρατες, ἐκκεκώφωκε τὰ ὦτα καὶ ἐμπέπληκε Λύσιδος." καὶ ἔτι κεκώφωνται χωρὶς τῆς εκ, ἀφ' οὗ καὶ ἀόριστος ἐκωφώθην, ἀπὸ ἑτέρου πάλιν αὐτὰ θέματος ἀχρήστου τοῦ κωφόω κωφῶ. τὸ δὲ πρᾶγμα κωφότης λέγεται ὡς χωλότης καὶ τυφλότης. λέγεται καὶ κώφωσις.

Just as from the adjective *chōlos* (lame) is derived the verb *chōleuō* (be lame), just so from the adjective *kōphos* (mute/deaf) is derived the verb *kōpheuō* (be mute), from which the imperfect is *ekōpheuon* and *kōpheusō* is the future. And the middle pluperfect is *ekkekōphein* with an irregular inflection and with addition of the prepositional prefix *ek*, from the unused base-form *kōpheō kōphō*, in accordance with the conjugational pattern of *lelaka*. (Example:) Synesius [*Epist.* 5, p. 14, 16 Garzya = *Epist.* 4, p. 640 Hercher] "but the filthy creature had become deaf." Perfect tense *ekkekōphēmai*, Euripides: "Have the swords fallen dumb at the sight of her beauty?" And the word is also found as *ekkekōphōmai* and *ekkekōphōken* in the active, meaning "caused to be deaf." [Plato, *Lysis* 204c7–d1] "So then, Socrates, he has deafened our ears and filled them with Lysis." And also *kekōphōntai* without the *ek*, from which also the aorist *ekōphōthēn*, these being again in turn from another unused base-form *kōphoō kōphō*. The thing produced is called *kōphotēs*, formed like *chōlotēs* and *tuphlotēs*. The noun *kōphōsis* is also used.

The form of the version found in Y is almost exactly matched in a Naples manuscript that is being studied by a young scholar in Venice.[103]

Two additional notes explicitly ascribed to Planudes have been located in other manuscripts in the collation conducted so far.[104]

Hec. 145 (γονάτων): οὕτω λαμβανομένη ἔξωθεν ἡ διά συντακτέον· οὐ γὰρ τὰ γόνατα ἔμελλε παρακαλεῖν, ἀλλὰ δι' ἐκείνων ἱκετεύσειν ἐκεῖνον. οὕτω νοεῖ τὰ περὶ τούτου ὁ κύρις Μάξιμος. Gu

Thus, with the preposition *dia* taken from outside, is it to be construed. For she was not about to beg his knees, but rather by his knees she was going to supplicate that man. This is how master Maximus understands this point.

---

[103] I owe knowledge of this to F. Pontani. He reports that the manuscript gathers "excerpts and notes that probably originated in Planudes' environment" and that this excerpt lacks the phrase ὡς καὶ ἐνταῦθα. So either the excerpt was an observation of general import that has been applied to the passage by Y² by adding that phrase, or the compiler has taken it from a codex of *Orestes* and made it more general by omitting the phrase. On these two possibilities see also the glosses in gB presented in Chapter 3, section 3, n. 92.

[104] These scholia were already noted by Turyn 1957: 57 and 66.

Hec. 167 (ἀπολέσατ' ὠλέσατ'): καὶ ἀμφότερα μικρὰ γράφει ὁ κύριος Μάξιμος. XoYf

Master Maximus writes both verbs with short vowel (omicron) (rather than long [augment omega]).

XoYf (like XXaXbY) have ἀπόλεσατ' ὠλέσατ' in the text and an omega above the omicron of the first word. The Moschopulean note on the phrase is ἀπώλεσα ἀντὶ τοῦ ἔφθειρα καὶ ἀντὶ τοῦ κοινῶς ἐχάωσα, showing that the indicative interpretation was assumed by Moschopulus. A scholion found so far only in Pr shows that at least some interpreters viewed the forms with omicron as potentially either indicative without augment or imperative: τὸ ἀπολέσατε ἢ ἀπὸ μόνης τῆς ἀγγελίας ἐφονεύσατέ με, ἢ χάριν ὑμῖν [ἡμῖν Pr] ὁμολογήσω ἐὰν φονεύσητέ με ("*apolesate* means either 'by your announcement alone you have destroyed me' or 'I will be grateful to you if you kill me'"). On the other hand, a note added in V by V³ recommends the omicron spelling and imperative interpretation if ἐνεγκοῦσαι is taken in a certain way:

> εἰ μὲν ἔστι τὸ ἐνεγκοῦσαι ἀντὶ τοῦ μηνύσασαι, γράφεται τὸ ἀπωλέσατε μέγα τὸ πω. εἰ δὲ ἔστιν πρὸς τὸν χορὸν τὸ ἐνεγκοῦσαι ἀντὶ τοῦ ὑπομείνασαι γράφεται τὸ ἀπολέσατε μικρὸν τὸ πο, ἀντὶ τοῦ ἀφανίσατε.
>
> If *enegkousai* is used for "having reported," then the reading is *apōlesate* with omega in *pō*; but if *enegkousai* pertains to the chorus, meaning "having endured," then the reading is *apolesate* with omicron in *po*, equivalent to (imperative) "destroy."

We cannot say which view Planudes favored, but if his choice of short vowels is correctly reported, he did not have a grasp of the dactylic meter here.

These notes are predominantly of the teachers' style, offering etymologies (*Hec.* 1, 2b, *Or.* 220) or derivation from root form (*Or.* 1287), vocabulary building (distinctions of sense, alternative senses of the same word or related words, and comparison of similar words: *Hec.* 12, *Or.* 221, 223, 291, 1065, 1287), explanation of a metaphor or an idiom or otherwise unusual usage (*Hec.* 3, 71, 80, 87, *Or.* 220, 919, 1284), apparent difficulties of syntax (*Hec.* 145, 759) or tangentially relevant grammatical lessons (*Hec.* 84, 973, 1287), and simple short paraphrase (*Hec.* 85, 752, 759, *Or.* 1284). Only one note, the last discussed, recommends a reading (*Hec.* 167). Only one Planudean note evokes mythographic background, in a very concise way: *Hec.* 2a, on the division of realms among Zeus and his brothers after the overthrow of the Titans. If the ascriptions to Planudes are accurate and the views are conveyed correctly, they show him mainly engaged, as far as *Hecuba* and *Orestes* are concerned, in fairly elementary instruction, and one needs to look elsewhere to detect the strengths of his erudition and his devotion to classical literature.

Turyn also believed that the non-Moschopulean notes found in Yf, some of which are shared with Y, should be taken to be Planudean.[105] These I take at present to be anonymous teacher's notes, glosses and paraphrases, either Palaeologan or going back to the 12th century (since both manuscripts share teachers' scholia from the set to be discussed in Chapter 3). But nothing definitive can be said until collations of scholia have been completed for the entirety of all three triad plays in the main Moschopulean and Thoman witnesses and in YYfYnGu and others.[106] Similarly, Turyn claims a Planudean source for some non-Moschopulean and non-Thoman scholia written by Gr and Gu and Yv, often shared by Y, but his inferences are shaky because he takes insufficient account of the wider existence in various *recentiores* of teachers' annotations showing the same preoccupations, instead jumping right to the conclusion that notes of this type reflect Planudean influence.[107] Günther has already objected to Turyn's extension of the evidence for Planudes to additions in Yf and Yn.[108] He offers a more cautious assessment of what might be additional Planudean notes included in some 14th-century Moschopulean witnesses like Xo.[109] We are, as just stated, not yet in a position to evaluate these issues definitively. At present I will end this chapter by offering three examples where there is already some additional evidence. The rhetorical analysis represented by the discussion of ἀπόθεσις in Sch. Hec. 313 in Gr (Dindorf I.296, 19–21) has parallels in PrRSa, and a long note here in Pr and V³ largely overlaps with a note in the A-commentary on *Prometheus* (Sch. 36a Herington): this is likely to reflect an interest of Byzantine teachers earlier than Planudes. The discussion of blending inspired by the false reading κραθεῖσαν in *Hec.* 219 (Dindorf I.272, 17–20) is not just in Y and Gu, but is shared by PrRw, and is closely related to item 10 in the set of pre-Palaeologan teachers' scholia edited in the next chapter. The distinction between βωμός and ναός is described in various terms by notes attached to *Hec.* 144 in RGuY² (none of these in Dindorf), but it is found earlier in a lacunose mention in *Et. Gud.* 401, 43–45 Sturz s.v. ναός and in Tzetzes' verbose scholion on *Il.* 1.439 (no. 95) beginning διαφέρει ναός ἄδυτον τέμενος καὶ βωμός and in his shorter Sch. Arist. Plut. (recens. 2) 659.[110]

In general, I would argue that the teaching of the Euripidean triad was widespread, as the number of *recentiores* manuscripts indicates, and there will have been teachers modifying traditional scholia and adding new ones, especially par-

---

[105] Turyn 1957: 56–60.
[106] Turyn made hardly any inspection of Yn, and I have not yet studied it at all.
[107] Turyn 1957: 64–66, 70–72.
[108] Günther 1995: 31–32.
[109] Günther 1995: 65–71.
[110] Interest in this distinction is clearly an extension of the ancient tradition of explaining the distinction between βωμός and ἐσχάρα seen in Ammonius and others as well as in Photius ε 2041 s.v. ἐσχάρα, Sch. Eur. Phoen. 274, and other scholia.

aphrases and those of the teachers' note variety. Such teachers were active before the Palaeologan revival, and some of their notes may well have survived until then. We therefore need either reliable ascriptions or really secure and unique stylistic evidence in order to assign a note to a particular name like that of Planudes, and such evidence is not forthcoming in most of what Turyn claimed as probably Planudean. One may also ask why, if much of the anonymous material in manuscripts like YYfGrGu is to be taken as Planudean in origin, so few notes are so labeled in Y and there are only the two notes cited above where ὁ κύρι(ο)ς Μάξιμος is credited within the note itself. In the next chapter we will look at more evidence that suggests that the practice of annotation for teaching of Euripides existed in the 12th century (and earlier) as well as the Palaeologan era.

Chapter 3

The Extra Exegetical Material in Sa and the Teaching Tradition

1. THE PRELIMINARIES PRECEDING *HECUBA* IN Ssa

Beginnings of bookrolls and codices are especially subject to damage, and it is not surprising that the hypothesis to *Hecuba* (often along with some part of the beginning of the poetic text) is missing from many manuscripts. Likewise, the *Life* (or *Lives*) *of Euripides*, the sort of text usually placed before the beginning of a collection of an author's works, is not found in any of the older manuscripts and survives only in relatively few witnesses from the late 13th century onward, from which it has been edited with detailed apparatus by Kannicht in *TrGF* V:1, Testimonia A1, I–IV. To be specific, B has lost the first 522 lines of *Hecuba* as well as any preliminary texts it may originally have contained, while the Euripidean portion of M starts with the beginning of *Hecuba* but lacks any hypothesis or other preliminary material.[1] O is like M in lacking arguments to the first play, although, despite its very sparing annotation, it does include arguments for six other plays (not for *Rhesus*, which has only the list of *dramatis personae*). V also is mutilated at the beginning, and the original survives only from *Hecuba* 32 onward. Several of the *recentiores* are likewise defective in the beginning.

Two *recentiores* in which not only the *Life* but also additional preliminary matter survives are S and Sa. Some of this extra material is not known from elsewhere. In both, the sequence of elements is scrambled, perhaps as a result of mistaking the continuity or discontinuity of texts placed in separate columns or added in marginal spaces in the exemplar. The following listing shows the shared sequence of several items found in Sa, fols. 95r–97r, and in S, fols. 117r–119r.

---

[1] For the question whether these were already lacking in the exemplar from which M was copied, see Chapter 4.

1. *Vita Euripidis* IA, lines 1-37 Kannicht, with heading γένος καὶ βίος εὐριπίδου. (Sa 95r, lines 1-30; S 117r, lines 35-36, 117v, lines 1-30)

2. *Vita Euripidis* IB, lines 42-59. (Sa 95r, lines 30-32, 95v, lines 1-14; S 117v, lines 30-40, 118r, lines 1-6)

3. hypothesis of Aristophanes of Byzantium, lines 19-21 Diggle (omitting last sentence τὰ περὶ Πολυξένην ... ἐν Πολυξένῃ, which was placed here from Sch. Hec. 1 [Schwartz I.10, 7-8] by Wilamowitz). (Sa 95v, lines 15-17; S 118r, lines 6-8)

4. the epitome-style hypothesis, lines 1-18 Diggle, both with the heading αὕτη δέ ἐστιν ἡ ὑπόθεσις; at the end of the epitome, after κατάρξαντα, Sa only adds ἤγουν τῆς ὠμότητος. (Sa 95v, lines 17-32; S 118r, lines 8-22)

5. a *problēma* about the appearance of the soul of Polydorus (essentially a scholion on the opening of the play).[2] (Sa 95v, lines 32-34, 96r, lines 1-3; S 118r, lines 22-27)

> ἀποροῦσι τινὲς λέγοντες πῶς, τῶν ἄλλων ψυχῶν μὴ ἀνιουσῶν μετὰ τὸ κατιέναι ἅπαξ πρὸς Ἅδην, ἡ ψυχὴ τοῦ Πολυδώρου ἀνήει. καὶ φαμὲν ὅτι οὐδέπω καθαρσίων ἔτυχε καὶ ἐπὶ τούτω οὐδὲ τῷ Ἅδῃ προσεδέχθη οὐδ' εἴσω τῶν πυλῶν εἰσήει τοῦ Ἅδου, ἀλλ' ἄχρι τῶν πυλῶν φθάσασα, ἐπεὶ καθαρσίων οὔπω τετύχηκε, πρὸς τὴν μητέρα πάλιν ἀνήει ὡς τάφου τύχῃ καὶ καθαρσίων.

> Some express puzzlement, saying how it is that, whereas the other souls do not come up after once going down to Hades, the soul of Polydorus came up. And we say that he did not yet receive purifying rituals and on this account he was not even accepted in Hades, nor did he enter within the gates of Hades, but having reached just to the gates, since he had not yet received purifying rituals, he went back up to his mother in order to obtain a tomb and purifying rituals.

6. last lines of *Vita Euripidis* IA (lines 38-41 Kannicht),[3] with the heading περὶ τῆς τελευτῆς εὐριπίδου. (Sa 96r, lines 3-6; S 118r, lines 27-31)

7. *Vita Euripidis* II, 60-68 Kannicht (more on Euripides' death), running on without break from item 7. (Sa 96r, lines 6-16; S 118r, lines 31-35, 118v, lines 1-5)

8. *Vita Euripidis* IV, 90-112 Kannicht, following the previous without break. (Sa 96r, lines 16-28; S 118v, lines 5-18)

9. a note on the origin of the word τραγῳδία (with close affinity to part of

---

[2] There is no close parallel for this in TLG texts or in manuscripts of Euripides collated so far. For some, Polydorus' ghost raised the question of whether it was substantial or not, and this question was connected to the possible meaning of ἥκω in the scholion on *Hec.* 1 from SSa quoted in Chapter 2 (preceding note 17); compare the scholion of Thomas Magister (I.219, 30-35 Dindorf) and also Moschopulus' paragraph περὶ τοῦ εἰδώλου (= I.204-205 Dindorf).

[3] In his apparatus Kannicht does not report S as carrying this item or the next, but it does.

the entry in *Et. Magn.* s.v.,[4] but with corruptions). (Sa 96r, lines 29–35; S 118v, lines 18–26)

περὶ τραγῳδίας ἔνιοι ταῦτα φασί· τοῖς πρῶτον νικήσασι τρύγα δοθῆναι κατ' ἀρχὰς ἆθλον καὶ ἀπὸ τούτου κληθῆναι τραγῳδίας [τρυγῳδίας *Et. Magn.*]. τρύγα δὲ ἐκάλουν οἱ παλαιοὶ τὸν νέον οἶνον. ἦν δὲ τὸ ὄνομα τοῦτο κοινὸν καὶ πρὸς τὴν τραγῳδίαν καὶ πρὸς τὴν κωμῳδίαν, ἐπεὶ οὔπω διεκέκριτο[5] τὰ τῆς ποιήσεως ἑκάτερα. ἔνιοι δὲ οὐ τρυγῳδίαν ἀπὸ τῆς τρυγός, ἀλλὰ τραγῳδίαν ὠνομάσθαι λέγουσι. τράγος γὰρ ὡρίσθη τοῖς νικήσασιν. ὕστερον δὲ τὸ μὲν κοινὸν ὄνομα μόνη ἔσχεν ἡ τραγῳδία, ἡ δὲ κωμῳδία ὠνομάσθη ἐπειδὴ πρότερον κατὰ κώμας ἔλεγον αὐτὴν ἐν ταῖς ἑορταῖς τοῦ Διός [Διονύσου *Et. Magn.*] καὶ τῆς Δήμητρος, ἢ ἀπὸ τοῦ κωμάζειν.

Concerning *tragōdia* some say this: that to those who first won victories unfermented new wine (*trux*, root *trug-*) was given as a prize in the beginning and from this it was called *tragōdia* [*trugōdia Et. Magn.*]. And the ancients used to call new wine *trux*. And this name was applied in common to tragedy and comedy, since the two different genres of poetry had not yet been separately categorized. Some others say that it was (originally) named not *trugōdia* from *trux*, but *tragōdia*: for a goat was established as prize for the victors. And later tragedy alone took over the shared name, and comedy was named because previously they used to recite it in various villages (*kōmai*) in the festivals of Zeus [Dionysos *Et. Magn.*] and Demeter, or it was named from reveling in a band of celebrants (*kōmazein*).

10. six short poems on Euripides. First there is an iambic trimeter couplet said to be by Ion (*Anth. Gr.* 7.47 Beckby), then four epigrams in elegiac couplets (the first two, presented as separate in SSa, together make up *Anth. Gr.* 7.43 Beckby; then 7.44 and 7.48 Beckby), and finally a poem in hexameters (Christodorus, *Anth. Gr.* 2.1, 32–35 Beckby). (Sa 96r, lines 35–36, 96v, lines 1–10; S 118v, lines 26–37)

11. a series of six old scholia on *Hec.* 1 and *Hec.* 3. Specifically, they are the following scholia from Schwartz: I.12, 13; I.10, 2–8; I.11, 9–18; I.12, 14–15; I.11, 19–12, 9; I.12, 16–27. (Sa 96v, lines 11–34; S 118v, line 37, 119r, lines 1–24)

12. genealogical/mythographic note on Xuthus, Creusa, Ion, and Achaeus. In view of the close similarity of this information to a somewhat longer note ex-

---

[4] *Et. Magn.* gives several possible derivations, among which are (764, 10–16) ἢ ἀπὸ τῆς τρυγὸς τρυγῳδία. ἦν δὲ τὸ ὄνομα τοῦτο κοινὸν καὶ πρὸς τὴν κωμῳδίαν· ἐπεὶ οὔπω διεκέκριτο τὰ τῆς ποιήσεως ἑκατέρας· ἀλλ' εἰς αὐτὴν ἓν ἦν τὸ ἆθλον, ἡ τρύξ· ὕστερον δὲ τὸ μὲν κοινὸν ὄνομα ἔσχεν ἡ τραγῳδία· ἡ δὲ κωμῳδία ὠνόμασται, ἐπειδὴ πρότερον κατὰ κώμας ἔλεγον αὐτὰ ἐν ταῖς ἑορταῖς τοῦ Διονύσου καὶ τῆς Δήμητρος, ἢ παρὰ τὸ κωμάζειν.

[5] S before correction and Sa have διέκριτο, which might be a Byzantine pluperfect without reduplication (Jannaris 1897: §736–737, 740; Schwyzer 1934–1971: I.779). But *Et. Magn.* and S after correction attest the full form (S also has supralinear αι at the end indicating a variant error κέκριται). In this text I have refrained from adding iota subscripts, but I have changed the scribes ὠνομᾶσθαι to ὠνομάσθαι.

plaining the word "Achaeans" in *Iliad* 1.2,⁶ this is probably a displaced teacher's note on Ἀχαιοί in *Hecuba* 35. (Sa 96v, lines 34–45, 97r, lines 1–2; S 119r, lines 24–26)

Ζοῦθος ὁ τοῦ Αἰόλου ἀδελφὸς ἀπῆρε Κρέουσαν τὴν Ἐρεχθέως θυγατέρα· καὶ ἐξ αὐτῆς ἐγέννησε Ἴωνα καὶ Ἀχαιόν. καὶ ὁ μὲν Ἴων κατῴκησεν ἐν ταῖς Ἀθήναις, ὁ Ἀχαιὸς δὲ ἐν τῇ Ἑλλάδι.

Xuthus the brother of Aeolus carried away Creusa the daughter of Erechtheus. And from her he sired Ion and Achaeus. And Ion resided in Athens, Achaeus in (the city) Hellas.

13. after the heading εὐριπίδου ἑκάβη, followed by *dramatis personae*, a laconic summary of the plot. (Sa 97r, lines 2–7; S 119r, lines 26–30)

τὸ δρᾶμα τοῦτο τὴν ταφὴν Πολυδώρου Πολυξένης τε τὴν σφαγὴν διαγράφει καὶ τῶν Πολυμήστορος ὀμμάτων [ὁ add. Sa] δίκην οἵαν δεδρακὼς εὗρεν ἀντιμισθίαν.

This drama describes the burial of Polydorus and the sacrificial slaughter of Polyxena and punishment of the eyes of Polymestor, what sort of punishment, having acted, he got as recompense.⁷

For this stretch of text Sa and S are clearly following the same source.⁸ After item 14, however, they differ. Before starting the text of *Hecuba* itself in the lower third of fol. 97r, Sa has teachers' scholia on four passages of *Hecuba*: on 90 χαλᾷ (ὁπλὴ χηλὴ καὶ ὄνυξ διαφέρει ..., also attested by Y²); on 130 σπουδαὶ δὲ λόγων (paraphrase σπουδαὶ αἱ λογικαὶ ἔριδες τῶν μαχομένων περὶ τῆς θυγατρός τῆς ἑκάβης, again shared by Y²), on 131 ἴσαι πως (shared with Y²

---

⁶ Sch. D Hom. Il. 1.2 Ἀχαιοῖς: τοῖς Ἕλλησιν. Ζοῦθος ὁ Αἰόλου παῖς ἀγόμενος Κρέουσαν τὴν Ἐρεχθέως θυγατέρα ἔσχεν ἐξ αὐτῆς δύο παῖδας, Ἴωνα καὶ Ἀχαιόν. ὧν ὁ μὲν Ἴων ᾤκησεν Ἀθήνας. ὁ δὲ Ἀχαιὸς φόνον ἐμφύλιον δράσας παρεγένετο εἰς Θεσσαλίαν· καὶ κυριεύσας τῆς χώρας τοὺς ὑποτεταγμένους ἀφ' ἑαυτοῦ προσηγόρευσεν Ἀχαιούς. Ἕλληνες δὲ κοινῶς πάντες οἱ τῆς Ἑλλάδος ἐκλήθησαν ἀπὸ Ἕλληνος τοῦ Διός. πρῶτοί τε οὕτως ἐλέγοντο οἱ ἐν Θεσσαλίᾳ ἄνθρωποι. οὐ μὴν ἅπαντες, ἀλλὰ μόνοι οἱ ἐν Ἑλλάδι τῇ πόλει. ἔπειτα μεγάλα δυνηθέντος τοῦ Ἕλληνος καὶ τῶν τούτου παίδων, ἀπ' αὐτοῦ πάντες ἐκλήθησαν Ἕλληνες.
⁷ One might wonder whether this is a distant descendant of the lost laconic plot summary of Aristophanes of Byzantium, but it does not seem accurate enough, and the word ἀντιμισθία at least is late Greek, common in Christian authors. The wording of the last phrase is doubtful, and possibly something has been lost: for instance ὀμμάτων τὴν φθορὰν (καὶ?) οἵαν δίκην ἀνόσια δεδρακὼς ("and the destruction of the eyes of Polymestor and? what sort of penalty he got as recompense for having done unholy deeds").
⁸ Sa alone has added two marginal notes on 96r: one concerns the word φαιῷ in item 7 (ἤτοι πορφυρῷ; in Plut. *Mor.* 184a, 489a, and Pollux 7.48 the two colors are in contrast, since one puts off purple robes in order to don black ones in mourning); the other concerns θράκας in item 8 (θράκας ἀπὸ τοῦ θρακὸς τοῦ ὀρφέως, a claim without parallel in other attested derivations).

and others), and on 109 τύμβου (τύμβος ἡρίον μνῆμα καὶ τάφος διαφέρει ..., also attested by Y²).⁹ As an afterthought, in smaller script, two other notes were squeezed into the space between the end of the scholion on 109 and the first verses of the play. One is grammatical and not firmly rooted in the text; its classification of tenses as "complete" vs. "incomplete" has no ready parallel that I know of.¹⁰

> ἡ ὁριστικὴ ἡ εὐκτικὴ καὶ ἡ ἀπαρέμφατος εἰσὶ τέλειαι ἐγκλίσεις. ἡ δὲ προστακτικὴ καὶ ὑποτακτικὴ εἰσὶν ἀτελεῖς.
>
> The indicative, optative, and infinitive are complete moods [i.e., occur in the future as well as present, aorist, and perfect], but the imperative and subjunctive are incomplete [i.e., do not occur in the future].

The other introduces a word not attested yet elsewhere (προλόγισις), and perhaps applies to the opening of the play (although conceivably it could be meant to comment on line 59, the beginning of Hecuba's monody).

> πᾶσα μονῳδία καὶ προλόγισις, οὐ μὴν πᾶσα προλόγισις καὶ μονῳδία.
>
> Every *monōdia* is also a *prologisis*; however, it is not the case that every *prologisis* is a *monodia*.

The lesson taught by this note is uncertain. *Monōdia* in later Greek can mean any threnetic discourse, even one in prose. *Prologisis* ought to mean something like "delivery of a prologue-speech."¹¹ Even granted that many tragic prologues show us a suffering character complaining of her or his situation, it still seems odd to say "Every speech expressing grief is also a prologue delivery, but not every prologue delivery is a speech expressing grief." But for teachers of Euripides there was some contention around the term *monōdia*, to judge from the insistence on not using the term loosely shown in Sch. Andr. 102:¹²

> μονῳδία ἐστὶν ᾠδὴ ἑνὸς προσώπου θρηνοῦντος· ὥστ' οὔτε τὸ [Andr. 1] "Ἀσιάτιδος γῆς σχῆμα" μονῳδία ἐστί· τραγῳδεῖ γὰρ καὶ οὐκ ᾄδει· οὔτε τὰ ἐν Θεοφορουμένῃ ᾀδόμενα· οὐ θρηνεῖ γάρ.

---

⁹ Three of these items are edited and discussed below. The notes on 90 and 109 are items 5 and 6 in a short list of glosses in gB presented in section 3 below; the note on 131 is item 15 in the Miscellany discussed in section 2 below.

¹⁰ ἐντελής alone is associated with the indicative mood in opposition to all other moods on a much different basis in ps.-Herodian, *παρεκβολαὶ τοῦ μεγάλου ῥήματος* 4, 12–15 La Roche.

¹¹ *LBG* provides a few (also very rare) words of similar formation, but they do not give much help: προλογιστής, "one who gives an introductory speech"; προλόγιν, "introductory speech"; προλόγισμα/προλογισμός, "preliminary consideration, reckoning in advance."

¹² Note that the text of this note has been heavily emended by Schwartz, but his corrections seem necessary.

A *monōdia* is the song of one character lamenting; thus neither is "pride of the Asiatic land" a *monōdia*, because Andromache is declaiming in tragic fashion and not singing, nor is the part sung in *Theophoroumene*, because the character is not mourning.

From folio 97v onward Sa continues with the text of the triad plays and select old scholia on them, with some scholia found only in *recentiores*, including a few teachers' notes, and many glosses.

S, for its part, follows item 14 above, at the bottom of folio 119r, with a second recording of the epitome (μετὰ τὴν τῆς Ἰλίου πολιορκίαν ... κατάρξαντα), which is finished in lines 1–10 of 119v. After that begin the text of and scholia on the triad. S also differs from Sa, however, in having other preliminary texts copied before item 1 in the listing above. Eight lines from the bottom of 114v the text and scholia of Oppian's *Halieutica* end, and material directly or tangentially related to Euripides begins, which I now list in summary form.

A. S 114v, last 7 lines, through 115v, line 31: ἐτυμολογίαι καὶ ἄλλ' ἄττα τοῦ πρώτου δράματος τοῦ Εὐριπίδους τοῦ περὶ τῆς Ἑκάβης (Etymologies and some other annotations of the first play of Euripides, about *Hecuba*), a collection of 32 notes that will be the subject of the next section of this chapter.

B. S 115v, lines 32–40, 116r, lines 1–30: an untitled short treatise describing terms for metrical feet, using in part the same order and examples as found in listings attached to the works of Dionysius Thrax and Hermogenes.[13] But the author of the listing in S has added etymologies for many of the terms, such as the following:

διὰ τοῦτο δὲ σπονδεῖος ἐκλήθη ἐπειδὴ ἐν ταῖς σπονδαῖς τῶν θεῶν εἰώθασι μετὰ τούτου τοῦ μέτρου λέγειν τὰς ᾠδάς.

It has been named *spondeios* for this reason, because in the libations (*spondais*) to the gods they are accustomed to recite songs with this meter.

μολοττὸς δὲ ἀπὸ Μολοττοῦ τοῦ υἱοῦ Πύρρου καὶ Ἀνδρομάχης· τὰς ᾠδὰς γὰρ λέγουσιν[14] ἐν τοιούτῳ μέτρῳ ἐν τῷ ἱερῷ τῆς Δωδώνης περὶ τὴν Ἤπειρον πρὸς μνήμην Μολοττοῦ· ἐκλήθη γὰρ ὕστερον.[15]

---

[13] Among TLG texts see the version in *GrammGr* I:1.117–119 (Uhlig) and that in *Rhetores Graeci* (Walz 1832–1836: 7:2.989–990).

[14] I have emended S's λέγει.

[15] I have not yet investigated this text in full detail, but can say that the two etymologies quoted are not closely paralleled in any texts in the TLG. Checking two other etymologies, I found that those for dactyl and anapaest are similar to statements in Aristides Quintilianus, *De musica* 1.15, and indeed Aristides' treatise is a text that offers etymologies of most of the metrical terms, so it is somehow a distant source. The etymology for dactyl in S's text seems to have been known later to Arsenius (cent. 5, 80b, *Paroem. Gr.* II.356).

(It is called) *molottos* after Molottus the son of Pyrrhus and Andromache. For they recite songs in such a meter in the shrine of Dodone in Epirus in memory of Molottus. For it got its name later.

C. S 116r, line 31-38, through 117r, line 35: a treatise on genres of ancient poetry entitled Ἰσαακίου τοῦ τζέτζου ἐξήγησις εἰς τὸν Εὐριπίδην (Isaac Tzetzes' interpretation for Euripides). The work is nowadays assigned to Ioannes Tzetzes, despite the heading in the manuscript,[16] and has nothing particular to do with Euripides, except as general background for teaching and reading ancient poetry. The text has been edited from Lycophron manuscripts by E. Scheer.[17] The presence of this Tzetzean material invites the speculation that text A or text B or both may have some connection to Tzetzes as well, and therefore it has seemed worthwhile to study in more detail the group of notes that form A, which I will henceforth in this chapter refer to as the Miscellany.

2. THE MISCELLANY OF NOTES ON *HECUBA* IN S

The Miscellany was mentioned without further analysis by Alexander Turyn in his description of S, Salamanca, Biblioteca Universitaria 31. The first half of the codex contains Oppian's *Halieutica* with scholia, and Oppian's *Cynegetica* with the paraphrase of Eutecnius. At the end of the *Halieutica* (fol. 79) the scribe Ioannes Kalliandros[18] recorded that he had finished copying "the present book" (meaning *Halieutica*?) in June 1326, and there is no reason to believe that completion of the rest of the codex falls far from that date. This Miscellany contains 32 notes. All of them can be attached to specific words or lines within the first 600 lines of *Hecuba*, and they represent various types of teachers' scholia,

---

[16] Wendel 1948: 1979-1980 skilfully marshalls the evidence that indicates that the ascription of the Lycophron commentary and of this treatise was a sort of dedication by Ioannes to his deceased brother Isaac. This text has considerable overlap in content and wording with Ioannes' verse introduction to poetry (Wendel 1948: 1987-1988), which is edited by Koster 1975: 84-109 and Pace 2011.
[17] Scheer 1908: 1-4. This is TLG work 5030.01. I think it probable that ἐξήγησις is an error for εἰσήγησις (introduction to Euripides), from the common confusion of ἐξ/εἰς. In the Lycophron tradition, according to Scheer's text, the treatise appears before the *Life* and a hypothesis to the poem, and the only heading is the general one εἰς τὸν Λυκόφρονα σχόλια Ἰσαακίου γραμματικοῦ τοῦ τζέτζου (followed by four hexameters also crediting Isaac with making the obscure clear).
[18] Vogel and Gardthausen 1909: 172; Turyn 1957: 96; *PLP* 10352. The contents of the codex are described in detail by Tovar 1963: 21-25, but his identification (21 n. 1) of the scribe of S with the scribe Ioannes Anagnostes of Vienna, Phil. Gr. 219, is not to be accepted (for the latter see *PLP* 91272). See also the remarks of Martínez Manzano 2008 (on the Oppian portion) and 2015: 131-132 and Lám. 17 for a sample of the scribe's hand (not from the Euripides part). I examined the manuscript in person for several hours in 2011, and subsequently obtained excellent color digital images of the Euripidean portion, which made further study much more accurate.

including etymologies, διαφέρει-notes, and σημαίνει-notes (the types illustrated in Chapter 2). The fact that the notes are all on *Hecuba* and cover only the first half of the play appears to be typical of scholia intended for students beginning their study of tragic poetry, but one cannot rule out the possibility that the limitation is due rather to some other process. It is possible, for instance, that the original author provided notes beyond line 600 of *Hecuba*, but that the compiler only needed the earlier ones, or had a damaged manuscript as his source, or suspended the work for an unknown reason. Some damage or loss in the source is suggested at any rate by the fact that that the last item is left incomplete, now ending in mid-sentence.

There are two ways such a collection of notes might have come about. First, the teacher may have kept a running record of additional remarks that he developed as he taught *Hecuba*, not intending his remarks to compete with or replace the scholia and glosses that he and his students also drew upon to understand the ancient text. (This appears to be what we have in a couple of pages of scholia on various lines of *Phoenissae* found in the 6th-century P. Würzburg 1.)[19] Second, the author of the notes may have added them in the margins of a manuscript, perhaps one with traditional annotation already present, placing them as near the relevant line of the play as the previous notes would allow or marking their reference points with symbols. Subsequently, they could easily be recognized as distinct from the original annotation by features such as the color of the ink, their position on the page, and the difference of the hand. In this scenario, someone later wanted to retain the notes of this particular teacher and transcribed just those notes from the manuscript into a single sequence such as we find in S.

On the whole, the second scenario is more likely. The Würzburg scholia on *Phoenissae* have lemmata, but the notes of our miscellany do not, so that their application to specific passages of *Hecuba* would in some cases be difficult to understand unless they were on the page with the poetic text, either in alignment with the relevant verses or linked with reference symbols to particular words. Moreover, upon further investigation, it has emerged that there are a few manuscripts in which some of these notes are not presented in one collection, but individually at or close to the lines to which they belong. It is more likely that they have this dispersed positioning because that is where the notes were found in an ancestor than that someone had the grouped arrangement of the Miscellany and worked to distribute them individually to appropriate positions.

A definitive understanding of the nature and fortune of these annotations will not be reached until my collations of *Hecuba* manuscripts are more complete. But enough has been done with select Palaeologan-era copies (especially

[19] Essler et al. 2013.

PrRSaY) to make tentative conclusions useful. The first point to make about the Miscellany itself is that for this material S is a *codex descriptus*, a copy of a surviving manuscript, Laurentianus plut. 31.03.[20] I owe this recognition to Professor Teresa Martínez Manzano of the University of Salamanca.[21] The source manuscript has not been deemed a "Euripidean" manuscript either in Turyn's great work[22] or by those after Turyn who have studied the tradition of the Euripidean triad, since there are no Euripidean tragedies in it, only the Miscellany and the short metrical treatise (item B above; it does not carry item C). This codex was written in 1287 by Manuel Spheneas,[23] and has been known as B of Aeschylus[24] and Z of Oppian; for the Euripides portion I have given it the siglum Sb. Like S, Sb contains the two Oppian works (fol. 1r-145r) before the Miscellany, which occupies two folios, 145v and 146r, while the metrical treatise (B) covers most of 146v. Folios 147r-v are blank except for some short jottings on the verso, then there are a few pages of scriptural exegesis (148r-150v), followed by the *Life of Aeschylus* and Aeschylean triad (151r-205v).

A prima facie case that the Miscellany in S is copied from Sb is suggested by the studies devoted to the tradition of Oppian. Fajen's study of the tradition of the *Halieutica* presents evidence that his s (our S) is descended from Z (our Sb), although s has incorporated some corrections from another source.[25] For *Cynegetica* Boudreaux established that Q (our S) is copied from M (our Sb).[26] In addition, in connection with the suspicion of a connection with Tzetzes for the Miscellany, it may be noted that Fajen's Z belongs to the group of manuscripts in which the set of scholia is plausibly characterized as containing some Tzetzean material.[27]

The same relationship of descent from Sb can be established for the Miscellany in S. The most telling indications are the following:

---

[20] Open-access online images available at the Biblioteca Medicea Laurenziana's site teca.bmlonline.it (where it is wrongly said to be of the 14th century). Bibliography on the manuscript through the year 2004 is also available there.

[21] Martínez Manzano had studied S for another purpose shortly before I visited Salamanca in 2011, and she kindly shared her knowledge with me in correspondence carried out after my visit.

[22] Turyn 1957: 101 n. 183 does in fact mention it once as an Aeschylean manuscript in another connection.

[23] On this scribe see *PLP* 27256; Turyn 1972: I.55-56; Moraux 1976: 282-286.

[24] Note that since Turyn 1943: 54-55 it has been known that folios 210-231 of Laurentianus plut. 86.03 (containing the *dramatis personae* and poetic text of *Persae* with old scholia) were originally part of the same codex as 31.03 (where the last page, 205v, has the hypothesis of *Persae*), and B has been used to refer to both parts.

[25] Fajen 1969: 38-39.

[26] Boudreaux 1908: 30-31.

[27] Fajen 1969: 32-33. There is, unfortunately, no adequate edition yet of the scholia on *Halieutica*, so any inferences about Tzetzes' contributions are at present no more than speculative.

1. There are two omissions in S that cover full lines of the text as written in Sb (see items 19 and 29 in the edition below). Neither omission involves *saut du même au même*, which is the case with the omission in item 15 caused by the two occurrences of δηλοῖ in proximity.

2. In item 15, Sb has προσισότητα treated as one word (instead of πρὸς ἰσότητα) and with the σό written in such a tight ligature that it is easy to understand how the scribe of S (or of any intervening copy) read the ligature as an omega with two closed loops and wrote the non-word προσιώτητα.

3. In item 13, S's σκῆπος is an attempt to make some sense of Sb's unknown form σκῆμος (the correct reading is σκῆνος, as is implied by the etymology, and attested in PrY²).

4. In two places where S has a superior reading, they are simple and obvious corrections: in item 4, S restores ἀντίφρασις for Sb's ἀντίφασις within an explanation of a series of compounds in -φρασις; in item 11, S writes the correct dative πλεονασμῷ (as is usual in such etymologies) for Sb's πλεονασμοῦ.

5. Item 9 presents an interesting case: in S an extra step is added to the syllogism above the line (along with the addition in the margin of its conclusion, which S had omitted), indicating either that someone has pedantically expanded the note or that S had access to some other source.

6. Less certain is the evidence of item 21. If the author of the note intended to quote the whole line *Ajax* 293 γύναι γυναιξὶ κόσμον ἡ σιγὴ φέρει, then Sb suffers from haplography in omitting γύναι; S had the same omission initially, but the original hand in S changed the first part of γυναι/ξὶ (divided at line-end) to γύναι by adding an acute to upsilon and then supplied γυναι in the left margin of the next line to provide the orphaned letters ξὶ with the needed syllables. But it is possible that the original author deliberately quoted this well-known line without the opening vocative the better to make his point about the generalization being universal and not directed to a character. If so, S's restoration of it is pedantic, but easy, and is paralleled in Y²'s version.

Turyn already reported that part of the Miscellany is found in Sa (of around 1300).[28] We have already seen above that Sa shares a long sequence of unusual prefatory material before *Hecuba* with S, although Sa has not included the Miscellany in that position. In Sa the Euripidean triad, written by one Theodorus,[29] is preceded by Oppian's *Halieutica* (written by a different scribe). The text of *Phoenissae* (by Theodorus) ends on folio 178v, while 179r–v are taken up with the last scholia on *Phoenissae* and a poem of 14 Byzantine dodeca-

---

[28] Turyn 1957: 97. No more is known of this Theodorus (*PLP* 7404).
[29] *RGK* III 224; *PLP* 7404.

syllables addressed to Euripides. On 180r the same scribe[30] begins the Miscellany, writing out the heading and the first three notes in full, but after several words of the fourth note he stops. The rest of that page was later crammed with an unrelated text by a different hand.[31] In addition, as mentioned earlier, Sa has item 15 from the Miscellany (along with other teachers' notes) among the scholia appended to the prefatory material on 97r. Items 11 and 17 of the Miscellany also occur in Sa, written near the lines to which they refer.

One other among the *recentiores* has been found so far to contain items from the Miscellany: Pr (Reims, Bibliothèque Municipale 1306), dating, like Sa, from around 1300 or a little earlier. Pr has eleven of the scholia from the Miscellany, distributed among other scholia in approximately the correct order. Moreover, Pr has 52 additional notes of the same character, far more than the number of additional notes found elsewhere. It is therefore a major source for this kind of grammatical note, and it is an unanswerable question whether any of the others in Pr came from the same source as those in the Miscellany. Most of these notes in Pr are on *Hecuba* (including some after line 572, the last line providing a lemma for the Miscellany), but to date a few have been found for *Orestes* too.[32] Although R (Vaticanus graecus 1135) has no notes matching those in the Miscellany, it does carry some similar notes shared with Sa or S, and RSSa also contain some syntactic notes of the type "Why did the poet say X rather than Y?" (illustrated in the previous chapter), which is another form that reflects teaching practice. Since R was written in Southern Italy before 1300, it is likely to be free of the influence of Planudean scholarship in Constantinople and of contemporary teachers in the capital. This fact, along with the date of Sb (1287) and the degree of corruption in the tradition of some of these notes, makes it most likely that many of these grammatical notes in the *recentiores* predate the Palaeologan renaissance, that is, that they derive from school practice in the 12th century or earlier.[33] This is also suggested by the similarities of some notes to remarks found in Tzetzes and Eustathius, or to elements of the Oppian scholia that possibly have some connection to Tzetzes.

---

[30] I agree with Turyn's implicit attribution of the top lines on 180r to Theodorus, but in *RGK* he is recorded as present only up to 179v.

[31] Yet another hand is responsible for copying item 1 again near the bottom of the page (a *Schriftprobe*?); this occurred at some time before the crammed text was added, for the latter is filled in around it.

[32] Note that Pr has been collated thoroughly for all of *Hec.* and for *Or.* 1–500, but only sporadically for the rest of *Or.* and for *Phoen.* See Chapter 2 above, just after note 25, for an argument that the current data suggest the situation will not change greatly once complete collations are finished.

[33] Note the similar argument made by Herington 1972: 43–44 about the A-commentary on Aeschylus, where again the precise dating of Laur. plut. 31.03 to 1287 is very important. Teresa Martínez Manzano, in her email communication with me about S and Sb, also emphasized the importance of the early date of the Laurentian witness as evidence that it reflects a pre-Palaeologan source.

Somewhat later than PrRSa, the Naples manuscript Y is another important witness of the transmission of teachers' scholia. Both Moschopulean and Planudean material has been entered by Y and Y^2, and Y^2's activity shows an effort to gather various exegetic material.[34] As part of that effort Y^2 added 12 items from the Miscellany, one more than Pr. Some of Y^2's additions are shared by the hand V^3, working on Vat. gr. 909 probably in the first decades of the 14th century. V^3 has four notes from the Miscellany plus two more that are extremely similar in content.

It is now time to turn to providing an edition of the Miscellany, with some commentary on the possible origins of the erudition in these notes (sophomoric though it may appear in some cases) and with citation of some comparanda. The 32 notes are presented here in the order found in Sb, which is mostly in the order of the apparent lemmata, and the evidence of S is recorded, despite its status as *descriptus*, to illustrate exactly how it compares to Sb. The apparatus here excludes most orthographic and trivial variants. Three further preliminary notes need to be made. (1) I have referred to the "apparent lemmata" because for some notes, if we had only the evidence of Sb, we would be uncertain which line of the play inspired the teacher/scholar to make the comment. With the help of identical or similar notes found so far in manuscripts like Y and Pr and Sa, it is possible to be somewhat more secure in assigning a lemma and line number. (2) As to the violations of order, they are perhaps not surprising in a casually gathered set apparently harvested from the margins of a source manuscript.[35] In four cases, the lemmata that are out of order are from lines very close to each other: item 2 on line 7 and item 3 on line 6; item 10 on line 89 and item 11 on line 86; item 25 on line 481 and item 16 on line 480; item 29 on line 553 and item 30 on line 549. Minor dislocations like this are not hard to explain: if these notes were originally added in the margin in a text already supplied with regular scholia, they might end up positioned in such a way (for instance, one on the left of the text and one on the right) that their order was easily reversed. In three cases, however, the dislocation is more pronounced: items 7 to 10 refer respectively to lines 59, 83, 71, 89; item 17 on line 195 is between item 16 on line 132 and item 18 on 174; item 32, the last, follows four sequential notes on lines 543, 549, 553, 572, but concerns line 334 (and thus belonged between items 21 and 22). These larger dislocations could be the result of the compiler realizing at various points that he has missed a note, which would be easier to do, once more, if they were small notes crowded into marginal spaces in a codex that already had regular

---

[34] See Chapter 2, section 3.
[35] See Essler et al. 2013: 69, 73–75, 84–85, 92 for the violations of order in the P.Würzburg 1 scholia on *Phoenissae*.

scholia before these were added. (3) The separation of the notes is usually shown in Sb by placing a cross at the end of the note and leaving a little extra space before the first word of the next one; but for item 1 the cross appears at the beginning and the normal scholion-ending punctuation (:~) occurs at its end; also, from item 23 onward the scribe writes in slightly smaller script and with tighter line-spacing and word-spacing in order to complete the set on folio 146v, so in that section only the cross separates one note from the next. S omits some crosses, uses the scholion-ending punctuation a few more times than Sb, and rarely has extra space between one note and the next. In S someone using red ink has subsequently made the divisions much clearer by adding at the beginning of each note an angle bracket, formed like a large majuscule gamma with a small stroke creating a little triangle inside the junction of the vertical and horizontal strokes; in a few places the same dividing mark has been added within a note to mark logical segments, as with the different technical terms explained in sequence in the long item 4.[36]

Heading:

ἐτυμολογίαι καὶ ἄλλ' ἄττα τοῦ πρώτου δράματος τοῦ Εὐριπίδου τοῦ περὶ τῆς Ἑκάβης.

Etymologies and some other annotations of the first play of Euripides, about *Hecuba*.

1. *Hec.* 1 κευθμῶνα

¹κευθμών ἐτυμολογεῖται ἀπὸ τοῦ κεύθω τὸ κρύπτω· ²τοῦτο δὲ ἀπὸ τοῦ εἴκω τὸ ὑποχωρῶ καὶ τοῦ εὔω τὸ φωτίζω· ³ὅθεν δηλονότι τὸ φωτίζον ὑποχωρεῖ.

SbSSa(twice in Sa); 1 ἐτυμολογεῖται om. Sa (both places)

Keuthmōn is derived from *keuthō* meaning *kruptō* (conceal). And this word is from *eikō* meaning *hupochōrō* (withdraw) and from *euō* meaning *phōtizō* (illuminate). (*Keuthmon* is thus something) from which, clearly, that which gives light withdraws.

This first note is of the etymological variety. The very obvious first part of the note is comparable to *Et. Gud.* 317, 42–46 Sturz s.v. κευθμών. The much more unusual second part is not found in the standard etymological dictionaries, but is nearly identical (and perhaps derived from) Sch. Oppian. Hal. 1.389 κευθομένην· κρυπτομένην, κεκρυμμένην. κευθομένην ἀπὸ τοῦ εἴκω τὸ ὑπο-

---

[36] In S there is a very sparing use of red ink up to fol. 130v (up to *Hec.* 532) and none after that. Red is used for the brackets mentioned in the text (which also appear sometimes among the marginal scholia to divide one from the another) and for a very few marginal labels of a few letters and a few missing *notae personae*. There is thus very little basis for saying whether the entries in red are by Kalliandros; I am inclined to judge that they are not.

χωρῶ καὶ τοῦ εὕω τὸ φωτίζω, ὅθεν τὸ φωτίζον ὑποχωρεῖ. This kind of eccentric etymologizing represents, I believe, some teachers' effort to impress students and colleagues with their ability to play the "game" of clarifying vocabulary by producing a striking derivation. The game was well enough known that in many cases the etymology is incomplete, and the recipients are expected to be able to fill in the steps. The kappa of *keuthō* is seen as a remnant of the verbal root of *eikō* and the *eu* is interpreted as coming from *euō*. In a fuller explanation the scholar would refer to *apokope* of the initial letters of *eikō* (so that only the kappa is left) and to the arbitrary extension of the word at its end with a theta (by what in this system was termed *pleonasmos*).

2. *Hec.* 7 ξένου

¹διαφέρει ξένος φίλος ἑταῖρος. ²ξένος γάρ ἐστιν ὁ ἀπὸ ξενίας φίλος, ³φίλος ὁ ἀεὶ προσφιλής, ⁴ἑταῖρος δὲ ὁ ὑποταγάτος ὁ ὑποτακτικῶς διακείμενος τινὶ καὶ προσφιλὴς ἐκείνῳ, ⁵γίνεται δὲ ἀπὸ τοῦ ἐθὰς ὁ συνήθης ἐθάρος καὶ προσθέσει τοῦ ι καὶ τροπῇ τοῦ δασέος εἰς ψιλὸν ἑταῖρος. ⁶διὸ καὶ τὸ δασὺ πνεῦμα φυλάττει, σημεῖον τῆς ἐκλείψεως τοῦ δασέος συμφώνου.

SbSSa; 6 ἐκλείψ- Sa, ἐκλήψ- Sb, ἐκκλήψ- S

Xenos, philos, hetairos differ in meaning. For a *xenos* is someone who is a friend from a hospitality relationship; a *philos* is the person who is always friendly/dear; a *hetairos* is one who is subject, who is disposed in a subordinate position toward someone and is friendly to that person; and *hetairos* is derived from *ethas* meaning *sunēthēs* (familiar), producing *etharos*, and by addition of the iota and change of the aspirated consonant to unaspirated, *hetairos*. For this very reason the word keeps the rough breathing, as an indication of the reduction of the aspirated consonant.

This note combines the διαφέρει-type with etymologizing of one of the terms discussed. From its position in the sequence in the Miscellany,[37] it is probably to be attached to the occurrence of ξένου in *Hec.* 7, although there are several other places in the play where φίλος or ξένος occurs. On the other hand, most of the note concerns the word ἑταῖρος, which does not appear in *Hecuba* at all. As we have seen in Chapter 2, the word in the text is simply a jumping off point for the teacher to make a point that he considers useful and an opportunity to display his erudition and validate his authority. There is a close parallel to the differentiation of *xenos, philos, hetairos* and to the etymology of the last word in Sch. Opp. Hal. 1.380: σημείωσαι ὅτι ξένος, φίλος καὶ ἑταῖρος διαφέρει· ξένος ἐστὶν ὁ

---

[37] *Hec.* 7 ξένου as lemma is also suggested by the fact that Moschopulus provided here a more sober note remarking on ξένος and φίλος: ξένος κυρίως ὁ φίλος, ὃν ἐπὶ τῆς πατρίδος τις ποιήσεται ἀπὸ ξένης ἐλθόντα, ἁπλῶς δὲ καὶ ὁ φίλος.

ἀπὸ ξενίας φίλος, φίλος δ' ὁ ἐν συμποσίῳ παρὰ τὸ πίνω, πίνος καὶ φίλος, ἑταῖρος ὁ ὑποτακτικῶς διάγων τινὶ καὶ προσφιλὴς ἐκείνῳ γενόμενος· ἀπὸ τοῦ ἐθὰς ὁ συνήθης ἐθάρος, καὶ προσθέσει τοῦ ι καὶ τροπῇ τοῦ δασέος εἰς ψιλὸν ἑταῖρος· διὸ καὶ τὸ δασὺ ἔχει πνεῦμα, σημεῖον τῆς ἐκθλίψεως τοῦ δασέος συμφώνου. This version also offers an etymology of φίλος from πίνω, to drink, which is attested elsewhere only in the late lexicon of pseudo-Zonaras (s.v. φίλος, 1809, 23), which perhaps derives it from the Oppian scholion.[38] Similarly, the treatment of ἑταῖρος features the made-up word ἔθαρος, which the TLG cites only from Sch. Oppian and a fragmentary late lexicon (of which Nicephorus Gregoras has been suggested as compiler). Other differences between the two versions are that ours adds the middle Byzantine word ὑποταγάτος (or ὑποταγᾶτος), attested a few times from the 12th century onward, and that ours uses ἔκλειψις where the other has ἔκθλιψις for the process that substitutes tau for the theta. For the equivalence of ἔκλειψις with the more common ἔκθλιψις to indicate omission of a letter, there are parallels in scholia and lexica.[39] For elimination of an aspiration, however, ἔκθλιψις τοῦ δασέος or the like appears four times in TLG (*Epimerismi Homerici*, Sch. Opp. Hal.), but ἔκλειψις τοῦ δασέος is unattested. Thus F. Pontani may be correct to suggest that the ἐκλήψεως or ἐκλείψεως is a corruption of ἐκθλίψεως. Or the non-standard extension of the meaning may indicate the writer's limited command of the erudite vocabulary.

3. *Hec.* 6 χθονός

χθὼν ἡ γῆ ἀπὸ τοῦ γῶ τὸ χωρῶ· ἡ χωρητικὴ πάντων.

SbSSa

Chthōn means *gē* (earth), (which latter is) from the verb *gō* meaning *chōrō* (have room for): meaning she who has room for all things.

Again the occurrence of one word in the text induces a comment on the derivation not of that word, but of a related one. This is a widely attested etymology for γῆ, but closest verbally is Sch. Opp. Hal. 1.567: γαίης καὶ γῆς πόθεν γίνεται; παρὰ τὸ γῶ τὸ χωρῶ, ἐξ οὗ καὶ γῆ ἡ χωρητικὴ πάντων. Note in this fuller version the question-and-answer form.

---

[38] Is this derivation omitted from our miscellany because it is too fanciful or not transparent enough as stated?
[39] Cf. Sch. Yf Hec. 334 οὔμοί: οἱ ἐμοί· ἔκλειψις καὶ κρᾶσις (where in Pr we find οὔμοὶ μὲν ἔκθλιψις καὶ κρᾶσις); Sch. rec. Arist. Nub. 782a θείνω, θενῶ, καὶ ῥῆμα εἰς μι θνῆμι· ὁ μέλλων θνήσω, ὁ παρακείμενος τέθνεικα, καὶ ἐκβολῇ τοῦ κ τέθνεια καὶ ἐκλείψει τοῦ ι τέθνεα, ἡ μετοχὴ ὁ τεθνεώς; Sch. Hom. Od. 17.343 Dindorf οὖλον] ὅλον, κατὰ ἔκλειψιν τοῦ υ; Sch. Pind. Ol.1.84g; a few times in *Epimerismi Homerici* and *Et. Gud.*

4. *Hec*. 8 Χερρονησίαν πλάκα

¹διαφέρει φράσις περίφρασις παράφρασις μετάφρασις ἔκφρασις ἀντίφρασις καὶ σύμφρασις· ²φράσις μέν ἐστιν ἡ ἁπλῶς λέξις. ³περίφρασις ἡ περισσὴ φράσις, ὡς τὸ βίη ἡρακληείη. ⁴παράφρασις ἡ ἐναλλαγὴ τῶν λέξεων τῶν αὐτῶν κατὰ τὸ ποσόν, ὡς τὸ "μῆνιν ἄειδε θεὰ" τὴν ὀργὴν εἰπὲ μοῦσα. ⁵μετάφρασις ἡ ἐναλλαγὴ τῶν λέξεων κατὰ τὸ ποσὸν πλειόνων ἢ ἐλαττόνων μετὰ ῥητορικοῦ κάλλους, ὡς ποιεῖ ὁ μεταφραστής. ⁶ἔκφρασις ἡ λεπτομερὴς διήγησις ἡ ἐναργῶς καὶ εἰς ὄψιν ἄγουσα ἡμῖν τὸ διηγούμενον ὅπως ἔχει θέσεως, ὡς ἔκφρασις ἱεροῦ ἀλεξανδρείας ἢ πόλεων ἢ ἄλλων χωρῶν. ⁷ἀντίφρασις ἡ δι' ἐναντίων λέξεων φράσις. ὁ ἀργυροῦς αἰθίοψ. καὶ εὐήθης ὁ μωρός. ⁸σύμφρασις δὲ ἡ συνακολούθησις τοῦ λόγου ἢ λέξεων σύνθεσις, ὡς νοβελισιμοϋπέρτατος.

SbS, 1-5 (through κάλλους) Sa; 3 ἡρακλέη SbSSa | 8 νοβελισιμουπερτατος (no diacritics) Sb, νοβελίσιμο ὑπέρτατος S

Phrasis, periphrasis, paraphrasis, metaphrasis, ecphrasis, antiphrasis, and *sumphrasis* differ. *Phrasis* is an expression pure and simple. *Periphrasis* is an expanded, roundabout expression, such as "the strength of Heracles." *Paraphrasis* is the substitution of words that are the same in quantity (as the originals), as "Sing, goddess, of the wrath" (can be paraphrased as) "Speak, muse, of the anger." *Metaphrasis* is the substitution of words that are more or fewer in quantity (than the originals) with the accompaniment of literary adornment, in the fashion of (Symeon) Metaphrastes. *Ecphrasis* is a detailed description that is done with vivid clarity and presents to our vision how the thing being described is situated, such as an ecphrasis of a shrine of Alexandria or of cities or other places. *Antiphrasis* is an expression using opposite terms: "the silvery Ethiopian," or the fool (termed) "of good character." *Sumphrasis* is the connected sequence of speech or composition of terms, such as *nobelisimohupertatos* (most noble and highest).

The assignment of this phrase to line 8 is encouraged by the position of the note in the sequence and by the fact that Zm (from the Thomano-Triclinian circle) glosses Χερρονησίαν πλάκα with περίφρασις. It also makes sense that the first compound term in the long series is the one inspiring the inclusion of this explanation. As a whole, the note is a slightly shortened and modified version of a section of a text called περὶ τρόπων ποιητικῶν[40] and ascribed to Georgius Choeroboscus (9th cent.), but as transmitted it must be later than the 10th century since it cites Symeon Logothetes/Metaphrastes. The final example is printed as νωβελήσιμος ὑπέρτατος in Spengel's edition, but συνακολούθησις as a grammatical term refers to the continuous flow of discourse between two words (such that a final acute on the first is changed to a grave). This phrase must rather be an example of a compounded word, the second meaning offered, even

---

[40] §14, Spengel 1853–1856: III.251, 9–31.

though no other example of this compound is known.⁴¹

5. *Hec.* 31 σῶμ'

¹σῶμα σημαίνει δύο· ²τὸ ζῶν παρὰ τὸ σῆμα καὶ σημεῖον εἶναι τῆς ψυχῆς, ³καὶ τὸ τεθνηκὸς παρὰ τὸ σῆμα καὶ σημεῖον εἶναι τοῦ ποτὲ ζῶντος.

SbSY²; 1 σημαίνει δύο om. Y² | 3 first καὶ om. Y² | παρὰ τὸ σῆμα om. SbS | σημεῖον] μνημεῖον Y² | ποτὲ om. Y²

Sōma has two meanings: that which is living, derived from its being a marker/"tomb" and sign of the soul, and that which is dead, from its being a tomb and sign of what was once living.

Here Y² reflects a sounder tradition of this note in respect to including the second παρὰ τὸ σῆμα, since παρὰ τὸ is needed to govern the second εἶναι. μνημεῖον of Y² perhaps has more point than a repeated σημεῖον, but the writer may have wanted the exact repetition, and in the parallels about to be cited Tzetzes has σημεῖον whereas Eustathius and Moschopulus use μνημεῖον.⁴² This note belongs to the σημαίνει-type, with etymology added. The connection of σῶμα and σῆμα is very old and was passed on from Plato to later philosophers and theologians. It occurs in the etymological dictionaries and various scholia, often in connection with the Aristarchan doctrine that Homer does not use σῶμα of a living body and with etymologies of δέμας connecting δέμας to δέω. Indeed, it is in connection with δέμας that we find a similar phrasing in Sch. Opp. Hal. 1.576 δέμας μὲν τὸ ζῶν σῶμα παρὰ τὸ δεδεμένον εἶναι τῇ ψυχῇ, σῶμα δὲ <u>παρὰ τὸ σῆμα καὶ μνημεῖον εἶναι τοῦ ποτὲ ζῶντος</u>, ἤγουν τὸ λείψανον, λαμβάνονται δὲ καὶ ἀντ' ἀλλήλων καταχρηστικῶς, as well as in Tzetzes' Sch. Il. 1.115 (no. 69) καὶ δέμας μὲν τὸ ζῶν λέγων, ἐτυμολόγει παρὰ τὸ δεδέσθαι καὶ συνεστηκέναι. τὸ δὲ τεθνηκὸς λέγων δέμας πάλιν παρὰ τὸ δεδμῆσθαι καὶ δαμασθῆναι καὶ διαλυθῆναι. καὶ σῶμα δὲ πάλιν τὸ ζῶν παρὰ τὸ σῶον εἶναι καὶ σώζεσθαι. <u>τεθνηκὸς δὲ παρὰ τὸ σῆμα καὶ σημεῖον εἶναι τοῦ ποτὲ ζῶντος</u>. δέμας νῦν τὸ ζῶν σῶμα. Another comparandum is a remark of Eustathius *in Il.* 1.115 (I.98, 18–22) ἰστέον δὲ ὅτι σημειοῦνται οἱ παλαιοὶ τὸ δέμας τὸν μὲν ποιητὴν ἐπὶ ἐμψύχου ἀεὶ τιθέναι σώματος ὡς συνδεδεμένου τῇ ψυχῇ καὶ δι' αὐτῆς συνεστῶτος, τὸ δέ γε σῶμα ἐπὶ ἀψύ-

---

⁴¹ The Byzantine honorific νωβελίσσιμος is borrowed from Latin and is attested over 80 times in TLG as of August 2017, with various spellings (omega or omicron, one lambda or two, one sigma or two, -ήσιμος or -ίσιμος). On this term, see Bury 1911: 35–36, who says its use as a separate title (rather than standard epithet of the title Caesar) goes back to the 4th century.

⁴² If the repetition of σημεῖον is an error, that process could also have caused the insertion of ποτὲ in SbS, but ποτὲ is probably original, since it appears in several parallel passages, quoted in the text and in the next note.

χου τουτέστιν ἐστερημένου ψυχῆς <u>διὰ τὸ σῆμα καί, ὡς ἄν τις εἴποι, μνῆμα γενέσθαι τοῦ ζῶντός ποτε</u>.[43]

6. *Hec.* 47 τλήμων

τλῶ τὸ καρτερῶ καὶ ταλῶ· καὶ ἀπὸ μὲν τοῦ τλῶ γίνεται τλήμων, ἀπὸ δὲ τοῦ ταλῶ γίνεται τάλας.

SbS

Tlō meaning *karterō* (endure) and *talō*. And from *tlō* comes *tlēmōn*, while from *talō* comes *talas*.

This note could rather be assigned to line 20 τάλας, with another disruption in sequence, but if the sequence is correct, then this is the lemma that occurs between 31 and 59. The etymologies offered here go back to antiquity, and we have brief versions in Orion 152, 7 Sturz τάλας· παρὰ τὸ τάλλω, καὶ τλῶ κατὰ συγκοπήν, and Orion 152, 8 τλήμων· τλῶ, τλήσω, τλήμων. The affinity to Eustathius, who like our note has ταλῶ instead of τάλλω, should also be noted: *in Il.* 17.167–169 (IV.33, 8–12). τὸ δὲ "οὐκ ἐτάλασσας" σκώπτει μὲν ὡς ἀταλαίπωρον καὶ οὐ τλήμονα τὸν Ἕκτορα, γίνεται δέ, ὡς καὶ ἀλλαχοῦ ἐφάνη, ἀπὸ τοῦ ταλῶ, ἐξ οὗ τὸ τλῶ κατὰ συγκοπήν. ὅθεν καὶ τὸ τλῆναι καὶ ὁ τλήμων καὶ ὅσα τοιαῦτα. ἐκ δὲ τοῦ ταλῶ ταλάσω ἀποβληθέντος τοῦ κατὰ τὸν μέλλοντα τελευταίου φωνήεντος ὁ τάλας γίνεται (see also Eust. *in Od.* 1.87 [I.23, 3–6]).

7. *Hec.* 59 ἄγετ'

διαφέρει τὸ ἄγω καὶ τὸ φέρω ὅτι τὸ μὲν ἄγω ἐπὶ ἐμψύχων λέγεται ἀκοντὶ ἀγομένων, τὸ δὲ φέρω ἐπὶ ἀψύχων βασταζομένων.

SbS; ἑκοντὶ SbS | ἀψύχων] ἐμψύχων a.c. Sb

Agō and *pherō* differ in meaning, because *agō* is applied to animate beings led along against their will, while *pherō* is applied to inanimate objects being carried in one's hands.

The traditional teacher's explanation of the difference between φέρω and ἄγω simply contrasts inanimate and animate objects: Ammonius 4 ἄγειν καὶ φέρειν διαφέρει. ἄγεται μὲν γὰρ τὰ ἔμψυχα· φέρεται δὲ τὰ ἄψυχα. Ὅμηρος [*Od.* 4.622]· "οἱ δ' ἦγον ⟨μὲν μῆλα⟩, φέρον δ' εὐήνορα οἶνον"; Choeroboscus *Epimer. in Psalmos* 73, 25–29, τί διαφέρει τὸ ἄγω τοῦ φέρω; ὅτι <u>τὸ μὲν ἄγω ἐπὶ</u>

---

[43] For an example later than our note, see Sch. Mosch. in Batrachomyomach. 81: δέμας σημαίνει δύο· ... ὡσαύτως καὶ <u>σῶμα σημαίνει δύο·</u> τὸ ζῶν καὶ τὸ τεθνηκός. καὶ τὸ μὲν ζῶν ἐτυμολογεῖται ἀπὸ τοῦ σῶον εἶναι, ... <u>τὸ δὲ τεθνηκὸς παρὰ τὸ σημεῖον καὶ μνημεῖον εἶναι τοῦ ποτε ζῶντος</u>.

ἐμψύχων λαμβάνεται, ὡς τὸ "ἄξετε δὲ Πριάμοιο βίην." τὸ δὲ φέρω ἐπὶ ἀψύχων, ὡς τὸ "οἵ δ' ἦγον μὲν μῆλα φέρον δ' εὐήνορα οἶνον"; *Et. Gud.* 551, 16-19 Sturz φέρω τοῦ ἄγω διαφέρει· τὸ γὰρ φέρω ἐπὶ ἀψύχων τάσσεται· τὸ δὲ ἄγω ἐπὶ ἐμψύχων· φέρω τὸ βιβλίον, ἄγω τὸν ἄνθρωπον·.... . For the additional point about the unwillingness of the animate objects, however, we need to turn to Tzetzes Sch. Il. 1.366 (no. 39): ταύτην δὲ τὴν Ὑποπλάκιον Θήβην ἐπορθήσαμεν καὶ ἤγομεν καὶ ἠνδραποδίσαμεν, ὡς ἐν αἰχμαλώτων μοίρᾳ τὰ πάντα ἐνταῦθα. διαφέρει γάρ, ἔφην, τὸ ἄγω τοῦ φέρω· τὸ μὲν γὰρ ἄγω, ἐπὶ ἐμψύχων λέγεται βιαίως ἀγομένων, τὸ δὲ φέρω ἐπὶ ἀψύχων καὶ βασταζομένων. Tzetzes' βιαίως provides the clue to the original form of item 7: ἑκοντὶ contributes nothing useful and must be a corruption of ἀκοντὶ.

8. *Hec.* 83 ἔσται

¹ἔσται τοῦ γενήσεται διαφέρει ²ὅτι τὸ μὲν ἔσται τίθεται ἐπὶ τῶν ὄντων μὲν γενησομένων δὲ καί τι ἕτερον, ³τὸ δὲ γενήσεται τίθεται ἐπὶ αἰτίας τῶν μελλόντων γενήσεσθαι.

SbSY²V³; 1 τὸ prep. Y²V³ | διαφέρει τοῦ γενήσεται transp. Y²V³ | 2-3 ὅτι τὸ μὲν γενήσεται ... γενήσεσθαι, τὸ δὲ ἔσται ... γεγενημένων δέ (om. καί τι ἕτερον) transp. Y²V³ | 2 τίθεται om. Y²V³ | γενησομένων Mastronarde, γεγενημένων SbSY²V³ | 3 αἰτίας Y², αἰτίας τῆς V³, αἰτία SbS

Estai differs from *genēsetai* because the former is used in reference to things that exist but will also become something different, but *genēsetai* is used in reference to the cause of things that are going to come into existence.

In their eagerness to give students a clear rule or to show off a novel perception, teachers in antiquity and in Byzantium, just as today, may propound an oversimplification or an implausible claim. This appears to be the case here, although the claimed distinction goes back to at least the Roman Imperial period. We may compare Herennius Philo, *De diversis verborum significationibus* (epitome) (72) ἔσται τοῦ γενήσεται διαφέρει. ἔσται μὲν γὰρ καὶ τὰ νῦν ὄντα, γενήσεται δὲ τὰ γενέσεως τευξόμενα, οἷον "νέος πρεσβύτης ἔσται," "τῷ ἀτέκνῳ παῖδες γενήσονται"; *Epimerismi Homerici*, s.v. ἔσσεται: τὸ δὲ ἔσται διαφέρει τοῦ γενήσεται, ὅτι τὸ μὲν ἔσται ἐπὶ τῶν ὄντων νῦν τάσσεται, τὸ δὲ γενήσεται ἐπὶ τῶν οὐκ ὄντων, ὡς τὸ "γενήσονται τῷ πρεσβύτῃ παῖδες" (οὐκ ὄντες γὰρ θέλουσι γενέσθαι) καὶ "ὁ νέος πρεσβύτης ἔσται"; Ammonius, *de adfin. vocab. diff.* 193 ἔσται τοῦ γενήσεται διαφέρει. ἔσται μὲν γὰρ τὰ καὶ νῦν ὄντα, γενήσεται δὲ τὰ γενέσεως τευξόμενα, οἷον "νέος πρεσβύτης ἔσται, τῷ δ' ἀτέκνῳ παῖδες γενήσονται." ἄλλως· ἔσται μὲν γὰρ τὸ ὑποκείμενον, οἷον "ὁ παῖς ἔσται ἀνήρ," γενήσεται δὲ τὸ ἀόριστον.[44] In our version as presented in SbS, the transmitted perfect

---

[44] See also, e.g., Sch. D Hom. Il. 14.3, Eust. *in Il.* 6.252 (I.326, 15-18).

γεγενημένων καί τι ἕτερον ("things that exist and/but have become something else") makes no sense, since the whole point of the future tense is that things have not yet become something else.[45] The comparanda suggest that the participle is supposed to be future γενησομένων, as emended and translated above. If this note refers to *Hecuba* 83 ἔσται τι νέον, as indicated by its position as written by V³ and Y²,[46] then the distinction is shown to be not always valid by the usage in 83 itself, where the meaning is "some (terrible) new thing is going to happen."

9. *Hec.* 71 μᾶτερ ὀνείρων

¹μητέρα τῶν ὀνείρων λέγει τὴν γῆν διότι, ὥς φασιν οἱ παλαιοί, ἐκ τῆς γῆς γίνονται οἱ ὄνειροι· ²πῶς δὲ ἐκ τῆς γῆς, ἄκουσον διὰ συλλογισμοῦ· ³εἰ οἱ ὄνειροι ἐκ τῶν βρωμάτων, τὰ δὲ βρώματα ἐκ τῆς γῆς, ἄρα οἱ ὄνειροι ἐκ τῆς γῆς.

SbS; 1 τὴν γῆν om. S | 3 (after βρώματα) ἐκ τῶν καρπῶν οἱ δὲ καρποὶ add. s.l. S | ἄρα κτλ om., add. in marg. S

The speaker (or the poet) calls the earth "mother of dreams" because, as the ancients say, dreams are born from the earth. How from the earth? Hear the answer by a syllogism: if dreams come from food consumed, and food consumed comes from the earth, then it follows that dreams come from the earth.

This note provides us with one of the most intriguing possible connections to Tzetzes. The suggested explanation is original, differing from those in the old scholia. There we find that χθών in *Hec.* 70 was replaced by νύξ in some texts, and so we have explanations both of "mother of dreams" in apposition to Night, explained on the basis that dreams come at night or are children of Night according to Hesiod, or in apposition to Earth, explained on the basis that dreams are sent up from Hades or from the ground. The connection of dreams with the term βρώματα as adopted in our note is shared by two texts in the current TLG. One is later than our usage, in a paraphrase by Maximus Planudes of some lines of the now-fragmentary 12th-century verse romance *Aristarchus and Callithea* by Constantinus Manasses, fr. 152a (Planudean excerpt §34):[47]

---

[45] Or "makes no sense to us"? One must consider the possibility that the author of the note was not particularly competent and thought that the perfect participle conveyed the meaning intended. The version without καί τι ἕτερον in the other witnesses still seems to me defective, since one needs "things that are *about to be* [scil. something else] but have already come into being."

[46] In V it is added at the bottom of fol. 4r, containing *Hec.* 71–94, and in Y it is added on fol. 94r in a gap between two marginal scholia of the first hand, fairly close to the level of *Hec.* 83.

[47] Mazal 1967: 55, 203.

ὅτι οὐ μόνον αἱ ἡμεριναὶ φροντίδες εἴδωλα ἑαυτῶν καθ' ὕπνους ἀνατυποῦσιν, ἀλλὰ καὶ <u>βρωμάτων πλήθη καὶ ποιότητες</u> καὶ χυμὸς πλεονάσας καὶ δειλία καὶ νόσος θορυβώδεις φαντασίας ποιεῖ.

Not only do one's thoughts during the day fashion images of themselves during sleep, but also quantities and qualities of food consumed and a humor that has become too abundant and cowardice and sickness create disturbing dream-visions.

βρωμάτων is Planudes's own term: the original verses exist here and Manasses used the much more common word τῶν τροφῶν, which is so ordinary that it is frequently a gloss on poetic words that mean food.[48] The other attestation goes back to the 12th century and is in fact in a letter of Tzetzes. Here Tzetzes writes to the emperor reporting to him a dream that he interprets as foretelling a military victory. At the beginning he declares that he often has prophetic dreams and says his dreams are not those of a glutton or drunkard (*Epist.* 58):[49]

ἐγὼ γὰρ ὁ ἀνάξιος δοῦλος τοῦ κράτους σου [Hom. *Il.* 1.202] "οὔτε τι μάντις ἐὼν οὔτ' οἰωνῶν σάφα εἰδώς" οὐδ' ὑπάρχων ἀββᾶς ἢ παπᾶς ἢ τῶν ἄλλως ἀρετὴν μετερχομένων τινά, ὀνείρους δὲ ἄντικρυς μαντείας καὶ χρησμῳδήματα βλέπων ἐνίοτε γινώσκω τὰ τούτων ἀποτελέσματα. <u>οὐδὲ γὰρ ἐκ βρωμάτων ἢ κραιπάλης καρηβαρῶν</u> καὶ κατόχιμος ὕπνῳ γινόμενος ὀνειροπολῶ, ἀλλὰ νήφων τε καὶ ἀκραίπαλος καὶ μηδὲ καθεύδων σχεδόν.

For I, the unworthy servant of your power, "neither being at all a prophet nor with exact knowledge of bird-omens," nor being an abbot or pope or anyone who pursues some (special) virtue in another way, (I) having dreams that are absolutely like prophecies and oracular pronouncements sometimes, understand the outcomes predicted by these. For I do not dream with my head heavy because of food consumed or because of overindulgence in wine and in a state where I am possessed by sleep, but I do so sober and abstemious and almost not sleeping at all.

This coincidence of word-choice and of subject matter is intriguing in itself, but two further points also may be reminiscent of Tzetzes. First, although the question-and-answer form is a reflection of oral teaching methods that we find in older and younger scholia, as seen in the previous chapter, the use specifically of ἄκουσον as we see here is paralleled in scholia in the TLG only in several of Tzetzes' notes on Aristophanes. Second, the jaunty tone of this note recalls Tzetzes' supremely confident style. Yet despite these pointers, the author of this

---

[48] Fr. 152 ὄνειροι γὰρ ὡς τὰ πολλὰ φαντασιοκοποῦσιν, / ἀνατυποῦντες εἴδωλα καὶ ζωγραφοῦντες τύπους / τῶν ἀκουστῶν καὶ θεατῶν ἡμερινῶν πραγμάτων· / πολλάκις δὲ καὶ <u>τῶν τροφῶν ποιότητες καὶ πλήθη</u> / καὶ πλεονάζοντες χυμοὶ καὶ νόσοι καὶ δειλίαι / ἐπάγειν δύνανταί τισιν ὀνείρους ταραχώδεις. "Dreams in general present visions of fantasies, / shaping images and depicting the forms / of the daily affairs one has heard or seen. / And often also the quality and quantity of foodstuffs / and humors too abundant and illnesses and episodes of cowardice / are able to bring upon some people disturbing dream-visions."

[49] Leone 1972: 84, 23–85, 8.

note has glossed over the medical or physiological doctrine to which Tzetzes himself is alluding in his letter. Consumption of food is sometimes said to prevent dreaming, or at any rate to produce disturbing, untruthful, or unprophetic dreams,[50] and Tzetzes is boasting that his dreams are prophetic because he has eaten little (and drunk little and is not in a deeply stuporous sleep inaccessible to true dreams). Hecuba's dream, like all dreams in tragedy, is to be understood by the audience as true, but the author of this note has emphasized the influence of food. So it looks like this syllogism is a hasty display of cleverness, more likely by someone other than Tzetzes, but perhaps familiar with his style.

It is also significant that there is evidence suggesting that Maximus Planudes knew of the explanation given in this item. In the previous chapter we saw the Planudean/Moschopulean note on this same line.[51] This gives two possible explanations, of which the second, ascribed to unnamed "others," uses the same syllogistic sequence: "or according to others, because nourishment (αἱ τροφαί) comes from the earth, sleep results from our nourishment, and dreams come from sleep." The note labeled as Planudean in Y stops at that point, but all the main Moschopulean witnesses have the additional phrase, clinching the syllogism, "therefore dreams come from earth." That addition makes it even more similar to the item in the Miscellany. Furthermore, Planudes uses three stages of derivation (earth > nourishment > sleep > dreams), while the note in Sb has only two steps (earth > nourishment > dreams), omitting sleep. It is curious that the supralinear addition in S brings an additional step as well, but not the same one (earth > crops > nourishment > dreams). Either addition makes the connection between earth and dreams more pedantically transparent, but it is not clear whether one should consider Sb to have lost something by corruption or conclude that both longer versions are free elaborations similar to other modifications routinely made in the copying of such scholia.

10. *Hec.* 89 κρίνωσι[52]

¹διαφέρει σύγχυσις μίξεως· ²σύγχυσις μὲν γάρ ἐστιν ἡ τῶν ὑγρῶν ἕνωσις οἷον οἴνου καὶ ὕδατος καὶ τῶν τοιούτων, ³μίξις δὲ ἡ τῶν ἀντιτύπων καὶ σκληρῶν, ἤγουν σίτου καὶ κριθῆς, κέγχρου καὶ λινοκόκκου, καὶ τῶν ὁμοίων.

SbSPr; 2 μὲν om. Pr | οἷον ... τοιούτων om. Pr | 3 κέγχρου Pr, κεχρ() Sb, μέχρι S[53]

---

[50] For references and some further discussion see Mastronarde 2017b.
[51] See Chapter 2 above, at note 91.
[52] In Pr this note is continued (with δὲ added after διαφέρει) from another note on 89 κρίνωσι· τουτέστιν διαχωρίζουσιν ὡς οἱονεὶ συγκεχυμένως τυγχάνοντα.
[53] Sb suspends χρ above κε and attaches a prominent abbreviation stroke to the rho, which S took as an iota, while misreading the kappa as mu.

Sungchusis (pouring together) differs in meaning from *mixis* (mixture). For *sungchusis* is the uniting of liquids, like wine and water and such things, but *mixis* is the uniting of solids and hard things, for instance wheat and barley, millet and flaxseed, and similar things.

Like several other notes in the Miscellany, this one contains an idiosyncratic doctrine. Stobaeus 1.17.4 quotes Chrysippus for Stoic philosophical/scientific distinctions among παράθεσις, μῖξις, κρᾶσις, σύγχυσις, but in that scheme *parathesis* corresponds to *mixis* in our note, and *krasis* corresponds to *sungchusis*, and Stoic *sungchusis* is something else (a mixture in which the original elements do not retain their nature and cannot be separated again). Philo, *De confusione linguarum* 182–187, follows the same learned tradition in defining *sungchusis* and comparing it to *mixis* (of dry solids) and *krasis* (of wet substances). In ordinary usage, however, *mixis* and *sungchusis* appear as synonymous alternative glosses of φυρμός in *Et. Gud.* 559, 40 Sturz s.v, and *mixis* appears as gloss for *sungchusis* in Hesych. σ 2204. The definition and examples given here for *sungchusis* are most closely paralleled in scholia on *Hec.* 219[54] that, starting from the false reading κραθεῖσαν, say that its use is from a metaphor for liquids being mixed (τῶν συγκιρνωμένων) and united (forms of ἑνόω are used: compare ἕνωσις above), following traditional teaching about *krasis*. Only the version in Arsenius' edition (not located in any manuscript collated so far) brings in the contrast with *mixis* and the examples for dry solids: κιρνῶ ἐνεστώς, κεράσω μέλλων, κεκέρακα παρακείμενος, ἐκράθην δεύτερος ἀόριστος, κραθεὶς μετοχή. λέγεται δὲ κρᾶσις ἐπὶ τῶν ὑγρῶν, οἷον οἴνου καὶ ὕδατος καὶ τῶν τοιούτων, μίξις δὲ ἐπὶ ξηρῶν, σίτου, κριθῆς καὶ τῶν ὁμοίων.

11. *Hec.* 86 ταρβεῖ

> ¹τάρβος σημαίνει τὸν φόβον. ²τρισσῶς δὲ λέγει ὁ Ἡρωδιανός· ³πρῶτον ἐκ τοῦ ταράσσω τάραβος καὶ ἐν συγκοπῇ τάρβος ἀπὸ τοῦ ταράσσειν τὴν ψυχήν. ⁴δεύτερον ἐκ τοῦ τρέπω· ὁ δεύτερος ἀόριστος ἔτραπον τράπος καὶ τάρβος· ⁵οἱ γὰρ εὐλαβούμενοι φεύγουσι. ⁶τὸ τρίτον ἐκ τοῦ τείρω τὸ καταπονῶ· ὁ δεύτερος ἀόριστος ἔταρον τάρος καὶ πλεονασμῷ τοῦ β τάρβος καὶ ἐξ αὐτοῦ ῥῆμα ταρβῶ.
> SbSY²PrSa; 3 ἀπὸ τοῦ] παρὰ τὸ Y²PrSa | τὴν ψυχήν om. S | 6 first τὸ om. Y²PrSa | πλεονασμοῦ Sb

Tarbos means fear. Herodian explains it in three ways. First, as derived from *tarassō* (strongly agitate), whence (noun) *tarabos*, and with syncope *tarbos*, from the fact that it strongly agitates the soul. Second, as derived from *trepō* (turn): the second aorist is *etrapon*, whence (noun) *trapos* and then *tarbos*. For those who are wary of something turn in flight. Third, as derived from *teirō*, meaning oppress

---

[54] Various versions of this observation are found in Rw, Pr, Y, and Gu (the last is Dindorf I.272, 17–20). Turyn 1957: 72 claimed the observation was a "Planudean comment."

with toil. The second aorist is *etaron*, whence (noun) *taros* and with superfluous addition of beta *tarbos*, and from it the verb *tarbō*.

This bit of Herodianic doctrine is from the tradition of the *Etymologica*. Although the *Et. Gen.* has only one derivation and does not name Herodian,[55] versions similar to ours are attested in the *Et. Magn.* and *Et. Gud.*[56] A version that is almost verbatim the same as ours, however, is found in Sch. Aesch. Septem 289f Smith, attested in manuscripts that give expanded versions of the A-commentary (Smith's Nc, end of 13th century; W, beginning of 14th century; Ya, dated 1413). The only difference in wording is that our version in SbS uses ἀπὸ τοῦ in the first explanation while the *Septem* scholion, like Y²PrSa, uses the alternative παρὰ τό. Such an addition to the basic A-commentary probably comes from a middle-Byzantine teaching tradition, like ours. We may note how in the ancient and medieval tradition of etymologizing the fact that three different "plausible" derivations can be offered for the same word did not call the validity and usefulness of the methodology into question.[57]

12. *Hec.* 97 δαίμονες

θεοὶ τῶν Ἑλλήνων λέγονται οἱ ἐπουράνιοι, δαίμονες δὲ οἱ καταχθόνιοι, ἥρωες δὲ οἱ βροτοὶ μὲν ὄντες, θεῶν δὲ τυγχάνοντες σύγγονοι.

SbSPr; τῶν ἑλλήνων om. Pr

The gods of the Greeks are those spoken of as the dwellers in heaven, whereas *daimones* are the ones beneath the earth, and heroes are beings who are mortal but are coincidentally kinsmen of gods.

The lemma is assigned because Pr places this between notes on 99 and 100. This is another idiosyncratic observation. Although the junctures θεοὶ ἐπουράνιοι and δαίμονες καταχθόνιοι are commonplace, they do not elsewhere appear in a differentiating definition quite like this, which also has the pedantic quality of being expressed absolutely. Arsenius also prints a scholion about the distinction between *theoi* and *daimones* on *Hec.* 164, but this note ends with a prudent

---

[55] *Et. Gen.* A (Vat. gr. 1818) and B (Marcianus gr. 304) have ταρβῶ· τὸ φοβοῦμαι παρὰ τὰ τάρβος, τοῦτο παρὰ τὸ ταράσσειν τὴν ψυχήν.

[56] *Et. Magn.* 746, 25–33 s.v. τάρβος: σημαίνει τὸν φόβον, τρισὶ παραγωγαῖς ὁ Ἡρωδιανὸς τοῦτο ὑπέβαλε. πρῶτον, ἐκ τοῦ ταράσσω τάραβος· καὶ συγκοπῇ, τάρβος, παρὰ τὸ ταράσσειν τὴν ψυχήν. β′, ἐκ τοῦ τρέπω, ὁ β′ ἀόριστος, ἔτραπον, τράπος καὶ τάρβος· οἱ γὰρ εὐλαβούμενοι φεύγουσι. τρίτον, ἐκ τοῦ τείρω, τὸ καταπονῶ, ὁ β′ ἀόριστος, ἔταρον, τάρος· καὶ πλεονασμῷ τοῦ β, τάρβος· καὶ ῥῆμα, ταρβῶ· τάρβησάν τε, ἀντὶ τοῦ ἐφοβήθησαν. Cf. *Et. Gud.* 522, 46–53 Sturz. The new edition of *Et. Symeonis* has not yet reached this point.

[57] On more than one etymology for the same word cf. Sluiter 2015: 902–903, 912.

phrase recognizing that the distinction is not absolute: λέγονται δὲ καταχρηστικῶς θεοὶ καὶ οἱ δαίμονες.[58]

13. *Hec.* 99 σκηνὰς

¹σκηνὴ ἡ τέντα κατὰ ἀρχαϊσμόν· ²οἱ γὰρ ἀρχαῖοι δερματίνους ἐποίουν τέντας· ³σκῆνος γὰρ τὸ δέρμα.
SbSY²Pr; 1 ἡ τέντα] ἐνταῦθα Pr | 3 σκῆνος Y²Pr, σκῆμος Sb, σκῆπος S
Skēnē means tent (*tenta*) in ancient usage. For the ancients made tents out of skins (*dermatinous*). (The word is so used) because *skēnos* is skin (*derma*).

The assignment to this line is suggested by the sequence and by Pr, in which this note follows one on 98;[59] the noun σκηνή occurs also in *Hec.* 53, 733, 1289, 1293. Again this is an observation that has no ready parallels for its particular formulation. The correct reading is given by Y²Pr, and Sb's σκῆμος is a corruption of that. There is a small blot on the ημ in Sb, but the surviving trace is surely a mu ligatured to the following omicron. S's σκῆπος may be a misreading caused by the blot in Sb or a failed effort to make some sense; σκῆπος does in fact appear as an invented word used in the etymology of κῆπος from σκάπτω (*Et. Magn.* and *Et. Gud.* 319, 56–62 Sturz s.v. κῆπος). τέντα is a Byzantine word borrowed from Latin, and a late gloss on σκηνή in a few places. Compare the scholion (neither Moschopulean nor Thoman) attested in Gr[60] on *Hec.* 616: σκηνωμάτων· κατὰ τοῦτο λέγεται καὶ σκήνωμα τὸ τοῦ ἀνθρώπου σῶμα διὰ τὸ πρὸς χρόνον βραχὺν κατοίκησιν εἶναι τῆς ψυχῆς. σκηνὴ γὰρ καὶ σκήνωμα ἡ πρὸς χρόνον βραχὺν ὡς ἔτυχε γενομένη οἰκία, ἤγουν τέντα ἢ ἄλλο τι τοιοῦτον.

14. *Hec.* 103 δοριθήρατος

¹δορίκτητος καὶ δοριθήρατος ἰῶτα, δορυάλωτος δὲ ψιλόν. ²κλίνεται δὲ τὸ δόρυ τοῦ δόρυος καὶ τοῦ δόρατος καὶ τοῦ δορός, ³ὡς τὸ γόνυ τοῦ γόνυος γόνατος καὶ γουνός.
SbSY²Pr; 2 second and third τοῦ om. Y²Pr | 3 τοῦ om. Y²

---

[58] The source of this note has not been located, and it may be Arsenius' own: θεοὺς ὑψηλότερόν τι τάγμα ἡγοῦντο τῶν δαιμόνων· ὃν γὰρ λόγον ἔχουσιν οἱ ἥρωες πρὸς τοὺς λοιποὺς ἀνθρώπους, ὑψηλότεροί τινες δοκοῦντες καὶ ὑπερέχοντες, τὸν αὐτὸν λόγον καὶ οἱ θεοὶ πρὸς τοὺς δαίμονας, ὑψηλότεροί τινες δοκοῦντες τούτων εἶναι. λέγονται δὲ καταχρηστικῶς θεοὶ καὶ οἱ δαίμονες. It is partly reminiscent of a passage in Proclus *in Pl. rem publ. comm.* II.331, 15–18: ἐξ ὧν ἐν Κρατύλῳ [397D] τῶν δαιμόνων καὶ τῶν ἀνθρώπων ἐν μέσῳ τὸ τῶν ἡρώων ἔταξεν φῦλον, ὡς οἱ δαίμονες τῶν ἡρώων ὑπέρτεροι κατὰ τὴν οὐσίαν, οὕτω τοὺς ἥρωας τῶν ἀνθρώπων ὑψηλοτέρους θέμενος.

[59] In Y it is in the top margin of fol. 94r (the page on which *Hec.* 53–111 are copied) and is followed by item 11 on 86 τάρβος.

[60] Also in the 15th-cent. manuscript Laur. plut. 31.25, with three trivial variants. This note was already published in Matthiae and Dindorf.

Doriktētos and *dorithēratos* are spelled with iota, and *dorualōtos* is spelled with the simple letter (upsilon) [that is, not the diphthong pronounced the same way, *oi*]. The declension is nominative *doru*, genitive *doruos* and *doratos* and *doros*, on the pattern of *gonu* with genitive *gonuos*, *gonatos*, and *gounos*.

This item can be assigned to *Hecuba* 103 δοριθήρατος, since the scribes of Pr and Y² locate it there. Grammarians' instructions of this kind, such as those about where to write ι and where to write ει instead, go back to antiquity, but the need for such instruction expanded in Byzantine times because of further possible confusions. No parallel dealing with the δορι-/δορυ- compounds is present in current TLG texts. There is a usage to be noted here that is characteristic of Byzantine teaching and not well attested in lexicons: ψιλόν alone may refer telegraphically to spelling something with epsilon or upsilon as opposed to the digraph with similar pronunciation (αι or οι).[61] This usage of ψιλόν is attested in 12th-century teachers and scholars. In his note on Thuc. 1.123.1 (Luzzato 1999: 47) ψιλόν τις ἐξώρθωσεν ..., Tzetzes refers to someone who wanted to read προφέρετε instead of προφέρεται, whereas Tzetzes recommends keeping the latter. In his note on Thuc. 2.102.5 (Luzzato 1999: 96) τὸν Ἀλκμέωνα ... ψιλὸν μέγα γράφουσι ("write with epsilon omega"), he is discouraging the spelling ἀλκμαίονα or ἀλκμαίωνα. Compare Eust. *in Od.* 21.145 (II.255, 6-7) ἵνα εἶεν δύο ῥήματα, κέω διὰ ψιλοῦ καὶ καίω διὰ διφθόγγου; and for application to οι/υ see also *Et. Gud.* 385, 8-9 Stef. s.v. δύω· παρὰ τὸ συνδεδέσθαι ἑτέρῳ ἀριθμῷ. καὶ γράφεται τὸ δυ ψιλὸν καὶ δίφθογγον κτλ. (on δύο/δύω vs. δοιώ).[62] What is unusual in our item, however, is that ψιλόν is just a short way of saying υ ψιλόν, even though the contrast here is not being made with οι, but with iota. Is the imprecision a sign of the mediocre erudition of the author of this note?

15. *Hec.* 131 ἦσαν ἴσαι πως

¹τὸ "Ἴσαι πῶς" δηλοῖ τὴν τελείαν ἰσότητα. ²τὸ δὲ "Ἴσαί πως" δηλοῖ τὸ ἄνισον μὲν τῆς ἐκείνων λογομαχίας πλησιότητα δὲ κεκτημένον, ὡς ἂν εἴπῃς, καὶ πρὸς ἰσότητα.

---

[61] The merging of the pronunciation of οι with υ is known from the Roman period and in Byzantium. Eventually in Byzantine times both collapsed into the same sound as ι/η/ει, as in modern Greek. Nevertheless, the memory of the shared sound of υ/οι was carried on by the very name of the letter upsilon.

[62] See also Dickey 2007: 265 s.v. ψιλός. In a personal communication, Ilias Nesseris reports that this kind of usage is seen in 12th-cent. school material when orthography of various words is concerned, citing an example from Vat. Pap. gr. 92 in which a short grammatical piece following an unpublished *schedos* of Ioannikios reads: οἴοντ(αι) νομίζουσι δίφθογγ(ος)· ὕονται βρέχοντ(αι) ψιλ(όν)· οἴωντ(αι) τὸ μεμόνωντ(αι) ... υἴωνται γεγέννηνται ψίλωσον (note ψιλόω = write with upsilon and not with omicron iota).

SbSSaY²; 1 τὸ ... ἰσότητα om. Y² | 1-2 δηλοῖ ... δηλοῖ om. Sa | τὴν τελείαν ... δηλοῖ om. S | 2 μὲν om. Y² | πλαγιότητα Sa, πλουσιότητα Y² | κεκτημένον Sa, -μένων SbS, -μέν() Y² | καὶ om. SaY² (rightly?) | προσιώτητα S

Isai pōs [with a circumflex on the omega] indicates complete equality. But *isai pōs* [with no accent on the omega] indicates the aspect of their verbal dispute that is unequal but possesses some proximity, one might say, even to equality.

This comment is quite specific to the passage, although it contemplates in the first alternative a construction that should not readily have occurred to anyone (perhaps for this reason the first sentence was omitted deliberately by Y²). I have not yet found any parallel for the explanation, which is meant to contrast the sense if πῶς is interrogative (allowing "equal" to be taken in an absolute sense) with the sense if πως is the enclitic (softening the implication of the adjective "equal"). The note is seriously defective in S and, differently, in Sa. As noted above, S's non-word προσιώτητα is a misreading based on Sb's writing style.

16. *Hec.* 132 κόπις ἡδυλόγος

"κόπις ἡδυλόγος" ὁ κεκο(μ)ψευμένα καὶ ὡς ῥητορικῶς κεκομμένα καὶ ἀπεξεσμένα εἰς κάλλος ἔπη λαλῶν.

SbS; ἀπεξεσμένα Mastronarde, ἀπεξευμένα SbS

"Sweet-talking prater (*kopis*)" is the man who speaks words that are prettified and as if in a rhetorical manner cut up (root *kop*-) (into short phrases) and polished to be beautiful.

This note too is more specific to its passage than many others. It is possible that transmitted ἀπεξευμένα (a form not found in TLG) is an *ad hoc* formation of the perfect of ἀποξέω or ἀποξύω, but is it more likely to be a corruption for ἀπεξεσμένα (or ἀπεξυσμένα; both are attested forms), misspelled under the influence of the preceding κεκο(μ)ψευμένα. The juncture of εἰς κάλλος with ἀποξέω occurs a few times in Gregorius Nazianzenus (e.g., *orat.* 18, *PG* 35: 1004, 41-43 ὥσπερ ἀνδριάντα πνευματικὸν, εἰς κάλλος ἀπεξεσμένον πάσης ἀρίστης πράξεως), and thereafter in about twenty passages in authors of the 6th to the 14th centuries.

17. *Hec.* 195 δόξαν

δόξα σημαίνει τρία· δόξα ἡ τιμή, δόξα ἡ δόκησις, καὶ δόξα ἡ γνώμη.

SbSSa

Doxa has three meanings: there is *doxa* meaning honor, *doxa* meaning appearance, and *doxa* meaning judgment/decision.

This note could apply to 117 or 370 instead; its position in the Miscellany perhaps suggests 117, but in Sa it follows a scholion on 195 and item 19 (on 176), so 195 is the most likely reference. The closest comparable passage is Sch. Hec. 489

in Pr: δόξα σημαίνει τρία· τὸ δόγμα τὴν δόκησιν καὶ τὴν τιμήν.[63] Compare also Sch. rec. Aesch. Pers. 28 (Dähnhardt): δόξῃ: γνώμη ἢ φιλοτιμίᾳ ἢ ἐνυποστάτῳ δοκήσει καὶ πείσματι ψυχῆς. A somewhat different approach to the distinction between only two of the meanings appears in pseudo-Zenodorus, τῶν περὶ συνηθείας ἐπιτομή 254, 1-2[64] δόξα, παρὰ τῇ συνηθείᾳ τιμή, παρὰ δὲ τῷ ποιητῇ ἡ κατὰ ψυχὴν ἔννοια καὶ δόκησις; and Eust. in Il. 10.324 [III.81, 4-8] ἰστέον δὲ ὅτι, ὥσπερ κλέος παρὰ τῷ ποιητῇ οὐ κοινότερον ἡ τιμή, ἀλλὰ ἡ φήμη παρὰ τὸ κλύω ... οὕτω καὶ δόξα οὐ κατὰ τοὺς ὕστερον ἐπὶ τιμῆς, ἀλλὰ ἔννοια κατὰ ψυχὴν καὶ δόκησις καὶ οἴησις.

18. *Hec.* 174 ἄϊε

> ¹τὸ ἀκούω ὅταν λέγηται ἀντὶ τοῦ ἐνωτίζομαι γενικῇ συντάσσεται, ὅταν δὲ ἀντὶ τοῦ συνιῶ αἰτιατικῇ. ²ὡσαύτως δὲ καὶ τὸ συνιῶ ἀντὶ τοῦ ἀκούω γενικῇ, ὡς τὸ [*Psalms* 5:2] "σύνες τῆς κραυγῆς μου" ἀντὶ τοῦ ἄκουσον. ³ὅταν δὲ ἀντὶ τοῦ εἰς νοῦν βάλλω αἰτιατικῇ.
> SbSPr; 2 δὲ om. Pr | 3 λάβω Pr

> The verb *akouō* (hear), when it is used as equivalent of *enōtizomai* (hearken to) is construed with a genitive object, but when it is used as equivalent to *suniō* (understand), with an accusative. In like fashion the verb *suniō* meaning the same as *akouō* (hear) is construed with genitive, as in "perceive my cry" instead of "hear it," but when meaning the same as *eis noun ballō* (cast into one's mind), with an accusative.

The verb ἀκούω appears many times in the play, but the position of the note in Pr and in the sequence of the Miscellany points to 174, as does the fact that the phrase ἄϊε ματέρος αὐδάν here apparently reminded the commentator of the much-quoted biblical verse *Psalms* 5:2. Euripides does not use συνίημι in *Hecuba*, but it is noteworthy that Pr has the gloss σύνες above ἄϊε, while the gloss ἄκουε is used by both Moschopulus and Thomas. A more detailed comment on the case usage with ἀκούω in *Suda* α 939 s.v. includes the phrase εἰ δὲ τὸ ἐνωτίζομαι τοῖς ὠσὶ μόνοις, μετὰ γενικῆς. Remarks about the case usage with συνίημι are found in *Suda* σ 1576-1577 and in a dozen places in Eustathius' Homeric commentaries. In Sch. Opp. Hal. 3.3 the same quotation from *Psalms* is used in a grammatical note to explain the different senses of a genitive or accusative complement with ξυμβάλλεο.[65] As for the variants εἰς νοῦν βάλλω vs.

---

[63] This Pr scholion was published (with τιμήν misreported as τύχην) by Matthiae (whence Dindorf) from La.
[64] Edited by E. Miller 1868 (the pagination is from the reprint in Latte and Erbse 1965).
[65] Part of the note reads ὅταν συντάσσῃς συμβάλλεο καὶ σύνες, πρέπον συντάσσειν τινῶν τῶν θεσμῶν τῶν νομίμων καὶ ὡρισμένων τύπων καὶ μηχανῶν, λέγω τῶν εἰναλίων, ἢ τῶν ἰχθύων,

λάβω (Pr), the classical Greek usage would be middle βάλλομαι, but the active verb emerges in this phrase in later Greek, especially in less educated styles (the phrase with the active form occurs twice in Sch. Opp. Hal. as a gloss on ἀκούω); so βάλλω is perfectly acceptable here, although λαμβάνειν εἰς νοῦν is also very common.

19. *Hec.* 176 ψυχάς

> ¹ψυχὴ λέγεται καὶ ἡ συνδεδεμένη τῷ σώματι ἤγουν τὸ θεῖον ἐμφύσημα. ²λέγεται καὶ ἡ τοῦ ἀνθρώπου ζωή, ὡς εἶπε καὶ ὁ θεὸς τῷ διαβόλῳ περὶ τοῦ Ἰώβ· ³[*Job* 1:12] "πλὴν τῆς ψυχῆς αὐτοῦ μὴ ἅψῃ," ἤγουν τῆς ζωῆς αὐτοῦ, τουτέστι μὴ θανατώσῃς αὐτόν.
>
> SbSᵃSᵇPrSaV³; 1 λέγεται δὲ ψυχὴ transp. V³ | συγγεγενημένη V³ | 1–3 ἐμφύσημα … πλὴν om. Sᵃ (one full line in Sb) | 3 αὐτοῦ ψυχῆς transp. SᵇSa
>
> *Psuchē* is used both for the spirit bound together with the body, that is, that which was breathed into man by God. And it is used of the life of a human being, as God said to the devil concerning Job: "but do not touch his *psuchē*," that is, his life, that is, don't kill him.

S has this twice: Sᵃ is the version in the Miscellany, while Sᵇ is found in the scholia block at the top of fol. 124v (containing *Hec.* 165–204). Pr has the note near 176, whereas V³ has added in the bottom margin of fol. 6r, near 182 ψυχάς, and has used the lemma ψυχάς (so V in 182, but in 176 V has ψυχῆς). The wording of the quoted example is the rendering found in Christian fathers (Ioannes Chrysostomus, PG 49.262, 31; 61.124, 37; Ioannes Damascenus (?), PG 95.609, 1), whereas in *Septuagint* the passage reads τότε εἶπεν ὁ κύριος τῷ διαβόλῳ "ἰδοὺ πάντα, ὅσα ἔστιν αὐτῷ, δίδωμι ἐν τῇ χειρί σου, ἀλλὰ αὐτοῦ μὴ ἅψῃ." No close parallel has been found for the entire formulation, but the juncture συνδεδεμένη σώματι used of the soul occurs in Flav. Josephus, *Bell. Jud.* 7.345, Eustratius, *in Arist. EN* 279, 23, a few other Byzantine texts, and the phrase θεῖον ἐμφύσημα is common in Christian writers. On the reciprocal concept of the body (esp. δέμας) being συνδεδεμένον τῇ ψυχῇ, see the comments on item 5 above.

20. *Hec.* 209 ὑποπεμπομέναν σκότον

> δύο εἴδη εἰσὶ τοῦ ὑπερβατοῦ· τὸ μὲν ἐστὶν ἐννοίας διακοπή, τὸ δὲ θεωρεῖται ἐν διακοπῇ λέξεως.
>
> SSbPr
>
> There are two kinds of hyperbaton. One is a splitting up of a thought, the other is observed in the splitting of a word.

ἡ τῶν ἁλιέων· τὸ συμβάλλω γὰρ, ἤτοι τὸ συνίημι γενικῇ, ὡς τὸ "σύνες τῆς κραυγῆς μου"· ὅταν δὲ ξυμβάλλεο καὶ νόει, ὅρα ἵνα συντάξῃς τινὰ τὸν θεσμὸν καὶ τὸν νόμον καὶ τὸ ἔθος.

The assignment of the lemma for this note is assured by its position in Pr and by the one-word gloss ὑπερβατὸν that appears above the ὑποπεμπομέναν in PrGu. The usage here pertains to having the preposition that is attached to the verb be taken as separable in sense, to govern σκότον.[66] The two types defined here are paralleled in Sch. Theocr. 2.95 ὑπερβατὸν κατὰ διακοπὴν λέξεως· ἔστι δ' ὅτε κατὰ διακοπὴν ἐννοίας γίνεται τοιοῦτον σχῆμα (from E, a 14th-century manuscript); Sch. Aj. 155b Christodoulou ὑπερβατὸν κατὰ λέξιν καὶ κατὰ δια⟨κοπὴν ἐννοίας⟩; but especially close is Eust. in Il. I.25 (I.47, 7-13) ὅτι <u>δύο εἴδη τοῦ ὑπερβατοῦ</u> σχήματος. <u>τὸ μὲν</u> γάρ <u>ἐστιν ἐννοίας διακοπὴ</u> οἷον· ὁ Ἀγαμέμνων, βασιλεὺς δὲ ἦν Ἑλλήνων, ἐραστῆς γέγονε Χρυσηΐδος. τὸ δὲ ἕτερον, [later addition: ὃ οὐδὲ κυρίως ὑπερβατόν ἐστιν, ὡς ἐν τοῖς ἑξῆς που τεχνολογηθήσεται],[67] <u>ἐν διακοπῇ λέξεως θεωρεῖται</u>, οἷον "λέων κατὰ ταῦρον ἐδηδώς," ἤγουν λέων καταφαγὼν ταῦρον, καὶ "διὰ τάφρον ἔβησαν," ἤγουν διέβησαν τὴν τάφρον, καὶ ἐνταῦθα τὸ "κρατερὸν δ' ἐπὶ μῦθον ἔτελλεν" ἤγουν ἐπέτελλε λόγον κρατερόν.

Identifying hyperbaton with a supralinear label of just the term is quite common in the *recentiores*, and the term is used with varied and sometimes loose reference. Here are examples that have been collated so far (again, with more from *Hecuba* than from other plays):

Hec. 91 ἀπ' ἐμῶν γονάτων σπασθεῖσαν, V³: referring to tmesis.

Hec. 98 σπουδῇ πρὸς σ' ἐλιάσθην, RS: used with somewhat unclear reference. Perhaps it treats this as verbal tmesis, but perhaps it is a misunderstanding, or an unclear way of shortening the gist of the old scholion on 104 that takes the phrase 104 οὐδὲν παθέων ἀποκουφίζουσα as separated from the main verb in 98 by hyperbaton.

Hec. 292 αἵματος κεῖται πέρι, Gr (not Moschopulean): prepositional anastrophe.

Hec. 339, V³PrGu: here some teachers' approach was to say that the accusative γόνυ could depend on πρόσπιπτε only if one assumed a hyperbaton for πίπτε πρὸς γόνυ; otherwise, they suggest, γόνυ should be taken as a truncated dative form, since they propound as a rule that προσπίπτω takes only the dative case. The same issue recurs at *Hec.* 737 προσπέσω γόνυ, where Rf has ὑπερβατὸν, Gu says to take the verb as separable elements (κατὰ διάλυσιν), and Moschopulus in his interpreting paraphrase perhaps assumes the same solution (πρὸς τὸ γόνυ προσελθοῦσα πέσω).

---

[66] A related, but different grammatical approach is offered in Sa, advocating interpreting the governance as γᾶς ὕπο rather than ὑπὸ ... σκότον: ἀντιστροφὴ ὁ τρόπος, ὡς τὸ νέων ὡς καὶ ὄρνιθες ὥς.

[67] Eust. *in Il.* 12.13 (III.343, 13–14) notes that the use of the term for διακοπὴ λέξεως is accepted by teachers of reading and literature, but rejected by experts in rhetoric (γραμματικοῖς μὲν θελητόν, τεχνικοῖς δὲ ῥήτορσιν οὐκ ἀρέσκει).

Hec. 555, Pr: marking the intrusion of the ὡς τάχιστ'-clause between subject and verb in οἱ δ' ... μεθῆκαν.

Hec. 857, Gu: splitting of a thought, ὑπερβατὸν μέχρι καὶ τοῦ [863] διαβληθήσομαι, apparently so labeling the roundabout way that 857 ἔστιν γὰρ ἧ introduces the explanation of Agamemnon's qualm about assisting Hecuba.

Hec. 900 νῦν δ', οὐ γὰρ ἵησ', Pr: marking the interposed γάρ-clause.

Hec. 1172 ἐκ δὲ πηδήσας, Gu: splitting of a word in the tmesis.

Phoen. 1165 ναί, πρός σε τῆσδε μητρός, Thoman: on the intrusion of σε.[68]

21. *Hec.* 254–255 ἀχάριστον ὑμῶν τὸ σπέρμα ὅσοι ...

¹διαφέρει τὸ ὡραῖον τοῦ γνωμικοῦ ὅτι τὸ μὲν ὡραῖον ἀπόφασίς ἐστι καταγομένη πρὸς πρόσωπον, ὡς τὸ "ἀχάριστον ὑμῶν τὸ σπέρμα ὅσοι δημηγόρους ζηλοῦτε τιμάς"· ²ἐπήγαγε γὰρ τὸ ὑμῶν· ³ὃ καὶ κατὰ παντός ἐστιν ὅτε ῥηθήσεται. ⁴τὸ δὲ γνωμικὸν ἀπόφασίς ἐστι μὴ ἀφορῶσα πρὸς πρόσωπον ἀλλ' ἀπολύτως ἀεὶ λεγομένη κατὰ παντὸς ὡς τὸ "γυναιξὶ κόσμον ἡ σιγὴ φέρει."

SbSY²Pr; 1 τιμὰς om. SbS | 2 γὰρ] δὲ Y² | 3 κατὰ πάντα Y² | 4 μὴ om. (ἔστιν scr.) Y² | ἀλλ' om. Y² | διαπαντός Pr | γύναι γυναιξὶ Y², p.c. S

The label "beautiful" [*hōraion*] (on a passage) differs from the label "gnomic" because the beautiful passage is a declaration directed to a person/character, as for example "An ungrateful lot you all are, who want to be political leaders!" [*Hec.* 254–255; tr. Kovacs]. For the speaker/poet added "you." Which statement will also sometimes be applied to everyone. In contrast, the gnomic passage is a declaration that is not aimed at a person/character but always said absolutely applying to everyone, for example, "Silence is an adornment for women" [Soph. *Ajax* 293].

I find no parallel for this comment in TLG, although the basis of the distinction is well established in the traditional teaching about γνῶμαι vs. χρεῖαι (e.g., Aelius Theon, *Progymn.* 96, 19ff.).[69] This item is unusual in that it actually addresses a feature of the annotation of tragedies in many manuscripts. Quotable passages are often marked in the margin (or occasionally above the line when the noteworthy phrase begins within a line) with an abbreviation for *gnōmikon* (gnomic), usually gamma-nu with an omega written above them, or with one for *hōraion* (beautiful), a large omega with an extra tall rho superimposed. At *Hec.* 254–255 we actually do find *hōraion* in several manuscripts, including M from the 11th century, SaPrY from the Palaeologan era, and some Moschopulean wit-

---

[68] Compare also the old scholia at *Hipp.* 678 (trying to deal with transmitted τὸ ... πάθος παρὸν, where Wilamowitz's πέραν is nowadays accepted); at *Hipp.* 1127 (on the anastrophe of μέτα); at *Andr.* 1188 (a desperate alternative among the interpretations of ἐμὸν γένος in a tangled lyric sentence, which is marked as corrupt by Diggle).

[69] For more references see Lausberg 1998: §§1117–1120.

nesses,[70] and we also find *gnōmikon* in the margin of some Sophocles manuscripts at *Ajax* 293.[71] One might think that the example from *Ajax* is "directed to" someone since it is actually addressed to Tecmessa, [72] but the author's point is rather that the statement itself contains no second-person reference. On the other hand, the example from *Hecuba* is expressed with second-person verbs. It would require considerably more study of these markings in the manuscripts to determine whether the distinction drawn was widely recognized or is an overprecise pedantic one.[73]

22. *Hec.* 359 δεσποτῶν ὠμῶν

¹διὰ τί εἶπε "δεσποτῶν ὠμῶν" πληθυντικῶς καὶ ἐπήγαγεν ἑνικῶς "ὅστις με ἀργύρου ὠνήσεται"; ²διότι κἂν καὶ δύο φέρει ὁ ζυγὸς κἂν καὶ δύο πρόσωπα εἰσὶν ὁ ἀνήρ τε καὶ ἡ γυνή, ἀλλ' οὖν ἑνικῶς ἐκφωνοῦνται τὸ ζεῦγος καὶ τὸ ἀνδρόγυνον. ³καὶ διὰ μὲν τοῦ πληθυντικοῦ ἐδήλωσε τὰς δύο ὑποστάσεις τὸν ἄνδρα καὶ τὴν γυναῖκα, διὰ δὲ τοῦ ἑνικοῦ τὴν τῆς σαρκὸς συμφυΐαν καὶ μίξιν αὐτῶν ⁴οἷα καὶ ὁ θεὸς τοῖς πρωτοπλάστοις φησὶ [*Gen.* 2:24] "καὶ ἔσονται οἱ δύο εἰς σάρκα μίαν."

SbSY²PrV³; 1 ὑπήγαγεν V³ | ἀργύρω SbS | ἐπωνήσεται PrV³ | 2 first κἂν καὶ] κἂν SbSY² | second κἂν om. Y² | τε om. Pr | οὖν] ὅμως V³ | ἐκφωνεῖται Y² | 3 ἑνικῶς Pr | τῆς σαρκὸς] διὰ σαρκὸς SbS | εὐφυΐαν Pr | 4 τῷ πρωτοπλάστῳ SbS(πρωπλάστω)

Why did she/he say "cruel masters" in the plural and follow it up in the singular with "whoever [sing. form] will purchase me with silver"? Because even though the yoke bears two creatures and even though a man and his wife are two persons, nevertheless the yoke-team and the man-woman couple are spoken of as singular. And through the plural the speaker has indicated the two substances, man and woman,

---

[70] This list is based on a cursory survey of a selection of witnesses and there are undoubtedly others.

[71] I do not have access to more than a few Sophocles manuscripts; checking the images at hand, I found it in K = Laur. 31.10 (= O of Eur., 12th century), and Ven. Marc. gr. 468 (Zg = F of Eur., around 1300).

[72] On the doubt whether γύναι was omitted accidentally or deliberately, see above for the discussion preceding n. 28.

[73] ὡραῖον is much rarer than γνωμικόν. A perusal of some of the plays in B revealed ὡραῖον in three passages of *Hipp.*, one of which (384 or 383-384) is also marked with γνωμικόν, another of which seems deserving of being termed gnomic but is not so labeled (436 αἱ δεύτεραί πως φροντίδες σοφώτεραι), and the third of which appreciates a nice phrase that is not gnomic (596 φίλως καλῶς δ' οὐ τῆνδ' ἰωμένη νόσον). In R, I noted that at *Or.* 823 γνωμικόν and ὡραῖον markings appear together (not entered at the same time; probably the latter came first), and at *Phoen.* 460-461 ὡρ() is written beside 460 (addressed to the two sons) and γνω() beside 461 (461-464 are universalizing). In T, a survey of the marks on *Hecuba* located fifteen passages with γνωμικόν (all impersonal and universalizing) and three passages with ὡραῖον, *Hec.* 751 (containing a first-person condition), 814 (containing a first-person generalizing "we mortals"), 1250 (second-person verb addressed to Polymestor). So Triclinius may have accepted a distinction like the one propounded in the Miscellany.

but through the singular the growing together of the flesh and merging of them, just as God says to the first created ones [*Gen.* 2:24] "and the two will be as one flesh."

For the question-and-answer form of the annotation, see Chapter 2. The passage from *Genesis* is also quoted in *Matthew* 19:5, *Mark* 10:8. No passage comparable to this note is found in TLG, but it may be observed that the the juncture of ὑπόστασις and συμφυΐα in such a context is borrowed from Byzantine explanations of the oneness of the Holy Trinity: most of the discussions using these two terms are later than the 12th century, but a few earlier examples occur, such as Leo VI (*Homil.* 7, 276–280) and Michael Psellus (*Orationes hagiographicae* 3a, 565–568). This is another example of an unnecessarily abstruse explanation displaying the teacher's skills. It is the third quotation of the Bible in these notes (see items 18 and 19 above).

23. *Hec.* 417 οἰκτρὰ

¹διαφέρει οἰκτρὸς τοῦ ἀθλίου· ²οἰκτρὸς γὰρ λέγεται ὁ ἄξιος ἐλέους· ³ἀπὸ τοῦ οἴκτος ἡ ἐλεημοσύνη· ⁴ἄθλιος δὲ ὁ πολλὰ δεινὰ πάσχων καὶ ὑπομένων· ⁵ἀπὸ τοῦ ἀθλῶ τὸ καρτερῶ.

SbSSaY²Lr;[74] 1 οἰκτρὰ Y² | 2 γὰρ λέγεται om. S | 4 δεινὰ om. Sa

Oiktros (pitiful) differs from *athlios* (miserable). For *oiktros* is used of the person who is worthy of pity, and is from *oiktos*, which means sense of pity. But *athlios* is used of the person who is experiencing and enduring many terrible sufferings, and it is from *athlō*, meaning *karterō* (show strong endurance).

The note is placed at 417 by both Y² and Lr, but Sa has it on fol. 105v between notes on 336 and 342, so may have meant it to be connected with 339 οἰκτρῶς. But 417 is the only line where both adjectives occur together (ἄθλιος elsewhere *Hec.* 322, 423, 811). As for the doctrine, it is very artificial (a teacher's overreaching precision), since scholiasts often gloss one with the other, as is also clear from *Et. Gud.* (422, 7 Sturz) s.v. οἰκτρῶς· ἐλεεινῶς, ἀθλίως and *Suda* ε 782 ἐλεεινῶς: οἰκτρῶς, ἀθλίως. The postclassical heteroclite genitive ἐλέους used here is attested from Polybius and the *Septuagint* onward.

24. *Hec.* 420 ἐλευθέρου

λέγεται ἐλεύθερος ὁ ἀκαταδούλωτος, καὶ λέγεται ἐλεύθερος καὶ ὁ καλῶς καὶ εὐτυχῶς καὶ ἐλευθερίως τραφείς.

SbSY²; λέγεται om. (both places) Y² | second καὶ om. Y² | εὐτυχῶς καὶ καλῶς transp. Y²

---

[74] This and the note on *Hec.* 481 (#25) are the only notes in the Miscellany previously published: Matthiae (whence Dindorf) edited them from Lr (fol. 16v, fol. 18r), a codex containing a partial set of Moschopulean scholia, dated 1431 by the scribe Ioannes. On this codex see Turyn 1957: 125 and Günther 1995: 83. A cursory review of the online images of this manuscript did not reveal any other notes from the Miscellany.

Eleutheros (free) is applied to the person who has not been reduced to slavery, and *eleutheros* is applied also to the person who is brought up nobly and fortunately and in a liberal manner (*eleutheriōs*).

Forms of ἐλεύθερος also appear in *Hec.* 234, 291, 367, 550, 754 (where Yf glosses with ἀκαταδούλωτον), 864, and 869; but Y² places the note at this line. The word ἀκαταδούλωτος is Byzantine, found especially in medieval writers. Knowledge of this note seems to be reflected in Gu, which has at this line ἤγουν ἀκαταδουλώτου, ἢ εὐτυχῶς καὶ καλῶς τραφέντος, ἤγουν βασιλέως (not Moschopulean or Thoman).

25. *Hec.* 481 ἀσίαν

ὅτι εἰς τρία μέρη διαιρεῖται ἡ οἰκουμένη ἅπασα· εἰς Ἀσίαν, εἰς Λιβύην, καὶ εἰς Εὐρώπην.

SbSY²V³Lr; σημειωτέον prep. V³ | ὅτι om. Y², app. Lr | εἰ add. before εἰς S | μέρη app. om. Lr | ἡ οἰκ. ἅπασα] Sb, ἡ οἰκ. SY², ὅλη ἡ οἰκ. V³, πᾶσα ἡ γῆ app. Lr | εἰς ἀσίαν] εἰ ἀσίαν S

(Take note) that the entire inhabited world is divided into three parts: into Asia, into Libya (Africa), and into Europe.

The threefold division is already discussed in Herodotus 2.16, 4.42; [Arist.] *De mundo* 339b21–22; Polybius 3.37.2; and there are scholia on various authors that have statements close to this one. Particularly close in wording is Geminus, *Elementa astronomica* 16.3 διαιρεῖται δὲ ἡ καθ' ἡμᾶς οἰκουμένη εἰς μέρη τρία, Ἀσίαν, Εὐρώπην, Λιβύην.

26. *Hec.* 480 κέκλημαι

ἀντέγκλισις λέγεται ὅταν χρόνος ἀντὶ χρόνου ληφθῇ ὡς τὸ κέκλημαι ἀντὶ τοῦ κληθήσομαι· ἐλήφθη ὁ παρακείμενος ἀντὶ τοῦ μέλλοντος.
SbS

Antenklisis is the term used whenever a tense is taken in place of another tense, as *keklēmai* for *klēthēsomai*: the perfect tense has been taken in place of the future.

The notion that κέκλημαι in this passage is to be taken as equivalent to κληθήσομαι is an established part of the teaching tradition, first attested in M (11th century) but probably used in classroom teaching for many centuries before that, perhaps going back as far as the early Roman empire or Hellenistic times. Around 1300 Moschopulus simply borrows the earlier gloss, while Thomas Magister has a more elaborate note in which he suggests that the substitution is more precisely for the future perfect middle-passive (not the future passive) and also contemplates a second possibility, that the verb could be interpreted as replacing an aorist ἐκλήθην.

ἢ τὸ κέκλημαι ἀντὶ τοῦ κεκλήσομαι κατὰ ἀντιχρονισμόν, ἢ ἀντὶ τοῦ ἐκλήθην. ἀφ' οὗ γὰρ τῆς πατρίδος ἐξελήλαται πορθηθείσης, ἀπὸ τούτου τοῦ καιροῦ εἰς δουλείαν ἐτάχθη, εἰ καὶ μήπω ἐπέβη τοῦ τόπου οὗ δουλεύειν ἔμελλεν. ZZaZbZmTGu

Either (perfect form) *keklēmai* is used in place of (future perfect form) *keklēsomai* by substitution of tense (*antichronismos*); or it is used in place of (aorist passive) *eklēthēn*: for from the moment when she has been driven out of her sacked fatherland, from this moment she was assigned to slavery, even if she had not yet stepped upon the location where she was going to be a slave.

Thomas uses the traditional grammarian's term for a substitution of one tense for another: ἀντιχρονισμός. ἀντέγκλισις is not to be found in the TLG at present. When I first transcribed this note from S I found the spelling ἀντέκλισις and wondered whether this was simply a mistake for ἀντίκλισις, but Sb proved to have ἀντέγκλισις, and I have since found this noun in other sources:

Hec. 480: κληθήσομαι ἀντέγκλισις, χρόνος ἀντὶ χρόνου. PrV³

Hec. 163 στείχω: τὸ στείχω ἀντέγκλισις, ὁ ἐνεστὼς ἀντὶ μέλλοντος. δηλοῖ δὲ τὴν βαρβαρώδη⁷⁵ καὶ σόλοικον φωνήν. Pr

Hec. 163 στείχω: ἀντέγκλισις ἀντὶ τοῦ μέλλοντος ἐνεστώς. δῆλον δὲ τὸ βάρβαρον τῆς ἑκάβης. V³

I suspect that the one instance of ἀντίκλισις in TLG, Sch. Opp. Hal. 1.59 (ἐλόωσιν· κινοῦσιν, ἄγουσιν, ἐλαύνουσιν, ἐλαυνέτωσαν, ἐλαύνουσιν, ἀντίκλισις in Bussemaker's 1849 edition) may actually be ἀντέγκλισις, or should be corrected to that—a hypothesis that can be tested only if the Oppian scholia are someday more thoroughly investigated. The problem with this word is that its meaning is somewhat unexpected. There was already an accurate term for substitution of tense, *antichronismos*, since *chronos* means tense. *Enklisis*, on the other hand, normally means verbal mood, and we would expect *antenklisis* to mean substitution of one mood for another, not one tense of the indicative for another tense of the indicative. So is our teacher simply mediocre in talent, and abusing the term by making *enklisis* carry a vaguer meaning such as "inflectional form of a verb"? Or is this rather a sign of adaptation at a lower level of teaching to the realities of

---

⁷⁵ The claim that the usage reflects Hecuba's barbarian status is fanciful, apparently based on the notion that στείχω is present indicative (although "substitution of mood" would actually apply if the comment were about the equivalence of a deliberative subjunctive and a future indicative). The form is recognized as subjunctive and legitimate Greek in a note from the Thoman circle found in ZmGu, perhaps reacting to a teaching tradition in which some espoused interpretation of στείχω as present indicative: ἰστέον ὅτι ὑποτακτικὸς ἐνεστὼς μέλλοντος καὶ ἐνεστῶτος σημασίαν ἔχει· τὸ στείχω γὰρ ἐνεστὼς ὂν [ὢν Zm a.c., Gu] ἐνταῦθα μέλλοντα ἐμφαίνει· ὁ δὲ παρακείμενος καὶ ἀόριστος [scil. ὑποτακτικὸς] μέλλοντα μόνον. "Note that the present subjunctive conveys the meaning of future and present. For *steichō*, being present, here indicates the future. In contrast, the perfect and aorist (subjunctives) indicate the future only."

Byzantine Greek? By this I mean that the future in colloquial Greek had reached its medieval form of a periphrasis with θα or να (as we find it in some late glosses that abandon their classicizing veneer). In glossing, moreover, subjunctives and optatives may be glossed with an apparent ancient future, and futures may be glossed with a subjunctive or optative. So whoever first used this rare term may have felt that the future was a different *enklisis* compared to the perfect indicative.[76]

27 *Hec.* 484 *personae nota* for Talthybius

¹Ταλθύβιος λέγεται παρὰ τὸ θάλλειν ἐν τῇ βοῇ. ²εὐρυβόας γὰρ ἦν καὶ κήρυξ τῶν Ἀχαιῶν, Θαλθύβοος καὶ τροπῇ τοῦ δασέος εἰς ψιλὸν καὶ τοῦ βραχέος εἰς δίχρονον Ταλθύβιος.

SbS;[77] 2 θαλθύβοος Mastronarde, θαλθύβιος SbS

Talthubios is so called by derivation from flourish (*thallein*) in the shout (*boē*). For he was broad-voiced and herald of the Achaeans. (Originally, the word was) *Thalthuboos*, and by shift of the aspirate (theta) to the unaspirated consonant (tau) and of the short-only vowel (omicron) to the vowel capable of two lengths (iota), (it became) *Talthubios*.

Surviving ancient sources have nothing to say about the etymology of this proper name. Grammarians' interest in the word is revealed only in the assertion that the syllable βι is spelled with an iota (*Epimerismi Homerici* and *Et. Gud.* 521, 24–30 Sturz s.v. Ταλθύβιος). The only other place where an etymology is discussed is in Eustathius, in a wider demonstration of etymologies being meaningful in proper names in Homer, *in Il.* 1.320 (I.171, 10-20):

ὅτι ὥσπερ καὶ ἕτερα πολλὰ τῶν κυρίων ὀνομάτων οἰκείως ταῖς προσωπικαῖς ἐνεργείαις ὠνομασμένα κατὰ τὴν λεγομένην φερωνυμίαν κεῖνται παρὰ τῷ ποιητῇ, οὕτω καὶ ἐπὶ τῶν βασιλικῶν ἐνταῦθα κηρύκων γέγονε. Ταλθύβιον γάρ τινα καὶ Εὐρυβάτην κήρυκας τοῦ βασιλέως φησὶ καὶ ὀτρηροὺς θεράποντας, ὅ ἐστι σπουδαίους, παρὰ τὸ ὀτρύνω ἢ ἀπὸ τοῦ τρῶ, τὸ δειλιῶ καὶ συστέλλομαι, πλεονασμῷ τοῦ ο. <u>παρῆκται δὲ Ταλθύβιος μὲν ἀπὸ τοῦ θάλλειν κατὰ τὴν βοήν, οἱονεὶ θαλθύβιος</u>· Εὐρυβάτης δὲ παρὰ τὸ εὐρὺ βάζειν. καὶ ἐν Ὀδυσσείᾳ δὲ κῆρυξ ὁμοίως Εὐρυβάτης Ἰθακήσιος. καὶ Τρωϊκός δέ τις

---

[76] Possibly relevant is a note by V³ on *Hec.* 344 προσθίγω saying ἀντιχρονία ἀντὶ τοῦ προσθί[ξω]. But probably the author of this note thought that προσθίγω was present indicative. The term ἀντιχρονία (instead of the usual ἀντιχρονισμός) is attested only twice in TLG, in notes on *Hec.* 729 (τοῦτο τὸ σχῆμα ἀντιχρονία λέγεται, referring to the interpretation that ἐῶμεν is used for εἴωμεν and ψαύομεν for ἐψαύσαμεν) and *Or.* 82 ἀντὶ τοῦ ὁράσεις, ἀντιχρονία, on ὁρᾷς) edited from Lp by Matthiae (and Dindorf), both scholia using the normal sense of one tense replacing another.

[77] Note that Y², although it does not carry the full note, seems aware of it in providing this gloss above the character's abbreviated name: ἀπὸ τοῦ θάλλειν ἐν τῇ βοῇ.

κῆρυξ Περίφας λέγεται ὡς περιττῶς φωνῶν. ὁ δ' αὐτὸς καὶ Ἠπύτου υἱὸς παρὰ τὸ ἠπύειν καὶ αὐτοῦ κληθέντος ὡς κήρυκος. ἠπύειν γὰρ τὸ φωνεῖν. καὶ αὐτὸ δὲ τὸ κῆρυξ ἐκ τοῦ γηρύω τὸ φωνῶ παράγεται.

Note that just as many other proper names are found in the poet named in a manner suited to the characters' activities, in accordance with the so-called (trope of) name-bearing (*pherōnumia*), just so it has occurred here in reference to the royal heralds. For he says that a certain Talthybius and Eurybates were heralds of the king and his nimble (*otrērous*) servants, nimble meaning good ones, derived from the verb "set in motion" (*otrunō*), or from the verb *trō* meaning be fearful and constrain oneself, with arbitrary addition of omicron. And Talthybius (*Talthubios*) is derived from flourish (*thallein*) in respect to the loud cry (*boē*), as if it were *Thalthubios*. Eurybates is derived from speaking widely (*euru bazein*). And in the *Odyssey* similarly the Ithacan herald Eurybates. And a certain Trojan herald is called Periphas, as one speaking exceptionally (*perittōs phōnōn*). And this same character is also son of *Ēputos*, derived from the verb "speak loudly" (*ēpuein*), a man who was himself so named as being a herald. For *ēpuein* means to speak. And the word herald itself (*kērux*) is derived from *gēruō* meaning speak.

Now, Eustathius' comprehensive review of heralds' names, each with its own etymology, might seem to be a *tour de force* of etymologizing erudition in the medieval manner, and so one might think that he originated these etymologies and that the note in the Miscellany borrows from him. In that case, the borrower has clarified the steps of etymology on his own, inspired by Eustathius' more telegraphically expressed suggestion. On the other hand, it seems more natural that the etymology was at first more explicit (as in many in the *Epimerismi Homerici*) and that Eustathius has truncated it. The issue is complicated by the fact that we need to emend the Miscellany's version so that it contains explicitly the form Θαλθύβοος, which is the starting point of the etymological process, since (1) the second part is derived from βοή, (2) the preceding sentence paraphrases with εὐρυβόας, and (3) the steps themselves mention the necessary change of omicron to iota. If -βοος is the original version, was it already corrupted to -βιος at the time when Eustathius read it? Or did Eustathius write -βιος through a lapse of mind or of pen, or just to abbreviate the steps of derivation?[78] It is frustrating not to be able to be more definite about what the relationship to Eustathius is here, but there is one. Eustathius has some relation to the next item as well, and there it seems clearly more likely that he is reporting an etymology already proposed by someone else.

---

[78] Θαλθύβιος was indeed written here by Eustathius in the original, visible online (Laur. plut. 59.02, fol. 28r, line 15 of the main text). For the latest argument that this is indeed an autograph manuscript see Cullhed 2012.

28. *Hec.* 543 φάσγανον

φάσγανον ἀπὸ τοῦ γάνυσθαι ἐν τῷ φόνῳ.
SbS

Phasganon (sword) is derived from being gleaming (*ganusthai*) in the act of killing (*phonos*).

This is the first instance of φάσγανον in the play; it recurs at 718, 876, 1161. A longer note that is similar occurs at 543 in Pr:[79]

φάσγανον τὸ ξίφος τὸ ἐν σφαγαῖς γανυσκόμενον, ἢ παρὰ τὸ φάος καὶ τὸ γάνος τὸ στίλβον, οἷόν τι σκεῦος γεγανωμένον. ὅτι δὲ γανόω ἐστὶ τὸ λαμπρύνω, καὶ Ἄρατος περὶ Κασσιεπείας ὅτι μὴ λαμπρὴν τὴν φάνσιν φησί· αὕτη δὲ καὶ Ἀνδρομέδα θυγατέρες Κηφέως· [*Phaen.* 1.190–191] "οὐ γάρ μιν πολλοὶ καὶ ἐπημοιβοὶ γανόωσιν / ἀστέρες, οἵ μιν πᾶσαν ἐπιρρήδην στιχόωσιν."

Phasganon, meaning sword, (so called as) that which is made gleaming (*ganusthai*) in slaughter (*sphagais*), or else derived from *phaos* (light) and *ganos* (gleam), that which shines, like a kind of implement that has been polished to a sheen (*geganōmenon*). And note that *ganoō* means *lamprunō* (make bright); and Aratus (gives an example) about Kassiepeia because he says her shining is not bright (this heroine and Andromeda are daughters of Cepheus): "for the stars that make her shine are not many and they alternate, the stars whose rows outline clearly her whole form."

The first alternative assumes that the pieces making up φάσγανον are σφαγ with metathesis (φασγ) and γαν. The second sees instead, for the first part, φάος as the origin of φασ by loss of one letter. The note's origin as a teacher's comment is demonstrated by the additional remark on γανόω, and its display of learning in quoting Aratus, strictly irrelevant to the *Hecuba* passage. Traditional etymological sources do not try to explain the second half of the word. Some offer a choice between a derivation of the whole from σφαγή and one from the φα- form of root φον- (e.g., *Et. Magn.* s.v. φάσγανον), or cite just one of these choices (e.g., Hesych. π 2098 πεφάσθαι· πεφονεῦσθαι, καὶ ἀνηρῆσθαι. ὅθεν καὶ φάσγανον and φ 303 φάσγανον· ξίφος, παρὰ τὸ φάσαι, ὅ ἐστιν ἀνελεῖν). Others combine the two by saying that φάσγανον is from σφάζω, which in turn is from the φα- stem of root φον- with pleonastic sigma added at the beginning (e.g., *Epimerismi Homerici* on *Il.* 1.190). Our note in the Miscellany is so truncated that it is difficult to infer whether ἐν φόνῳ is meant to evoke

---

[79] The first sentence alone of this scholion is added in V by the Palaeologan hand V³; a version omitting the third sentence αὕτη ... Κηφέως was added by a late hand in B. Various corruptions in Pr are not recorded here.

σφαγή/σφάζω or the φα- root or the combined explanation. What is interesting, however, is that the only source that tries to explain γαν as a separate element, apart from our Euripidean scholia in the Miscellany and Pr, is Eustathius, *in Il.* 7.191 (II.441, 9–13):

> εἰ δὲ χαίρει ἐνταῦθα ὁ Αἴας τῇ πρὸς Ἕκτορα μάχῃ, ἔχομεν καὶ νῦν ἀφορμὴν ἐντεῦθεν ἐτυμολογεῖν τὴν χάρμην, ὅ ἐστι τὴν μάχην, ὡς τῶν ἀνδρείων χαιρόντων αὐτῇ. καίτοι ἕτεροι ὥσπερ φάσγανον ἀπὸ τοῦ σφαγαῖς γάνυσθαι καὶ μάχαιραν ἀπὸ τοῦ αἵμασι χαίρειν, οὕτω καὶ χάρμην ἀπὸ τοῦ χαίρειν αἵμασιν εἰρῆσθαί φασι.
>
> If in this place Ajax delights in his battle with Hector, we have now too a justification for etymologizing *charmē* from this, *charmē* which means battle, on the grounds that valorous men delight in it. Yet others say—analogous to the way they explain *phasganon* as from being gleaming in slaughter (*sphagais ganusthai*) and *machaira* as from delighting in bloodshed (*haimasi chairein*)—that *charmē* too has been so named from delighting in bloodshed (*chairein haimasin*).

Since Eustathius disagrees with and ascribes to others the second approach to *charmē*, it is most plausible that he also has taken from an earlier lost source the connection of φάσγανον with γάνυσθαι, the same source from which it has reached the Miscellany. We are once again in the context of 12th-century (or earlier) grammarians' erudition.

29. *Hec.* 553 ἐπερρόθησαν

> ¹διαφέρει φλοῖσβος ῥόθος καὶ βρόμος. ²φλοῖσβος μὲν γάρ ἐστιν ὁ ἐν ἡσυχίᾳ τῶν κυμάτων ἀποτελούμενος ἦχος, ῥόθος ἡ ἐξ ἀντωθήσεως καὶ ἀντικρούσεως αὐτῶν ταραχὴ γινομένη. ³βρόμος δὲ ὁ τοῦ πυρὸς ἀποτελούμενος ἦχος ὅταν ἐν αὐτῷ εἰσβάλωσί τινες συρφετόν.
>
> SbS; 1–2 καὶ βρόμος ... ταραχὴ om. S [= one full line in Sb] | 3 τινες om. S
>
> *Phloisbos*, *rhothos*, and *bromos* differ in meaning. For *phloisbos* is the murmur produced in a calm condition of wave action, *rhothos* is the tumult arising from the counter-thrust and crashing together of waves, and *bromos* is the sound of fire produced whenever people throw sweepings into it.

This combination of statements seems not to be paralleled, nor is the specific wording closely paralleled elsewhere. For the first word, however, cf. [Herodian.] *Partitiones* 147, 15–16 Boissonade: πλὴν τοῦ φλοιός, τὸ λέπος· φλοῖσβος, ὁ λεπτὸς ἦχος τοῦ κύματος. The third definition reflects an old doctrine that βρόμος is used κυρίως of fire, based on Homeric usage and stated dozens of times in learned sources. This pairing of the nouns ἀντώθησις and ἀντίκρουσις does not occur in current TLG texts, but once again Pr and Y² show a special affinity to the notes of the Miscellany in having the same phrase ἐξ ἀντωθήσεως καὶ ἀντικρούσεως in a scholion on *Hec.* 116, though in describing breakers themselves rather than their roar.

καλῶς εἶπεν ἔριδος κλύδων, ὅτι καὶ ἡ ἔρις ἐξ ἀντωθήσεως καὶ ἐναντιώσεως ἀμφοτέρων τῶν μερῶν γίνεται, ὡς καὶ ὁ κλύδων ἐξ ἀντωθήσεως καὶ ἀντικρούσεως τῶν κυμάτων εἴωθε γίνεσθαι.

The poet used the phrase "breaking wave of strife" well (correctly, justifiably), because strife too comes about through the counter-thrust and opposition of both the parties, just as also a breaker usually comes about from the counter-thrust and crashing together of the waves.

30. *Hec.* 549 δέρην

¹δέρις ὁ τράχηλος ἀπὸ τοῦ δέρω τὸ ἐκδέρω· ²οἱ γὰρ παλαιοὶ τὰ τῶν προβάτων δέρματα ἐκ τοῦ τραχήλου ἐξέ(ρ)ρησσον.

SbS; 2 τὰ τῶν προβάτων δέρματα] τὰ πρόβατα S

Deris is the throat/neck, derived from *derō* meaning flay a hide. For the ancients used to strip off the hides of sheep from the neck.

This etymology is not innovative, but depends on Pollux 2.235 ἀπὸ δὲ τοῦ δέρματος ὀνόματα δορά, δέρις, δέρη καὶ δειρὰ διὰ τὸ ἐκεῖθεν τὰ ζῷα γυμνοῦσθαι τῆς δορᾶς (cf. *Et. Magn.* s.v. δέρρις: παρὰ τὸ δέρω, δέρις· καὶ πλεονασμῷ τοῦ ρ, δέρρις). Although Pollux supplied the detail about skinning of animals, our commentator has expressed it in terms of a custom of the ancients, and uses a juncture, ἐκρήγνυμι δέρμα, that is very rare, with only one other instance in TLG texts, Paulus, *Epit. med.* 6.52.3 (on the recommended thickness of the thread used for sutures: if it is too thick, the suture will burst the skin).

31. *Hec.* 572 πόνον

¹πόνος λέγεται καὶ ὁ κόπος καὶ ἡ θλίψις. ²λέγεται δὲ καὶ ἡ ἐνέργεια, ὡς καὶ ἐνταῦθα οὐδεὶς εἶχε τὸν αὐτὸν πόνον ἤτοι τὴν αὐτὴν ἐνέργειαν.

SbS; 2 αὐτὴν om. S

Ponos (toil) is used in the sense both of fatigue and of affliction. And it also is used to mean activity, as also here "no one had the same *ponos*," that is, the same activity.

I have not found a close parallel, but ἐνέργεια appears as a gloss on πόνον in PrV³ and Moschopulus uses ἐργασίαν, and for the doctrine of the second sentence compare the longer phrase that Moschopulus adds here: πόνος ἡ ὀδύνη καὶ ἀπὸ τούτου ἡ ἐργασία.

32. *Hec.* 334 αἰθέρα

¹ἄλλο αἰθὴρ καὶ ἄλλο ἀήρ· ²ἔστι δὲ ὁ αἰθὴρ ὑπεράνω τοῦ ἀέρος, ὁ αἰθὴρ δέ ἐστι θερμὸς καὶ ξηρός, ὁ δὲ ἀὴρ φύσει ψυχρὸς καὶ ὑγρός· ³μιγομένου γοῦν τοῦ

τοῦ ἀέρος ψυχροῦ τῷ τοῦ αἰθέρος θερμῷ καὶ τοῦ ὑγροῦ τῷ ξηρῷ γίνεται τὸ τοῦ καιροῦ κατάστημα εὔκραες. ⁴διὰ τοῦτο γοῦν γινομένων ὑπὸ τῆς γῆς ἀναθυμιάσεων ⟨ ... ⟩.

SbS; 3 ξηρῷ om., s.l. add. ξυρῷ S | 3-4 SSb have colon after κατάστημα, Sb also has punct. after εὔκραες | 4 γινομένων repeated after ὑπὸ τῆς γῆς S

Aithēr is one thing and aēr is another. The aithēr is above the aēr, and the aithēr is warm and dry, but the aēr is by nature cold and moist. At any rate, when the cold of the aēr is mixed with the warm of the aithēr, and the moist with the dry, the condition of the season turns out to be temperate. At least, for this reason when the rising vapors from under the earth occur ... [left incomplete].

In the sequence of the Miscellany this occurs at the very end, after the note on 572, but line 334 is the only place where αἰθήρ is used in this play, and ἀήρ does not occur at all. There is some similarity to a note on Opp. *Hal.* 1.418 recorded in Vári 1909: 24: ὁ αἰθὴρ ξηρὸς καὶ θερμός· ὁ ἀὴρ θερμὸς καὶ ὑγρός· τὸ ὕδωρ ὑγρὸν καὶ ψυχρόν· ἡ δὲ γῆ ψυχρὰ καὶ ξηρά. The juncture εὔκραες κατάστημα is not attested in current TLG texts. But Tzetzes in his *Allegories of the Iliad* does use similar words in close proximity. In *Allegories*, Proleg. 280 and 324, he associates Aphrodite with εὐκρασία, as the force that provides the needed proportion of mixture between Athena allegorized as ἀήρ (272) and Hera allegorized as τὸ λεπτότερον κατάστημα αἰθέρος (272), without which there is confusion and disturbance of the cosmos; at 23.46 he refers to Aphrodite as τὸ κατάστημα τὸ εὔκρατον.

If we look back over these 32 items, we find the distribution of types of lessons offered as follows:

διαφέρει-notes or equivalent distinctions between similar words (11 times, 3 times with διαφέρει): items 2, 4, 7, 8, 10, 12, 19, 21, 23, 29, 32

etymologies (10 times): items 1, 2, 3, 5, 6, 13, 16, 27, 28, 30

σημαίνει-notes or equivalent comparison of different possible meanings of one word (6 times, 3 times with σημαίνει): items 5, 11, 17, 18, 24, 31

grammatical remarks about spelling, accentuation, case, tense, or the like (6 times): items 14, 15, 18, 20, 22, 26

question-and-answer, explaining the appropriateness of the poet's phraseology (2 times): items 9, 22 (the latter with καλῶς εἶπε)

Item 25 on the threefold division of the earth is the only one that does not fit in any of these categories (but it may have been meant to remark on the distinction between Europe and Asia). It is thus easy to see that these notes belong to the overall genre of teachers' scholia.

If we consider the affinities of explanation and of verbal usage, we find the following connections, many pointing to the 12th century, although many explanations follow traditional methods that could go back earlier, even much earlier, in the teaching tradition.

Sch. Opp. Hal. (7 times): items 1, 2, 3, 5, 18, 26, 32

Tzetzes (5 times): items 5, 7, 9, 14, 32

Eustathius (7 times): items 5, 6, 14, 18, 20, 27, 28

tradition of *Etymologica* and lexica (8 times): items 1, 5, 6, 7, 8, 11, 18, 30

Sch. rec. Aesch. (2 times): items 11, 17

rhetorical source (2 times): items 4, 20

In addition, apart from the presence of some items (or extremely similar items) in PrSaY²V³, which occurs 21 times (items 1–3, 5, 8, 10–15, 17–25, 27), we can also see other evidence that a few notes or the doctrine contained in them may have been known to the circle of Planudes and Moschopulus or to the circle of Thomas and Triclinius or to Gu: items 4, 9, 18, 24, 31. Some of these could be coincidental similarity, and the most striking instance is the Planudean-Moschopulean note referring to the syllogism of how earth causes dreams, which appears in item 9.

As mentioned at the outset, the Tzetzean text entitled ἐξήγησις found in S in proximity to the Miscellany raises the question whether the Miscellany is also connected to Tzetzes. But there are more affinities to other sources, including Eustathius, and the connections to Tzetzes are plausibly interpreted as being reflections of knowledge of Tzetzes' oral teaching and/or writings rather than signs he compiled all or any large part of this group of notes. Moreover, the claim about dreams and food in item 9 appears to be less accurate and "scientific" than we might expect from Tzetzes based on his use of the idea in the letter quoted. We lack any revealing third-person claims that Tzetzes says such-and-such or other indications of the cantankerousness, pretended self-abasement, and criticism of others considered a hallmark of his personality. Even so, the 12th century seems a plausible context because of parallels with Eustathius and Tzetzes and with the A-commentary on Aeschylus and because of some verbal usages that seem firmly middle Byzantine since they are attested in authors from the 12th century onward. Even if the notes remain anonymous, they have something to tell us about teaching Euripides (or rather teaching with Euripides) in Byzantium.

3. THE TIP OF THE ICEBERG? A VOCABULARY LIST BASED ON *HECUBA* IN BARBERINIANUS GRAECUS 4

In medieval manuscripts blank folios or partial folios that occur between different works are sometimes filled, by the original scribe or a later one, with miscellaneous extracts or grammatical observations, including lexical observations. For instance, in R, the first section of the codex contains scholia only on *Hecuba* 1–981, 1076, 1200, 1213 and ends on the middle of folio 10v. In the blank space a later hand, probably one that also added some of the glosses on the triad plays later in the manuscript, has written a short narrative probably inspired by the mention of Orion in *Hec.* 1102, containing an implicit etymology of the name from his exile.[80]

> Οἰνοπίων [οἰνωπίων R²] ἐτύφλωσεν Ὠρίωνα καὶ <u>ἐκ τῶν ὁρίων</u> αὐτοῦ αὐτὸν <u>ἐξώρισεν</u> ὅτι τὴν θυγατέρα αὐτοῦ ἔφθειρε. καὶ(?)[81] Ὠρίων ἀπελθὼν εἰς Λῆμνον καὶ παρ' Ἡφαίστου ἵππον λαβὼν ᾧ ὀχούμενος ἤχθη εἰς τὰς Ἡλίου ἀνατολὰς καὶ τὸ τῶν ὀφθαλμῶν ἀνεκτήσατο φῶς.
>
> Oenopion blinded Orion and exiled him from his territory because he raped his daughter. And Orion, having gone off to Lemnus and obtained a horse from Hephaestus, riding on which, he was carried to the risings of the Sun and he regained the light of his eyes.[82]

Later, when the section containing the continous block of scholia on *Orestes* ends only one-third down the page on folio 101v (with τέλος τοῦ ὀρέστου and an ornamented stroke to fill the line), the main scribe of R has filled the rest of the page and also 102r with miscellaneous excerpts, before beginning the *Phoenissae* section with the argumenta on 102v. In this case the selections are quite heterogeneous, and only the first has a tangential relevance to the Euripidean triad:

1. (a corrupted extract from *Et. Symeonis* s.v. δρᾶμα)[83]

> δρᾶμα τὸ πρᾶγμα· λέγεται δὲ δράμα [corrected from or to δράμα] καὶ τὸ τῶν θεατρικῶν μιμήλως [sic] γινόμενον, ὡς ἐν ὑποκρίσει δῆθεν τὸ [s.l. τὰ] ἐκ συσκευῆς καὶ κακουργίας δρώμενον [s.l. δρώμενα].

---

[80] I owe this observation to F. Pontani.

[81] Little is left of this word, but the traces seem to be part of the vertical of kappa and a grave accent and the size of the space available suits the size of the καί-abbreviation as seen in adjacent lines.

[82] The translation assumes anacoluthon; this could be avoided by taking καὶ τὸ ὀφθ. ἀνεκτ. φῶς as the main clause with adverbial καί, but "he even regained" seems clumsy to me, and if one insists on removing anacoluthon I would prefer to delete the last καί. This narrative is unique in saying Orion got a horse to ride to the east. This is probably a rationalized version, since the other sources say Orion (a giant) got someone to carry on his shoulder and guide him as he apparently made his way east on foot: ps.-Apollodorus 1.27, Lucian, *de domo* 28 with Sch. Luc. on this passage; Sch. Nic. *Ther.* 15a.

[83] *Et. Symeonis* δ 348 Baldi: ποίημα, πρᾶγμα· παρὰ τὸ δρῶ, τὸ ἐνεργῶ, ἀφ' οὗ καὶ δρᾶσαι καὶ πρᾶξαι, ὁ παθητικὸς παρακείμενος δέδραμαι, καὶ ἐξ αὐτοῦ δρᾶμα. λέγεται δὲ δράματα τὰ ὑπὸ τῶν θεατρικῶν μιμήλως γινόμενα, ὡς ἐν ὑποκρίσει καὶ τὰ ἐκ συσκευῆς καὶ κακουργίας δρώμενα κατά τινος ὑπό τινων, δράματα.

Drama the action: And drama is also used for the business of theatrical performers occurring with mimetic representation, as that which is done through intrigue and knavery (is said to be done) in (insincere) pretence.

2. (a moralizing narrative about Daedalus and Icarus)[84]

ἦν ἄρα καὶ Δαίδαλον οὐκ εἰς καλὸν τῆς τέχνης ἀπόνασθαι. καὶ πᾶς ὁ θέλων γνῶναι τὰ κατ' αὐτὸν τὸ τοῦ παιδὸς Ἰκάρου πάθος ἀ⟨να⟩λογίζου μοι. οἷς γὰρ οὐ μετρίως πολλάκις τὴν τῶν Κρητῶν ἐλυμαίνετο Δαίδαλος τοῖς οἰκείοις ἀθέσμοις μηχανουργήμασιν εἰς ὀργὴν ἐκμαίνει τὸν Μίνωα. καὶ ὃς ἐζήτει τοῦτον τῆς [τοῦ R] κακοτέχνου τέχνης ἀμύνασθαι. μανθάνει τοίνυν οὗτος τὴν βασιλέως ὀργὴν καὶ πῶς ἂν ἐκφύγῃ ταύτην ζητεῖ. πρὸς [app. πρὴν R] τὴν τέχνην οὐκοῦν καὶ πάλιν ἀφορᾷ τὴν αὐτοῦ, κἀκεῖθεν ἐθέλει λαβεῖν τὴν βοήθειαν. ἔνθεν τοι κηροπλάστους ἐπιτεχνάζεται πτέρυγας αὑτῷ [αὐτῷ R] τε καὶ Ἰκάρῳ τῷ ἐξ αὐτοῦ, καὶ διαπόντιον πειρῶνται τὴν πτῆσιν ποιήσασθαι. ἀλλ' οὗτος μὲν ἅτε [ἄτε R] πανουργότατος ὢν οὐκολίγα τε τῇ τέχνῃ καὶ τῷ χρόνῳ πρὸς δεινότητα(?) βοηθούμενος, μικροῦ καὶ αὐτοῦ τοῦ ὕδατος ψαύων ἐφίπτατο. Ἴκαρος δὲ νεώτερόν τι φρονῶν πρὸς τὴν τῶν ἀετῶν ἄντικρυς ἐρίζειν πτῆσιν ἐβούλετο· τοῖς ὠκυπτέροις [a.c. -ην] ἰσοφαρίζειν ἐπόθει. καὶ μέχρι αἰθέρος πτερίσσεσθαι ἤθελεν. ὑπερεφρόνει τὸν Ἥλιον ἀεροβατῶν, οἷς οὐκ ἔλαβε κατὰ νοῦν τὸ τῶν πτερύγων ἐπείσακτον, ἀλλ' ἔσχε λήθην ὡς κηρῷ τὰ πτίλα συνήρμοστο καὶ ὡς οὐδόλως φέρει κηρὸς τὴν ἐξ Ἡλίου ἐκπύρωσιν, ἀλλὰ χαυνοῦται καὶ τὸ σκληρὸν ἀποτίθησιν. ἀποδι{α}σκεύει[85] τοίνυν τὰς ἀκτῖνας διακαεῖς ὁ Ἥλιος πρὸς αὐτόν. ἐκτήκει τὸν κηρόν. ἐπεισάκτους ἀπελέγχει τὰς πτέρυγας, καὶ διασκίδναται τὰ πτίλα, καὶ καταπίπτει πρὸς τὸ πέλαγος Ἴκαρος, τῶν κηροπλάστων ἐκείνων ὠκυπτέρων διαρρυέντων αὐτῷ. καὶ δίδωσιν ἐξ αὐτοῦ τὸ πέλαγος ἐκεῖνο κατονομάζεσθαι. καὶ κἂν ἀχανεῖ πελάγει αὐτὸς κατεβυθίσθη πεσών, ὅμως ὁ τοσοῦτος χρόνος οὐκ ἔσχε λήθης ἐναποκρύψαι βυθῷ τὸ πάθος τὸ κατ' αὐτόν.

It was, after all, possible even for Daedalus to get no good benefit from his skill. Anyone who wants to learn his story, consider, please, the experience of his son Icarus. For through the actions in which he often excessively outraged the land of the Cretans by his own lawless devisings, Daedalus maddens Minos to anger. And he sought to take vengeance on him for his evil-contriving skill. Now then, Daedulus learns of the king's anger and seeks a way to escape it. Therefore once again he looks to his own skill, and from that he wishes to obtain rescue. Consequently, he contrives wings of molded wax for himself and Icarus, his offspring, and they try to make their winged journey across the sea. But because he was so cunning and was helped toward extreme expertise in no small measure by his skill and his age,

---

[84] This does not match any text currently in TLG.

[85] I owe this correction to F. Pontani; ἀποδισκεύω is used by Byzantine writers with objects like φῶς, πῦρ, and ἀκτῖνας, and the juncture ἀκτῖνας διαδισκεύειν appears in Eustathius *in Il.* 2.190 (I.290, 38–39), but also in others.

Daedalus flew almost touching the water itself. Icarus, on the other hand, with his youthful rashness, wanted no less than to compete with the flying of eagles: he longed to match himself with the swift-winged. Journeying through the sky, he thought himself greater than Helios, in which he did not remember the artificial nature of his wings, but he forgot that the feathers were glued together with wax and that wax by no means endures the fiery heating that comes from Helios, but wax is weakened and loses its hardness. So then, Helios hurls against him his rays burning with fire. He melts the wax. He fully exposes the wings as artificial, the feathers are scattered, and Icarus falls to the sea, since those wax-molded swift-flying wings had dissolved for him. And he (Helios) grants that that sea be named for him. And even though Icarus himself fell and was sunk in the depths of the yawning sea, nevertheless the so great passage of time has not been able to conceal in the depths of oblivion what happened to him.

3. (a line of Aristophanes, *Nubes*)

ἐκ τοῦ Ἀριστοφάνους [*Nub.* 37]: δάκνει μέ τις δήμαρχος ἐκ τῶν στρωμάτων.

From Aristophanes: Some deme-boss in the bedding is biting me.

4. (philosophical/doctrinal extract)[86]

τὸ μὲν γὰρ ἄλλος καὶ ἄλλος ἐπὶ τῶν προσώπων λέγεται, τὸ δὲ ἄλλο{ς} καὶ ἄλλο ἐπὶ τῶν φύσεων. οἷον ἵνα σαφέστερον τὸ ὄνομα ἐκθήσομαι· Πέτρος καὶ Παῦλος· ἄλλος μὲν γὰρ καὶ ἄλλος· δύο γὰρ πρόσωπα εἰσίν. οὐκ ἄλλο γὰρ καὶ ἄλλο· μία γὰρ φύσις αὐτῶν ὁ ἄνθρωπος. οὕτως καὶ ἐπὶ πατρὸς καὶ υἱοῦ δογματιστέον· ἄλλος μὲν γὰρ καὶ ἄλλος· δύο γὰρ πρόσωπα, οὐκ ἄλλο δὲ καὶ ἄλλο· μία φύσις ἡ θεότης.

The expressesion "*allos* and *allos*" (one and another) is used of individual persons, but "*allo* and *allo*" (one thing and another thing) is used of natures. I mean, so that I may explain the term more clearly: Peter and Paul. For (they are) "*allos* and *allos*": for they are two persons. For they are not "*allo* and *allo*": for they have a single nature, "man." Thus too one must lay down the doctrine applying to Father and Son. For (they are) "*allos* and *allos*": for (they are) two persons, but not "*allo* and *allo*": their single nature is divinity.

5. (definition of Latin-derived terms)[87]

κουστωδία τὸ πλῆθος τῶν στρατιωτῶν, κοῦστος γὰρ λέγεται ὁ φύλαξ.

Koustōdia is the large group of soldiers, for a guard is called *koustos*.

---

[86] There is no close parallel in TLG, but the idea expressed is commonplace in discussions of the unity of the Trinity. The use of Peter and Paul is paralleled in Gregor. Nyss. *ad Graecos ex communibus notionibus* 3:1.30–32 (Mueller) in a discussion of their common οὐσία as ἄνθρωπος vs. their differences in accidental qualities of each πρόσωπον.

[87] Cf. *Συναγωγὴ λέξ. χρησ.* κ 448 κοῦστος· φύλαξ; κ 449 κουστωδία· τὸ δεσμωτήριον, ἢ τὸ τῷ δεσμωτηρίῳ ἐπικείμενον στράτευμα, σύστημα, στρατιωτικὸν στῖφος. (Both also in Photius and Suda.)

6. (etymology from *Et. Gud.* 471, 23 Sturz)

ποδάγρα διὰ τὴν πολλὴν ἀγριότητα.

Podagra (gout) (is so named) because of the great fierceness (of the pain).

7. (well-known statement of Hippocrates on seven ages of man)[88]

ἰστέον ὡς κατ' Ἱπποκράτη τοῦ ἀνθρώπου ἑπτὰ εἰσὶν ὧραι, ἃς ἡλικίας καλοῦσιν.

Note that according to Hippocrates there are seven ages of man, which we call age-brackets (*hēlikiai*).

8. (calculation of timing of Easter)[89]

χρὴ ἐπιτηρεῖν τῷ Ὀκτωβρίῳ μηνὶ πότε ἐστὶν ὁ ιδ τῆς σελήνης καὶ ἐξ ἐκείνης τῆς ἡμέρας τοῦ Ὀκτωβρίου ἀριθμεῖν ἡμέρας ἑκατὸν ὀγδοήκοντα β καὶ ὅπου ἂν φθάσῃς ἐν αὐτῇ τῇ ἡμέρᾳ ἐστι τὸ ἅγιον πάσχα.

One must watch during the month of October for when it is the 14th day of the moon's cycle, and from that day of October count 182 days, and wherever you come to, holy Easter/Passover is on that very day.

9. (verbal distinction from Ammonius, *in Porphyrii isagogen*, CAG 4:3.67, 20–21)

μειονέκτης μὲν ἐστιν ὁ ἧττον τοῦ δέοντος ἑαυτῷ τί περιποιῶν, πλεονέκτης δὲ ὁ πλέον τοῦ δέοντος.

A "less-haver" (*meionektēs*) is the man who claims something less for himself than what it due, the "more-haver" (*pleonektēs*) the one who claims more than is due.

10. (verbal distinction from Ammonius, *in Porphyrii isagogen*, CAG 4:3.67, 23–68, 1)

ἠλίθιος μέν ἐστιν ὁ ἧττον κινούμενος, ἀκόλαστος δὲ ὁ μᾶλλον καὶ ἀτάκτως κινούμενος.

The term *ēlithios* ("foolish") applies to the one who is less agitated, but *akolastos* ("undisciplined, licentious") to the one who is agitated more and in a disorderly way.

---

[88] Hippocrates, *de septimanis* 5 οὕτω δὲ καὶ ἐπ' ἀνθρώπου φύσιος ἑπτὰ ὧραι εἰσὶν ἃς ἡλικίας καλέομεν· παιδίον· παῖς· μειράκιον· νεηνίσκος· ἀνὴρ· πρεσβύτης· γέρων. This is cited by Philo Judaeus, Iamblichus, and Christian writers, and in various scholia, sometimes with καλοῦσιν, sometimes with καλέομεν/καλοῦμεν.

[89] I am not aware of any other example of calculating Easter/Passover from the full moon after the autumnal equinox (the full moon in October) rather than from the full moon after the vernal equinox.

Manuscript catalogues often do not give much detail about such filler material, so it may be only by accident that one discovers the content and rationale of such excerpts, which are often relevant to teaching or as evidence of the circulation of particular texts or bits of knowledge. While inspecting Vaticanus Barberinianus graecus 4 (siglum gB for Euripides),[90] an early 14th-century codex containing, among other texts, gnomologies from the works of the three tragedians and of Aristophanes as well as other ancient poets, I came upon a short list of ten lexicographic glosses of the same types as seen in the Miscellany discussed in the previous section of this chapter. These glosses matched or treated the same topic as teachers' scholia I had collated in *Hecuba* 1–177 and were mostly in the order of appearance in that text. Thus it became clear that this list was in fact related to the reading of or teaching of the opening of Euripides' play, even though there is no heading mentioning Euripides or *Hecuba*. Already in the papyri we find vocabulary lists or lexicographical works based on Homer with the entries in the order in which the words occur in the epics, and such an ordering characterizes the main version of the *Epimerismi Homerici*, the other being an alphabetic reordering of the lemmata.[91] Lists of Homeric words are easily recognized because of the nature of Homeric *Kunstsprache*. But a list based on Euripides, much of whose vocabulary is less markedly poetic, would not announce itself so openly. Thus the previous skeletal descriptions of this list give no indication of that connection and do not even quote enough to make one suspect it.[92]

The Euripidean gnomology in gB is divided into two parts: (1) excerpts from the select plays outside the triad on folios 9v–18r; (2) excerpts from the triad plays on folios 26r32v. Folios 1r–9r contain five short treatises, the last of which, περὶ τῶν ἐν τῷ ἡρωικῷ μέτρῳ εὑρεθεισῶν κοινῶν συλλαβῶν, ends with its final line at the top of 9r, leaving an ample space on this page for some kind of filler.[93] The filler here is by the main scribe of the manuscript. Each item has a rubricated initial and ends with the usual closing punctuation :~. The lines of *Hecuba* to which the notes are related are 16, 24, 21–22, 59, 90, 109, 144, 142, 132, 177, and it is possible to speculate that where the notes are slightly out of order, they were copied from a codex in which lines 21–24 at least fell on the

---

[90] Excellent recent images of this manuscript are online at digi.vatlib.it.
[91] On glossaries see for example those on the *Odyssey* discussed by Pontani 2011: 117–126, with further references. For the *Epimerismi Homerici* see Dyck 1983–1995.
[92] Capocci 1958: 3 states "Sequuntur (f. 9) glossae quaedam lexicographicae, ut videtur. Inc. Τὸ κεῖσθαι γενικόν ἐστιν ὄνομα. καὶ δηλοῖ (cfr. Schoell-Studemund, I, p. 183 in adn.), des. καὶ ἀεὶ ἀκμάζον, ταῖς συμφοραῖς:~." The reference is to a note in Schoell and Studemund 1886: 1:182–183 ending "Deinceps sequitur in B: τὸ κεῖσθαι γενικόν ἐστιν ὄνομα etc."
[93] This term may be misleading, however, since it is possible that the scribe is copying miscellaneous grammatical and metrical items that were already collected in a source manuscript along with the gnomological anthologies that follow.

same page, and likewise 132–144. As with the Miscellany, the disorder is easier to understand if these were additional teachers' notes crowded in available spaces around pre-existing blocks of text and scholia. It is also noteworthy that in the gB version of items 2 and 3 the portion that refers to the actual text is eliminated, making the note more general and portable; and the same generality is seen in gB's version of item 1 compared to the very similar scholion in SSa.[94] We may now present the items with some comment on their affinities. Where gB gives a partial version, I have presented the fuller version and indicated what gB omits.

1. *Hec.* 16 ἔκειθ'

   τὸ κεῖσθαι γενικόν ἐστιν ὄνομα καὶ δηλοῖ τρία· τὸ ἀνίστασθαι, τὸ καθῆσθαι, καὶ τὸ ἀνακεῖσθαι.

   Keisthai ("to lie") is a general term and means three things: to stand upright, to sit, and to be placed upright.

Compare the closely similar but more clearly expressed Sch. SSa Hec. 16 τὸ κεῖσθαι σημαίνει τρία, τὸ καθέζεσθαι, τὸ ἵστασθαι, καὶ αὐτὸ τὸ κεῖσθαι {ἐνταῦθα}. ἐνταῦθα δὲ τὸ ἔκειτο ἀντὶ τοῦ ἵστατο δεῖ νοεῖν. ("*Keisthai* has three meanings: to sit, to be standing, and to lie itself. And here one must understand *ekeito* to be used for "it was standing.") Several commentators on Aristotle's *Categories* remark on the three species of κεῖσθαι, e.g., Ammonius, *In Arist. Cat.* 93, 1 κεῖσθαι δέ ἐστιν ἡ τοιάδε τοῦ σώματος θέσις, τούτου δὲ εἴδη τρία, ἀνακεῖσθαι καθῆσθαι ἑστάναι, whence similar statements are to be found in Phot. *Amph. epist.* 146, 12–13, Psellus, *Opuscula logica etc.* 50, 112–115.

2. *Hec.* 24

   [1]ἀντινομία λέγεται ὅταν δύο νόμοι ἐναντιοῦνται ἑαυτοῖς ἐν ὑποθέσει καὶ θάτερος τὴν νικῶσαν σπεύδει λαβεῖν, ὅπερ κἀνταῦθα. [2]νόμος γὰρ ἦν τὸν προσφυγόντα τῷ βωμῷ σώζεσθαι. [3]ἕτερος δὲ νόμος μὴ παραβαίνειν τοὺς ὅρκους. [4]προσέδυ Πρίαμος τῷ θεοδμήτῳ ναῷ· [5]ὁμόσαντες Ἕλληνες εἰ πορθήσειαν Τροίαν μὴ φείσασθαι μηδ' ἐμβρύου ἄρρενος· [6]ἀνηρέθη οὖν Πρίαμος ὑπὸ Νεοπτολέμου ἐντὸς βωμοῦ. [7]καί ἐστι τοῦτο ἀντινομία.

   Y², 1–2 only SSa, 1 only gB (om. ὅπερ κἀνταῦθα)

   Antinomia is spoken of when two laws/rules are opposed to each other in their suggestion, and one of the two seeks eagerly to take the winning position [*the rest*

---

[94] Of course, the process could also work in the opposite direction: a general lexical observation could be tied to a particular passage by adding ὡς ἐνταῦθα or the like to show which of the several meanings is used in the text currently being studied. So a lexical nugget could pass back and forth between list and commentary, just as glosses could pass between compiled lexicographic works and corpora of scholia on an author.

added in witnesses other than gB], exactly as here. For there was a rule that one who had fled to an altar be saved. A second rule was not to contravene oaths. Priam entered the god-established shrine. The Greeks, having sworn an oath that if they should sack Troy they would not spare any male, even one in the womb. So then, Priam was killed by Neoptolemus within the shrine. And this is a case of *antinomia*.

Antinomia is referred to hundreds of times in the traditon of Hermogenes and his commentators, but never in these terms. The use of ναός and βωμός here points to their equivalence for the writer, which suggests why some were eager to explain the difference between the terms in classical Greek (see item 7 below).

3. *Hec.* 21–22 Ἕκτορὸς ἀπόλλυται / ψυχὴ

> ¹διττή ἐστιν ἡ ἀπώλεια, ἡ μὲν παντελὴς διὰ πυρὸς ἀφανισμός, ὡς ἐπὶ ξύλου καὶ τῶν ἄλλων, ²ἡ δὲ ἀπὸ τόπου εἰς τόπον μετάβασις, οἷον ἀπώλεσέ τις χρυσὸν, ³οὐ κατὰ τὴν οὐσίαν ἀλλοιωθέντα, καὶ ἀπολεσθέντος τοῦ χρυσοῦ, ⁴ἀλλ᾽ ἀπὸ τῶν χειρῶν τοῦ ἀπολέσαντος μεταπεσόντα εἰς ἄλλου χεῖρα. ⁵τοιαύτη καὶ ἡ τῆς ψυχῆς τοῦ Ἕκτορος ἀπώλεια, ἤγουν ἀπὸ τοῦ ὅλου σώματος μερισμὸς καὶ ἀφανισμὸς ψυχικός.

Sa, 1–4 only gB; 1 ἀφανισμοῦ gBSa | 2 τίς gB | 3 ἀπωλεσθέντα gBSa | 4 ἀπωλέσαντος gBSa

Destruction (*apōleia*) is twofold, one being complete disappearance by fire, as is the case of wood and the other things, the other a movement from place to place: for instance, suppose someone lost (*apōlese*) gold, it not being altered in respect to its essence, the gold having been destroyed, but having been transferred from the hands of the man who lost it to the hand of another. [*added in source other than gB*] Such too is the destruction of the soul of Hector, that is to say, separation from the whole body and disappearance of the soul.

In Sa this note has been displaced so that it appears between Sch. Hec. 156 and 160, but the wording of sentence 5 (omitted by gB) points exactly to the correct lemma. There is no close parallel. In the first sentence, transmitted ἀφανισμοῦ must be corrected because διὰ must govern πυρός (the phrase (ὁ) διὰ πυρὸς ἀφανισμός is found several times from Plutarch onward), and this matches the two later nominatives, μετάβασις in the parallel clause and ἀφανισμὸς ψυχικός at the end in the longer version. In the third sentence, one could treat τοῦ χρυσοῦ as an intrusion to be deleted, but its presence is hard to explain, so I have preferred to emend the participle before it to genitive and punctuate to create a parenthetic addition.

4. *Hec.* 59 ἄγετ᾽

> τὸ ἄγω ἐπὶ ἐμψύχου λέγεται, τὸ δὲ φέρω ἐπὶ ἀψύχου.
> ἀψύχου ... ἐμψύχου gB

agō is used of a living object, but *pherō* of an inanimate one.

With correction of the transposition error, this is like *Et. Gen.*, Choeroboscus, etc., as cited for Miscellany, item 7, in section 2 above. Compare that item (in SbS) and also Sch. V³ Hec. 59 ση(μείωσαι) ὅτι τὸ ἄγω / [ἐπ]ὶ ἐμψύχου λέγεται, τὸ δὲ φέρω ἐπὶ ἀψύχου.

5. *Hec.* 90 χαλᾷ

¹ὁπλὴ χηλὴ καὶ ὄνυξ διαφέρει. ²ὁπλὴ μὲν γὰρ ἡ τῶν ἵππων καὶ τῶν λοιπῶν ζώων τῶν ἐχόντων ἄτμητον τὸν ὄνυχα. ³χηλὴ δὲ ἡ τῶν χοίρων τῶν ἐχόντων μεμερισμένον τὸν ὄνυχα. ⁴ὄνυξ δὲ ἡ τῶν ἀνθρώπων καὶ τῶν λοιπῶν τῶν ἐχόντων μεμερισμένους τοὺς ὄνυχας. ⁵οἷον λύκων κυνῶν καὶ λοιπῶν.

SaY², gB; 1 καὶ om. Y², gB | διαφέρει om. Y² | 2 γὰρ om. Y² | ἵππων gB, ἀλόγων SaY² | 2-3 ἄτμητον ... ἐχόντων om. Y² (because of the omission, μὴ has been added later above μεμερισμένην in a very faint ink) | 2 τὸν om. gB | 3 ἡ om. Sa | μεμερισμένην τὴν ὄνυχα Y², gB | 4 ἡ om. SaY² | after λοιπῶν add. ζώων Y² | 5 οἷον and καὶ λοιπῶν om. Y²

Hoplē, *chēlē*, and *onux* differ. For *hoplē* is the hoof/nail of horses and the other creatures having their nail undivided; *chēlē* is that of swine who have their hoof/nail divided (in two); *onux* is that of human beings and the other animals that have their (multiple) nails divided. For instance, of wolves, dogs, and others.

Careful scholarship recognized that these words were sometimes interchangeable, but the pressure of the etymologizing system led to simplifications like this διαφέρει-note. Cf. Apoll. Soph. *Lex. Hom.* 114, 21 μώνυχας μονώνυχας, ἐπεὶ ἡ ὁπλὴ τοῦ ἵππου ὥσπερ ὄνυξ ἐστίν· οἱ γὰρ βόες χηλὰς ἔχουσιν; Hesych. o 1030 ὁπλή· ὄνυξ κτήνους. ἄλλοι ἐπὶ ποδῶν ἀνθρώπου. ἢ χηλή; Photius o 404 ὁπλαί· αἱ πυξίδες· τῶν ἵππων οἱ ὄνυχες; *Suda* o 464 ὁπλή· ὁ κυκλοειδὴς ποῦς τῶν κτηνῶν, οἷον βοῶν, προβάτων καὶ τῶν λοιπῶν τῶν ἐχόντων μικροὺς ὄνυχας ἐν τοῖς τῶν ποδῶν ὀπισθίοις. κυρίως δὲ ἐπὶ ἵππων. Ἀριστοφάνης δὲ ἐπὶ τῶν χοίρων ὁπλὴν εἴρηκε. καὶ Σιμωνίδης· ὁπλὰς ἐκίνει τῶν ὀπισθίων ποδῶν. καὶ Ἡσίοδος ἐπὶ βοῶν ὁπλάς. καὶ τὸ ἐναντίον ἐπὶ ἵππου· νύσσοντες χηλῆσιν; *Et. Gud.* 566, 22-25 Sturz χηλὴ δὲ ἐπὶ τῶν διονύχων ζώων, οἷον, διχέλη τις οὖσα, ἀπὸ τοῦ ἐσχίσθαι, ὡς τὸ ὁπλῆ ἡ ἁπλῆ, ἐπὶ ἵππων καὶ ἡμιόνων; cf. Sch. vet. Arist. Ach. 740a (ΕΓ³) τὰς ὁπλὰς τῶν χοιρίων: οὐ μόνον Ἀριστοφάνης ἐπὶ τῶν χοίρων ὁπλὰς εἴρηκεν, ἀλλὰ καὶ Σιμωνίδης ὁμοίως ἐπὶ χοίρου "ὁπλὰς ἐκίνει τῶν ὀπισθίων ποδῶν" καὶ Ἡσίοδος ἐπὶ βοῶν "μήτ' ἄρ' ὑπερβάλλων βοὸς ὁπλήν," καὶ τὸ ἐναντίον ἐπὶ τοῦ ἵππου "νύσσοντες χηλῆσιν"; Sch. Tri. Arist. Ach. 740b (Lh) οὗτος ὁπλὰς ἐπὶ χοίρων εἶπεν, Ἡσίοδος δὲ ἐπὶ βοῶν, "μήτ' ἄρ' ὑπερβάλλων βοὸς ὁπλήν," καὶ τὸ ἐναντίον χηλὴν ἐπὶ ἵππου "νύσσοντες χηλῆσιν." ὁπλαὶ μὲν γὰρ κυρίως ἐπὶ τῶν ὁλοκλήρους ἐχόντων τοὺς ὄνυχας, οἷον ἵππων ὄνων ὀρέων καὶ τῶν τοιούτων, χηλαὶ δὲ ἐπὶ τῶν διῃρημένους, βοῶν φημὶ καὶ αἰγῶν καὶ προβάτων καὶ τῶν τοιούτων. καὶ Λουκιανὸς ἐκφράζων τὸν Πᾶνά φησι "καὶ σκέλη τραγικὰ καὶ δίχηλα καὶ οὐρὰν ὑπὲρ τὰς πυγάς." οὗτοι δὲ ἐναντίως ἐχρήσαντο.

6. *Hec.* 109 τύμβου

¹τύμβος ἡρίον μνῆμα καὶ τάφος διαφέρει. ²τύμβος γάρ ἐστι ἐν ᾧ τὸν θανόντα καίουσιν ὡς ἐκ τοῦ τύφω τὸ καίω. ³ἠρίον δὲ ὁ ἐν τῇ γῇ τάφος ἀπὸ τοῦ ἔρα ἡ γῆ. ⁴μνῆμα δὲ τὸ ἔνδοξον μνήμην ἐμποιοῦν. ⁵τάφος δὲ ὁ διὰ λίθων εὐτελῶν μικρὸν ἐπανεστηκὼς τῆς γῆς.

SaY², gB (9r); 1 τύμβος ... διαφέρει om. Y² | καὶ om. gB | 2 γάρ ἐστιν gB, μέν ἐστι Sa, om. Y² | ὡς gB, γίνεται δὲ Sa, om. Y² | 3 δὲ om. Y² | ἀπὸ τοῦ ἔρα ἡ γῆ om. Sa | 4 δὲ om. Y² | 5 δὲ om. Y² | λίθων] λιτῶν Sa | μικρόν τι ὑπανεστηκὼς Sa

Tumbos, ērion, mnēma, and *taphos* differ. For *tumbos* is that in which they burn the dead person, as derived from *tuphō* meaning burn. *Ērion* is the grave in the earth, derived from *era* meaning earth. *Mnēma* is that which creates glorious memory (*mnēmē*). *Taphos* is the one made of humble stones that rises a little above the earth.

This fourfold distinction is not paralleled in TLG, but some parts of it are. τάφος is a standard gloss for both τύμβος and ἠρίον, and μνῆμα is a gloss for ἠρίον, while the etymologies involving τύφω and ἔρα are attested in (e.g.) *Suda* τ 1158, *Et. Gud.* 248, 52 Sturz. Also partly comparable is Sch. rec. Arist. Plut. 729b (alpha) "τύμβος" ὁ τάφος ὁ ὑπερέχων τῆς γῆς κατὰ κύκλον, ὥσπερ "ἠρίον" τὸ κατὰ γῆς καὶ μὴ ὑπεριστάμενον; (beta) "τύμβος" ὁ τάφος ὁ τῆς γῆς ὑπερέχων ἐν σχήματι ἡμισφαιρίῳ, ὥσπερ καὶ "ἠρίον" τὸ κατὰ γῆν μνημεῖον μὴ ὑπερέχον.

7. *Hec.* 144 ἴθι ναούς, ἴθι πρὸς βωμούς

ναὸς βωμὸς διαφέρει· ναὸς ἐν ᾧ προσεύχονται, βωμὸς ἐν ᾧ θύουσι τοὺς βόας.

Naos and *bōmos* differ.[95] *Naos* is that in which people pray, *bōmos* is that in which they sacrifice cattle (*boes*).

Again Y² offers (above the line) the closest parallel, giving a shorter version with the two items reversed: βωμὸς ἐν ᾧ θύουσι, ναὸς ἐν ᾧ προσεύχονται. The distinction is expressed differently in V with ναὸς λέγεται ἔνθα εἰσὶ τὰ εἴδωλα, βωμὸς δὲ ἔνθα θ[ύου]σιν; in R with βωμὸς λέγεται τὸ θυσιαστήριον, ναὸς δὲ ἡ ἐκκλησία; and in Gu with καθολικώτερον τοῦ βωμοῦ ναός· μέρος γὰρ τοῦ ναοῦ βωμός. θύειν and derivatives are naturally found often in conjunction with βωμός, but the derivation from βοῦς implied in our note seems not be be found elsewhere. A more detailed set of distinctions (with a correct etymological connection of βωμός with βάσις, as in *Suda* β 493) is offered by Tzetzes Sch. Il.

---

[95] One could consider ναὸς βωμοῦ διαφέρει, "*naos* differs in meaning from *bōmos*," but sometimes διαφέρει appears with asyndetic nominatives, a few times with three terms (as διαφέρει ξένος φίλος ἑταῖρος in item 2 of the Miscellany, section 2 above), but for two terms I have found so far Sch. SSa Hec. 126 παρθένος σώφρων διαφέρει.

1.440 (no. 95, on ἐπὶ βωμὸν) διαφέρει ναός ἄδυτον τέμενος καὶ βωμός· ναὸς τὸ ὅλον ἱερόν· ἄδυτον, νῦν τὸ βῆμα, ἔνθα δύνειν καὶ ὑπεισέρχεσθαι οὐκ ἔστι τὸν κοινὸν ὄχλον, ἀλλὰ μόνους τοὺς ἱερεῖς· τέμενος, ἄλσος ἢ προάστειον ἢ κηπίον ἀφιερωθὲν ἢ καὶ στρατιώταις χαρισθὲν ἀποτμηθὲν ὑπὸ δημότου· βωμὸς δέ, βωμίδας ἢ βαθμίδας ἔχουσα λίθους βάσις ὑψηλή, ἢ μονολίθους καὶ αὐτοφυεῖς ἔχουσα τὰς βαθμίδας, ἢ ναστὴ καὶ κτιστὴ σύνθετος, ἐν αἷς πρὶν ὡλοκαύτουν καὶ ἐθυσίαζον .... The distinction was needed because some contemporaries used the two terms as synonyms, as in item 2 of this list.

8. *Hec.* 142 μαστῶν

> μαστὸς τῆς γυναικὸς σ̅ καὶ τ̅ γράφεται, ἀπὸ τοῦ μεμεστωμένος εἶναι γάλακτος· μασθὸς δὲ ὁ τοῦ ἀνδρὸς σ̅ καὶ θ, ἀπὸ τοῦ μὴ ἐσθίεσθαι.
>
> *Mastos* ("breast") of a woman is written with sigma and tau, derived from its being filled full (participle of *mestoō*) with milk. *Masthos*, that of a man, (is spelled with) sigma and theta, derived from not being eaten (*mē esthiesthai*).

Most similar this time is the note in SSa: μαστὸς ὁ τῆς γυναικὸς, παρὰ τὸ μεστὸς εἶναι γάλακτος. μασθὸς δὲ ὁ τοῦ ἀνδρὸς θ, διὰ τὸ μὴ δύνασθαι ἐσθίεσθαι; comparable, but with a less explicit derivation of the second term is Sch. RSa Hec. 424 μαστὸς μετὰ τοῦ σ̅τ̅ ἐπὶ γυναικὸς λέγεται διὰ τὸ μεστὸς εἶναι γάλακτος, μασθὸς δὲ μετὰ τοῦ σ̅θ̅ ἐπὶ ἄρρενος· ὁ γὰρ τοῦ ἄρρενος μαστὸς κενός ἐστι γάλακτος. Different derivations, from θῶ = θηλάζω or from μαδάω, are seen in Sch. Tzetz. Lycophron 1328 μασθὸς ὁ ἀνδρεῖος παρὰ τὸ μὴ θηλάζεσθαι ἢ ἐσθίεσθαι, μαστὸς δὲ ὁ γυναικεῖος παρὰ τὸ μεστὸς εἶναι γάλακτος; *Suda* μ 250 μασθὸς καὶ μαστός: κυρίως ἐπὶ γυναικός, καταχρηστικῶς δὲ καὶ ἐπὶ ἀνδρός. τὸ μὲν μασθὸς ἀπὸ τοῦ θῶ, τὸ θηλάζω· τὸ δὲ μαστὸς διὰ τὸ μεστὸς εἶναι γάλακτος ... ; Eust. *in Il.* 4.123 (I.714, 21ff.) μαζὸς δὲ καὶ ἐπὶ ἀνδρῶν ἰδοὺ κεῖται, ὥστε οὐκ ἐπὶ μόνων λέγεται γυναικῶν. δοκεῖ δὲ γενέσθαι ἐκ τοῦ μαδός κατὰ φανερὰν στοιχειακὴν τοῦ δ καὶ τοῦ ζ συγγένειαν. μαδᾷ γὰρ φύσει ἀναγκαίως ἅπας μαζός, ὁ καὶ μασδὸς Δωρικῶς καὶ μαστὸς διὰ τοῦ τ καὶ μασθὸς δὲ διὰ τοῦ θ λεγόμενος. χρῆσις δὲ τοῦ μαδοῦ, ἐν οἷς Ἡρακλείδης, εἰπὼν ἐκ τοῦ ἔδω τὸ ἔσθω γίνεσθαι Δωρικῶς τροπῇ τοῦ δ εἰς θ ... .

9. *Hec.* 132 κόπις

> κόπις λέγεται ὁ ἡδυλόγος καὶ λάλος, ἐξ οὗ καὶ κοπίδας τὰς τῶν λόγων τέχνας.
>
> gB (9r), partial Y²ᵐᵃʳᵍ; κόπις ... οὗ καὶ om. Y² | κοπίδας *Et. Magn.*, κόπιδας gBY²
>
> *Kopis* is used to describe the one who talks sweetly and is glib; derived from it (we use) *kopides* to refer to the arts/tricks of discourse.

Cf. *Et. Gud.* 337, 56–338, 2 Sturz κόπις, σύντομος, ὀξὺς τῷ λόγῳ, ἢ λάλος, ὅθεν καὶ ὁ δημοκόπος καὶ κόβαλος, καὶ κατεστωμυλημένος, κόβαλοι λέγονται· καὶ τὰς τῶν λόγων τέχνας κοπίδας ἐκάλουν· "μὴ τὸν Πυθαγόραν εὕρομεν ὄντων ἀληθινῶν κοπίδων"· Εὐριπίδης "πρὶν ὁ ποικιλόφρων κόπις ἡδυλόγος δημοχαριστής"; *Et. Magn.* 529, 25–30 κόπις: Εὐριπίδης, "ὁ ποικιλόφρων κόπις ἡδυλόγος δημοχαριστής". σύντομος, ὀξὺς τῷ λόγῳ, ἤγουν λάλος· ἔνθεν καὶ ὁ δημοκόπος καὶ κόβαλος. καὶ τὰς τῶν λόγων τέχνας κοπίδας ἔλεγον.

10. *Hec.* 177 νέον

> τὸ νέον σημαίνει δύο, τὸ πρόσφατον καὶ τὸ νεαρὸν καὶ †ἀναντήρητον† καὶ ἀεὶ ἀκμάζον ταῖς συμφοραῖς.
>
> The term *neon* ("new") has two meanings: that which is fresh and new, and that which is young and new and †undeniable† and always blooming in misfortunes.

The explanation offered in gB has two faults. Not only does ἀναντήρητον (a vulgar medieval spelling of ἀναντίρρητον, "undeniable") give poor sense (the alternative meaning needed is "unwelcome," not "irrefutable"), but the article preceding νεαρὸν suggests that νεαρὸν begins the explanation of the second sense, whereas in fact νεαρός is often paired with πρόσφατος by Greek authors, and they are synonymous glosses in the lexicographic tradition[96] and must have been so intended in the original version of this note. At least part of the truth is evident from the versions of this found in Pr at this line and in Sch. Aesch. Sept. 370g reported from the Aeschylean codices W (early 14th cent.) and Ya (dated 1413):

> τὸ νέον σημαίνει δύο, τό τε πρόσφατον καὶ νεαρὸν καὶ τὸ ἐναντίρρητον καὶ κακὸν καὶ ἀεὶ νεάζον ταῖς συμφοραῖς.
>
> Pr, Aesch. codd. WYa; τὸ νέον om. Ya | ἐναντίον Pr | καὶ κακὸν transp. to follow νεαρὸν Ya | at end add. ὡς Εὐριπίδης "ἰὼ μᾶτερ μᾶτερ τί βοᾷς, τί νέον" κηρύξουσ' ἦλθες WYa

The loss of καὶ κακὸν in gB is presumably related to the false placement of the same words in Ya (transpositions are often related to omission, as they may represent a reinsertion of the lost word(s) in the wrong place). Consideration of *utrum in alterum* suggests that ἐναντίρρητον is the original and Pr has simplified it to ἐναντίον, perhaps deliberately. But it is worth noting that this is the only instance of ἐναντίρρητος so far known, the compound is oddly formed,

---

[96] The facts of usage did not stop the etymologists from drawing a distinction between them (irrelevant to their use in explaining νέον in our example), connecting νεαρός with freshly drawn water (ἀρύειν) and πρόσφατος with meat (φάσαι = φονεύσαι): ps.-Ptolemaeus *de diff. vocab.* 100 (Ambros. E 26 sup.) or 404, 29–405, 2 (Ottobon. gr. 43 and Vat. gr. 197); Herennius Philo *de diversis verborum signific.* v 121.

and its natural sense would be "spoken in opposition" (not really apposite here) rather than *nefasto* as suggested in *DGE* and *gegenteilig, widersprechend* as in *LBG*. Perhaps what lies behind it is ἐναντίον καὶ ἄρρητον, "untoward and unspeakable."

Once again, we can observe the community of interest between the compiler and author(s) of these items on the one hand and the grammatical tradition and scholia mostly attested in *recentiores* on the other. Of the manuscripts of Euripidean scholia, the ones with the most affinities are the same as seen earlier in this chapter and in the previous: Sa (6 items of similarity); Y² (5); S (3); R (2); V, V³, Pr, Gu, and the Miscellany of Sb (1 each). Connections to the etymological tradition are found for 5 items, while other typical comparanda come from the scholia on Aristophanes (2), the scholia on Aeschylus (1), the rhetorical tradition (1), Tzetzes (1), and Ammonius the commentator on Aristotle (1), who, it may be recalled, was the source of two items in the short list of glosses in Barberinianus gr. 4 described above.

How many other lists of this nature may lurk in the filler pages of manuscripts without having been recognized as related to the teaching or reading of a specific text, we cannot say.

Chapter 4

On Venetus Marcianus Graecus 471 (Codex M of Euripides)

1. THE PROBLEM OF DATING

The parchment manuscript Venetus Marcianus graecus 471[1] is well known under the siglum M in editions of Euripides and of the Euripidean scholia. Along with B and H, M is one of the three earliest extant medieval witnesses for Euripides. It now preserves the triad plays and *Andromache* with ample annotation and *Hippolytus* (lines 1–1234) with much sparser annotation. In many recent editions and works on the textual tradition of Euripides, a date in the 11th century has been assigned to M, but older sources assign it to the 12th, as does Mioni's catalogue of 1985,[2] and as late as 2010 André Tuilier reasserted his belief in a late 12th-century date.[3] The same manuscript contains on its first 19 folios Dionysius Periegetes' hexameter poem *Orbis Descriptio* with extensive annotation, produced at the same time by the same scribe or scribes as the Euripides part, and the only scholar who has thoroughly studied the tradition of the Dionysius Periegetes accepted the 12th-century dating.[4]

Even for the purposes of editing the plays of Euripides or the associated scholia, it does not make much difference which of these two dates is likelier to be true. In either case this witness is older than the fall of Constantinople in 1204, which is often a watershed of significance in the tradition of Greek authors. On the other hand, for Byzantine studies, it is important to have a more secure an-

---

[1] Also referred to as Z. 471 or 471 Zanetti; to summon the manuscript in the Library one also needs the Numero di collocazione 765.
[2] Mioni 1985: 260–262.
[3] Tuilier 2010, briefly reasserting without additional arguments the view he espoused in Tuilier 1968 and Tuilier 1972.
[4] Tsavari 1990: 198–199. Marc. gr. 471 was unknown to or ignored by earlier editors of Dionysius, and when first described in Livadaras 1960 was dismissed by him as of no significance.

swer to the question of dating. Byzantinists are making increasing use of codicological studies to improve our understanding of education and intellectual pursuits in relation to social status and networking, and for anyone interested in the reception of classical poetry and prose as it varied over time between the invention of minuscule and 1204, reliable dating is essential.[5] Should the manuscript be taken as evidence for the state of copying, teaching, and scholarship in the 12th century[6] or is it instead relevant to the previous era?

The problem has another aspect as well, related to the discipline of medieval Greek palaeography. As experts in Greek palaeography know, in comparison to the situation in Latin palaeography, it is much harder to locate in space and time many surviving Greek manuscripts. The situation has improved tremendously in the past 50 years, for several reasons: more dated manuscripts of the 13th and 14th centuries have been illustrated in important volumes by Turyn and others; hundreds of named scribes are better known because of the *Repertorium der griechischen Kopisten*; new manuscript catalogues bring better information; several major European libraries have made large numbers of Greek manuscripts visible on the web, and more are being added every year. But for the period before 1200 there is still much uncertainty about many manuscripts, because of the conservative nature of minuscule, the underrepresentation of pagan texts in the subset of dated manuscripts from this period as well as in the subset of manuscripts with scribal signatures, and the conservative tendency of scholars to accept datings first proposed 150–300 years ago. Because the copies of classical authors are very likely to be written in less formal and more varied hands than the sorts of formal and calligraphic minuscule scripts used in esteemed Christian and liturgical works, some of the early authorities on Greek palaeography and the older catalogues tended to assign to the 13th or 14th century manuscripts that are now accepted to be earlier. To take two examples from the Euripides tradition, B was considered to be of the 13th century by Schwartz when he edited the old scholia in 1887–1891 (whereas modern researchers mostly place it in the 11th century),[7] and Laurentianus plut. 31.10 (O of Euripides, K of Sophocles) was thought to be of the early 14th century,[8] whereas the scribe Ioannikios is

---

[5] For recent examples see Nesseris forthcoming, Bernard 2014, Gaul 2011, Olsen 2009.

[6] My interest in the question of dating was prompted by the forthcoming work of Ilias Nesseris on higher education in Constantinople in the 12th century, where the question is raised whether M might be taken as evidence for the nature of interest in Euripides in the 12th century. I am grateful to him for allowing me to read his 2014 Ioannina dissertation on the subject.

[7] The 11th-century date of B has recently been endorsed in the detailed expert description of the manuscript (dated 19/09/2012) that accompanies the excellent open–access online images available at http://gallica.bnf.fr/ark:/12148/btv1b84526627.

[8] The date is still given as 1301–1400 at http://teca.bmlonline.it, where open-access images have been available since 2010. Compare the case of Laur. plut. 31.03 (our Sb in the previous chapter), also

now known to have been active around 1175, or according to the most recent research, probably a couple of decades earlier.[9]

In the case of M, it is not clear how many of the scholars who record the date as 12th century have actually considered the matter, as opposed to simply repeating the date given by a previous authority. An outlier in the discussion of the date is André Tuilier,[10] who proposed not only that M was produced quite late in the 12th century,[11] but also that B and H derive from the previous decades and are no earlier than 1150.[12] Tuilier's dating conforms to an idiosyncratic history of the textual tradition of Euripides that goes well beyond the limits of the scanty existing evidence, a reconstruction that has met with very little agreement. More than that, Tuilier never supported his dating by any detailed palaeographic argument.

The origin of the 12th-century date is the (by current standards, very primitive) 1740 catalogue of Greek manuscripts in the Biblioteca Marciana.[13] On page 249 the compilers record, before listing the contents very briefly, "in 4. membranaceus, foliorum 154. saeculi circiter XII." The 12th-century date is repeated in Wattenbach and von Velsen (who published an image of folio 26r),[14] in Spranger's facsimile,[15] and in Turyn,[16] who is cited by subsequent scholars,[17] and in the 1985 catalogue.[18] A 13th-century date was given by Gudeman, but one may wonder whether this is due to a misprint.[19] The first to object to the dating in the catalogue was T. W. Allen in his review of Spranger.[20] Allen provided the palae-

---

dated on the site as 1301–1400, though it is dated by the scribe to 1287, as has been known for many decades.

[9] On Ioannikios see in particular Wilson 1978 and 1983a, Degni 2008a, and Nesseris forthcoming.

[10] Tuilier 1968, 1972, 2010. See, however, the important reviews of Diggle 1971, 1974.

[11] Believing that M derives from a lost exemplar that was affected by the work of Ioannes Tzetzes and Eustathios, Tuilier 1968: 153 describes it as "des dernières décennies du XIIe siècle," or (154) "de la fin du XIIe siècle." See also Tuilier 1972: 138.

[12] For the latest examination of B, see note 7 above. Tuilier 1968: 138 ascribes B to the middle of the 12th century in the text, but in footnote 3 concedes that if the intermarginal scholia and γράφεται-variants of B are younger than the main text and main blocks of scholia (I see no reason to believe the original ones are), the original production could have been at the beginning of the 12th or even end of the 11th century. On H, which Tuilier 1968: 157 assigns "à la seconde moitié du XIIe siècle" (also Tuilier 1972: 138), see the response of Daitz 1970: 32–33 and 1979: 11 n. 5; we await the publication of new enhanced images of H and new studies by the Palamedes project, expected soon (see for now Albrecht 2012).

[13] Zanetti and Bongiovanni 1740.

[14] Wattenbach and von Velsen 1878: 14 with p. 48 (*non vidi*).

[15] Spranger 1935: 3rd unnumbered page of section I of the introduction to the facsimile.

[16] Turyn 1957: 84–85.

[17] E.g., Livadaras 1960: 104; Tsavari 1990: 198–199.

[18] Mioni 1985: 260–262. Mioni shows no awareness of the earlier dating proposed by Allen.

[19] Gudeman 1921: 663, 44: is XIII a misprint for XII?

[20] Allen 1937.

ographic introduction to the facsimile of Marcianus 474 (the Venetus of Aristophanes), produced an important monograph on Greek abbreviations, and worked with many manuscripts to produce his Oxford Classical Text of Homer. He noted: "I find on consulting my note-books that since 1889 I have referred it [Marc. 471] to the eleventh. It was written early in that century, before the Venetian Aristophanes (no. 474). It is as old as the Paris Euripides, grec 2713, which M. Omont puts in the same century." Zuntz agreed with Allen.[21] Matthiessen referred to the datings offered by Turyn and Tuilier and added "doch scheint mir die von T. W. Allen ... vorgeschlagene Datierung auf die erste Hälfte des 11. Jh. der Wahrheit näher zu kommen."[22] Nigel Wilson, writing on a different matter in 1973, describes M as "often but not universally assigned to the twelfth century"[23] without taking a position, and he did not mention M in his important discussion of scholarly hands of the 11th and 12th centuries a few years later.[24] Only in 1996, apparently, did he pronounce in print for the 11th-century date.[25] Much earlier, however, while I was working on *The Textual Tradition of Euripides' Phoinissai*, I met with him in 1979 and asked his opinion about the dating of this manuscript among others, and at that time he endorsed the 11th-century date.[26]

Since Spranger's facsimile was produced in very few copies and only two folios of M have been illustrated (in sources not readily available),[27] few scholars have been able to study the script of this codex, except by visiting the Marciana. After working at first with the black and white microfilm (and images I had digitized from it), in 2014 I obtained much superior color JPEG images at 300dpi of the entire manuscript, and I inspected it in person in March 2015.[28] I have done an initial collation of all the Euripidean scholia (greatly aided by the ability to

---

[21] Zuntz 1965: 35 n.†, ascribing MBH all to "the (early) eleventh century."

[22] Matthiessen 1974: 48.

[23] Wilson 1973a: 224.

[24] Wilson 1973a: 224; Wilson 1977.

[25] In the Addendum to p. 178 n. 7 printed in Wilson 1996: 278: "It should perhaps be added that there are no less than three early copies of Euripides which may be assigned with probability to the eleventh century (Paris gr. 2713, Marc. gr. 471 and the Jerusalem Palimpsest, Taphou 36)."

[26] Mastronarde and Bremer 1982: 2. Subsequently, this dating is also reflected in Diggle's OCT and Diggle 1991.

[27] For one see n. 14 above; the other is a plate of fol. 19r (end of Dionysius Periegetes) in Livadaras 1960, facing page 104.

[28] I take the opportunity to mention that when Spranger had his photographs produced, the parchment on several pages had small folds in it that obscured some letters. On a leaf inserted facing each folio with such a fold, Spranger indicated the readings that were obscure in the reproduction but that he had read in person by gently prying the fold open for a moment. At some point later than the 1930s, the manuscript has been conserved again and the folds are no longer a problem. The words Spranger deciphered are clearly visible on the 2014 images and on the original.

magnify the digital images) and looked over every page. The discussion that follows has two purposes: first, to identify what features of the script might provide evidence for one dating or the other (11th or 12th century; the proposal of the 13th century may safely be ignored); second, to provide further details of a palaeographic or codicological nature where the catalogue entry of Mioni can be supplemented.

2. GENERAL DESCRIPTION AND EVIDENCE FOR DATING

The main text of M, both for Dionysius Periegetes and for Euripides, appears to be the work of a single scribe writing in a fairly idiosyncratic, informal, and variable minuscule characterized by extensive intermixture of majuscule forms as well as cursive traits, while at the same time exhibiting restraint with respect to ascenders and descenders or exuberant flourishes. In both parts (Dionysius and Euripides) the ruling is similar and is destined for 29 or 28 lines of main text with commentary blocks in the upper, outer, and lower margins.[29] The scholia are in an ink of the same or a very similar tint, and the style of the script is very close to that of the main text, except in a much more condensed format and with frequent use of abbreviations. I see no evidence that the scholia, in general, are not by the same scribe who wrote the main text. (More difficult is the question whether some scholia are by another scribe whose hand is extremely similar.) The Dionysius part ends on 19r, the last sheet of its quire, with folio 19v originally blank.[30] The Euripides part starts with a new quire at folio 20r (*Hecuba* 1-28). It is fairly likely that the exemplar already lacked the *argumenta* to *Hecuba*, since the missing material is insufficient to fill a normal quire, even if one assumes the *Vita Euripidis* was also prefaced to *Hecuba*. Admittedly, however, these could have been copied in a separate quire of fewer sheets, later lost as a whole.[31]

Over the course of more than 300 surviving pages, the script shows a certain degree of variation. Overall, the impression suggests some affinity to the Perl-

---

[29] The ruling for 29 lines of main text occurs in the quires for Dionysius Periegetes (1r-19v) and in the first quire for *Hecuba* (20r-27v), but the remaining quires from 28r on are ruled for 28 lines (but on 99r-v the scribe uses only 27 lines, perhaps because of the length of the upper block of scholia). On the layout of text and annotation see Chapter 1, section 2, and the references in Chapter 1, n. 100.
[30] The epigrams of religious content added on 19v at some later time have been edited in a forthcoming publication by Fabio Cescon and Filippomaria Pontani.
[31] Note, however, that if the tally figures entered on 19v and 43v are by the original scribe, as I suggest below (see at note 57), then the tally of folios on 43v indicates that the *argumenta* to *Hecuba* were never present.

schrift identified by Herbert Hunger,[32] but in a relaxed form. In particular, the horizontal spacing of the letters on some pages is loose and variable, and on others is tighter and more regular. Some lines show a high level of uniformity in the loops of alpha, delta, omicron, omega, pi, and minuscule epsilon (alone and in ligature), but this is not consistently so, as some loops (esp. omicron) may be somewhat reduced. The proportion of the height of the core of the letters to the measurement from guideline to guideline is 1:4, which is also a characteristic of Perlschrift. In the main text the tops of the small letters hang from the ruling, except that sometimes the letters start to rise across the guideline farther to the right in the line, a tendency that would be a natural for a right-handed scribe. Although the style is more relaxed than fully calligraphic hands, it also shows a remarkable degree of restraint in controlling the size of the letters. The descenders of mu, nu, rho, phi, and chi are often short; majuscule lambdas usually project only a little above and below the height of letters like alpha and sigma; kappa is more often majuscule than minuscule, and the majuscule form usually projects little if at all above or below the normal letter height. Abbreviations are avoided for the most part in the main text: those that occur are usually at line-end for "justification" of the margin. The letters are formed with relatively plain strokes. There may be a hook on the bottom of rho (but many rhos have no hook), iota (especially the tall form), the ει ligature, and phi. Slight clubbing may be present on the left end of the horizontal of theta, tau, pi, and psi, and sometimes a slight lozenge is seen on the top left of majuscule kappa.

In his 1977 study Wilson showed how the scholarly hands of the 11th century, particularly from 1150 to the early years of the 12th century, allow some admixture of elements from cursive scripts. There are certainly elements of the script of M that reflect this trend, but again (especially in comparison to V of Aristophanes, Marc. gr. 474) the restraint of this scribe is noteworthy. Enlarged letters do appear, but as a very small percentage overall, especially if we consider the forms found in the middle of the regular lines of text. That is, initial letters are occasionally enlarged (not very much), final letters even less often, and several significant enlargements appear in exclamations that occur in short lyric lines or on a line by themselves as *extra metrum* in an iambic passage. For more details, see the next section.

Upsilon is the letter that is most often noticeable as larger than others. The scribe uses several forms of upsilon, as described in detail below. The form of interest here is of double or triple width, also dipping somewhat under the baseline, most often in ligature with pi. While this wide form may have suggested a date in the 12th (or 13th) century to some early palaeographers, a similar widened upsilon is already seen in the 10th century in Laur. plut. 32.09 (L of

[32] Hunger 1954: 22–32.

Sophocles, M of Aeschylus) and can be paralleled in dated manuscripts of the 11th century.[33]

Some indices that militate against a 12th-century date are the lack of broad open omegas, the scarcity of majuscule betas, the very low incidence of tall gamma or tau, the use of minuscule epsilon for well over 99% of the epsilons, and the rarity of enlarged lunate sigma or enlarged epsilon enclosing a following letter (such as pi or upsilon). It is also noteworthy that in the scholia this scribe ligatures a sigma at the end of εἰς, πρὸς, or an article with the initial letter of the next word (mostly pi and tau),[34] since in the 12th century Ioannes Tzetzes, at least, considered such ligatures that obscured word boundaries an obnoxious older practice.[35]

The "modern" letter forms that Canart and Perria identify as beginning to appear or becoming common in the 12th century (such as n-shaped eta, v-shaped nu, wide, open omega or omega "en petit pain") are absent from M.[36] The same can be said of those ligatures listed by them as beginning to appear in the 12th century (such as forms of αρ, γρ, το, τα).[37] M does not seem to fit easily in any of the categories suggested by Canart and Perria in their study of bookhands of the 11th and 12th century.[38] The script of M is less cursive and varied than the "corsiveggiante" type of Perlschrift; it is more joined and less uniform than the examples of rounding archaizing script from the first quarter of the 11th century. What is clear from their discussion, however, is that M's script has little in common with the various developments that set in late in the 11th and early in the 12th century. It would seem either to belong to the middle of the 11th century (or earlier in the century), or to be the product of a some-

---

[33] Examples from the 10th century: Laur. 32.09 (online) fol. 19r ὑπεράχθεο (Soph. El. 177), 20v λυπῶ (Soph. El. 355), 21r ὑπεικάθοιμι (Soph. El. 361); Paris gr. 438 (992, Lake IV 144, plate 246), in the scholia, line 14 of second marginal note, ὑπογραφικὰ, and penultimate full line at bottom, ὑποληπτέον; Lake I 16, plate 35 (962), line-initial; Lake III 94, plate 165 (997); Lake III 124, pl. 210 (961). From the 11th century examples may be seen in R of Aristophanes, and see also Vat. gr. 1675 (1018, Franchi de' Cavalieri and Lietzmann 1929, plate 20) col. 1, 13 ὑβρίζοντες, col. 2, 3 ὑβρίσομεν, 7 ὕβρις σοι, 8 ὑπερηφανίας, 25 σύμψυχον; Oxford Bodl. Auct. T.4.13 (Wilson 1973b: plate 35), fol. 42r, line 2 ὑπό (three times wider than in adjacent ἀξιούμενον), line 6 συνυπάρχει (second upsilon twice as wide as first). A notable example in B is a very wide upsilon in ὑμνεῖν at the beginning of a line (6th from the bottom on 83v).

[34] Similarly on fol. 78v, Phoen. 91, in the supralinear annotation ἱκεσίαις σου is written with the two sigmas forming the standard minuscule double-sigma ligature with the second sigma open. Note the similar double-sigma ligature in ὕβρις σοι in Vat. gr. 1675 (cited in the previous note). Such ligatures are also to be found occasionally in B: e.g., in τὰς χεῖρας, last line of 103v; εἰς τοὔπισθεν written with stigma ligature, 104r, 8 lines from bottom of side block; ζεύς σε, 95v, 11 lines from bottom.

[35] Luzzatto 1999: 21–24.

[36] Canart and Perria 1991: 72–74 with Fig. 1 on p. 117.

[37] Canart and Perria 1991: 74–76 with Fig. 2 on p. 117.

[38] Canart and Perria 1991: 76–102, especially 84–87, 100.

what later date by a scribe who is able to write smoothly while relaxing the traditional minuscule and at the same time not permitting many borrowings from cursive hands and only very rarely indulging in the exuberant strokes and contrasts of size that become more typical in the 12th century and later.

In addition, the abbreviation system[39] used in M probably favors a date in the 11th century. Obviously, refinements of dating based on abbreviation styles are a subject that deserves a modern treatment, since the previous studies are extremely old and partial. Nevertheless, I suspect that Allen's intuition about the date of M was not unrelated to his interest in, and familiarity with, abbreviations. The repertoire of abbreviations and the forms of them used by M are most closely paralleled in the scholia in B, and many of the most distinctive features are matched in a document from 1015 illustrated in Dolger.[40] As for specific features, the scribe uses abbreviations word-internally as well as at the end of words: for instance, a common form of πάντα in the scholia consists of a pi with the angular abbreviation for αν in the line, descending from the right of the cross-stroke of pi, followed by a tau in line with dots above and below the right side of its cross-stroke, or the tau with dots may be suspended, or τα may be represented by a simple horizontal with dots above and below (Plate 1, 1–2); similar is the occasional treatment of αν and ον before tau in active participle endings.[41] Two abbreviations that become rarer as time goes by are still common in M: the tilde-shaped supralinear omega is extremely common (and often used word-internally), while the straight supralinear stroke for alpha also occurs from time to time. On a few occasions one even finds these two with a small loop added at the right end of the stroke to represent αρ or ωρ (the former is also used rarely by B).[42] The scribe distinguishes between the abbreviations for ην, ιν (by addition of diaeresis dots), ειν (by doubling of the symbol), as some early minuscule scribes do not (Plate 1, 4–6).[43] The angle used in these three abbreviations is markedly assymmetrical (again similar to B's form), and I believe this favors an

---

[39] More details about the abbreviations (less revealing for dating) are given in the next section.

[40] Dolger 1948: 272–276 (#103). Points of similarity include the flattened compendium for ως, occasional iota adscript of somewhat reduced size, the shape and size of the s-form compendium for καί, and the form of suspended omega and its use even within a word.

[41] Another good example is ἐπιγινώσκειν with ωσ represented by an ως abbreviation above the nu and ειν abbreviation above kappa (Plate 1, 3).

[42] I regret that I failed to record the location of these rare forms in M; for the shapes, see Allen 1889: Plate II, last in fourth row and first in fifth row for αρ; Plate IX, third, fourth, and fifth examples in first row for ωρ. For examples of the αρ form in B, see Sch. Hipp. 426, 90v, 9 lines from bottom, in ἁμαρτημάτων; hyp. Andr., 145v, end of 10th line, in σπάρτην.

[43] E.g., R of Aristophanes uses the single symbol for both ην and ειν; B of Euripides usually has the doubled symbol for ειν but occasionally uses the single one in the older fashion (in these places, the intent of the relevant note more or less demands that the word be taken as an infinitive in ειν).

earlier rather than a later date. The rising left side of the angle is long, while the falling right side is short or very short; in contrast, in later centuries the two sides in ην/ιν tend to be almost equal, or the right side may be longer than the left, as is natural for a finishing stroke in later styles. Moreover, whereas the ειν abbreviation (mostly used for the infinitive ending) developed into two parallel oblique lines, M still has a pair of two-part angles juxtaposed, or (when quickly written) two diagonals each with a vestigial turn downward at the upper end. The technique of doubling a suspended final letter to indicate a plural is another habit that may or may not be relevant to date: the most common example of this is παι^{ΔΔ} indicated παῖδες or παῖδας, but note also (fol. 133v) στοι^{χχ} for στοιχείοις and (fol. 134r, third line from bottom, genitive plurals) παλαντι^{ΔΔ} παί^{ΔΔ} ἕνα (Plate 1, 7).[44]

Finally, there is a compendious form of εἰς (used when an article beginning with tau follows the preposition) that looks a great deal like a small epsilon loop attached to the upper left stroke of a chi (Plate 1, 8–10). This form is not common in M, since the scribe usually writes this sequence by using an ει ligature and then separately a stigma ligature. This abbreviation is discussed in Allen 1889: 13 and various forms are shown in the last two lines of his Plate III: the two at the end of the penultimate line are most similar to M's version, and these come from the 10th and 11th centuries; M's version differs in that the rising oblique stroke ligatures to the left end of the horizontal of tau rather than leading into the joining of the two strokes of tau, as in Allen's examples. Examples are also offered by Vitelli and Tsereteli.[45] Allen and Vitelli do cite some examples from the 12th century and later, so it is unclear whether this abbreviation contributes to the dating of M. But it may be noted that I have so far seen this form of abbreviation only in B[46] among the other Euripidean manuscripts.

Although, as noted, the script of B is similar in many ways to that of M, B may be earlier than M. One difference between them is that B uses so-called *Kleinunciale* or small majuscule for many of the scholia, whereas the M's scholia are in minuscule. One may compare R and V of Aristophanes: R uses small majuscule for scholia, but V uses minuscule, and R is regarded as the older of the two manuscripts. There has apparently been no adequate general study of the

---

[44] In B I have so far seen one apparent example of something similar: in the intermarginal Sch. Hipp. 141 positioned beside verse 142 ῥήματα is written ρ^{η}ρ^{η} (both rhos have an abbreviation stroke attached to the botttom of the descender).

[45] See Vitelli 1884: plate following page 14, items III.43–45 (in two of his examples the following word does not begin with tau); Vitelli 1884: 166, item 98; Tsereteli 1904: Table 4, the first in the fourth line of the entry for ΕΙC (10th century).

[46] Examples can be seen (in B online) on fol. 75r, εἰς τὴν χολὴν in intermarginal Sch. Phoen. 1256; on 75v, last full line, εἰς τὸ λυποῦν in Sch. Phoen. 1310; and on 83r, εἰς τὴν ἀττικὴν in the gloss above *Hipp.* 36. The joining to tau in B is positioned as in the examples in Allen 1889.

use of small majuscule.[47] Gardthausen notes its emergence, apparently in the 10th century, as a way of marking the distinction between marginal annotation and the main text, but his discussion occupies only a few lines, and he notes that the practice is not found in the period he defines as younger minuscule and that the approximate date at which the practice ended is unknown.[48] Curiously, M does use majuscule for a substantial portion of text in the hypotheses to *Andromache* and *Hippolytus*, though the hypotheses to *Orestes* and *Phoenissae* are in minuscule (*Hecuba*'s is absent entirely). Perhaps this is something that could not have occurred in the 12th century, but it would take a thorough survey of paratexts in classical manuscripts to confirm such a suspicion.

Another possible clue that M belongs to the 11th century and not later is the treatment of silent iota. M never has an iota subscript or even an adscript that is small and lowered with respect to the usual baseline. It does, however, have some very short silent iotas, resting on or above the baseline, and obviously different in size from the preceding α, η, or ω. This reduced iota, however, does not rule out a date in the 11th century, since there are dated parallels.[49] Furthermore, the scribe also sometimes adds a tiny iota above the line to the right of the

---

[47] Exploring the distribution of majuscule and minuscule in the commentaries or scholia in early minuscule codices that have such annotation would seem to be a desideratum. It does not seem to be the case that majuscule is used only when the amount of annotation is relatively small (as in M of Aeschylus = L of Sophocles). Early examples with dense annotation in majuscule: Lake IX 333, pl. 606 (Vat. Urb. gr. 35, before 914, Arist. *Categories*), Lake X 383, pl. 724 (Grottaferrata La Badia cod. B.a.4, before 991, St. Maximus); also another image of Vat. Urb. gr. 35 ca. 900 (Follieri 1969: pl. 18); Vat. gr. 1 of ca. 900 (images online at persistent URL http://digi.vatlib.it/view/MSS_Vat.gr.1/0007), which has some pages with rather full margins—see 1r-v, 3v, 4v. I have also noted majuscule scholia in the Clark Plato (Oxon. Clarkianus 39, late 10th century). In Venetus A of Homer (Marc. gr. 454, late 10th century) the main body of annotation is in minuscule (with little abbreviation, since the format is so large), whereas majuscule is used for short notes and glosses that are added above the line, in the margin, or intermarginally. Such early examples of dense majuscule scholia militate against Herwig Maehler's notion that dense marginal commentaries were possible only after the invention of minuscule and were not practical with the majuscule script of late antiquity (Maehler 1993 and 2000, following Zuntz 1939).

[48] Gardthausen 1911–1913: II.159, ending with "Bis jetzt ist noch nicht festgestellt, bei welchem Jahr ungefähr die Grenzlinie lieft." For various aspects of the continued use of majuscule script and willingness in certain contexts to mix majuscule letters in minuscule script, see Degni 2008b, with references to earlier studies in the notes on 751–753. I consulted G. Cavallo by email on this topic, and he kindly told me, while emphasizing that he had not made a systematic study, that "il fenomeno di scrivere in maiuscoletta ('piccola onciale') i 'marginalia' di diversa specie compare in manoscritti in minuscola già nel terzo venticinquennio del secolo IX, persiste per tutto il X, diventa più raro nell'XI e tende a scomparire nel corso del XII. Quando—ma assai raramente—il fenomeno si incontra più tardi del secolo XII, esso è da considerare proprio di una scelta individuale del copista, ma non più un'usanza grafica. Talora, inoltre, si potrebbe trattare di un fenomeno imitativo ripreso da un modello più antico."

[49] E.g., Vat. gr. 1675 of 1018, illustrated in Follieri 1969: pl. 24.

tilde-form suspended omega, when an adscript is desired, although in most cases the adscript is omitted when the vowel is suspended. Of manuscripts I have studied, only B has a few examples of this small iota beside the suspended form.[50] An example of both approaches can be observed in M in the small extract shown in Plate 1, 11: the article τῷ has the iota beside the suspended omega, whereas the suspended omega alone appears on ἐναντίῳ (an error for ἐναντίον by assimilation of ending to the following words) and on δικαίῳ.

Finally, the scribe of M, particularly in the scholia, is remarkably prone to errors of breathing: for example, the majority of appearances of ἑξῆς are given a smooth breathing, ἐξῆς; ἴσος is as common as ἴσος. Occasionally an initial iota is simply ϊ with no breathing added. In addition, his accentuation of prefixed prepositions and prepositional phrases is quite inconsistent. There are many cases of univerbation of preposition with the following noun, with no accent on the preposition and sometimes no breathing on the noun if it begins with a vowel. Conversely, an accent sometimes appears on the prepositional prefix (mostly πρόσ-) of a compound verb form. The occurrence and the frequency of such a treatment of the diacritics reminds me of R of Aristophanes, and it is my impression that such departures from a consistent standard practice are less common later (until we meet particularly incompetent scripts of the 15th century or later).[51]

I have sought comparanda for the script of M in the collections of dated minuscule manuscripts, and I have found nothing really comparable later than the early years of the 12th century, while parallels for some features have been noted in manuscripts from the early 11th century or even the late 10th.[52] And the items from the early 12th century that share some characteristics with M also seem to be later than M because they have features such as freer and more ornate forms of the abbreviations, ειν abbreviated with two straight lines, and the suspended ου ligature more commonly or always in the form with a full loop (which is extremely rare in M, where suspended ου looks like a small upsilon: Plate 1, 3).[53] Of course, it is possible that we have a scribe who is extremely self-controlled and is suppressing most "modern" tendencies, but that is not very likely for the scholia, and the script is smoother and more flowing than what is seen in con-

---

[50] E.g., B 42r, τῶι, end of 3rd line of margin block; 44v, ἰαμβικῶι, end of 15th line of the margin block; 45v, ἵππωι, 2nd line after the divider ornament in the middle of the margin block; 110r, προλόγωι, side block, middle of page, 5th line of the scholion with ref ε.

[51] Again, an up-to-date account of scribal habits surrounding diacritics in early minuscule manuscripts, especially of the works of pagan authors, might be useful.

[52] Inmaculada Pérez Martín suggested to me in email communication that there are "coincidences, perhaps meaningful, in Vat. Pii II 21 (a. 1013, Lake VII 272, pl. 483–489), Par. gr. 438 (a. 992, Lake IV 144, pl. 245, 247) and Laur. 69.06 (a. 997, Lake X 368, pl. 689)."

[53] Two such examples are Vat. gr. 504 (1105, Lake VIII 304, pl. 555–556); Par. gr. 2659 (1116, Lake V 184, pl. 314).

servative or archaizing attempts at purer minuscule or Perlschrift from the 12th century on. I therefore believe that those modern scholars who accept that M is from the 11th and not the 12th century have been justified in doing so, and I estimate that it is later than R of Aristophanes and B of Euripides, but probably earlier than V of Aristophanes.[54]

3. DETAILED DESCRIPTION

A. Scribal Tallies and Quires

The first 19 folios of M contain Dionysius Periegetes, in three gatherings, originally of 8, 8, and 5 leaves, but two have been lost. The Euripides portion consists of 17 quires of 8, except that the last quire has lost its final folio, which would have contained *Hippolytus* 1235–1290. As noted above,[55] except for the first quire of *Hecuba*, the pages of the Euripides part are ruled for 28 lines of main text.

There is some evidence for the tallying of leaves in the separate sections.[56] After describing the preliminary sheets bound in the volume, which are irrelevant to the original, Spranger records: "The only ancient signature is κα τετράδια β φυλλά ε[57] (i.e. 21 = 2 quires, of eight leaves each, + 5 leaves) at the top left-hand corner of fol. 19b. Since one leaf is now missing before fol. 1 and another between fols. 16 and 17, this signature was written previously to the loss of these two leaves and of course previously to the numbering." Mioni too speaks of *vestigia antiquae foliorum subputationis*, and correctly notes that there is also a similar (but simpler) tally of leaves at the end of *Hecuba* on fol. 42v.[58] The tallies

---

[54] Fries 2017: 745 n. 3 has suggested that M belongs "earlier rather than later in the 11th century" because of affinities of script she detects in Paris, suppl. grec 469A (986 = Lake IV 142, pl. 242); Patmos, gr. 138 (988 = Lake I 18, pl. 37); and St. Petersburg, gr. 64 (994 = Lake VI 237, pl. 425–426).

[55] See note 29 above.

[56] Such a tally of leaves is not the same as the counting of lines in a book of poetry. The latter practice is discussed briefly in Irigoin 1984: 94, who judges it to be a habit revived by scholars of the 12th century. I am grateful to Robert Allison for an explanation of this kind of notation of the tally of leaves in a section of a manuscript.

[57] *Sic* Spranger with the incorrect accent: the scribe wrote κ̄α τετρά∆ β· φύ() ε̄:~. Understand φύλλα with the first numeral: "21 (leaves in all); (consisting of) two gatherings of four (folded sheets, thus eight leaves each), 5 (further) leaves." Spranger is not using "signature" in the sense that is now usual in codicology, designating the numbering on the first sheet of each gathering to keep track of the sequence of quires.

[58] Mioni 1985: 261. But he has an incorrect transcription or typographic error, printing φυλλα with no accent and giving the number as μγ'.

on 19v and 43v are of the same age, as Mioni implies, and in my opinion they are in the same ink and hand as the main text. The second occurs in the left margin opposite the end of *Hecuba* and reads φύλλα κ̄γ· (23 folios; so this count was made with the current state of *Hecuba*, lacking *argumenta*). At the ends of *Orestes* and *Phoenissae* there are similar tallies, but by a different hand (larger and cruder). On fol. 75r the note is damaged and appears to read φύ() λ̄[ ]. If we assume that the person who wrote this began his count at 43r, disregarding the portion of *Orestes* argumenta present on the last page of *Hecuba* (42v, already counted), the missing numeral ought to be β̄ or γ̄, to give 32 or 33, probably the latter, if 75r-v is being counted as one of the leaves (even though the arguments to *Phoenissae* begin in the last lines of 75r). On fol. 109r, intermarginally in the middle of the page at the last line of *Phoenissae*, the same cruder hand has written φύ() λ̄β. Assuming the count began at 76r, then one would have expected the count to be 34 rather than 32. Fol. 132v is too damaged at the bottom to allow us to determine whether a similar tally occurred at the end of *Andromache*, and the last folio of *Hippolytus*, 154v, is similarly damaged, and in any case it may not have been the last folio extant at the time this second hand was active, whether it was fairly close in date to the original hand of M or several generations later, since we do not know the date at which the last folio of the last (extant) quire was detached.

B. Use of Majuscule

Majuscule is used for headings (like play titles or headings of hypotheses) and also occurs for an extended stretch in the hypotheses and lists of *dramatis personae* of *Andromache* (109r-v) and *Hippolytus* (133r-v). This is somewhat odd, since the same items for *Orestes* and *Phoenissae* are in the usual minuscule (*Hecuba* has no argumenta). Was the scribe imitating a difference already seen in his exemplar(s)? Majuscule is also used often (but not always) for the scholia reference symbols that take a numeric form, and for numerals within the scholia, such as β̄ for δύο or for a form of δεύτερος. The scribe does not observe the practice of deliberately using majuscule in lemmata or in the first letter of a lemma or of a scholion, although an initial letter may coincidentally be majuscule from the normal admixture. As far as concerns such admixture of majuscule forms amidst minuscule, the practice with particular letters is detailed in the section on letter forms below. The minuscule seems to be somewhat purer in the text of the tragedies than in the smaller script of the scholia. As noted earlier, what seems noteworthy is the rarity of majuscule beta and majuscule epsilon.

C. Use of Enlarged Letters

The extra width of some instances of upsilon has already been mentioned in section 2 above, and the variants are described below under D (see Plate 2, 1-2).

Psi and zeta (in an angular form that looks like a reversed form of epigraphic three-bar sigma) are often tall, and angular 3-shaped zeta may also be somewhat enlarged. Enlargement (usually quite modest) also is seen occasionally in kappa, gamma, and lambda. Enlargements (usually slight) may also occur at the beginning of a line of the poetic text, and less often in the final letter of a line.

Enlarged tau is infrequent; when enlarged, its vertical extends slightly below the base line as well as far above the usual letter height. This form appears mainly as the second tau in ττ, but sporadically elsewhere, as for example *Hec.* 625 (30v) τίμιος, in *Or.* 4 (44r) τύχας; *Or.* 1140 (64v) κτανών; Sch. Phoen. 88 (78v, 2nd line from top of page) ἀγωνιστικ(ω)Τέρα (Plate 2, 3); *Phoen.* 809 (91v) τείχεσι. As far as I recall, there is only one instance of a tall tau that overlaps the center of omega:[59] on 128r in the right margin block of scholia, in Sch. Andr. 1014, τῶι (Plate 2, 4) contains this combination (the following word ἄρει happens to feature a majuscule epsilon of moderately enlarged size, also uncommon).

The lunate form of sigma is extremely rare in M, but a large one may be seen in συμφορᾶς in *Hipp.* 803 (Plate 2, 5), and on the same page the *personae nota* for Theseus (four times) consists of θη at normal size, with a suspended lunate sigma equal to or taller than the theta. The name is similarly written on other pages, and on fol. 151v, at *Hipp.* 1038 and 1045, the sigma is even larger. Compare the lunate sigma, somewhat enlarged, at line-end in *Or.* 3 (44r) φύσις. I have noted only two instances of ος written with large lunate sigma surrounding omicron (there may of course be a few more I missed): at line-end in *Phoen.* 1153 (97v) γόνος; and in Sch. Hipp. 205 (Plate 2, 6) γενναίος (phonetic error for γενναίως), not at line-end.[60]

As noted earlier, exclamations may be enlarged, especially if in isolation or written as part of a relatively short line of verse.[61] Here are some examples: ὤμοι αἴ αἴ, as part of a short line, *Hec.* 702 (32r); φεῦ, extra metrum, on its own line, last line of the page, *Hec.* 955 (36r); ἔα, extra metrum, with the letters not actually enlarged, but instead very widely spaced and with a large arc ligaturing the cross-stroke of epsilon to the bottom of alpha, as also in *Hec.* 1116 [ἔα] (39r) and *Andr.* 896 (126r); enlarged ὤ line-initial in ὤ γέρον *Or.* 544 (53v); φεῦ, extra metrum, on its own line, *Or.* 1052 (Plate 2, 7) and *Or.* 1154 (65r); ναί, extra metrum, on its own line, *Andr.* 242 (114v), with large majuscule nu and slightly enlarged minuscule αι, and the same again, *Andr.* 586 (120v); line-initial (and

---

[59] Gardthausen 1911–1913: II, Taf. 6–7 indicates that this ligature is attested in the late 10th and 11th centuries as well as in later centuries.

[60] See below under Epsilon for a (rare) similar treatment of lunate epsilon.

[61] For this practice, compare folio 59v of B, where *Phoen.* 161 ὁρᾷς; (beginning of a trimeter, but the last word of the old servant's speech; Antigone replies in antilabe) appears on its own line, centered and with letters twice or thrice as large as normal.

last line of page) καί with somewhat enlarged kappa but a large flourish beneath the line for αι, *Andr.* 807 (124r); enlarged αῖ αῖ ἔ ἔ with (the rare) majuscule epsilons, *Hipp.* 595 (144r).

A sample page with more than the usual frequency of enlargements is 138r, containing *Hipp.* 247-274. Here the anapaestic dimeters, shorter than the usual iambic trimeter lines, seem to invite some relaxation in regularity of size: note the larger than usual suspended omicron at line-end 252 (βίοτος), several wide upsilons (twice in ὑπερ-, but also in ὑγιείαι), somewhat large καί abbreviation (s-form) line-initial in 266, slightly larger (majuscule) phi line-initial 268, slightly larger nu at line-end 265. Even a page like this does not contain the number of flourishes and enlargements often seen in 12th-century scholarly hands. Moreover, almost every enlargement used in M can be matched by a similar occasional form in R of Aristophanes or in Laur. plut. 32.09 (L of Sophocles, M of Aeschylus): note, for instance, in Laur. 32.09, the slightly enlarged exclamation, line-initial, ὀᾶ *Persae* 116 (120r); ἔ ἔ ἔ ἔ *Sept.* 150, 158 (170v).

D. *Comments on Specific Letters*

In these comments I indicate the usual form or forms and the degree of admixture of majuscule, and remark on any variations, unusual traits, or use in ligatures. "Both forms" means both majuscule and minuscule.

Alpha: usually minuscule, rarely with a tail descending below loop (this tail is more common later in ms); majuscule alpha used in line-initial or scholion-initial position and occasionally within words; sometimes the diagonal ascender of the majuscule form is extended in a more pronounced way, but this is not very common. Later in the codex one notices from time to time a somewhat different minuscule alpha: where the loop is closed, the stroke above the crossing (normally very short) projects up and a little to the right in such a way that the character looks much more like the ευ-ligature: examples on 120v are supralinear Sch. Andr. 588, both alphas in ἅπαξ (Plate 2, 8); supralinear Sch. Andr. 600, second alpha in ἀνδράσιν.

Beta: predominantly minuscule, but a few majuscule forms. A sample of the rare instances in the poetic text: *Hec.* 37, 41, 50 (20v) τύμβ-; *Hec.* 168, (22v) βίος; *Phoen.* 1689 (107v: Plate 2, 9) ὤλβισ'; *Hipp.* 898 (149r) βίον. These betas are larger than the adjacent letters, of about the same vertical dimension as the scribe's phi; they have a rightward slant, and the larger bottom loop is flat and wide while the upper loop is narrow and tall.

Gamma: usually minuscule; majuscule form in γὰρ abbreviation and in γρ(άφεται), but not common in the poetic text. The very tall majuscule form is uncommon, but found here and there: e.g., *Hec.* 376 (26v) ζυγῷ and 384 (26v) ψόγον (where it seems that the original scribe erased a phi and entered the large gamma to fill the ample space), also in the *nota personae* ἀγαμε() in *Hec.* (as on 34v); *Or.* 1608 (73v) θυγατρός.

Delta: minuscule form predominates, the upper arc of the letter varies from a straight-up extension from the loop in ligature with omega or omicron, to a left slant (usually not exaggerated) in ligature with iota or alpha (or sometimes by itself); occasionally there is a more exuberant upper arc in δι, as *Hipp.* 946 (Plate 2, 12), *Or.* 1361, 1364 (68v); but the upper portion slants to the right and is shorter than usual in ligature with epsilon and indeed in most circumstances in the smaller script of the scholia (Plate 2, 10). Majuscule delta occurs mostly in suspension (ἐπειδ(ή)) or line-initially or in abbreviated δια in the scholia.

Epsilon: predominantly in minuscule form, and not usually enlarged when majuscule (Plate 2, 11). For examples of majuscule, see *Hec.* 58 (Plate 12, 11) φθείρει, *Hec.* 75 (21r) ὀνείρων; *Or.* 941 (61r) ἀνεῖται; the third example is almost as tall as a minuscule epsilon, but the other two rise above the guideline less than minuscule epsilon. There are, however, some large majuscule epsilons in the early pages containing Dionysius Periegetes. Sometimes later in the codex there are a few enlarged epsilons in abbreviations, or used when the arc encloses the pi of ἐπ- beginning a word: cf. Sch. *Hipp.* 73 (135r, third line of the right margin block, first word of the ἄλλως scholion, now very faint), ἐπιεικῶς, and in the poetic text *Hipp.* 946 (Plate 2, 12) ἐπειδή γ', 955 ἐπεί γ'.[62] Also note the very large majuscule epsilon above pi for περι in περιπαθεῖς on fol. 76r, 5th line (*arg. Phoen.*). Among the minuscule forms, one may note the open form in the ligature ευ, especially in σευ.

Zeta: both in the rounded 3-shape (extending above and below standard letter height, but not by much) and (less often, but especially used early in *Hec.*) in a much taller form, a 2-shape that is usually quite angular (thus resembling a reversed epigraphic three-bar sigma), extending well above and below the standard letter height. For example, both forms appear on 36r, the first in *Hec.* 935 προσίζουσ' (Plate 3, 1), the second in *Hec.* 949 ὀϊζύς (Plate 3, 2).

Eta: more often the short majuscule form than the taller h-shaped minuscule form; the proportion of majuscule forms seems to be even higher in the smaller script of the scholia.

Theta: closed oval majuscule form in most places, with good extension of the center stroke on either side of loop (extension to left even when no connection to previous letter; often slight clubbing on the left); open minuscule form found in ligatured σθαι and the like, and occasionally on its own.

Iota, both short and tall forms (greater extension upward, little or less extension below the baseline); many are plain verticals, but some have a slight

---

[62] Although they are not the same form as in M (where the epsilon is definitely majuscule and the pi lies within the large arc), the scribe of L of Sophocles, Laur. plut.32.09 (e.g., on 50v, *Ant.* 57, 74), already has forms of επ in which the minuscule epsilon portion of the ligature is larger than normal and features a more circular arc than usual.

clubbing at the bottom or a visible hook. For some extraordinarily tall versions, see, e.g., *Phoen.* 489 (85r) πύργοισι; *Phoen.* 919 (93v) πόλις (where the line above is short and the space above -λις is empty). In some ligatures iota extends below the line and has a hook on the descender, and rarely this form with extension only downward is found in isolation (a particularly long version four times in ἰώ in the poetic text on 82r). The silent iotas, when present, tend to be small, but similar smallness can be seen elsewhere (e.g., in τοι). As noted above in section 2, the reduced iota is not lowered with respect to the baseline of the regular characters and may be at mid-character height. Also as mentioned previously, when a dative ending ωι is suspended, usually we have just the suspended tilde-form of omega, and less often there is a very small iota placed next to it (Plate 1, 11). Diaeresis dots are used for genuine cases of syllabic diaeresis, except that occasionally the dots appear on an initial iota that has no breathing sign added: e.g., Sch. *Phoen.* 91 (78v) ϊκεσίαις; Sch. *Phoen.* 202 (80v) ϊερόδημοι (M's variant for ἱερόδουλοι); Sch. *Phoen.* 274 (81v) ϊκέτης; Sch. *Phoen.* 347 (82v) ϊσμηνὸς; Sch. *Phoen.* 836 (92r) ϊσόπεδον. This may be a reflection of older practice (before consistent application of breathing signs), or indicate uncertainty about which sign would be correct, since we have noted in the previous section the frequency of breathing errors in this manuscript.

Kappa: usually the majuscule form, but normally small in size, or if enlarged, with a vertical extending just slightly above and below the normal letter height. Occasionally kappa is formed in two non-tangent strokes (looking like ιc), but the scribe is usually careful to bring the two parts into contact (Plate 2, 1 vs. 3). For an example of a fairly tall vertical on majuscule kappa (but still with small right fork), see *Phoen.* 309 (82r) σκιάζων.

Lambda: in both majuscule and minuscule forms. The majuscule form rarely shows enlargement, but see, e.g., the line-initial lambda of *Andr.* 425 (117v) λάβεσθέ.

Mu: both majuscule and minuscule forms, in about equal frequency; minuscule with the descender straight down and fairly short, or if long, it may have club or hook.

Nu: both majuscule and minuscule forms, in about equal frequency; slightly slanted to right in both forms; the descender of the minuscule form is often short; note the joining of αν, for both minuscule and majuscule forms of nu, where the alpha's finishing stroke dips down below the line, then loops back upward to join the bottom of the left side of nu, occasionally with a visible but tiny loop at the joining (Plate 3, 3).[63]

Xi: the form used in isolation (and in ligature with alpha) has a straight horizontal top at midline (matching the height of characters without ascenders) and

---

[63] A similar way of joining majuscule nu with minuscule alpha is at least as early as the late 10th century (Gardthausen 1911–1913: II, Taf. 6, column 15 of row nu).

a stroke consisting of three arcs that extends far below the baseline (Plate 3, 4). In the εξ ligature (with pointed peak) it is tall, but not exaggeratedly so (Plate 3, 5).

Omicron: round, sometimes slightly reduced in size compared to adjacent letters.

Pi: both forms, but the minuscule version predominates in the poetic text; ππ ligature in both forms. In the majuscule form, the top stroke, like that of tau, sometimes has slight clubbing on the left end; the horizontal occasionally slants down on the right to ligature under following vowel, but this is less common than the normal form ligaturing with a straight extension of the horizontal. The majuscule form is used in the abbreviations for παρα described below.

Rho: minuscule either with straight descender (often short) or with hook at bottom; only rarely does the scribe continue from the descender of rho into a ligature with next letter.

Sigma: normally in the minuscule form; the double sigma ligature with second loop open is common. For enlarged sigma, see above, paragraph C.

Tau: normally small, and with its horizontal almost straight, sometimes with slight clubbing at the left; sometimes the top stroke may slant down to ligature under alpha (Plate 3, 6), but most instances of τα feature a straight horizontal meeting the top of alpha; in the scholia one sometimes sees ττ in the old cursive form looking like τγ (and this older form is more common than that consisting of regular tau followed by enlarged tau).

Upsilon: varies widely in size, especially in width, as mentioned above.[64] There is a normal-sized version, harmonious with the size of the standard loops (Plate 2, 1); a slightly widened version ligatured to a following letter (Plate 2, 1); a vertically reduced version, either narrow or a little widened, ligatured to a following letter (especially lambda in βουλ-, such that the first impression is often of βολ- when the writing is faint or the image not magnified for clarity; an example with kappa in Plate 3, 11); and a form of double or triple width, also dipping somewhat under the baseline, most often in ligature with pi, but also with tau, phi, mu. One of the widest examples is *Or.* 168 (Plate 2, 2) ἐξ ὕπνου, a phrase which occupies a line of its own.

Phi: the usual form is the double-looped minuscule one with a descender of variable length, comparable to that of rho, hooked to the right, and a minimized upper small loop that reduces the extension of the letter about the head line. More often than not, the main loop is asymmetrical, smaller on the right than on the left, sometimes with the impression that the bottom of the oval is squeezed upward in the middle (Plate 2, 9 and 11). Much less frequent is the majuscule form with simple oval and straight vertical through it. An open form occurs in

---

[64] For wide upsilons in 10th- and 11th-century hands, see note 33 above.

the ligature σφ and rarely elsewhere (Plate 2, 5 and 7).

Chi: usually close to symmetrical above and below the crossing of the strokes; thus the descenders are usually restrained (rarely, in the small script of the scholia, one or another of the lower strokes is extended a little more).

Psi: cross-shaped, resembly a tau with a noticeably long vertical ascender above the crossing and descending little or not at all below the baseline. The vertical stroke is usually clubbed or hooked at the top, and sometimes at the bottom. As with tau, the left end of the crossbar may present slight clubbing, while the right end occasionally bends down to ligature from below with the next letter (Plate 3, 7).

Omega: more often minuscule form with closed loops than majuscule form with open loops. In both, the two halves tend to be close to the same size. Occasionally the minuscule form shows a slight separation between the two loops.

Epsilon-iota ligature: the projection of the minuscule epsilon above the standard letter height varies: sometimes the projection is the normal size, sometimes it is reduced in comparison with isolated epsilon or epsilon in εσ ligature, and sometimes there is no projection at all above the joining of the curved and the straight strokes.

Epsilon-pi, epsilon-xi: both ligatures, when linked from the upper extension of epsilon, feature a sharp peak matching the height of the ascending tall letters (Plate 2, 2); but epsilon-pi is also often written as two letters in sequence, with the link formed by the horizontal of the epsilon continuing into pi.

Omicron-upsilon ligature: in both text and scholia the use of the full loop ου ligature is very rare, as the two letters are normally written out separately in the line. The suspended abbreviation for ου is a reduced υ (Plate 1, 3).

Other ligatures: most ligatures of horizontal strokes with the next letter are done in the standard way, but occasionally there is a more cursive form in which the horizontal right stroke is bent down to a diagonal that dips below the line and curves back up to join the next letter in the middle: this is found with ε, σ, τ, ψ, στ-ligature (Plate 3, 6–8); also δ as in δω three times in *Hec.* 1023–1024, 37v. Rho is not usually joined to the next letter, but here and there the scribe adopts a more cursive approach: the descender of rho continues into an arc rising to join the next letter: e.g., *Hec.* 1152 (Plate 3, 9) κόραι, *Or.* 502 (52v) μητέρα. This kind of flowing rho-ligature is a little more common later in the manuscript.

Accents and breathings: the acute and grave are usually small in size, but sometimes they are moderately lengthened when there is a lot of blank space above a word. Whereas the diagonal representing ου can sometimes be fairly long (at line-end), the grave does not share this degree of enlargement. The circumflex is also small, and there is a hastily written version of it in which the left part of the arc is much reduced, so that occasionally the result looks very much like a small grave with only slight curvature at one or both ends. Both curved and rectilinear breathings are used. The accents are never joined to breathings or to characters or abbreviations. The circumflex is sometimes on top of the breathing and sometimes beside it.

E. Abbreviations

Abbreviations are not at all common in the poetic text, and when used they are limited to the commonest items for case ending or the like, normally at line-end. The scholia, however, make very frequent use of abbreviations, word-internal as well as for endings. Among the common ones are those for αις, αν, ας, εν, ες, εις, ην, ης, ιν, ις, ον, ος, ου, ουν, ους, ων, and the sinuous downward tail indicating αι. Of the reduced signs, those of ἐστι and ὅτι and δέ are common, while there are only a handful of instances for εἶναι. The δέ symbol is usually the size of a letter, not tiny like a comma, as often in later scripts. Alpha can be represented either by a straight horizontal stroke or by the addition of two dots, above and below a horizontal (such as the right side of tau or theta). Omega is very often a supralinear tilde shape. In M the compendium for οις is usually much flatter than in other manuscripts of the scholia (but again B is comparable) and features an angle or near-angle rather than the smooth curve characteristic of more cursive hands (Plate 3, 10 and 11). The ους and ως compendia also seem to me unusual in their vertical compression (Plate 4, 1 and 2). The abbreviation for γάρ is routinely a majuscule gamma (not enlarged) with a rightward extension of the horizontal through which a diagonal is drawn, inclined from upper left to lower right (Plate 4, 3). For παρά (which is more often written out than abbreviated), one finds, not very often, pi with the slanted anchor sign above; but more often, especially later in the manuscript, a majuscule pi with the same sort of rightward extension of the top and crossing diagonal used in the compendium for γὰρ (Plate 4, 4).

The number of errors of case-ending in M's scholia indicates that earlier in the tradition similar abbreviations were in use, and because of the small size of many of the abbreviations, errors were easy (as between οις, ων, and suspended ω). Indeed, in comparing my own collations with Schwartz's, I found places where his different reading made me return to the image to determine who was right. Sometimes damage has blurred the ink and made the surviving trace too ambiguous to determine, but under magnification of the digital image one can usually see a reason to discriminate between the choices.

It is rare for the standard abbreviations to be enlarged, although this happens a few times with the diagonal for ον at line-end in the poetic text and (even in mid-line) for the arc representing ων. Some examples: *Or.* 901 (60r) λυπούμεν(ον); *Hec.* (24v) 280 πολλ(ῶν); *Or.* 799 (58v) ἀργεί(ων) [exceptionally wide] and 806 μυρί(ων), ὁμαινῶν(ων) (*sic*).

The unusual compendium for εισ (used before τ) that looks like εχ was illustrated above (Plate 1, 8-10). It is relevant to note the error in Sch. Hipp. 377 [376 Schwartz], where M has ἔχοντες κακόν for the correct εἰς τὸ κακόν, for this error must have arisen from the fact that in one of the ancestors of M someone misread as a truncation of ἔχοντες this same uncommon compendium. Other less common abbreviations in M are the compendia for αρ and ωρ described above.

Similarly, in M (as in some of the other witnesses of the scholia) there are several instances where διά and λείπει have been confused. This indicates that ancestor copies often used the abbreviations consisting of majuscule delta with a squiggly tail for διά and consisting of majuscule lambda with a squiggle for ει below it for λείπει. I noted at least one place where Schwartz, in collating M, misread one of these as the other, which proves how easy this is to do when reading the tiny script. Another error found a few times in M also derives from the use of abbreviation in the earlier tradition. The astrological symbol for the sun (☉)[65] was used at some point not only to replace various cases of ἥλιος, but also to abbreviate the name Apollo. For the symbol used for ἥλιος see Sch. Hipp. 128 (135v, end of second full line from bottom) and Sch. Hipp. 191 (137r, fifth line from top); but see Sch. Andr. 296 (115v, third line from top) for the same symbol standing for ἀπόλλων. The dual value of this symbol has led to those variants where a full form of ἥλιος has been written out instead of the corresponding case of Ἀπόλλων: Sch. Phoen. 101, 205, 235, 1102; compare V at, e.g., Sch. Or. 76 and 275, with ἡλίου for ἀπόλλωνος.

In the scholia of M there are also frequent instances of abbreviation by truncation of familiar words, such as λόγος, λέγει, λέγεται, forms of λαβεῖν, φέρω, ἀκούω, πόλις, πόλεμος, ποταμός, βασιλεύς and other βασιλ- words, παρθένον, δόξα. There is an isolated case of a different kind of abbreviation, the sort more common in grammatical texts, on fol. 71v, line 7, where προπερισπᾶται γὰρ παρακείμενος ὤν has a truncation of the name of the tense, π(αρα)κ(), and after προ represents περισπᾶται with an enlarged circumflex accent written within the line and surmounted by a horizontal stroke (Plate 4, 5).

Probably fewer than a dozen times in the codex the scholia feature the compendium consisting of a pi-tau combination with two vowels above, to represent παρά plus a form of the article. Usually the vowels are alpha and omicron to indicate παρὰ τό, an abbreviation often seen in the manuscripts of *Etymologica* for this familiar formula meaning "derived from" (Plate 4, 6).

F. The Scholia Reference System

In different parts of the manuscript, for the scholia that are written in the main blocks (top of page, outer margin, bottom of page), one may find alternatively

---

[65] Gardthausen 1911-1913: II.343; Mossay 1982.

letter-numerals as reference symbols or various non-character symbols (paralleled in other manuscripts, such as RV of Aristophanes).[66] On some pages with few scholia there are no reference symbols, with the scholia usually placed in the margin at the level of the relevant lemma. The symbols are more usually in the margin closely adjacent to the scholia block, but sometimes they are incorporated within the lines of the block before the lemma. Less frequently, the symbols are in the margin but considerably separated from the left edge of the scholia block, with the result that on such pages the signs may be obscured by damage to the edge of the leaf or even completely trimmed away. Scholia that are written intermarginally (that is, between the inner margin of the side block of scholia and the outer margin of the text) or in the inside margin sometimes have reference symbols and sometimes do not.

For most of the manuscript the scholia are properly placed on the same page as the relevant passage, but there is a section of *Phoenissae* (95r–105v) where this matching has been neglected, so that some scholia appear on the page before the relevant line in the text. Similarly, the sequence of numbering is usually started anew at alpha on each page, but in some sections (in *Andromache* and *Hippolytus* as well as *Phoenissae*) the first scholia on a page will complete a previous sequence (for instance, with δ through ζ), and then a new sequence will start with ᾱ later on that page. One may speculate that in such a case the scribe is retaining the numbering used in the exemplar while not being able to adhere to the same pagination of the sections of poetic text.[67] (For more exact details, see the Appendix to this chapter.)

G. Other Oddities

On fol. 23r (*Hec.* 173–201) four *notae* for the character Polyxena (πολ) are added to the right of text, although the *notae* for Polyxena and Hecuba are present in their normal place in the left margin of the text; on 27r (*Hec.* 404–433) the *notae* are to the right of text and absent in their usual location.

Sch. Andr. 224 in M (fol. 114r, starting in line 9 of the right margin block) contains two very unusual abbreviations, not used elsewhere in the codex (or in others being collated for this project, so far). Twice the word αὐτοῦ is represented by what looks like an iota with diaeresis and an overstroke (ὃς αὐτοῦ κατελήφθη and ὁ πατὴρ αὐτοῦ, Plate 4, 7–8), and there is an abbreviation for πρός (in πρὸς εὐριπίδην) that looks somewhat like M's ους compendium, but

---

[66] See Atsalos 1991 in general and especially for the illustrations he gives of a variety of symbols.
[67] Maniaci 2006: 287–288 notes some examples where a reference symbol is used within a sequence of letters as references in two manuscripts of Homeric scholia that are *gemelli*, so that the mixture of symbols must have been in their source, and she suggests that the different types indicate different sources.

placed in the line (Plate 4, 9). The latter can be found in collections of abbreviations.[68] The closest comparanda I can find for the former are the fifth and eighth (last) examples in the first line under the rubric ΑΥ in Tsereteli 1904: Plate 2, for which he gives a date in the 4th century!

M contains some long marks over Doric alphas (and one long alpha from crasis) by the original scribe. There are four such marks in *Phoenissae*, fourteen in *Hippolytus*, and one in *Andromache*. This phenomenon is also found 12 times in O of Euripides in the first 400 lines of *Orestes* only, and O also has one upsilon marked long as well. In B there are no long marks in the first five plays contained in the codex, but of the last two, *Alcestis* features about 100 marks, and there are several dozen in *Andromache* 1–956; in B these are applied not just to some Doric alphas and products of crasis, but also to words in iambic trimeters like ἀφῖκόμην, βαρύνομαι, δακρύματα. Much later, such marking, on all three dichronic vowels, is done in a more consistent way (but without absolute consistency) by Triclinius in his autograph T.[69]

M has a few shaped scholia. In some manuscripts with few scholia occupying an ample margin, scribes sometimes gave the block of lines a shape other than rectangular. For instance, by decreasing the length of each line, a triangle is formed, or a diamond shape can be created by starting with a very short line and gradually increasing the length, and at mid-point gradually decreasing line-length again. This is similar to the practice of tapering lines of text into a point at the end of a text or in a subscription. Many pages of M have too many scholia to allow such designs, but even when scholia are sparse, the scribe's regular practice is to distribute the available scholia at the top and bottom. Nevertheless, on three pages near the end of *Hecuba*, the scribe produces shaped scholia in the outer margin. Folio 38v has a mostly blank left margin and a blank bottom margin, and Sch. Hec. 1098 in the lower left is shaped like a cross. On 39r in the right margin of the upper half of the page, two scholia are written in a shaped block that consists of a narrow diamond shape of 9 lines (Sch. 1100 and the start of Sch. 1102), followed by two normal lines, and then by an upward-pointing triangle of 12 lines (finishing at the end of Sch. 1102). On 40r, the shaping is rather different: in a blank right margin, four scholia are written separately in narrow columns, and the notes themselves are arranged in a diamond pattern (12 lines in the top scholia, positioned in the middle, below that and to the left 10 lines with another note, at the same level but toward the right edge 7 lines of another

---

[68] Lehmann 1880: 87; Allen 1889: Plate VII, προc #9; Mioni 1973: 97.

[69] Exceptionally, V has written κηφήνᾱ at *Tro.* 192 (for κηφήν ἀ). In the Palaeologan witnesses I have (partially) collated so far, I have found only Hec. 5 κίνδῡνος in XXb. See now Fries 2017 for discussion of long and short marks added to many vowels in two Pre-Palaeologan manuscripts of Pindar.

note, and 8 lines in the bottom note, positioned centrally like the top note.[70]

Finally, there is a curiosity that appears to reflect the use of the codex in teaching Euripides at some date after its original production. A later hand I designate as M³ has added sporadic glosses, generally characterized by a darker ink and a much larger, cruder script than M¹ or than another fairly early hand designated M².[71] Among the additions made by M³ are eight marginal notations featuring a numeral and the word ἑρμηνεία, either in full or truncated (and in six instances with smooth breathing instead of rough; once with rough breathing, and the eighth example is damaged).

> 85v outer margin near end of text, at *Phoen.* 526 (choregus' couplet before the third *agōn* rhesis by Jocasta): ἑρμηνεία ἀ(?). The last sign is uncertain. It may be an alpha in a circle with an enlarged smooth breathing outside the circle, perhaps for πρώτη; but numeral alpha usually does not have a breathing, and the circle appears not to be quite complete.
>
> 92r, a little before middle of inner margin, at *Phoen.* 834 (the first iambic line of the third episode, entrance speech of Teiresias): [δε]υτέρα [ἑ]ρμηνεία.
>
> 95v middle of outer margin, at *Phoen.* 1019 (start of third stasimon): ε̄ ἑρμην().
>
> 98v middle of outer margin, at *Phoen.* 1200 (choregus' couplet after the messenger speech): γ̄ ἑρμηνεία followed by cross.
>
> 102v near end of text, outer margin, at *Phoen.* 1425 (choregus' couplet after first messenger rhesis): *? ἑρμηνεία (numeral partly cut off and faded at margin, trace of overstroke).
>
> 135v, outer margin at *Hipp.* 121 (beginning of parodos): γ̄ ἑρμηνεία.
>
> 138r, at *Hipp.* 267 (choregus starting iambic scene after anapaests of nurse): ε̄ θέκλας ἑρμηνει().
>
> 144r, at margin of *Hipp.* 601, right against end of line (Hippolytus bursting out from indoors at the opening of scene): β̄ ἑρμην(εία) εἰς τὰς θ**. After the two damaged characters or as part of the second there survives a diagonal, possibly a truncation stroke. There is not space enough for θεκλ, and the theta itself is also not certain (it could be the bottom of a closed epsilon).

There are two other markings by M³ that may be related, because they occur at the opening of scenes: on 82v the *nota personae* χορ (*Phoen.* 354, first iambic line after Jocasta's aria) is partly surrounded on the left and bottom by an odd

---

[70] Once again in this detail B and M are similar, since shaped scholia are also found in B: intermarginal scholia on 30r and 31v, and a few other pages; regular scholia on fol. 104v–107r (last pages of *Hipp.*; various shapes), 119v, 128v (penultimate page of *Med.*). Cavallo 2002: ix notes that shaped marginal annotations are mentioned by Cassiodorus around 500 CE.

[71] Perhaps M³ belongs to the 12th century, based on the shape of the s-form eta in ligature with mu in μη and the appearance of the ει ligature.

shape, and above is a possible omega, but also what looks like an enlarged rough breathing and perhaps a smooth one too;[72] on 89r there is a large circle with a cross inside it at *Phoen.* 690, the first line of the second episode.

In any case, it is unclear what *hermēneia* means in these annotations, but a possible speculation is that a teacher taught passages of these two plays, offering "interpretation," that is paraphrases and other explanations, and divided the treatment at structurally relevant points in the text. This does not explain, however, why the numbers are not in sequence for *Phoenissae* (and one number is duplicated). The mention of Thecla (there is no doubt that the word is θέκλας) perhaps refers to the famous Saint Thecla, who had a feast day on September 24. There were apparently two churches dedicated to her in Constantinople, but their identification is very uncertain,[73] and I know of no evidence for a school associated with either. This is a detail that I will have to leave to others to clarify, if that is possible.

---

[72] The couplet is gnomic, but I have never seen a γνωμικόν mark resembling this.
[73] One church, presumably the one described in Zonaras, *Epitome hist.* III.174 (Büttner-Wobst 1897) as renewed (ἀνεκαίνισε) by Justin II (565–578), is identified as the goal of a procession on the saint's feast day, September 24, where it is said to be in the Krithopolia (located south of Hagia Sophia, near the harbor of Sophia on the Sea of Marmora: Janin 1950: 99, 349): *Typikon* I.42, 21–25 (Mateos 1962), *Synaxarium ecclesiae Constantinopolitanae*, Sept. 24 (Delehaye 1902); Berger 2001: 76 n. 8 and map on 87. The second, according to Zonaras, *Epitome hist.* III.672 and Anna Comnena, *Alexias* 3.8.5–10, was founded by Isaac I Comnenus (1057–1059) within the palace (ἐντὸς τῶν βασιλείων in Zonaras) at Blachernae (in the northwest of the enlarged city, on the Golden Horn) to acknowledge his miraculous survival of danger in a storm on September 24. This one has been identified with the Atik Mustafa Pasha Mosque (near the Blachernae palace, but not within it), but this remains doubtful: Tunay 2001: 228–229.

APPENDIX TO CHAPTER 4

Numeration Sequence in Scholia References in M

In *Hecuba* the scribe uses a variety of non-character reference symbols. *Orestes* features the same system, but folios 51r–v have dense scholiation, and lemmata are there included in the scholia, but no reference symbols are used. *Phoenissae* continues the use of non-character symbols until folio 94r, but on 94v starts to use letter-numerals, and from this point the scholia sometimes end up on a different page from the relevant passage:

95r	after sequence α–θ, one symbol note and then α referring to a line on 95v
95v	β–ιδ for this page
96r	ιε–ιϛ then α–θ all for this page
96v	ι–ια and then α–ζ for this page, η for next
97r	θ and one symbol and α–ια for this page
97v	ιβ–ιγ and then α–η for this page
98r	θ–ιβ, α–ϛ for this page
98v	ζ–θ, α–ϛ for this page, ζ–ια for next page
99r	α–γ for this page, δ–ζ for next page
99v	η and α–δ for this page
100r	α for this page, β–ζ for next page
100v	one symbol and θ–ια, then α for this page, β–γ for next page
101r	δ–θ, α–β for this page, γ–ϛ for next page
101v	ζ–ιγ, α for this page, β for next
102r	γ–ιβ for this page
102v	ιγ, α–ζ for this page, η for next
103r	α–η for this page
103v	α–δ for this page, ε–ϛ for next
104r	ζ–θ, α–η for this page, θ for next
104v	ι–ιδ, α–β for this page, γ for next
105r	δ, α–γ for this page, δ for next
105v	ε–ϛ, α–γ for this page, δ for next
106r	ε–ζ, α–β (from this point to the end, the scholia are on the correct page)
106v	γ and one symbol

186

107r	one symbol and α–ε
107v	ϛ–ια, α–β
108r	γ used for a marg. sch., δ–ζ in upper block, then α–γ
108v	δ–ιβ
109r	one symbol for Peisander scholion

Andromache starts at 109v: the scribe first uses letters but shifts later. The scholia are on the correct page.

111v	first sch. on page uses θ (prev. page went up to η), other (widely spaced scholia) have no ref.
112r–v	a few symbols and some sch. without ref.
113r–v	symbols, except one β used among symbols on 113v
118r	use of letters returns
118v	ζ–θ, α–ζ
119r	no ref., few sch.
119v	α, then α–γ
120r	δ–η, α–γ
120v	δ–ε, α–ε
121r	ϛ–η, α–γ
121v	δ–ζ, α
122r	β–δ, α–β
122v	γ–ι, α
123r	β–ε, α
123v	β–ε
124r	α–ϛ
124v	sparse scholia, margins washed out, but reference symbols are visible in the text
125r	returns to letters, α–ζ
125v	η, α–δ and one symbol
126r	ε–ϛ, α–ε
126v	ϛ, α–ϛ
127r	ζ–η, α–ε
127v	ϛ–ζ, α–β
128r	γ–ϛ, α–γ
128v	δ–η
129v	α–γ
130r	δ–η with two symbols interposed between ζ–η, then α
130v	sparse, apparently no symbols
131r	α–δ
131v	α–ε
132r	α–ϛ
132v	ζ, α–δ

188   PRELIMINARY STUDIES ON THE SCHOLIA TO EURIPIDES

Hippolytus. The scholia are on the correct page.

133v	a couple of symbols interposed within the sequence α–η
134r	θ–ιγ, α–ζ
134v	η–ιβ, α–β
135r	γ–ς, α–δ
135v	ε–ιγ, α–ζ
136r	η–ις, α–γ
136v	δ–θ
137r	α–η, α
137v	β–ιγ
138r–139r	symbols used
139v	α–ζ or more (many washed out), one symbol interspersed
140r	symbols, sparse
140v–154v	too damaged to tell, or no scholia, or sparse scholia placed by relevant line with no symbols, or symbol used only for a lone item in upper margin

Plates

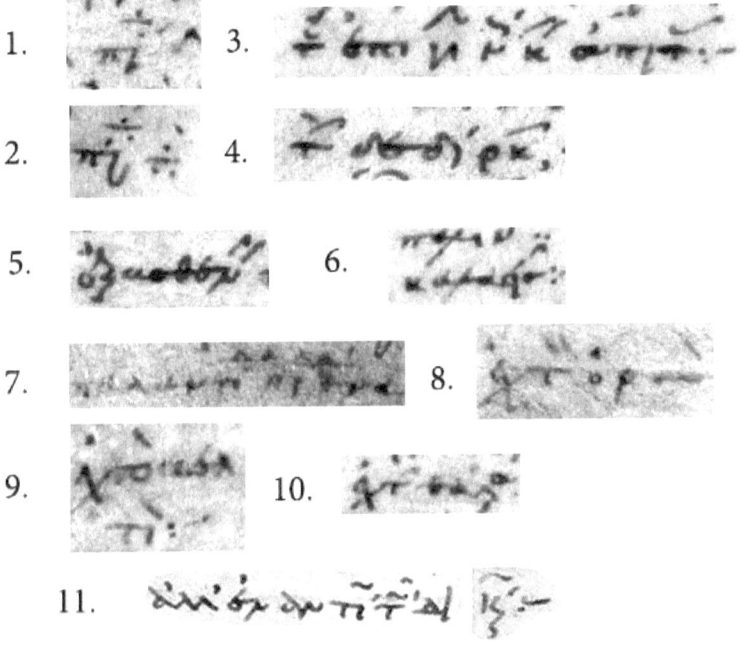

PLATE 1.
ABBREVIATIONS IN M

(1) πάντα, Sch. Or. 488, 52v line 7; (2) πάντα τὰ, Sch. Or. 382, 50v line 9 of side block; (3) τοῦ ἐπιγινώσκειν, ἅπαντας Sch. Phoen. 96, 78v line 13 of side block; (4) τὴν δε δίρκην, Sch. Phoen. 102, 78v line 15 from bottom of side block; (5) ἐξασθενεῖν, Sch. Phoen. 114, 79r line 3; (6) καλα εισιν, Sch. Hipp. 79, intermarginal beside line 8 from bottom of text; (7) παλαντι∆∆ παί∆∆ ἕνα, Sch. Hipp. 35, 134r line 3 from bottom, at end; (8) εἰς τὸν ὅρμον, Sch. Hec. 450, 24v line 5 of side block; (9) εἰς τὸ βέλτιον, Sch. Hec. 961, 36v in margin beside line 6 of text; (10) εἰς τὴν θάλα(), Sch. Phoen. 4, 76v line 2 from bottom of side block; (11) ἀλλ᾽ ἐναντίω τῶι δικαίω, Sch. Phoen. 526, fol. 85v line 7–8 of side block.

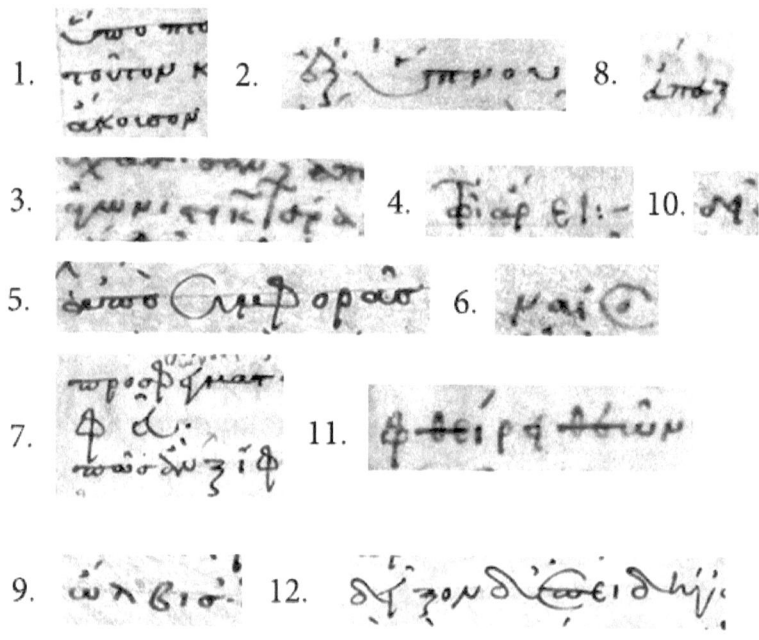

PLATE 2.
LETTER FORMS IN M

(1) ὕποπτο[ν] / τοῦτον κ[/ ἄκουσον, Hec. 1135-1137, 39v lines 10-12 of text; (2) ἐξ ὕπνου, Or. 168, 46v line 2 from bottom of text; (3) ἀγωνιστικωτέρα, Sch. Phoen. 88, 78v line 2; (4) τῶι ἄρει, Sch. Andr. 1014, 128r line 14 of side block; (5) ἀπὸ συμφορᾶς, Hipp. 803, 147v line 12 of text; (6) [γεν]ναίος, Hipp. 205, 137r line 14 from bottom of side block; (7) προσφθέγματ' / φεῦ / πῶς ἂν ξίφ[ος], Or. 1051-1053 (beginnings), 63r middle of text; (8) ἅπαξ, supralinear Sch. Andr. 588, 120v line 10 of text; (9) ὤλβισ', Phoen. 1689, 107v line 12 of text; (10) δεῖ, Sch. Phoen. 1684, 107v line 3; (11) φθείρει θεῶν, Hec. 58, 21r, line 1 of text; (12) δεῖξον δ' ἐπειδὴ γ', Hipp. 946, 150r line 9 of text.

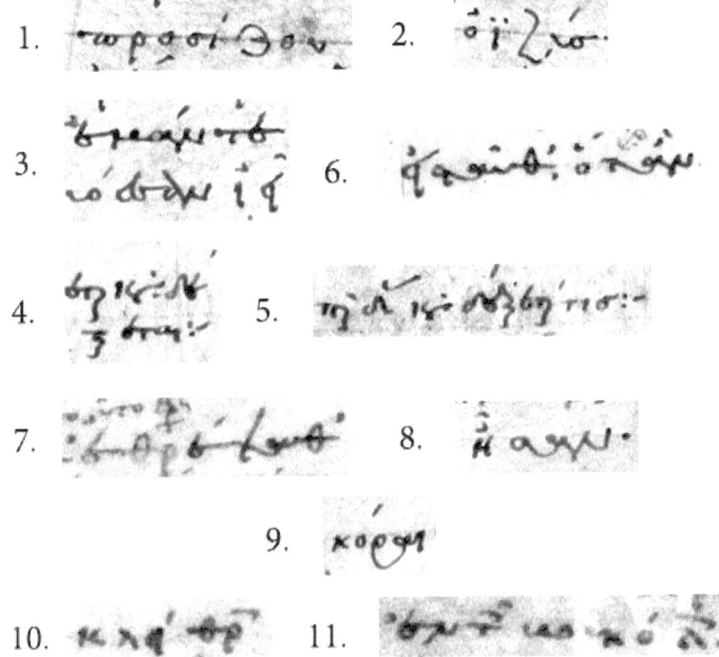

PLATE 3.
LETTER FORMS AND ABBREVIATIONS IN M

(1) προσίζου[σ'], *Hec.* 935, 36r line of text; (2) ὀϊζύς, *Hec.* 949, 36r line 21 of text; (3) ἐμάν τε / [δακρ]ρυόεσαν ἱεῖ[σα], *Phoen.* 322–323, 83r lines 4 and 3 from bottom; (4) [πιστώσ]εται καταδέξεται, Sch. Andr. 201, 113v; (5) παῖδας καταδέξεταί τις, Sch. Andr. 201, 113v line 12 of side block; (6) εἰς ταῦθ', ὅτᾶν, *Phoen.* 585, 86v last line of text; (7) ἐθρέψαθ', *Hec.* 424, 27r line 10 from bottom of text; (8) ἦσαν, *Hec.* 124, 22r line 11 of text; (9) κόραι, *Hec.* 1152, 39v line 3 from bottom; (10) κλείθροις, Sch. Phoen. 114, 79r line 1; (11) ἐν τοῖς βουκόλοις, Sch. Phoen. 102, 78v line 30 of side block.

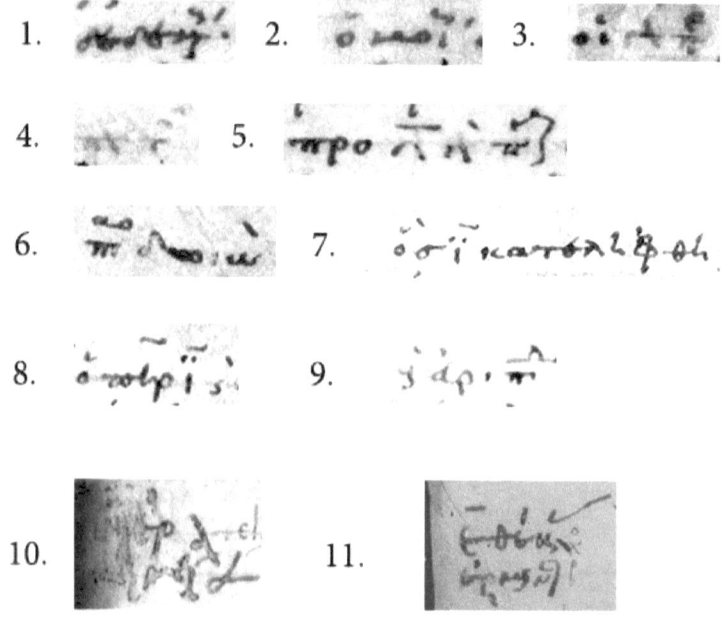

PLATE 4.
ABBREVIATIONS AND *HERMĒNEIA* NOTATIONS IN M

(1) δεδεμένους, Sch. Phoen. 114, 79r line 2; (2) ὁμοίως, Sch. Phoen. 129, 79r line 15 from bottom of side block; (3) οἱ γὰρ πε(ρί), Sch. Phoen. 102, 78v line 26 of side block; (4) παρὰ τῶν, Sch. Hipp. 98, 135r line 4 from bottom; (5) προ(περισπᾶται) γὰρ π(αρα)κ(είμενος), Sch. Or. 1525, 71v line 7; (6) π(αρ)ὰ τὸ δοιώ, Sch. Phoen. 156, 79v line 1 of bottom block; (7) ὅς (αὐτοῦ) κατελήφθη, Sch. Andr. 224, 114r line 18 of side block; (8) ὁ π(ατ)ὴρ (αὐτοῦ) καὶ, Sch. Andr. 224, 114r line 21 of side block; (9) (πρὸς) εὐριπίδ(ην), Sch. Andr. 224, 114r line 25 of side block; (10) [δε]υτέρα [ἑ]ρμηνεία, 92r margin at *Phoen.* 838; (11) ε̄ θέκλας ἑρμηνει(), 138r margin at *Hipp.* 267.

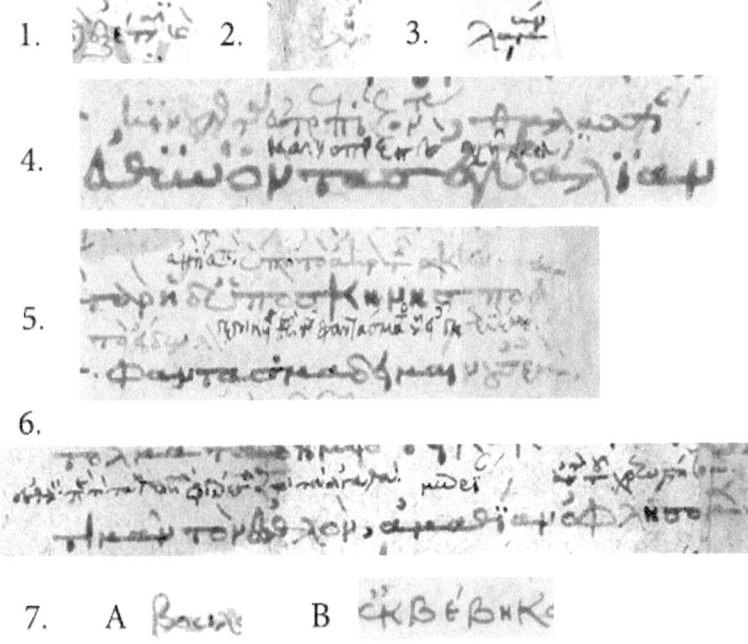

PLATE 5.
TRUNCATION IN V AND HANDS OF V

(1) [π]ρὸς ἐξέτα(σ)ιν καὶ, Sch. Andr. 702, 246v line 5 from bottom; (2) βούλη(σ)ις, Sch. Andr. 702, 246v line 2 from bottom; (3) λαμβ(ά)ν(ει), Sch. Andr. 696, 246v above line 11 of text; (4) A κινοῦντας and θαλασσίαν, B εὐτρεπίζοντας, V³ καινοπρεπὲς σχῆμα, Hec. 39, 3r line 8 of text; (5) A ὑπὸ τὸ ἄκρον τῆς σκηνῆς and τὸ εἴδωλον, B ἀντὶ τοῦ ἀπό, V³ δεδοικυῖα περὶ τοῦ φαντάσματος οὗ εἶδε περὶ ἐμοῦ, Hec. 53–54, 3v lines 3–4 of text; (6) A ἀντὶ τοῦ χρεωστήσομεν, B μωρίαν, V³ ἐσθλὸν· παρὰ τὸ τὰ θελητὰ φέρεσθαι ἤτοι τὰ ἀγαθὰ, Hec. 327, 8v line 3 of text; (7) A βουλο[ίμην], Med. 73, 120r line 2; B ἐκβέβηκ`, Med. 56, 119v line 5.

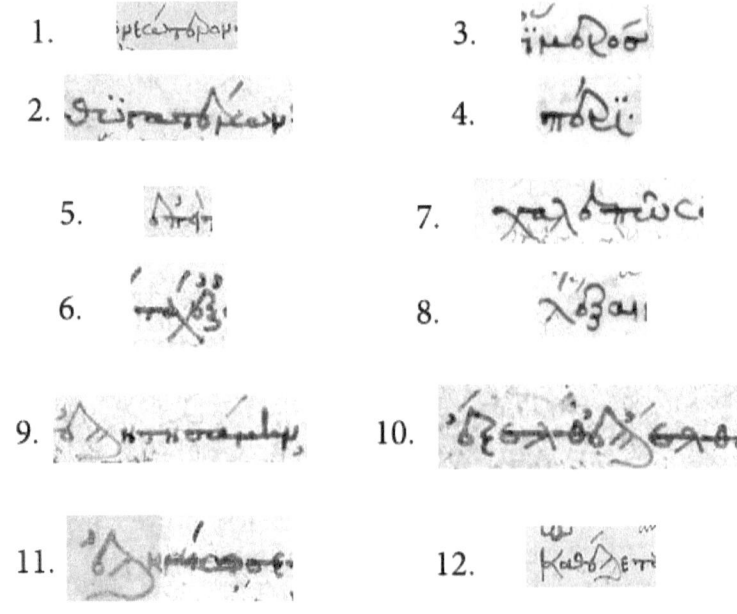

PLATE 6.
LIGATURES IN V

(1) νεώτερον (A), *Phoen.* 71, 69v line 1 of text; (2) θυγατέρων (A), *Or.* 250, 31r line 4 from bottom of text; (3) ἵμερός (B), *Med.* 57, 119v line 6 of text; (4) πέρι (B), *Med.* 66, 119v line 6 from bottom of text; (5) ἐπεὶ (A), Sch. *Or.* 390, 34v line 3 from bottom of side block; (6) τάχ' ἐξ (A), *Med.* 335, 127v line 4 from bottom of text; (7) χαλεπῶς (B), *Med.* 121, 121r line 3 from bottom of text; (8) λέξαι (B), *Med.* 58, 119v line 7 of text; (9) ἐξητησάμην (A), *Hec.* 49, 3r line 2 from bottom of text; (10) ἔξελθ' ἔξελθ' (A), *Hec.* 174, 6r line 10 from bottom of text; (11) ἐζημίωσε (A), *Or.* 578, 40r line 7 from bottom of text; (12) καθέζετ' (A), *Phoen.* 75, 69v line 5 of text.

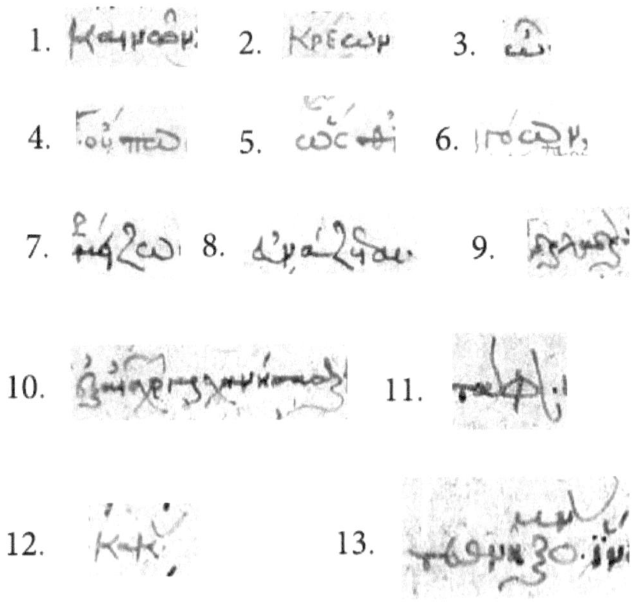

PLATE 7.
LETTER FORMS IN V

(1) καινῶν (A), *Med.* 76, 120r line 5; (2) κρέων (A), *Med.* 72, 120r line 1; (3) ὦ (A), *Med.* 82, 120r line 11; (4) οὔπω (B), *Med.* 59, 119v line 8 of text; (5) ὥσθ' (B), *Med.* 57, 119v line 6 of text; (6) γόων (B), *Med.* 59, 119v line 8 of text; (7) μείζω (B), *Med.* 43, 119r line 12; (8) εὐνάζεται (B), *Med.*18, 118v line 5 of text; (9) δηλαδή (A), Sch. Hipp. 331, 166v line 1 of bottom block; (10) ἐξ αἰσχρῶν μηχανήσασθαι (A), Sch. Hipp. 331, 166v line 5 of bottom block; (11) τάφον (A), Hyp. Alc., 197r line 5; (12) κακόν (A), Sch. Hipp. 348, 167r above line 5 from bottom of text; (13) τεθνηξόμενον (A), Hyp. Alc., 197r line 3.

Chapter 5

On Vaticanus Graecus 909 (Codex V of Euripides)

1. V AND PLANUDES?

The purpose of this chapter is to clarify the scribal history embedded within the manuscript V of Euripides, a very important witness for the study of Euripides and of the Euripidean scholia because of its inclusion of the text of, and scholia on, nine of the select plays. It took significant effort to copy the more than 600 pages of this codex from a source that was evidently sometimes hard or impossible to read. I believe that this effort probably took place in the period 1250–1280 (the dating suggested by Nigel Wilson),[1] before the full onset of Palaeologan interest in pagan literature spearheaded by Maximus Planudes in the capital and also pursued in Thessalonike in an erudite circle around Thomas Magister and Demetrius Triclinius. V continued to be used for study and teaching in the generation or two after its creation, as we can see both from the corrections in the text, ascribable to several different hands, and the many additional glosses and some discursive notes added by one or more cursive hands, mostly, perhaps, before 1320–1330,[2] and thus contemporary with the collecting of annotation from different sources that we see in Triclinius (T) and in Y, as well as a little later in Gr/Gu.

First, however, some discussion must be devoted to the once widely held view, still cited as authoritative in the Vatican catolgue entry in 1988,[3] that the manuscript is to be dated 1280–1300. This was the date proposed by Turyn, who also believed there were Planudean elements in the annotation of the later hand

---

[1] Wilson 1966: 342.
[2] Based on the fact that Y copied from V, along with the text of *Troades*, some of these cursive glosses that were not written by the original hands of V; see chapter 2, n. 75.
[3] Schreiner 1988: 108–109.

(V² for Turyn, but termed V³ here, as explained later) and that there might be Planudean influence even in the original production of the manuscript and its scholia. Specifically, Turyn suggested that some of the longer discursive scholia known only from V, marked as "recent" by Schwartz, might be "possibly Byzantine or Planudean influenced products."[4] That date was assumed by Vincenzo di Benedetto when he argued in more detail that the codex could be viewed as a product of a new Palaeologan humanism possibly associated with Maximus Planudes.[5] The arguments used by them about Planudes' characteristic interests (paraphrases, etymologies, distinction between similar words, grammatical usage) are weak because they did not (or could not) take sufficient account of the teaching tradition and the evidence for annotation of this kind earlier than 1200, discussed in Chapters 2 and 3. Where Turyn has referred generally to items marked as "recent" by Schwartz and found only in V, di Benedetto offered a list of specific examples, acknowledging that there were more pertaining to *Hecuba* than to *Orestes*. In particular, he argued that certain rather verbose scholia analyzing argumentation and psychology in dialogue in *Orestes* reflect this Planudean-era humanism. Indeed, the *Orestes* scholia do contain an unusual group of notes that reflect an interest in close readings of some dialogue scenes, readings that seek hidden motives in the choice of particular words and phrases and that assume subtle rhetorical skills in the speakers in the use of trickery and innuendo (πανουργία, ὑπόνοια).[6] But most of these are part of the "old" collection carried in MBC as well as V. Only a few are in V alone or V and one or another of the *recentiores* (their presence in witnesses other than V was not known when Di Benedetto wrote). Here we may consider briefly three of these V-scholia, which are among those singled out by Di Benedetto.

At *Orestes* 414 there is a scholion attested in MBCVPr that paraphrases the whole stichomythic exchange in *Orestes* 414–420. Following this in V only is an even more expansive analysis of these lines, with the lemma ἄλλως.

> Sch. Or. 414 ἄλλως: ὅρα τὸ εὐφυὲς τοῦ ποιητοῦ, πῶς δι' ἀμφοτέρων τῶν προσώπων τούτων, τοῦ Ὀρέστου καὶ τοῦ Μενελάου, τὰς ἐναντίας τῶν ἀνθρώπων δόξας ὑποδηλοῖ. ἐπεὶ γὰρ οἱ μὲν τῶν ἀνθρώπων λέγουσι τιμωρεῖν

---

[4] Turyn 1957: 75. "Byzantine" in Turyn's terminology (also used by di Benedetto) means "Palaeologan," a most unfortunate use of this adjective that arose among the classical scholars of earlier centuries.
[5] Di Benedetto 1965: 23–51. After identifying some characteristics of the nature of the text of the plays in V (such as incorporation of glosses or other simplifications) and believing these were somehow a matter of the learned scribe's choices, he concluded on p. 38: "il procedimento seguito da V è impensabile al tempo di Fozio o di Psello o anche all'epoca di Tzetzes."
[6] I plan to address this topic in detail elsewhere in the near future.

τὸ θεῖον τοῖς πάσχουσιν, οἱ δ' ⟨ὅτι οἱ θεοὶ⟩ ἀδιαφοροῦσι,[7] διὰ μὲν τοῦ Ὀρέστου τὸ βοηθεῖσθαι παρὰ τοῦ θείου τοὺς κάμνοντας συνίστησι, διὰ δὲ τοῦ Μενελάου σοφιστικῶς ἀπαγορεύει. ἐκεῖθεν δὲ τὴν ὑφὴν τοῦ λόγου προὐκατεσκεύασεν. εἰπόντος γὰρ τοῦ Μενελάου ἀπὸ τοῦ "οἶδα μὲν αὐτὰς, ὀνομάσαι δ' οὐ βούλομαι" καὶ καθεξῆς, τοῦ Ὀρέστου εἰς μομφὴν τῶν Εὐμενίδων κινηθέντος ὁ Μενέλαος τρόπον τινὰ τοῦτον ἀπεστρέψατο[8] εἰπὼν "αὗταί σε βακχεύουσι συγγενεῖ φόνῳ," δηλονότι ἃς κατευτελίζεις καὶ οὐ θέλεις καλεῖσθαι Εὐμενίδας, λέγων "εὐπαίδευτα δ' ἀποτρέπου λέγειν," ἤτοι ἀπόφευγε τὸ προστιθέμενον αὐταῖς ὄνομα, τὸ Εὐμενίδες, παρὰ τῶν εὖ πεπαιδευμένων καὶ σοφῶν λέγειν, καὶ λέγε δήπουθεν τὸ οἰκεῖον αὐταῖς ὄνομα ἤγουν αἱ ἀλάστορες, αἱ Τελχῖνες, αἱ φονεύτριαι. πρὸς τὸ βακχεύουσιν ὁ Ὀρέστης ἐπιτατικῶς εἶπε τὸ "οἴμοι διωγμῶν οἷς ἐλαύνομαι τάλας," ὁ δ' ἀντεῖπεν "οὐ δεινὰ πάσχειν δεινὰ τοὺς εἰργασμένους" ἤγουν μὴ τὰς θεὰς μέμφου, ἑαυτὸν δὲ τὸν αἴτιον τοῦ πάσχειν τὰ δεινὰ ὡς δεινὰ ἐργασάμενον. εἶτα ἐκείνου φεύγοντος τὴν πρᾶξιν καὶ πρὸς τὸν Φοῖβον ταύτην ἀναφέροντος ὁ Μενέλαος ἀπεστρέψατο μὴ εἶναι λέγων τὸ θεῖον ἀμαθὲς τοῦ καλοῦ καὶ τοῦ δικαίου. ἐκείνου δὲ ἐπιμείναντος τῇ ἐνστάσει καὶ λέξαντος ὅτι δουλεύομεν τοῖς θεοῖς, ἤτοι ποιοῦμεν ἃ παρ' αὐτῶν κελευόμεθα κἂν μὴ λίαν ἐπιστάμεθα τί πρᾶγμά εἰσιν οἱ θεοί, ὁ Μενέλαος τὸν οἰκεῖον βουλόμενος συστῆσαι λόγον ὅτι οὐκ ἐκ θεοῦ ἐκεῖνο, ἀλλ' ἐκ θυμοῦ τὸ πραχθέν, φησὶν ὅτι πάντως ἂν ἐβοήθησέ σοι ὁ θεός, εἴπερ καὶ προσέταξεν. ὡς δ' εἶπεν ἐκεῖνος μέλλει τὸ θεῖον, ἤτοι βραδύνει ἐν ταῖς ἀντιδόσεσι ταῖς φαύλαις τε καὶ ταῖς ἀγαθαῖς ὡς ὂν φύσει τοιοῦτον, σοφιστικῶς ἐκεῖνος ἐπήγαγε τὸ "ὡς ταχὺ μετῆλθόν σ' αἷμα μητρὸς αἱ θεαί," ἤτοι ἀπῄτησαν. ἔκλεψε δ' αὐτὸν διὰ τῆς μέσης ἐρωτήσεως τῆς "πόσον χρόνον δὲ μητρὸς οἴχονται πνοαί." ἀποκριθέντος δ' ἐκείνου τὸ πόσον τοῦ καιροῦ, ἀνεῖλεν ἐκεῖ τὸ "μέλλει τὸ θεῖον" διὰ τοῦ "ὡς ταχὺ μετῆλθόν σ' αἷμα μητρός." V

Differently explained: observe the natural talent of the poet, how through both these characters, Orestes and Menelaus, he suggests the contradictory opinions of humans. For since some people say that the divine avenges those who suffer, while others say that the gods are indifferent, through Orestes he affirms the view that those in distress are rescued by the divine, but through Menelaus he denies this through sophistic argumentation. From that point he made a preliminary exposure of the web of the argument. For after Menelaus has made his statements, from the line "I know them, but I do not want to name them" and what follows that, and Orestes has been moved toward reproach of the Eumenides, Menelaus in a certain way turned Orestes away from his point, by saying "these goddesses drive you mad because of kindred bloodshed," namely the goddesses whom you (Orestes) disparage and do not want to be called Eumenides when you say "avoid speaking, in the manner of a well-educated person," in other words, "avoid speaking the

---

[7] The supplement ⟨ὅτι οἱ θεοὶ⟩ is mine. V reads οἱ δ' ἀδιαφοροῦσι, the meaning of which would be inappropriate: "they neglect (their religious duties)" (a sense well attested in Christian authors), or (?) "they are indifferent (to possible divine punishment)."

[8] ἀπεστρέψατο Schwartz (exactly as used a few lines later in the note), ἀπεπέμψατο V.

name, Eumenides, that is applied to them by those who are well educated and wise, and say rather the name that is proper to them, that is, *alastores* (avenging demons), Telchines, murderesses." In response to "they drive you mad" Orestes said with intensity "Woe is me for the pursuit with which I am driven, wretched man," and the other said in contradiction "it is not a shocking thing for those who have done terrible things to suffer the same," meaning do not reproach the goddesses, but rather yourself, the one responsible for suffering terrible things because you did them. Next, when Orestes tries to disown the deed and refer it to Phoebus, Menelaus rejected this point by saying the divine is not ignorant of what is good and just. When Orestes persisted in the objection and said "we are slaves to the gods," that is, we do what we are commanded to do by them even if we don't really understand what the gods are, Menelaus, desiring to confirm his own argument that the act did not come from a god, but from strong emotion, says that by all means the god would have come to his rescue if he had in fact given the order. And when Orestes said "the divine procrastinates," that is, acts slowly both in bad and good repayments (for human action), because the divine is such by nature, Menelaus added sophistically the point "how swiftly the goddesses pursued you for the bloodshed of your mother," that is, demanded their due. He tricked Orestes with the intervening question, "how long since your mother breathed her last?" When Orestes replied with the quantity of time, Menelaus refuted at that point the claim "the divine procrastinates" with his "how swiftly the goddesses pursued you for the bloodshed of your mother."

This kind of analysis has no particular connection to Planudes, but is one that had been practiced for centuries in the scholiastic tradition. We saw, for instance, long notes by one Irenaeus on Medea's first speech to the chorus.[9] As for the language, the appeal to the notion of προκατασκευή (or προκατασκευάζειν), for instance, is attested well before the Palaeologan era in scholia to Thucydides, Demosthenes, Homer, Sophocles, and Euripides, and for long-winded scholia in which the term appears we may refer to Tzetzes, in his note on Hesiod, *Theogony* 1 (line 228), or again his scholion to Lycophron quoted in Chapter 2.[10] Furthermore, the close association of Telchines with Erinyes is found more than a dozen times in Middle Byzantine authors, and six instances occur in works of Tzetzes, four in other 12th-century authors, and the only earlier instance is in Libanius.[11] This note thus surely reflects one aspect of the teaching tradition, the use of ancient texts for the study of rhetorical tropes and techniques,[12] and the language suggests it is not ancient, but nothing connects it

---

[9] Sch. Med. 214 and 219 (above Chapter 1, at note 93).

[10] See Chapter 2, just above n. 71.

[11] Libanius, *Declam.* 40.2.80, 6–8 ἐκεῖνον τὸν γάμον Τελχῖνες ἐζεύξαντο, ἐκείνην τὴν παστάδα Ἐρινύες ἐπήξαντο.

[12] Apart from προκατασκευάζω, note the use of σοφιστικῶς, συνίστημι, ἔνστασις, and ἀναιρέω (perhaps also ἐπιτατικῶς).

to what we know of Planudes' teaching of Euripides, or dates it specifically to the Palaeologan era.

The other two notes we will look at are both shared by other witnesses.

Sch. Or. 416[13] Φοῖβος κελεύσας: ἀπὸ κοινοῦ οὕτως συντάξεις ὅτι ἐκέλευσεν ἂν τοῦτο ὁ Φοῖβος καὶ ἐπιστεύθης ἀληθεύειν, ἐὰν ἦν ἀμαθέστερος καὶ πλέον σοῦ ἀμαθὴς τοῦ καλοῦ καὶ τοῦ δικαίου. τοῦτο δὲ εἶπεν ὡς φαυλίσας τὴν ἀναφορὰν, ὡς τάχα ψευσαμένου τοῦ Ὀρέστου καὶ τούτῳ τῷ τρόπῳ φεύγοντος τὴν μομφὴν τοῦ μητρικοῦ φόνου. κρείσσων γὰρ ἂν ἦν ἡ αἰτία, ἐὰν ἦν αὕτη ὁ θάνατος τοῦ πατρός, τοῦ θεὸν ⟨* * *⟩. VPr

Phoebus having commanded: You will construe this *apo koinou* in this way, that Phoebos would have commanded this and you would have been believed to be speaking truly, if he (the god) were *amathesteros*, that is to say, more ignorant than you of what is fine and just. Menelaus said this as one who dismissed as unimportant the reference (of the action to the god) on the ground that perhaps Orestes made the story up and is trying in this way to escape the reproach for the murder of his mother. For the cause would have been greater, if this (the cause) were the death of his father, †the [gen.] god [acc.] (*left unfinished*)

Sch. Or. 424 οὐ σοφὸς: πρὸς ὃ κλαπεὶς ὁ Ὀρέστης εἰς κολακείαν αὐτοῦ προΰθετο τὸ οὐ σοφός, ἀληθὴς δ' εἰς φίλους ἔφυς κακός. τοῦτο δὲ τὸ ἔπος ἐναντιοφανές ἐστιν. ἐναντιοφανῆ δὲ λέγεται τὰ ῥητὰ τὰ μὴ τῇ ἄνωθεν ἑαυτῶν {τῇ ἀπάτῃ} κειμένῃ φράσει συναρμοζόμενα, νοήματι δὲ ἢ συντάξει θεραπευόμενα. σκόπει γὰρ ὅτι πρὸς ὕβριν ἐστὶ τοῦ Μενελάου τὸ οὕτως εἰπεῖν "οὐ σοφὸς ἔφυς, ἀληθὴς δὲ καὶ τέλειος κακὸς εἰς τοὺς φίλους" καί που δέον τὸν ἱκέτην ὑβρίζειν τὸν ἱκετευόμενον. θεραπεύεται δὲ τὸ ἔπος τῇ συντάξει οὕτως· οὐ σοφὸς κακὸς εἰς φίλους ἔφυς, ἀληθὴς δὲ ἔφυς σοφός. τὸ δὲ νόημα τοιοῦτον· σοφὸς μὲν ἀληθὴς λέγεται ὁ ὄντως σοφός, σοφὸς δὲ κακὸς ὁ σοφιστὴς καὶ ἀπατεὼν καὶ πιθανολογούμενος. λέγει τοίνυν αὐτῷ κολακικῶς ὅτι ⟨οὐκ⟩ ἐσόφισάς με, ὦ Μενέλαε, εἰπόντα βραδὺ εἶναι τὸ θεῖον πρὸς συνασπισμὸν ἀντειπὼν "ὡς ταχὺ μετῆλθόν σ' αἷμα μητέρος θεαί," οὐ δὲ ἀληθὴς εἶ σοφός, οὐ κακὸς σοφὸς εἰς φίλους, ἤγουν διὰ τῆς σοφιστείας καὶ πιθανότητος πλανήτης τῶν φίλων. VRw

Not wise: Tricked in relation to this (the sophistic move in the preceding lines 421–423), aiming to appeal to him (Menelaus) in a flattering way, Orestes offered the reply "not wise, but you are a true villain toward your friends/kin." This verse is one with an apparent contradiction. We speak of as apparently contradictory those things said that do not fit with the phrase positioned before them, but are ameliorated by thought or syntax. For observe that it is insulting to Menelaus to put it this way, "You are not wise, but a true and complete villain toward your friends/kin," as if it were the proper thing for the suppliant to disrespect the one he supplicates. But the verse is ameliorated by the syntax as follows: "you are not a clever villain

---

[13] I ignore here trivial variants; Schwartz rightly corrected ἀμαθῶς to ἀμαθὴς in the appositional glossing of ἀμαθέστερος.

toward your friends, but you are a true wise man." The thought is like this: One who is really wise is called a true wise man, but the sophist and deceiver and speaker of mere plausibilities is called a clever villain. So Orestes is saying to Menelaus by way of flattery that you did not trip me up sophistically, Menelaus, after I said that the divine is slow to help out, by saying "how quickly the goddesses pursued you for the bloodshed of your mother," but you are a true wise man, not a clever villain toward your friends, in other words, not one who misleads his friends with sophistry and plausibility.

That these notes do not originate at the time when V was first copied, but earlier, is suggested by their transmission in other witnesses, for it does not appear that any of the *recentiores* being used are descended from V itself. Both scholia also contain corruptions, again suggesting a process of transmission from an earlier codex. Although the first is marked in Pr with the usual scholion-ending punctuation after the nonsensical or lacunose τοῦ θεὸν, the careful scribe V has left after θεὸν an empty space of a half line of the full-width bottom block of scholia to show the lacuna, and he added, as he usually does, a marginal sign to indicate the lacuna.[14] In this case, his partner V[1] either forgot to try to decipher the damaged remainder of the note, or found it impossible to read anything in the damaged area of the exemplar. The second note is clearly a continuation of the analysis in the ἄλλως scholion on line 414. That is why Schwartz rightly accepted the odd κλαπεὶς in V (Rw has τραπεὶς, a banalization resulting from not understanding κλαπεὶς), which follows up on ἔκλεψε δ' αὐτὸν in the penultimate sentence of the earlier scholion.[15] There is also another corruption in the definition of ἐναντιοφανής, since after τὰ ῥητὰ τὰ μὴ the needed τῇ (Schwartz) is corrupted to τοῖς in V and omitted in Rw, and τῇ ἀπάτῃ is intrusive. Schwartz deleted ἄνωθεν ἑαυτῶν τῇ ἀπάτῃ, but without ἄνωθεν ἑαυτῶν the sense is insufficient.[16] As for the content, the second-person address in Sch. Or. 416 certainly fits the didactic style of teachers' notes, while the term ἐναντιοφανής is found nowhere else in published Greek scholia, rhetoricians, or teaching materials, although this Byzantine word is quite common in jurists and

---

[14] On this sign (⸖) see below at note 23.
[15] Schwartz also changed πρὸς ὃν of VRw to πρὸς ὅ.
[16] We would need προκειμένῃ, as in these two comparanda: Theodorus Dexius, *Epist.* 2.18, 69–70 καὶ τοιαύτη μὲν ἐπὶ τοῖς προκειμένοις ἀνωμαλία καὶ ἐναντιοφάνεια κρατήσει; *Scholia in Basilicorum Libros I–XI*, 12.1(CA).61.17, 2–3 λύει τὰς δοκούσας ἐγείρεσθαι ἐναντιοφανείας πρὸς τὸ προκείμενον. Instead of προ- our commentator has used "above themselves in the text." ἑαυτῶν was apparently difficult to read before modern cleaning of V, but it can now be seen clearly and agrees with Rw. The only source of difficulty now is that V originally began writing τη after ἄνωθεν, but corrected himself by writing an epsilon with wide ligature-loop covering τη and an alpha above the partially blotted eta.

also used in discussions of Christian doctrine.[17] The word συνασπισμός is common in its military sense from Hellenistic times onward, but the less common metaphorical sense, as here, is attested in ecclesiastical authors, and the word was used often in both senses by Michael Psellus and Eustathius (in his *Sermones* as well as Homeric commentary).

In any case, it seems quite clear to me that the interests and purposes detected in such notes by Turyn and Di Benedetto are simply those of the teachers who have given us many of the scholia, older and more recent, that are aimed at instruction. In these examples this ameliorating rhetorical analysis is likely to be from the 12th century or earlier rather than something contemporary introduced by the scribes of V. Moreover, not only in Sch. Or. 416, but in many places in V, it is evident that in the first production of this codex the partner scribes (about to be described in more detail) were using an older witness in which the scholia were sometimes damaged and partially illegible, leading the scribes of V to leave blank spaces or write an obviously corrupt text. As for the verbosity of some of the scholia in V, it is shared by some scholia in the 11th-century manuscript B and is perfectly conceivable for the 12th century, if we think of the examples of Eustathius and Ioannes Tzetzes. Likewise, the verbose elements in or related to the A-commentary on Aeschylus have been deemed to be of the 12th century or earlier.

Finally, it should be noted that good palaeographic grounds for fixing V to the period 1280–1300 are lacking. V's script is quite idiosyncratic. It has some mannered and enlarged features such as had been popular since the 12th century, but it does not closely resemble the informal and mannered and sometimes downright sloppy script of *recentiores* that are thought to come possibly from two decades 1280–1300. Turyn cited a few comparanda that are not convincing, or on current knowledge point to an earlier date.[18] There are very few dated literary manuscripts from the period 1204–1280 available for comparison.[19] I therefore reject the notion that the original production has any connection to

---

[17] There is even a jurist whose work was known under the pseudonym Enantiophanes, who is constantly cited in the scholia to the *Basilica*.

[18] Di Benedetto 1965: 42–43 admitted that the similarities with the script of Ambrosianus C 222 inf. (adduced by Turyn) were not probative, and recently that manuscript has itself been downdated to the late 12th century by Mazzucchi 2003 and 2004. I do not see much to connect the script of Laur. plut. 32.16 (another comparandum suggested by Turyn) with that of V (one can examine both online). Note also that Turyn 1957: 78 n. 126 thought that the "Planudean" writing style of his examples was closely related to the script of Ioannikios in Paris grec 2722 (16r–32v), but we now accept that Ioannikios belongs in the 12th century (see above Chapter 4 at n. 8). Although the overall impression of the scripts of V and of these pages of Par. gr. 2722 is quite different, I do detect some shared letter forms, especially with scribe V[1] in his most florid manner.

[19] Document #33 in Dolger 1948: 90–93, which he says is from the early 13th century with a script typical of the end of the 12th, seems to me similar to V in the set of abbreviations used and their form and also in some letter forms and ligatures, especially that for αρ.

Planudes or that its content militates in any way toward a date after 1280.[20] It is a separate issue that there may be a connection with Planudes in additions made by one or more cursive hands in the first decades of the 14th century.

2. THE PARTNER SCRIBES OF THE ORIGINAL PRODUCTION

It has been known since the 19th century that two scribes with very similar writing styles collaborated in producing codex V, although this fact has not been represented accurately in the catalogue entry.[21] Schwartz indicated this by his special treatment of the siglum A in his first volume and by his statement in the preface (I.vi) that *inde a fol. 118ᵛ codex a duobus librariis paene alterna vice descriptus est*. For the purposes of the discussion in this chapter, I will refer to the two hands as Hand A, or simply A, and Hand B, or simply B. In his apparatus criticus in volume 1 (triad plays) Schwartz used the siglum A^1 to indicate annotations or corrections added by Hand B on a page written by Hand A, while he used the unmodified siglum A to indicate annotation entered by Hand A. In his second volume (non-triad plays), however, he used the siglum A^1 only one time (Sch. Med. 19),[22] even though there are places where A wrote the notes on a page whose text had been written by B (or vice versa) and places where notes by A and by B are both present on the same page. In my own apparatus to the scholia, I convert Schwartz's A to the symbol used by modern consensus, V. I use V^1 where he used A^1 (except in one or two places where I don't agree that a phrase was added by Hand B). Unlike Schwartz, however, I also use V^1 for all scholia written in Hand B, no matter whether the poetic text of the page was written by A or by B, and I use V only for what is written by Hand A.

For much of the manuscript Hand A did most of the work (poetic text and marginal blocks of scholia), and then B corrected and supplemented in places where Hand A had difficulty deciphering what must have been a damaged or

---

[20] Another pointer to the earlier origin of the content in V is the fact that some of the Tzetzean material was already entered by the first hands (although most of it is connected to the later hand V^3): see above Chapter 2, section 2, on Sch. Hec. 1220, Sch. Med. 1201.

[21] Schreiner 1988: 107: *Fabularum textus necnon plerumque scholiorum ab uno eodemque scriba (an viro docto?) exaratus, sed invenies et scholia et glossas ab alia eiusdem temporis manu descripta.* Schreiner was apparently misled by Schwartz's restricted use of his siglum A^1 and did not attend to Schwartz's statement about the alternation of work in some parts of the manuscript. Cavarzeran 2016: 37 simply adopts Schreiner's view ("l'intero manoscritto è stato vergato da un unico copista").

[22] At Sch. Med. 19 (Schwartz II.143, 25–144, 3), Schwartz refers to Hand B as A and Hand A as A^1. The poetic text and the other 6 scholia on this page are by Hand B.

faint original. It would appear that there was an agreement between the two scribes that A would not try to decipher, but would leave space for, particularly damaged portions of the text of the annotations, leaving it to B (somehow more experienced, or with sharper eyesight?) to fill in as much as he could decipher, if he could decipher anything. When Hand A left a lacuna, he wrote a mark of omission in the outer margin of the page at the appropriate level. The omission mark is a dotted obelus (⁒),[23] and it is usually, but not always, blotted or crossed through after the lacuna is filled. In some parts of the manuscript, however, B wrote entire pages or provided all the marginal scholia around a text and glosses above a text written by Hand A. One wonders whether this occurred on pages where the marginal writing was particularly damaged, or where the entire written surface had suffered more than on most pages; but there could have been other reasons for B to relieve A at times. The pattern of succession of hands at some points suggests that B's review often followed immediately on A's completion of one page and that A did not continue further (sometimes even on the verso of the same sheet) until B had checked the page just written.[24] Schwartz had noted this alternation of work but gave no details. He also judged that when one corrected or supplemented the work of the other, the same exemplar was being used by both.[25] I believe that this hypothesis is likely to be correct.

The two hands are similar, and although sometimes B's additions are obvious because the ink is darker, in many places there is no strong difference between the appearance of the inks used by A and B. Furthermore, if the scribe continues writing for some time without dipping his pen back in the ink, the script just before he does refresh the ink can be remarkably fainter in appearance than the ink placed by the freshly-dipped pen, so that judging by apparent color can be unreliable at times, especially if one consults only a black-and-white image with poor resolution.[26] There is also the problem that whereas A is rather constant in

---

[23] Cf. McNamee 1992: 18 and Table 2.E; Atsalos 1991: 229 suggests the name lemniscus for this symbol.

[24] This is most evident in the copying of *Hippolytus*, where there are several pages (including some recto pages) where a few verses were added by B at the bottom of the text written by A (perhaps after determining that there were no more scholia to add and thus room for more lines of the text), and then A took account of the additional lines in beginning the next page at the correct line. For details, see the listing in the Appendix to this chapter. There is also one case where A himself changed his mind about the distribution of lines: *Hipp.* 546 πῶλον ἄζυγα λέκτρων was first written as the last on 172v, but then written instead first on 173r, probably because there was no room left on 172v for the scholia belonging to this line. The version on 173r was in this case fairly thoroughly erased. With autopsy under UV I could detect enough traces to see that the erased words are line 546 and are not comparable to the intrusive gloss found in manuscript A at this point (see Diggle's apparatus).

[25] Schwartz I.vi.

[26] An example: fol. 45v, a few lines above the end of the narrow left margin block, at the end of Sch. Or. 766, the letters φέρων ἔγκλημα look very much darker than the preceding πράγματι ἴδιον ἐπι, but here it is simply the case that all is the work of Hand A, but the ink for the first part of the phrase

his style of script, B is capable of a range of treatments, varying from a regularity of size close to A's manner to short stretchs of more ornamented and flowing letter forms of contrasting sizes. The easiest way to get an initial impression of the diagnostic differences is to look at the pages on which Hand B has written everything (or all the scholia) rather than to start from the short phrases and glosses added to the work of Hand A. In the Appendix to this chapter I give a listing of the division of work, which has not been done before.

Both hands use frequent abbreviation of endings in the scholia and glosses. Apart from the standard suspended abbreviations for final syllables, they often use truncation of familiar words (e.g., forms of βασιλεύς, λαμβάνω, βάλλω), sometimes in such a way that one cannot determine what ending was intended, although the fact of abbreviation is explicitly marked by the low oblique stroke added to the last letter expressed. Some truncated words leave off two syllables and give two suspended letters to indicate what is missing: for example (Plate 5, 1–3), ἐξέτασιν written ἐξέτ with low oblique stroke marking abbreviation and with suspended alpha ligatured to the ιν abbreviation, leaving the intervening sigma to be understood; βούλησις written as βουλ with low oblique stroke added to lambda and with small eta above it and the ις abbreviation above eta; λαμβάνει written λαμ with minuscule beta ligatured to nu and an acute accent above the mu.

I will now provide some indications of places where the different hands can be seen in juxtaposition in the interlinear annotation. Readers who want to understand the distinctions should equip themselves with a printed text of Euripides for orientation and then view the images at the DigiVat website at maximum magnification.

Fol. 3r (*Hec.* 32–50): above line 39 (Plate 5, 4) there are typical glosses by Hand A (V) κινοῦντας, θαλασσίαν, and κώπην, then right after κινοῦντας Hand B (V¹) has added in thinner and looser script εὐτρεπίζοντας (note the large arc and the straight downward link in the επ ligature). Under εὐτρεπίζοντάς and above the verse the cursive hand I refer to as V³ has crowded in καινοπρεπὲς σχῆμα. Then B is also responsible for σφάγιον at 41 and ἡ ψυχὴ προνοεῖται τὰ ἄτιμα μέλλοντα γενέσθαι at 42, with V³ supplementing the latter by adding ὡς ἀϋλότερον καὶ θειότερον καὶ καθαρώτερον.

Fol. 3v (*Hec.* 51–70): above the ends of line 53–54 (Plate 5, 5), A has written ὑπὸ τὸ ἄκρον τῆς σκηνῆς and εἴδωλον, B contributed ἀντὶ τοῦ ἀπὸ just to the left of the former, and V³ wrote δεδοικυῖα περὶ τοῦ φαντάσματος οὗ εἶδε περὶ ἐμοῦ to the right of the latter. Note the variation between the relatively sober βαστάζουσα

---

was nearly exhausted and the remainder of the phrase was made after redipping the pen. In contrast, a few lines below, the darker-appearing πρὸ ἐτῶν γὰρ δύο τῆς in Sch. Or. 772 actually is a supplement by Hand B.

above line 60 vs. the florid ὑμῶν δωρικὸν, both of which I assign to Hand B. At 66 the glosses ἐπιστηριζομένη ἐπαναπαυομένη are by A, but the paraphrase τὴν βραδεῖαν πορείαν καὶ ἔλευσιν αὐτῶν ἄρθρων προστιθεῖσα τῷ σκίπωνι is by B. At 69 A wrote ἀστραπὴ while B added αὐτὸν τὸν Δία ἐπικαλεῖται.

Fol 8v (*Hec.* 325–344): line 327 (Plate 5, 6) shows V³ writing ἐσθλόν· παρὰ τὸ τὰ θελητὰ φέρεσθαι ἤτοι τὰ ἀγαθὰ above the start of the line in his more disciplined mode, but still recognizable from the backwards-leaning epsilon, the very tiny omicron, and the very tiny loop on open theta; then in midline μωρίαν is by Hand B, recognizable by the typical omega and the size and shape of the αν loop as well as the finer pen stroke; and above the end of the line is Hand A's gloss ἀντὶ τοῦ χρεωστήσομεν.

Fol. 12r (*Hec.* 474–500): here the lower half of the right margin block contains four scholia, written by Hand B, out of order after A's entry of Sch. Hec. 497 φεῦ φεῦ γέρων κτλ. This is a particularly good example of some more flamboyant letter forms appearing sometimes, but not always, in B's contributions: the large lambda with a main diagonal that sweeps back at the top in an arc over the preceding letter, alphas of various sizes, some closed sigmas with enlarged belly, upright epsilons with two arcs as well as the usual lunate form, some omegas with backswept finishing stroke.

Fol. 33r (*Or.* 319–339): in the middle of the page, at Or. 328 ὀρεχθεὶς ἔρρεις, the rubricator[27] first placed a reference symbol over ρεχ of ὀρεχθεὶς, Hand A placed φθείρῃ over ἔρρεις, B then added ἐπιθυμήσας over ὀρεχθεὶς, but had to crowd it in between the reference mark and A's gloss; V³ then wanted to extend ἐπιθυμήσας by adding the clause found in the marginal scholion (ἐκτείνεται γὰρ ὁ ἐπιθυμῶν), and he had to start this addition above φθείρῃ instead of writing it on the same level after ἐπιθυμήσας.

It is my impression that the rubrication was generally left to Hand A. At least, in pages written by B the few majuscule initials added to the scholia and the *notae personarum* do not seem to differ from those on pages written by A (but these are only single letters, intentionally written with care). More significantly, on fols. 228r-v, where Hand B wrote the hypothesis to *Andromache* and the first lines of the play with their scholia, the rubricator supplying the heading ὑπόθεσις ἀνδρομάχης and the title εὐριπίδου ἀνδρομάχη and also (in between these two items) the list of *dramatis personae* certainly appears to be A rather than B. On the other hand, on fol. 261v, containing the hypothesis to *Troades*

---

[27] There are various places where it is clear that rubrication, including the addition of the reference symbols, preceded the entry of supralinear notes by hand A. Occasionally, the rubricator omitted the initials of the lemma and of the note as well as a reference symbol. Only a little evidence survives of the reminders to the rubricator of what was to be added, but we can still see on fol. 47r on the far outer edge of the page small letters, singly or in pairs, indicating what the rubricator had to supply in the line of the scholion on the same level. On most pages of V, however, the edges have been lost to damage and trimming.

and the first lines with the scholia all written by Hand B, the list of *dramatis personae* in red again looks like Hand A (and probably also the play title), but the red heading ὑπόθεσις Τρωάδων looks more like Hand B, to judge from the omegas.

A few examples of the variations in ink color may also be useful. Some of B's glosses are in a very light ink (or an ink that has faded more than others), as on fol. 29r, ὑπόσκηνον above *Or.* 147 ὑπώροφον, and συγκλίθητι above *Or.* 149 (second) κάταγε; with the latter we can also observe the later cursive hand working around the earlier gloss. One can also observe variations in the appearance of ink even when the same hand is involved: e.g., on fol. 26v Hand A apparently wrote the top block of scholia first (Sch. Or. 48, Sch. Or. 54, Sch. Or. 57), using the full width of the page, then continued with the lines of the text (48–68) in a partial-width column beneath the scholia, then added, at the top of the left-side column but in lighter ink, Sch. Or. 63 (which runs on into a scholion ἐδεδίει γὰρ κτλ on *Or.* 57 that is shared with several *recentiores*); similarly, on fol. 26r, two additional notes (Sch. Or. 41; a variant of Sch. Or. 36) have been added at the bottom after the block ending in Sch. Or. 47 and the ink used by A is lighter. Or for Hand B, compare Sch. Or. 915 (the last in the top block on fol. 50v), where the note is entirely written by B, but with the ink appearing grayish for the first 20 characters or so, but then blacker for the rest of the note. For change of hand and of ink within the same note or line, see, again in the top block of fol. 50v, Sch. Or. 916, which is begun by Hand A and finished by B (in blacker ink), or Sch. Or. 626 at the top on fol. 41v, in which the first line, from the lemma through ἔσχε δὲ παῖδας, is by B, the rest by A, but the last three words by B appear somewhat lighter, since the pen was running out of ink.

3. CHARACTERISTICS OF THE ORIGINAL HANDS

The A hand presents a strong impression of vertically compressed letters, with many letters also closely spaced horizontally; it also gives the impression of a disciplined horizontal continuity across the top of most letters, while the depth of letters is more uneven. The interlinear glosses of A are normally equally disciplined, with a similar horizontal evenness. On the other hand, various enlarged letters are occasionally used: e.g., some upsilons and omegas and phi loops are exaggerated in width. The B hand is capable of a similar level of control on some pages entirely written by B, but much more commonly gives an immediate impression of greater freedom and looseness, with more irregularities of letter size and more separation between letters, and more flourish strokes. In glosses B is capable of a wide variation of sizes and varying degrees of cursiveness. For an example of B at his most mannered style, full of flourishes, see the hypothesis to *Andromache* on fol. 228r, with some large looping characters or strokes suspended above the relatively small letters within the lines, particularly omega, epsilon, an enormous upper arc on delta, omicron with inset nu, and the abbreviations for καὶ and αν.

Script written by A usually features a lighter ink. For this ink, see most of the scholia on pages of *Orestes*, and both scholia and text on some pages, such as fols. 29r–31v, but this is by no means always the case (for a darker ink, see most of *Hecuba* on fols. 3r–23v). The strokes of the letters of Hand A are usually a little thicker and have less sharply defined edges, whereas the B scribe seems to have favored a pen tip that was kept much sharper, producing thinner, sharper strokes. But again where Hand A has dark ink, his strokes tend to be more sharply defined than on the pages with light ink. Hand B's script thus often appears darker, and in some cases he used a blackish ink. Both hands are capable of a variety of forms for many letters, and many forms are very similar, but I have found two elements most reliably diagnostic. (1) Hand A always gives a fairly strong impression of a straight horizontal at the level of the tops of standard letters, resulting partly from the consistent level and straightness of some crosspieces and partly from keeping the tops of loops in curved letters on or very close to the same level; Hand B, on the other hand, tends to give the impression of unevenness and variable height for the same letter elements. (2) The two differ in the treatment of omega, beta, and the ace-of-spades form of the epsilon-rho ligature (and often also the related shape of the joining of epsilon with xi, zeta, and sometimes pi), and differences are particularly telling when two or three of these diagnostics are found in combination. I now describe some letter forms for which some distinctions can be made or other features deserve to be noted.

Alpha: In A, usually minuscule, often with extreme flattening of the loop (Plate 5, 3; Plate 7, 10 and 12), but also majuscule, especially before nu. In B, there is a wider variation in size, and in more informal glosses minuscule alpha may be very flattened or very large; the majuscule form sometimes has a small loop but a fairly large oblique. Similar is the small alpha loop in B's mannered ligature αρ, as in the now extremely faint πάρεστι above *Hec.* 34 (fol. 3r); also of note in some tiny glosses by B is an initial alpha with an extra-long ligature stroke along the baseline leading to the next letter.

Beta: Similar in both hands, with a substantial descender on the upright and two well-formed loops forming the belly. A's tendency is to make the two loops more or less equally wide, or the bottom one half again the width of the upper, with the upper loop about twice as high as the lower one (Plate 5, 7 A). B has a strong tendency to use a beta in which the lower belly is noticeably wider than the upper loop and usually less flattened than A's (Plate 5, 7 B). There are, however, many betas in both hands that fall between the extremes and are not diagnostic.

Gamma: Both A and B use the minuscule form in a large majority over the majuscule, but Hand B is more prone to mixing in some tall majuscule gammas.

Delta: Hand A's delta is usually upright, but occasionally it features an extended slant leftward of the top arc. In B, the upper arc of delta may be upright (that is, the upper arc is more or less symmetrically above the lower loop), or tilted to the right; but B's delta is often written with a pronounced backward-leaning upper arc.

Epsilon: Hand A has its majuscule epsilon slightly enlarged, but it is less common than the minuscule form with closed lower loop. Hand B writes epsilon in various forms, but all upright, all majuscule except in ligatures. Usually the epsilon is lunate, but B has some formed with two arcs in some more informally written glosses (never, however, the backward leaning two-arc epsilon seen in V[3] and many Palaeologan hands).

Epsilon-ligatures: In both hands, the ει ligature is often quite tall (also when the circumflex accent is joined to it), and the εσ ligature is also somewhat enlarged. For the ερ ligature, Hand A favors a large ace-of-spades style with a distinct point and usually a symmetrical appearance; whereas B most often uses a less pointed, sometimes even rounded connection, and the two sides tend to be less symmetrical than in A's version (Plate 6, 1–2 vs. 3–4). But the ligature can look much alike when A uses a less sharp connection and B makes his sharper than usual. The επ ligature can be made with a similar shape for the top of epsilon and the joining stroke down to pi, with A favoring a sharp and symmetrical apex and B using a more mannered form with concavity on the right side (Plate 6, 5 vs. 7). As for the εξ ligature, both hands use a common form where the connecting stroke is very like that of the ace-of-spades ερ, but the differences are often less diagnostic: sometimes Hand A makes a sharper angular turn at the top, while B is apt to have a smoother turn or a sharp point but concave right side (Plate 6, 6 and 10 vs. 8). B's version also tends to be taller and wider, with its three right-side arcs aligned with a notional upright tangent. In addition, Hand A uses an unusual ligature of εξ that I have not seen elsewhere (Plate 6, 9–10).[28] It can easily be mistaken for επ, and Schwartz in fact did this a few times in reading the scholia on the first pages of *Hecuba* before recognizing the intent of this unusual form.[29] In *Hec.* 174 ἔξελθ' ἔξελθ' we even see the regular ligature followed by this unusual one (Plate 6, 10). The left half of the ligature is like that of the ace-of-spades style ερ, and the point is sharp as for that ligature; the right

---

[28] As far as I recall it is not used by Hand B. Nothing like it is illustrated in the tables of letter-forms in Gardthausen 1911–1913 (end of vol. II).

[29] One example is in Sch. Hec. 53 (fol. 3v), where for ἐξελθεῖν τὴν ἑκάβην of other manuscripts V reads τὴν ἑκάβην ἐξεληλυθέναι and Schwartz misreports ἐπεληλυθέναι.

side oblique extends straight to the baseline and then makes a large curve back to the left under the baseline, and the two perpendiculars added to this oblique stroke mark the letter as xi. Hand A also forms an εζ ligature in exactly the same way, but with only one perpendicular attached to the right oblique (Plate 6, 11–12).

Zeta: In A zeta is cursive and upright and very similar to xi (see above on the εζ combination), but Hand B makes not only a rounded form, but also a form similar to an Arabic two, with the lower two-thirds consisting of almost straight lines at an angle of just under 90 degrees and the top similar to an attached circumflex (Plate 7, 7–8); B also has a more florid version of zeta, but it too features angular transitions in the middle section.

Eta: In both hands, when minuscule, eta may be tall (especially in ligatures and initially) or short (especially word-internally), and when majuscule it is usually short, much less often slightly taller. Both hands also use the wavy form of eta in ligature after delta or mu (Plate 7, 9–10).

Iota: In both hands, three or four different heights are used for iota, from minimum small-letter height to very tall above and below.

Kappa: In both hands, kappa in the majuscule form (and also in the epsilon-kappa ligature) is enlarged both above and below the line (and in his freer moments B may enlarge it more noticeably). When the minuscule form is used, it has a tall initial vertical.

Lambda: In both hands, lambda varies from reaching slightly above and below the height of a standard small letter to being more markedly extended above and below. The stroke above the intersection of the two parts may be virtually straight or have a pronounced downturn in an arc.

Mu: some minuscule mus can be remarkably short in their upper portion (Plate 5, 3 and 6; Plate 7, 10).

Nu: In Hand B, in some more informally written glosses, the nu may take the v form, but normally it is minuscule with a clear descender separate from the cup (the descender is absent, as usual, in ligature after upsilon).

Xi: See above under Epsilon for the unusual form of εξ in Hand A.

Omicron: In hand A, the ους ligature is written with a very pronounced horizontal element (the loop may be open): see Plate 5, 5 δειμαίνουσ'.

Rho: Both hands sometimes have a form with straight descender and sometimes a form with a slight curve rightward. Joining to the following letter is rare, but in Hand B the descender of rho in such cases forms a smooth curve to join the middle of the bottom of the next letter or to join the top of a short iota. These hands do not use the form that is used in the cursive hands of the type seen at times in Y^2 and most of the time in V^3, namely, a rho with a descender that turns back to the left at bottom, sometimes with the whole letter tilting backwards.

Sigma: Hand A occasionally uses a slim lunate sigma extending far above and below the line, especially word-initially followed by upsilon. Many of A's lunate sigmas of regular size almost complete a full circle, since the two ends come close to meeting, while in Hand B such lunate sigmas tend to be more open.

Tau: Many taus in both hands are small, but occasionally there is a moderately tall tau, and in A one may find a few with only the leftward side of the cap. For some very tall taus, see the florid script of Hand B in the hypothesis to *Andromache* (fol. 228r), where a few extend far into the wide interlinear space and have a broad arc for the upper stroke, matching some of the other interlinear enlargements in those lines.

Omega: Both hands have omegas with the two loops open and omegas with the two loops closed. In Hand A the two halves are normally symmetrical (Plate 7, 1–3), whereas in Hand B they tend to have the right half wider than the left (Plate 7, 4–6). Most characteristic of B, however, is a form that appears in about half of his omegas: in this, the curve that forms the right side of the letter is continued in a backwards flourish above the letter. In other hands one would read such a stroke as a ligatured grave accent, but in Hand B this definitely appears on unaccented omegas.

Accents: In both hands, the acute and grave accents usually are rather long, but Hand A is, for once, more flamboyant in this regard than B, since his accents tend to be longer. This length applies as well to the extended stroke representing an acute in ligature with alpha, upsilon, or omega (e.g. τάφον, Plate 7, 11). But ligaturing of an accent with a letter of regular size in the line is not particularly common. Furthermore, acute and circumflex accents are rarely ligatured to a breathing sign, although they are ligatured to abbreviated signs in suspension. The circumflex is appended to the ων abbreviation to form two arcs side by side (Plate 7, 10 αἰσχρῶν). An odd and potentially confusing practice in regard to ligatured accents is the way that the oblique stroke representing ον may be continued from the bottom in two ways. Sometimes there is a curved hook of small or moderate length (τάφον, Plate 7, 11), which is merely a flourish with no meaning. In other instances, the upward turn is continued into a longer stroke to represent an acute accent on the final ον, and since the transition from one diagonal to the other is smoothed into a curve, the result looks rather like an enlarged compendium for ας (κακόν, Plate 7, 12). The same ligatured abbreviation occurs a few times when the acute accent actually belongs on a previous syllable and not on the final ον (as in τεθνηξόμενον, Plate 7, 13).

4. OTHER CORRECTORS AND THE CURSIVE HANDS

The other hands that added glosses in V are far more informal and cursive and similar to the glossing hands found in the *recentiores* of the very late 13th and early 14th centuries or to even later hands. In editions of Euripides where corrections to the text are cited it is sometimes hard to be sure which later hand is intended: V^2 in one edition may be the same hand labelled V^3 or something else in another. For the scholia and glosses, in short stretches Hand B at his most florid is sometimes hard to distinguish from one of the cursive hands, and Dindorf in fact a few times misleadingly identified a more florid example of Hand B as *manus recentissima*. Usually by paying attention to the form of rho and epsilon one can decide what is later than Hands A and B, but in words that are faded or damaged there is often doubt. I have spent many hours with the original and with the excellent recent online images trying to reach consistency in my identifications, but there remain frustrating uncertainties. My current judgment is that the hand identified as V^2 in, for instance, Diggle's OCT, reflects someone who mainly corrected the text, usually in a dark ink with large strokes, and contributed very few glosses. The cursive glossing and the carelessly written discursive scholia mostly found in the outer margins (and often damaged) I assign to V^3, and my usage seems to agree almost always with Diggle's use of V^3 in reporting γράφεται-variants and the like. The cursive notes can vary greatly in appearance, with different shades of ink and different fineness or crudeness of stroke, reflecting the state of the pen tip, the quality of the paper's surface in any given place, and the amount of abrasion and damage from moisture. When these different-appearing notes are studied under magnification, however, the letter forms are much the same, and I have concluded that one person may have worked on the manuscript repeatedly over a period of time, or more than one person using very similar informal scripts, so similar that it is futile to try to break down the identification beyond using V^3 for most of the later notes. V^3 did not confine himself to the triad plays, but also made corrections and additions in the other plays.[30] As mentioned before, the work of V^3 preceded the copying of *Troades* from V in Y, which may have occurred in the decade 1320–1330. V^3 then would be a contemporary of Triclinius.

There are some additional scholia that are later than V^3, generally in a larger and cruder script or using letter forms that suggest 15th-century (or later) hands. These I assign to V^{rec}. In addition, it is important to note that Schwartz reported some scholia from *Hec.* 1–31 on the replacement folio 2r–2v using only his standard siglum A. I report these instead as V^v, because although they are definitely not by the original hands, I agree with Schwartz's tacit assumption that the scribe of this very damaged replacement page was trying to transcribe the origi-

---

[30] Note that Cavarzeran 2016 uses the siglum V_2 for my V^3. Because of the difficulty of deciphering V^3 using older images and without prolonged scrutiny of the whole codex, Cavarzeran has made a number of mistakes in reporting what V^3 wrote (see next note for an example) and has sometimes not recognized when V^3 has added words to extend a shorter gloss written by V or V^1.

nal, damaged leaf of V before discarding it. In doing so, however, V^v transcribed any additional scholia of V³ that were on those pages without making any distinction between them and the original scribes' work, so we can no longer verify exactly which items on these pages were written by one of the original scribes and must make inferences, where possible, based on attestation in other witnesses.

I provide here very briefly some main characteristics of the cursive hand(s):

Beta: with two separate small loops attached at top and bottom of the vertical stroke.

Delta: with reduced loop, even with the loop flattened so as to have no white space, and the upper part tilted right and sometimes short, producing a strong similarity to sigma.

Epsilon: backward sloping epsilon when not in ligature.

ει ligature: upright, with its loop sometimes small.

ερ ligature: with smooth arc, open rho loop.

εσ ligature: like an inverted U with narrow σ on right.

Theta: loop often closed, flat, easily confused with another letter.[31]

Nu: angular v-shape.

Omicron: may be joined to pi, either suspended from the horizontal or above it.

Rho: when not in ligature, written with its lower stroke turning horizontal under the loop and with a serif at the end; sometimes tilted back so that the tail almost parallels the baseline.

σθ: may have a very flattened sigma loop.

Tau: τοῦ formed with tau and above it a fountain-like abbreviation of ου and the circumflex.

Regular use of diaeresis on iota and upsilon in all positions.

Frequent use of double stacking of the letters of suspended endings: for example, σηκώσας with second sigma above kappa and ας abbreviation above sigma; λόγοις with gamma above the omicron and οις above gamma.

---

[31] For instance, in Sch. Hipp. 48c Cavarzeran, V³'s θήσω has been misreported as μίσω partly because of the way this scribe makes many of his thetas.

APPENDIX TO CHAPTER 5

The Distribution of Work between Hands A and B

Since previous discussions have not given many details about this, except what can be inferred from Schwartz's use of A^1 (modern V^1) in his first volume (but not his second), I here record the distribution of the writing of V between Hand A and Hand B. The following lists are only about the original hand and take no account of additions made by V^2, V^3, or later hands, but it may be noted that V^3 did not confine his glosses and scholia to the triad plays (and recall that V^{2*}'s glosses are very few, as opposed to V^2's corrections in the text of the plays).

In all three triad plays, the text and main scholia blocks and many interlinear annotations are generally the work of Hand A. Therefore, it is necessary only to list the contributions of Hand B for these plays.

Hecuba
Hand B's role in *Hecuba* is minimal. None of the text of the play is by B, and there are no places where B fills in a lacuna left by A. B's glosses are widely scattered, but B does supply a few scholia in the margin. On several pages of *Hecuba* Hand A used a sharper pen tip, and in some short glosses one may be quite uncertain which of the two is responsible for the word if it does not contain a particularly diagnostic letter form.

12r: Sch. Hec. 483, 484, 491, 497 are all written by B.
16r: Sch. Hec. 675, 679, 680 by B.
16v: Sch. Hec. 707 λείπει, 710, and an addition to Sch. Hec. 709 appear to be by B.
20v: the scholia (all on *Hec.* 1156) in the upper half of the page are by Hand B, those in the lower half by A (on *Hec.* 1151, 1153, 1155, 1157).
21r: Sch. Hec. 1160 πῶς δοκεῖς is by Hand B.
22v: Sch. Hec. 1236 (top of margin block), 1270 (bottom of margin block; the note belongs to a line that appears on the facing folio) are by B, but Sch. Hec. 1238 (between the two, with gaps) is by A.

Orestes
The text of *Orestes* is always written by Hand A. Hand B added glosses sporadically, and neither the darkness of the ink nor the sharpness of the pen stroke is a reliable criterion, so that in some short glosses containing no good diagnostic letter form, there may be uncertainty about which hand is responsible. In such doubtful cases, the gloss is usually assigned to Hand A.

24v: Hand A filled in the space left vacant after the *argumenta* by adding miscellaneous scholia; at the bottom, Hand B used the empty last half-line to add a grammatical note about ἀφαίρεσις, συγκοπή, and ἀποκοπή, which I assign to *Or.* 69 κείνου because of a nearly identical note on κείνοις in Sch. Opp. Hal. 1.186.
27v: Sch. Or. 101 αἰδώς added at end of bottom block by Hand B.
29v: the gloss ὁ θάνατος was written above 190 ὁ πότμος by B, but A added the rest of the annotation to the right, εἰ μὴ γὰρ κτλ.
31v: lacuna filled in by B in Sch. Or. 247, 259.
32v: the ending of νοσ* is corrected by B to νοσεῖν in Sch. Or. 314.
33v: lacuna filled in by B in Sch. Or. 341, 345.
34v: lacuna filled in by B in Sch. Or. 392.
35r: lacuna filled in by B in Sch. Or. 410 (also a correction made), 417.
37r: lacuna filled in by B in Sch. Or. 456, 457; all of Sch. Or. 458 added by B.
38r: lacuna filled in by B in Sch. Or. 501.
38v: lacuna filled in by B in Sch. Or. 517.
40r: Sch. Or. 585 and 590 added by B.
41r: lacuna filled in by B in Sch. Or. 621.
41v: lacuna filled in by B in Sch. Or. 626.
42v: lacuna filled in by B in Sch. Or. 665.
43r: all the marginal scholia on this page are by B (Sch. Or. 671, 672, 685, 687, 688).
43v: after Hand A wrote most of the scholia on the page, B added three notes, in four and a half lines at the bottom: Sch. Or. 688 (a second version, for which he uses a lemma from 690 and has a reference symbol to 690), 693, 694.
44r: B added Sch. Or. 712 (the space for the lemma is left blank), and the beginning of Sch. Or. 714, but was unable to supply (or forgot to supply) the lemma of 715, for which space had been left.
44v: B wrote Sch. Or. 727 at the end of the top block.
45v: lacuna filled in by B in Sch. Or. 766.
46r: B wrote Sch. Or. 775, and a lemma for Sch. Or. 779, but could not decipher any of the content of 779 and left blank space. Lower in the column Sch. Or. 773, 781, 782 are by A.
47v: note that all scholia on this page are by Hand A, and by some error Schwartz gave the siglum A¹ (Hand B) for Sch. Or. 811.
48v: this page has one short scholion by A and also the lemma of Sch. Or. 841 without the note itself; B corrected A's μασθὸν in the lemma to μαστὸν.
50r: lacuna filled in by B in Sch. Or. 911.
50v: B contributed all of Sch. Or. 915, half of 916, and part of 918.
51r: B fills the bottom third of the side margin block with Sch. Or. 941, 944.
51v: the short first scholion, appearing near the top of the margin block, is by B, while the rest of the margin and the bottom block is filled by A.
52v: Sch. Or. 982 and, at the end of the bottom block, Sch. Or. 991 are by B, as well as the lemma and opening lines of Sch. Or. 983 added in blank space.
53r: in the top margin B added an unrooted note about Atreus, Thyestes, and Aerope, which Schwartz assigned to line 1009 (on 53v), where Aerope is mentioned; the

scribe may have meant it to go with 996–1000, where the curse on the house and Atreus are mentioned. Small lacunae are filled in by B in three scholia on Or. 999.
53v: lacunae at the ends of Sch. Or. 1007 and 1017 are filled in by B.
54r: lacuna filled in by B in Sch. Or. 1018, 1030.
55r: the first two notes on the page, as well as the last, are by A, but B added in between Sch. Or. 1065, 1072, 1074, 1075 (the last two run together as one).
56r: B filled in a lacuna in the first half of Sch. Or. 1094 and added the second half; Sch. Or. 1098 is also by B, followed, after a large gap, by further scholia by A lower on the page.
57v: scattered scholia by A on the page, but B added Sch. Or. 1156 ἕνα φησὶν κτλ.
58v: for Sch. Or. 1204, the last word of the lemma and the first two-thirds of the note itself were added by B.

Phoenissae

Once again, the text of the play is entirely the work of Hand A. Hand B fills in lacunae and adds a few scholia.

67r: lacunae are filled in by B in Sch. Phoen. 8, 11, 13 (two separate gaps), 21.
67v: for Sch. Phoen. 31 the lemma is by A, but the scholion itself is added by B.
68r: on this page all the notes in the upper and lower blocks (Sch. Phoen. 31, 33, 36, 42, 43) are by B (there are no notes by A or B in the side block), and there are some blank spaces left in some of them where the source was unreadable.
69r: lacuna filled in by B in Sch. Phoen. 53, 61.
70r: lacuna filled in by B in Sch. Phoen. 88.
70v: lacuna filled in by B in Sch. Phoen. 111 ἄλλως (a blank left unfilled in Sch. Phoen. 111), 114 (3 gaps filled in, and a supralinear addition).
71r: in the first damaged line the traces of διηρκοῦντο (in the completion of Sch. Phoen. 114 ἄλλως from the previous page) appear to be more widely spaced and partially enlarged, suggesting the word was added by B; a single word is supplied by B in Sch. Phoen. 125, and at the bottom the last line is by B, adding Sch. Phoen. 130 with lemma (the rubricator never added the initial letters of the lemma or note).
71v: lacuna filled in by B in Sch. Phoen. 138.
72r: B supplies the lemma to Sch. Phoen. 148 and perhaps also the supralinear addition near the end of the note. The first six lines of the top block are by Hand A, but B squeezes in one more line and then writes all the scholia in the side margin block and the bottom block, Sch. Phoen. 151, 155, 157, 159, 160, and between Sch. 155 and 156 a second version of Sch. Phoen. 150.
73r: lacuna filled in by B in Sch. Phoen. 175.
74r: three lacunae of various extents filled in by B in Sch. Phoen. 208.
75r: lacuna only partially filled in by B in Sch. Phoen. 234.
77v: at four places Hand A has written next to scholia in the left margin block the symbol that normally means omission; in three the mark has been crossed out but one cannot detect Hand B in the associated line.[1] In Sch. Phoen. 341 it is possible that

---

[1] Such marks are usually, but not always, deleted when the lacuna is filled.

τὸ δὲ may have been added, but the hand is consistent and the lighter shade of the ink could be due simply to normal variation as the ink is discharged from the pen tip. In Sch. Phoen. 347 ἄλλως the adjacent line seems to be all by A and written at one time; near the end of the same note there is a gap left in the text, not filled in later (οἱ ποταμ is missing), and the sign in the margin is intact. Beside Sch. Phoen. 354 there is another sign, crossed out. It seems that in the three instances where the sign has been crossed out, it was used to indicate uncertainty on the part of scribe A, reminding scribe B to check this passage, and apparently B could not improve on what A wrote and either B or someone later crossed out the symbol.

78r: Sch. Phoen. 370 ἄλλως is added at the end of the side margin block.

79v: A left several blank spaces on this page, but only once, in Sch. Phoen. 421, is part of the space filled in by words supplied later by B.

92r: several lacunae are left and marked with symbols in Sch. Phoen. 822–823 (which are run together as one), but not filled in.

100v: at the end of the bottom block, a grammatical scholion is added by Hand B, writing in his most informal manner: Sch. Phoen. 1147 γυμνίτης ὁ πτωχὸς ῑ, καὶ ἔστιν ἡ εὐθεῖα ὁ γυμνίτης. γυμνήτης δὲ εἶδος ὅπλου, η̄, καὶ ἔστιν ἡ εὐθεῖα γυμνὴς γυμνήτης.[2]

110r: the word λέγω in Sch. Phoen. 1485 ἄλλως (12th line of the note as laid out in V) appears to be smaller and lighter than the words around it, apparently because squeezed in later. But the hand looks more like A than B.

116r: in Sch. Phoen. 1722 Hand B adds εἰμὶ after κατὰ τὴν ἰσχὺν, but the addition is in the marginal space and there was no space left or sign of omission added by A.

After the triad plays, up to fol. 263v (that is, up to *Tro.* 85), B appears more often, and sometimes writes entire pages. From 264r to the end (most of *Troades* and all of *Rhesus*), Hand B makes no more appearances. The following lists for the select plays describe all the remaining pages of the manuscript.

Medea
117v (*arg. Med.*): all A.
118r (*arg. Med., dramatis personae, Med.* 1–13): text and scholia in block by A, interlinear glosses by B.
118v (*Med.* 14–31): text, most scholia, glosses by B, one scholion added by A (a fuller version of Sch. Med. 19, already written by B in shorter form).
119r (*Med.* 32–51): text, most scholia, glosses by B, three scholia in margin added by A (Sch. Med. 40, 43, 43 ἄλλως).
119v (*Med.* 52–71): text and glosses by B, scholia by A.
120r (*Med.* 72–89): text and scholia by A, glosses by B.
120v (*Med.* 90–108): text by A, scholia and glosses by B.
121r–125v (*Med.* 109–274): all B.

---

[2] The content of this note is not paralleled in any text currently in TLG, but there is a passage in ps.-Herodian that mentions γυμνίτης among the set of nouns ending in -ίτης.

126r (*Med.* 275-290): *Med.* 275-286 by B, 287-290 by A, and the one scholion and the glosses on this page are by A.

126v-142v (*Med.* 291-860): all A. There are a few glosses that may either be by Hand B or be by V³ (see, e.g., *Med.* 341 on 128r, *Med.* 702, 704 on 138v). Note that on 142r the penultimate scholion in the block (partial version of Sch. Med. 837) has been crossed out by the rubricator, because the fuller version of it is on 142v; the rubricator mistakenly started to cross out the last scholion as well (Sch. Med. 835), but stopped in the middle, and the cursive hand V³ later added a note in the margin to explain that the crossed-out words in Sch. 835 were to be read and not ignored (τοῦ καλλινάου [the lemma] μὴ ὡς(?) ὄχλημα(?) παραβλεπτέον ἀλλ' ἀναγνωστέον).

143r (*Med.* 861-880): text A, scholia and glosses all B except for Sch. Med. 861, 864 in the first lines of the top block by A. Note that B enters on this page a repetition of Sch. Med. 851, although the verse is on 142v and A already included the note there.

143v (*Med.* 881-900): text B, no scholia, a few glosses by A. Note that the rubricator crossed out the last two lines (*Med.* 899-900) because 144r starts with 899 (by A).

144r-147r (*Med.* 899-1036): all A, except for a few glosses added by B (but on 147r the majority of glosses are by B).

147v (*Med.* 1037-1054): text by A, Sch. Med. 1039, 1043, 1044 by A in the top third of the margin block, the rest in the margin along with those in bottom block by B, glosses by B.

148r (*Med.* 1055-1074): all B except one note, Sch. Med. 1055, at top by A.

148v-149v (*Med.* 1075-1135): all B.

150r-151r (*Med.* 1136-1194): text and scholia by A, glosses by both hands.

151v (*Med.*1195-1213): all by B.

152r (*Med.* 1214-1234): text by A, scholia and glosses by B.

152v (*Med.* 1235-1254): text by A except last line, *Med.* 1254, by B; scholia and glosses B.

153r-v (*Med.*1255-1294): all by B.

154r (*Med.*1295-1314): text by A, sparse scholia and glosses by B.

154v (*Med.* 1315-1334): all by B.

155r-156v (*Med.* 1335-1419): all by A.

Hippolytus

157r (*arg. Hipp., dramatis personae*): all by A.

157v (*arg. Hipp., Hipp.* 1-12): text by A, scholia and glosses by B.

158r-159v (*Hipp.* 13-78): all by B, except a few glosses on the 159v by A. Note that the rubricator has crossed out the last line, *Hipp.* 78, because it is written first on the next page, where the associated scholion will fit.

160r (*Hipp.* 78-95): text, and two glosses on 78, by B, scholia and rest of glosses by A.

161r-168r (*Hipp.* 96-387): all by A.

168v (*Hipp.* 388-404): text by A, except *Hipp.* 403-404 by B; top margin Sch. Hipp. 384, 385 by A, side margin Sch. Hipp. 387-401 by B, glosses by B.

169r (*Hipp.* 405-424): text B, but *Hipp.* 421-424 by A; scholia by A, a few glosses by B.

169v–172v (*Hipp.* 425–545): text and scholia by A, a few glosses by A, fewer by B.[3]
173r (*Hipp.* 546–567): text and glosses A, except *Hipp.* 565–567 by B (with gloss on 565), scholia by B.
173v–174r (*Hipp.* 568–611): all B.
174v–175r (*Hipp.* 612–644): all A.
175v (*Hipp.* 645–664): text by A, except *Hipp.* 663–664 by B; scholia and glosses by B.
176r (*Hipp.* 665–678): all B.
176v–178r (*Hipp.* 679–742): all A.
178v (*Hipp.* 743–757): text and glosses by A, except *Hipp.* 757 (and gloss on it) by B; scholia by B, except lemma for first, Sch. Hipp. 744, by A.
179r (*Hipp.* 758–777): all B.
179v–181v (*Hipp.* 778–874): all A.
182r (*Hipp.* 875–890): text by A, scholia and glosses by B.
182v (*Hipp.* 891–910): all B.
183r (*Hipp.* 911–931): text by B, except *Hipp.* 930–931 by A, scholia and glosses by A.
183v–185r (*Hipp.* 932–1007): all A.
185v–186v (*Hipp.* 1008–1067): text by A, scholia and glosses by B.
187r–187v (*Hipp.* 1068–1104): all B.
188r (*Hipp.* 1105–1122): text by B, except *Hipp.* 1122–1123 by A; scholia and glosses by A.
188v–196v (*Hipp.* 1123–1466): all A.

Alcestis
197r–198v (*arg. Alc.*, *Alc.* 1–59): all A.
199r–208v (*Alc.* 60–430): all B, including some sparse scholia. Many pages have been trimmed down in conservation to just the text column; presumably they had no scholia, since the surviving top and bottom areas are without scholia, and (to judge from other trimmed pages in V) the conservator would probably have attempted to keep damaged margins if there had been writing on them.
209r–216r (*Alc.* 431–709): all A.
216v–220v (*Alc.* 710–881): all B, including sparse scholia.
221r–227v (*Alc.* 882–1159): all A.
228r (*Alc.* 1160–1163): top third of the page with the end of *Alc.* is by A, but B takes over on the same page for the next play.

Andromache
228r (*arg. Andr.*): the bottom two-thirds, where *Andr.* begins, are by B (but the heading of the hypothesis is probably A as rubricator).
228v–229v (*arg. Andr.*, *Andr.* 1–51): all B (except that *dramatis personae* and play title in red seem to be by A serving as rubricator).

---

[3] See above, n. 24, on the removal of *Hipp.* 546 from the bottom of 172v in order to keep the line with its scholion on 173r.

230r (*Andr.* 52–71): text by B, scholia and glosses by B, except Sch. Andr. 63 and two glosses on *Andr.* 65 by A.

231r–258v (*Andr.* 72–1191): all A, except for a two short scholia on 257v: Sch. Andr. 1157 κατὰ τὸ σιωμώμενον κτλ is written by B above the first half of that line; in the margin where A added the omitted lines 1150–1152, B adds a gloss on 1150 ὀξυθήκτῳ and also fills in a short lacuna left by A in the text of 1151.

259r–261r (*Andr.* 1192–1288): text by A, scholia and glosses by B.

Troades

261v–263v (*arg. Tro., Tro.* 1–85): all B, except that the *dramatis personae* and play title in red seem to be by A serving as rubricator, although the heading of the hypothesis, also in red, is apparently B.

264r–295r (*Tro.* 86–1332): all A.

Rhesus

296r–315v (*arg. Rhes., Rhes.* 1–940): all A.

BIBLIOGRAPHY

Items in the Bibliography are referred to in the text and notes by the author's name and the date. For names that appear without date (such as Matthiae, Dindorf, Schwartz, Diggle, and Kovacs) see the Abbreviations and Sigla in the front matter.

Agiotis, N. 2013. "Tzetzes on Psellos Revisited." *Byzantinische Zeitschrift* 106: 1–8.
Albrecht, F. 2012. "Ein *Novum Supplementum Euripideum*? Die unbekannten Seiten des Euripides-Palimpsestes *Codex Hierosolymitanus Sancti Sepulchri* 36." *Aevum* 86: 3–27.
Allan, W. 2000. *The Andromache and Euripidean Tragedy*. Oxford.
Allegrini, S. 1971–1972. "Note di Giovanni Tzetzes ad Eschilo." *Annali della Facoltà di Lettere e Filosofia dell'Università di Perugia* 9: 219–33.
Allen, T. W. 1889. *Notes on Abbreviations in Greek Manuscripts*. Oxford.
———. 1937. Review of Spranger 1935, *JHS* 57: 109.
Alpers, K. 2001. "Lexicographie." In G. Ueding et al., eds., *Historisches Wörterbuch der Rhetorik*, 5: 194–210. Tübingen.
Andres, G. de. 1968. *Catálogo de los Códices Griegos Desaparecidos de la Real Biblioteca de El Escorial*. El Escorial.
Arnesano, D. 2008. *La minuscola "barocca": Scritture e libri in Terra d'Otranto nei secoli XIII e XIV*. Università del Salento, Dipartimento dei Beni delle Arte e della Storia. Fonti medievali e moderne, 12. Galatina.
Arsenius 1534. Arsenius of Monembasia [Aristobulus Apostolis/Apostolius], *Scholia in septem Euripidis tragoedias ex antiquis exemplaribus ab Arsenio collecta et nunc primum in lucem edita*. Junta, Venice. (For a digital copy at books.google.com, with pages in reverse order, and many duplicate pages, https://books.google.com/books?id =6vlPAAAAcAAJ)
Arsenius 1544. Reprinted (among other times and places) Basel 1544 by Hervagius, *Scholia in septem Euripidis tragoedias ex antiquis exemplaribus ab Arsenio archiepiscopo Monembasiae collecta nuncque denuo multo quam antea emendatiore in lucem edita*. Hervagius, Basel. (Digital copy accessible at the Österreichische Nationalbibliothek, http://data.onb.ac.at/rec/AC10297615)
Atsalos, B. 1991. "Les signes de renvoi dans les manuscrits grecs." In Harlfinger and Prato 1991: 211–231.

Atsalos, B., and Tsironi, N., eds. 2008. *Actes du VIe Colloque Internationale de Paléographie Grecque (Drama, 21-27 septembre 2003).* Vivlioamphiastis - Annexe, 1. Athens.
Bachmann, L. 1828. *Anecdota Graeca e Codd. Mss. Bibl. Reg. Parisin.* 2 vols. Leipzig.
———. 1832. *Scholia in Homeri Iliadem* I. Leipzig.
Bagordo, A. 1998. *Die antiken Traktate über das Drama, mit einer Sammlung der Fragmente.* Beiträge zur Altertumskunde, 111. Stuttgart and Leipzig.
Baldi, D. 2011. "Ioannikios e il *Corpus Aristotelicum.*" *Revue d'Histoire des Texts*, n.s. 6: 15-26.
Barnes, J. 1694. *Euripidis quae extant omnia: Tragoediæ nempe XX, praeter ultimam omnes completae: Item Fragmenta aliarum plusquam LX tragoediarum; Et Epistolae V nunc primum et ipsae huc adjectae: Scholia demum doctorum virorum in septem priores tragoedias, ex diversis antiquis exemplaribus undiquaque collecta et concinnata ab Arsenio Monembasiæ Archiepiscopo.* Cambridge. (Digital copy accessible at the Österreichische Nationalbibliothek, http://data.onb.ac.at/rec/AC09846700)
Barrett, W. S. 1965. "The Epitome of Euripides' *Phoinissai*: Ancient and Medieval Versions." *CQ* 15: 58-71.
Belardinelli, A. M. 2000. "A proposito dell'uso e della funzione dell'*ekkyklema*: Eur. *Hipp.* 170-266, 808-1101; Men. *Asp.* 309-399, *Dysc.* 689-758a." *Seminari Romani di Cultura Greca* 3: 243-265.
Berger, A. 2001. "Imperial and Ecclesiastic Processions in Constantinople." In Necipoğlu 2001: 73-87.
Bernard, F. 2014. *Writing and Reading Byzantine Secular Poetry, 1025-1081.* Oxford.
Bevilacqua, F. 1973-1974. "Il Commento di Giovanni Tzetzes à Sopocle." *Annali della Facoltà di Lettere e Filosofia dell'Università di Perugia* 11 [published 1975]: 557-570.
Bianconi, D. 2005. *Tessalonica nell'età dei paleologi. Le pratiche intellettuali nel riflesso della cultura civica.* Dossiers byzantins, 5. Paris.
Bietenholz, P. G., and Deutscher, T. B. 1985. *Contemporaries of Erasmus. A Biographical Register of the Renaissance and Reformation. Vol. 1. A-E.* Toronto.
Blinkenberg, C. 1915. *Die Lindische Tempelchronik.* Kleine Texte für Vorlesungen und Übungen, 131. Bonn.
Boudreaux, P. 1908. *Oppien d'Apamée, La Chasse.* Bibliothèque de l'École des Hautes Études, Sciences historiques et philologiques, 172. Paris.
Braswell, B. K. 2011. "Didymus on Pindar." In S. Matthaios, F. Montanari, and A. Rengakos, eds., *Ancient Scholarship and Grammar. Archetypes, Concepts and Contexts.* Trends in Classics - Supplementary Vol. 8, 181-197. Berlin and New York.
Breithaupt, M. 1915. *De Parmenisco grammatico.* Leipzig.
Broggiato, M. 2001. *Cratete di Mallo. I frammenti: Edizione, introduzione, e note.* Pleiadi. Studi sulla letteratura antica, 2.
Bury, J. B. 1911. *The Imperial Administrative System in the Ninth Century, with a Revised Text of the Kletorologion of Philotheos.* The British Academy Supplemental Papers I. London.
Büttner-Wobst, T. 1897. *Ioannis Zonarae Epitomae Historiarum Libri XIII-XVIII* [= *Ioannis Zonarae Epitomae Historiarum Libri XVIII*, ex recensione M. Pinderi, tomus III]. Corpus Scriptorum Historiae Byzantinae. Bonn.
Canart, P., and Perria, L. 1991. "Les écriture livresques des XIe et XIIe siècles." In Harlfinger and Prato 1991: I.67-118 with plates II.51-68.

Capocci, V. 1958. *Codices Barberiniani Graeci*. Tomus I: *Codices 1–163*. Vatican City.
Carrara, P. 2007. "Editori e commentari di Euripide della prima età ellenistica." In R. Prestagostini and E. Dettori, eds., *La cultura letteraria ellenistica: Persistenza, innovazione, trasmissione*. Quaderni dei Seminari Romani di Cultura Greca, 10: 247–255. Rome.
Cavallo, G. 1992. "La storia dei testi antichi a Bisanzio. Qualche riflessione." In J. Hamesse, ed., *Les problèmes posés par l'édition critique des textes anciens et médiévaux*, 95–111. Louvain-la-Neuve.
———. 2002. "In limine." In Fera et al. 2002: vii–xii.
———. 2008. "Qualche riflessione su livelli di istruzione, categorie di lettori e pratiche di lettura a Bisanzio." In Atsalos and Tsironi 2008: I.247–257.
Cavarzeran, J. 2016. *Scholia in Euripidis Hippolytum. Edizione critica, introduzione, indici*. Sammlung griechischer und lateinishcher Grammatiker, 19. Berlin and Boston.
Cohn, L. 1903. "Dionysios 141." *RE* 5:1: 985–986.
———. 1905. "Eirenaios 7." *RE* 5:2: 2120–2124.
Csapo, E., and Slater, W. J. 1995. *The Context of Ancient Drama*. Ann Arbor.
Cullhed, E. 2012. "The Autograph Manuscripts Containing Eustathius' Commentary on the *Odyssey*." *Mnemosyne* 65: 445–461.
———. 2015. "Diving for Pearls and Tzetzes' Death." *Byzantinische Zeitschrift* 108: 53–62.
Daitz, S. G. 1970. *The Jerusalem Palimpsest of Euripides: A Facsimile Edition*. Berlin.
———. 1979. *The Scholia in the Jerusalem Palimpsest of Euripides: A Critical Edition*. Heidelberg.
Degni, P. 2008a. "I manoscritti dello 'Scriptorium' di Gioannicio." *Segno e Testo* 6: 179–248.
———. 2008b. "Tra maiuscola e minuscolo nei secoli X e XI: Alcune riflessioni." In Atsalos and Tsironi 2008: I.751–770.
Delehaye, H. 1902. *Synaxarium ecclesiae Constantinopolitanae (e codice Sirmondiano nunc Berolinensi)*. Acta Sanctorum, 62. Brussels.
Del Fabbro, M. 1979. "Il commentario nella tradizione papiracea." *Studia Papyrologica* 18: 69–132.
Di Benedetto, V. 1965. *La tradizione manoscritta Euripidea*. Proagones: Studi, 7. Padua.
Dickey, E. 2007. *Ancient Greek Scholarship. A Guide to Finding, Reading, and Understanding Scholia, Commentaries, Lexica and Grammatical Treatises, from Their Beginnings to the Byzantine Period*. Oxford.
Diggle, J. 1971. Review of Tuilier 1968. *Classical Review* 21: 19–21.
———. 1974. Review of Tuilier 1972. *Gnomon* 24: 746–749.
———. 1991. *The Textual Tradition of Euripides' Orestes*. Oxford.
Dindorf, L. 1825. *Euripidis Fabulae cum annotationibus*. 2 vols. Leipzig.
Dolger, F. 1948. *Aus den Schatzkammern des Heiligen Berges. 115 Urkunden und 50 Urkundensiegel aus 10 Jahrhunderten*. Munich.
Drachmann, A. B. 1903–1927. *Scholia vetera in Pindari carmina*. 3 vols. Leipzig.
Duffy, J. 1998. "Tzetzes on Psellos." In C.-F. Collatz, et al., eds., *Dissertatiunculae criticae. Festschrift für Günther Christian Hansen*, 441–445. Würzburg.

Dyck, A. 1981. "On Apollodorus of Cyrene." *Harvard Studies in Classical Philology* 85: 101–106.
———. 1983–1995. *Epimerismi Homerici*. 2 vols. Sammlung griechischer und lateinischer Grammatiker, 5:1–2. Berlin and New York.
———. 1986. *Michael Psellus. The Essays on Euripides and George of Pisidia and on Heliodorus and Achilles Tatius*. Byzantina Vindobonensia, 16. Vienna.
Eitrem, S., and Amundsen, L. 1957. "From a Commentary on the 'Troades' of Euripides: P. Oslo Inv. No. 1662." In *Studi in onore di Aristide Calderini e Roberto Paribeni, 1956–1957*: II.147–150. Milan.
Elsperger, W. 1907. *Reste und Spuren antiker Kritik gegen Euripides gesammelt aus den Euripidesscholien*. Philologus Supplementband 11: 1. Leipzig.
Erbse, H. 1969–1988. *Scholia Graeca in Homeri Iliadem (scholia vetera)*. 7 vols. Berlin and New York.
Essler, H., Mastronarde, D., and McNamee, K. 2013. "The Würzburg Scholia on Euripides' Phoenissae. A New Edition of P.Würzb. 1 with Translation and Commentary." *Würzburger Jahrbücher für die Altertumswissenschaft*, n.F. 37: 31–97.
Fajen, F. 1969. *Überlieferungsgeschichtliche Untersuchungen zu den Halieutika des Oppian*. Beiträge zur klassischen Philologie, 32. Meisenheim.
Fera, V., Ferraù, G., and Rizzo, S., eds. 2002. *Talking to the Text: Marginalia from Papyri to Print*. Percorsi dei classici, 4. Messina.
Ferroni, L. 2011. "I manoscritti della Συναγωγή Planudea." *Studi Classici e Orientali* 57: 327–353.
Flamand, J.-M. 2017. "Aristobulo (Arsenio) Apostoli: Notizie biografiche." In L. Ferreri, S. Delle Donne, A. Gaspari, and C. Bianca, eds., *Le prime edizioni greche a Roma (1510–1526)*. Répertoires et Inventaires, 2. Turnhout.
Follieri, E. 1969. *Codices graeci Bibliothecae Vaticanae selecti temporum locorumque ordine digesti commentariis et transcriptionibus instructi*. Exempla Scripturarum, IV. Vatican City.
Formentin, M. R. 1995. *Catalogus codicum Graecorum Bibliothecae Nationalis Neapolitanae*, 2. Rome.
Franchi de' Cavalieri, P., and Lietzmann, J. 1929. *Specimina codicum graecorum vaticanorum*. Berlin.
Fries, A. 2017. "For Use in Schools: Prosodical Marks in Two Pre-Palaeologan Manuscripts of Pindar." *GRBS* 57: 745–770.
Fuhr, M. 1841. *Dicaearchi Messenii quae supersunt*. Darmstadt.
Gallavotti, C. 1934. "I Codici Planudei di Teocrito." *Studi Italiani di Filologia Classica* n.s. 11: 289–313.
Gardthausen, V. 1911–1913. *Griechische Paläographie*, 2. Aufl. Leipzig.
Gaul, N. 2007. "The Twitching Shroud: Collective Construction of *Paideia* in the Circle of Thomas Magistros." *Segno e Testo* 6: 263–340.
———. 2008. "Moschopulos, Lopadiotes, Phrankopulos (?), Magistros, Staphidakes: Prosopographisches und Methodologisches zur Lexicographie des frühen 14. Jahrhunderts." In E. Trapp and S. Schönauer, eds., *Lexicologica Byzantina*. Super alta perennis. Studien zur Wirkung der Klassischen Antike, 4: 163–196. Göttingen.

———. 2011. *Thomas Magistros und die spätbyzantinische Sophistik. Studien zum Humanismus urbaner Eliten in der frühen Palaiologenzeit.* Mainzer Veröffentlichungen zur Byzantinistik, 10. Wiesbaden.
Geanokoplos, D. J. 1962. *Greek Scholars in Venice. Studies in the Dissemination of Greek Learning from Byzantium to Western Europe.* Cambridge, Mass.
Geel, J. 1846. *Euripidis Phoenissae cum commentario edidit Jacobus Geel. Scholia antiqua in Euripidis Tragoedias partim inedita partim editis integriora adiunxit C. G. Cobetius.* Leiden.
Gibson, C. 2002. *Interpreting a Classic. Demosthenes and His Ancient Commentators.* Berkeley.
Grünbart, M. 2005. "Byzantinische Gelehrtenelend—oder: Wie meistert man seinen Alltag?" In L. M. Hoffmann and A. Monchizahdeh, eds., *Zwischen Polis, Provinz und Peripherie: Beiträge zur byzantinische Geschichte und Kultur.* Mainzer Veröffentlichungen zur Byzantinistik, 7: 413–426. Wiesbaden.
Gudeman, A. 1912. "Helladios 2." *RE* 8:1: 98–102.
———. 1919. "Kallistratos 38." *RE* 10:2: 1738–1748.
———. 1921. "Scholien." *RE* 2A: 625–705.
Günther, H.-C. 1995. *The Manuscripts and the Transmission of the Paleologan Scholia on the Euripidean Triad.* Hermes Einzelschriften, 68. Stuttgart.
Harding, P. 2006. *Didymos on Demosthenes: Introduction, Text, Translation, and Commentary.* Oxford.
Harlfinger, D., and Prato, G., eds. 1991. *Paleografia e codicologia greca. Atti del II Colloquio internazionale (Berlino-Wolfenbüttel, 17–21 ottobre 1983).* Biblioteca di Scrittura e Civiltà. Alessandria.
Haupt, M. 1876a. "de Minucio Pacato qui et Irenaeus." *Opuscula* II: 434–440. Leipzig.
———. 1876b. "de Helladiis Alexandrino et Besantinoo." *Opuscula* II: 421–427. Leipzig.
Heimannsfeld, H. 1911. *De Helladii Chrestomathia quaestiones selectae.* Bonn.
Henry, P., ed. 1959–1977. *Photius. Bibliothèque.* 8 vols. (+ v. 9 Index). Paris.
Herington, J. 1972. *The Older Scholia on the Prometheus Bound.* Mnemosyne Suppl. 19. Leiden.
Hermann, G. 1812. *Draconis Stratonicensis Liber de metris poeticis. Ioannis Tzetzae Exegesis in Homeri Iliadem.* Leipzig.
Holwerda, D. 1976. "Zur szenisch-technischen Bedeutung des Wortes 'ὑπόθεσις' anlässlich einer Bemerkung des Aristophanes von Byzanz zu Eur. *Hipp.* 171." *Miscellanea Tragica in honorem J. C. Kamerbeek,* 173–198. Amsterdam.
Hunger, H. 1954. *Studien zur griechischen Paläographie.* Biblos-Schriften, 5. Vienna.
Ippolito, A. 2005. "Parmeniscus." *LGGA.*
Irigoin, J. 1984. "Livre et texte dans les manuscrits byzantins de poètes. Continuité et innovation." In C. Questa and R. Raffaelli, eds., *Il libro e il testo: Atti del convegno internazionale di Urbino, 20–23 settembe 1982,* 85–102. Urbino.
Janin, R. 1950. *Constantinople Byzantine. Développement urbain et répertoire topographique.* Achives de l'Orient chrétien, 4. Paris.
Jannaris, A. N. 1897. *An Historical Greek Grammar, Chiefly of the Attic Dialect as Written and Spoken from Classical Antiquity down to the Present Time, Founded upon the Ancient Texts, Inscriptions, Papyri and Present Popular Greek.* London and New York.

Kaster, R. A. 1988. *Guardians of Language: The Grammarian and Society in Late Antiquity*. Berkeley.
Keaney, J. 1971. "Moschopulea." *Byzantinische Zeitschrift* 64: 303-321.
Koster, W. J. W. 1975. *Prolegomena de comoedia [SchArist* 1:1A]. Groningen.
Latte, K., and Erbse, H. 1965. *Lexica Graeca Minora*. Hildesheim.
Lausberg, H. 1998. *Handbook of Literary Rhetoric. A Foundation for Literary Study*. Leiden and Boston.
Lehmann, O. 1880. *Die tachygraphischen Abkürzungen der griechischen Handschriften*. Leipzig.
Leone, P. A. M. 1968. *Ioannis Tzetzae historiae*. Naples.
—————.1972. *Ioanni Tzetzae epistulae*. Leipzig.
Livadaras, N. A. 1960. "Ἡ παράδοσις τοῦ κειμένου τῆς οἰκουμένης περιηγήσεως τοῦ Διονυσίου ἐν τοῖς κώδιξι τῆς Μαρκιανῆς Βιβλιοθήκης." *Thesaurismata* 3: 103-139.
Lolos, A. 1981. *Der unbekannte Teil der Ilias-Exegesis des Iohannes Tzetzes (A 97-609)*. Beiträge zur klassischen Philologie, 130. Königstein.
Lucarini, C. M. 2013. "Il monologo di Medea (Eurip. Med. 1056-1080) e le altre 'Medee' dell'antichità." *Annali della Scuola Normale di Pisa, Classe di lettere e filosofia*, ser. 5, 5.1: 163-196.
—————. 2016. "L'ἐκκύκλημα nel teatro greco dell'età classica." *Hermes* 144: 138-156.
Ludwich, A. 1917. "Über den Homerischen Glossen Apions." *Philologus* 74: 205-247.
Luzzatto, M. J. 1999. *Tzetzes lettore di Tucidide. Note autografe sul Codice Heidelberg Palatino Greco 252*. Paradosis, 1. Bari.
McNamee, K. 1992. *Sigla and Select Marginalia in Greek Literary Papyri*. Papyrologica Bruxellensia, 26. Bruxelles.
—————. 2007. *Annotations in Greek and Latin Texts from Egypt*. American Studies in Papyrology, 45. New Haven.
—————. Forthcoming. *Commentaria et Lexica Graeca in Papyris reperta* I.2.5.1: *Euripides*. Berlin.
Maehler, H. 1993. "Die Scholien der Papyri in ihrem Verhältnis zu den Scholiencorpora der Handschriften." In F. Montanari, ed., *La philologie grecque à l'époque hellénistique et romaine: Sept exposés suivis de discussions*, 95-127. Genève (repr. in H. Maehler, *Schrift, Text und Bild: Kleine Schriften*, ed. C. Láda and C. Römer. *Archiv für Papyrusforschung, Beiheft* 21 (2006) 79-99).
—————. 2000. "L'évolution matérielle de l'hypomnèma jusqu'à la basse époque." In M.-O. Goulet-Cazé et al., eds., *Le commentaire entre tradition et innovation: Actes du colloque international de l'Institut des traditions textuelles (Paris et Villejuif, 22-25 septembre 1999)*, 29-36. Paris.
Magnelli, E. 2003. "Un nuovo indizio (e alcune precisazioni) sui drammi 'alfabetici' di Euripide a Bisanzio tra XI e XII Secolo." *Prometheus* 29: 193-212.
Malzan, G. 1908. *De scholiis Euripideis quae ad res scaenicas et ad histriones spectant*. Darmstadt.
Maniaci, M. 2002. "'La Serva padrona': Interazioni fra testo e glossa sulla pagina del manoscritto." In Fera et al. 2002: 3-35.
—————. 2006. "Problemi di *mise en page* dei manoscritti con commento a cornice: L'esempio di alcuni testimone dell'*Iliade*." *Segno et Testo* 4: 211-297.

Martínez Manzano, T. 2008. "Die Aufenthalte des Andreas Darmarios in Madrid und Salamanca und ihre Bedeutung für die 'Recensio' der Philostrat- und Oppianscholien." *Rheinisches Museum für Philologie*, N. F. 151: 400–424.

———. 2015. *Historia del Fondo Manuscrito Griego de la Universidad de Salamanca*. Obras de Referencia, 37. Salamanca.

Mastronarde, D. J. 1988. *Euripides. Phoenissae*. Bibliotheca Scriptorum Graecorum et Romanorum Teubneriana. Leipzig.

———. 1994. *Euripides: Phoenissae*. Cambridge Classical Texts and Commentaries, 29. Cambridge.

———. 2002. *Euripides. Medea*. Cambridge Greek and Latin Classics. Cambridge.

———. 2017a. "Text and Transmission." In L. K. McClure, ed., *A Companion to Euripides*, 11–26. Chichester.

———. 2017b. "Food and Dreams: Ioannes Tzetzes Reading Euripides?" In *A Maurizio Bettini. Pagine stravaganti per un filologo stravagante*, 239–242. Milan.

Mastronarde, D. J., and Bremer, J. M. 1982. *The Textual Tradition of Euripides' Phoinissai*. UC Publications: Classical Studies, 27. Berkeley.

Mateos, J. 1962. *Le Typicon de la Grande Église, Tome I: Le cycle des douze mois*. Orientalia Christiana Analecta, 165. Rome.

Matijašić, I. 2014a. "Timachidas di Rodi e la *Cronaca di Lindo*." *Annali della Scuola Normale di Pisa. Classe di Lettere e Folosofia*, ser. 5, 6:1: 91–112.

———. 2014b. "Timachidas di Rodi. Introduzione, edizione dei rammenti, traduzione e commento." *Annali della Scuola Normale di Pisa. Classe di Lettere e Folosofia*, ser. 5, 6:1: 113–185.

Matthaios, S. 1999. *Untersuchungen zur Grammatik Aristarchs: Texte und Interpretationen zur Wortartenlehre*. Hypomnemata, 126. Göttingen.

———. 2015. "Philology and Grammar in the Imperial Era and Late Antiquity: An Historical and Systematic Outline." In *BCAGS* 184–296.

Matthiessen, K. 1974. *Studien zur Textüberlieferung der Hekabe des Euripides*. Bibliothek der klassischen Altertumswissenschaften, n.F., 2. Reihe, 52. Heidelberg.

———. 2001. Review of Günther 1995. *Gnomon* 73: 484–487.

Mazal, O. 1967. *Der Roman des Konstantinos Manasses. Überlieferung, Rekonstruktion, Textausgabe der Fragmente*. Wiener Byzantinische Studien, 4. Vienna.

Mazzucchi, C. M. 2003. "Ambrosianus C 222 inf. (graecus 886): Il codice e il suo autore. Parte prima: Il codice." *Aevum* 77: 263–275.

———. 2004. "Ambrosianus C 222 inf. (graecus 886): Il codice e il suo autore. Parte seconda: L'autore." *Aevum* 78: 411–440.

Meccariello, C. 2014. *Le Hypotheseis Narrative dei Drami Euripidei: Testo, Contesto, Fortuna*. Pleiadi, 16. Rome.

Medda, E. 2001. *Euripide. Oreste*. Milan.

Meijering, R. 1987. *Literary and rhetorical theories in Greek scholia*. Groningen.

Meliadò, C. 2005. "Helladius [3]." *LGGA*.

Merro, G. 2008. *Gli scoli al Reso euripidea*. Orione: Testi e Studi di Letteratura Greca, 2. Messina.

Messeri Savorelli, G., and Pintaudi, R. 2002. "I lettori dei papiri: Dal commento autonomo agli scholii." In Fera et al. 2002: 37–57.

Miller, E. 1868. "Zénodore." In *Mélanges de littérature grecque*, 407–412 [reprinted in Latte and Erbse 1965: 253–258]. Paris.
Mioni, E. 1973. *Introduzione alla Paleografia Greca*. Università di Padova. Studi Bizantini e Neogreci, 5. Padova.
———. 1985. *Bibliothecae divi Marci Venetiarum codices Graeci manuscripti. Thesaurus antiquus, 2: Codices 300–625*.
Mirhady, D. C. 2001. "Dicaearchus: The Sources, Text and Translation." In W. W. Fortenbaugh and E. Schütrumpf, eds., *Dicaearchus of Messana. Text, Translation, and Discussion*. Rutgers University Studies in Classical Humanities, 10, 1–142. New Brunswick, N. J., and London.
Montana, F. 2006. "Timachidas." *LGGA*.
———. 2007–2008. "Callistratus." *LGGA*
———. 2011. "The Making of Greek Scholiastic *Corpora*." In F. Montanari and L. Pagani, eds., *From Scholars to Scholia. Chapters in the History of Ancient Greek Scholarship*. Trends in Classics - Supplementary Volumes, 9, 106–161. Berlin.
———. 2013. "Il commentario all'*Iliade* P.Oxy. LXXVI 5095 e gli *scholia exegetica*." *Zeitschrift für Papyrologie und Epigraphik* 184: 11–20.
———. 2014a. "Introduction: From Types to Texts." *Trends in Classics* 6: 1–14.
———. 2014b. "Anything but a Marginal Question: On the Meaning of παρακείμενον σχόλιον and παραγράφεσθαι." *Trends in Classics* 6: 24–38.
———. 2015. "Hellenistic Scholarship." In *BCAGS* 60–183.
Moraux, P. 1976. *Aristoteles Graecus. Die griechischen Manuskripte des Aristoteles*. Peripatoi, 8. Berlin and New York.
Mossay, J. 1982. "La signe héliaque. Notes sur quelques manuscrits de S. Grégoire de Nazianze." In L. Hadermann-Misguich and G. Raepsaet, eds., *Rayonnement Grec: Hommages à Charles Delvoye*. Université Libre de Bruxelles. Faculté de Philosophie et Lettres, 83: 273–284.
Necipoğlu, N. 2001. *Byzantine Constantinople. Monuments, Topography and Everyday Life*. The Medieval Mediterranean: Peoples, Economies and Cultures, 400–1453, 33. Leiden and Boston.
Nesseris, I. Forthcoming. English translation with revisions of volume 1 of his 2014 Ioannina dissertation Η Παιδεία στην Κωνσταντινούπολη κατά τον 12ο αιώνα.
Nickau, K. 1966. *Ammonii qui dicitur liber De adfinium vocabulorum differentia*. Leipzig.
Novokhatko, A. 2015. "Greek Scholarship from its Beginnings to Alexandria." In *BCAGS* 3–59.
Nünlist, R. 2009. *The Ancient Critic at Work: Terms and Concepts of Literary Criticism in Greek Scholia*. Cambridge.
———. 2012. "Homer as a Blueprint for Speechwriters: Eustathius' Commentaries and Rhetoric." *GRBS* 52: 493–509.
Olsen, B. M. 2009. "The Reception of Classical Literature in the Early Middle Ages." In *Copyists, Collectors, Redactors and Editors. Manuscripts and Editions of Late Byzantine and Early Modern Greek Literature*, 423–443. Herakleion.
Pace, G. 2011. *La Poesia Tragica. Edizione critica, traduzione e commento*. Speculum: Contributi di Filologia Classica. 2nd. ed. Napoli.
Pagani, L. 2004. "Asclepiades [1]." *LGGA*.
———. 2007–2009. "Crates [1]." *LGGA*.

―――. 2013. "Dionysios [9]." *LGGA*.
―――. 2014. "Through the Warping Glass: A Reconsideration on Venetus A Subscriptions and the Birth of Scholiography." *Trends in Classics* 6: 39–53.
Papathomopoulos, M. 2007. *ΕΞΗΓΗΣΙΣ ΙΩΑΝΝΟΥ ΓΡΑΜΜΑΤΙΚΟΥ ΤΟΥ ΤΖΕΤΖΟΥ ΕΙΣ ΤΗΝ ΟΜΗΡΟΥ ΙΛΙΑΔΑ*. Athens.
Pearson, L., and Stephens, S. 1983. *Didymi in Demosthenem Commenta*. Stuttgart.
Pertusi, A. 1951. "Intorno alla Tradizione manoscritta degli Scolii di Proclo ad Esiodo V: Scolii Planudei e Bizantini inediti alle 'Opere.'" *Aevum* 25: 342–352.
Pfeiffer, R. 1968. *History of Classical Scholarship from the Beginning to the End of the Hellenistic Age*. Oxford.
Pontani, F. 2011. *Sguardi su Ulisse: La tradizione esegetica greca all'Odissea*. 2nd ed. Pleiadi, 13. Rome (1st ed. 2005, Sussidi eruditi, 63. Rome).
―――. 2015. "Scholarship in the Byzantine Empire (529–1453)." In *BCAGS* 297–455.
―――. 2016. "Thoughts on Editing Greek Scholia." In E. Göransson et al., eds., *The Arts of Editing Medieval Greek and Latin Texts: A Casebook*, 312–337. Toronto.
Regali, M. 2007. "Minucius Pacatus Irenaeus." *LGGA*.
―――. 2008. "Phrynichus Arabius." *LGGA*.
Rusten, J. S. 1982. "Dicaearchus and the *Tales from Euripides*." *GRBS* 23: 357–367.
Schaefer, G. H. 1811. *Gregorii Corinthii et aliorum grammaticorum Libri de Dialectis Linguae Graecae, quibus additur nunc primum editus Manuelis Moschopuli Libellus de Vocum Passionibus*. Leipzig.
Scheer, E. 1908. *Lycophronis Alexandra, Vol. 2: Scholia Continens*. Berlin.
Schoell, R., and Studemund, W., eds. 1886. *Anecdota varia graeca et latina*. 2 vols. Berlin.
Schrader, H. 1864. *De notatione critica a veteribus grammaticis in poetis scaenicis adhibita*. Bonn.
Schreiner, P. 1988. *Codices Vaticani Graeci. Codices 867–932*. Vatican City.
Schwyzer, E. 1934–1971. *Griechische Grammatik*, ed. A. Debrunner et al. 4 vols. Handbuch der Altertumswissenschaft, Bde. 2:1:1–4. Munich.
Slater, W. J. 1986. *Aristophanis Byzantii Fragmenta*. Berlin.
Sluiter, I. 2015. "Ancient Etymology: A Tool for Thinking." In *BCAGS* 896–922.
Smith, O. L. 1980. "The A Commentary on Aeschylus: Author and Date." *GRBS* 21: 395–399.
―――. 1982. *Scholia graeca in Aeschylum quae exstant omnia. Pars II, fasc. 2: Scholia in Septem adversus Thebas continens*. Leipzig.
―――. 1996. "Medieval and Renaissance Commentaries in Greek on Classical Greek Texts." *Classica et Mediaevalia* 47: 391–405.
Smyth, H. W. 1921. "The Commentary on Aeschylus' *Prometheus* in the Codex Neapolitanus." *Harvard Studies in Classical Philology* 32: 1–98.
Spengel, L. 1853–1856. *Rhetores Graeci*. 3 vols. Leipzig.
Spranger, J. A. 1935. *Euripidis quae in codice Veneto Marciano 471 inveniuntur phototypice expressa*. Florence.
Stephanus, P. 1602. *Euripidis Tragoediae quae extant. Cum Latina Gulielmi Canteri interpretatione. Scholia doctorum virorum in septem Euripidis tragoedias, ex antiquis exemplaribus ab Arsenio Monembasiae archiepiscopo collecta* [Paris] (Digital copy accessible at the Österreichische Nationalbibliothek, http://data.onb.ac.at/rec/AC12115219).

Stroppa, M. 2008. "Lista di codici tardoantichi contenenti *hypomnemata.*" *Aegyptus* 88: 49–69.

——. 2009. "Some Remarks Regarding Commentaries on Codex from Late Antiquity." *Trends in Classics* 1: 298–327.

Tovar, A. 1963. *Catalogus Codicum Graecorum Universitatis Salamantinae. I: Collectio Universitatis Antiqua.* Acta Salmanticensia, Filosofía y Letras, Tomo XV, Núm. 4. Salamanca.

Trendelenburg, A. 1867. *Grammaticorum graecorum de arte tragica iudiciorum reliquiae.* Bonn.

Tsavari, I. O. 1990. *Histoire du Texte de la Description de la terre de Denys le Périégète.* ΔΩΔΩΝΗ: ΠΑΡΕΡΤΗΜΑ, 28. Ioannina.

Tsereteli, G. 1904. *De compendiis scripturae codicum Graecorum praecipue Petropolitanorum et Mosquensium anni nota instructorum.* (Plates volume, rev. ed.). Saint Petersburg.

Tuilier, A. 1968. *Recherches critiques sur la tradition du texte d'Euripide.* Études et Commentaires, 68. Paris.

——. 1972. *Étude comparée du texte et des scholies d'Euripide.* Études et Commentaires, 77. Paris.

——. 2010. "Remarques sur les fondements historiques et rationnels de l'édition critique des drames d'Euripide." *Revue des Études Grecques* 123: 881–895.

Tunay, M. 2001. "Byzantine Archaeological Findings in Istanbul during the Last Decade." In Necipoğlu 2001: 217–234.

Turyn, A. 1943. *The Manuscript Tradition of the Tragedies of Aeschylus.* New York.

——. 1949. "The Sophocles Recension of Manuel Moschopulus." *Transactions and Proceedings of the American Philological Association* 80: 94–173.

——. 1957. *The Byzantine Manuscript Tradition of the Tragedies of Euripides.* Illinois Studies in Language and Literature, 43. Urbana.

——. 1964. *Codices graeci vaticani saeculis XIII et XIV scripti annorumque notis instructi.* Codices e Vaticanis selecti, 28. Vatican City.

——. 1972. *Dated Greek Manuscripts of the Thirteenth and Fourteenth Centuries in the Libraries of Italy.* 2 vols. Urbana.

Valckenaer, L. C. 1755. *Scholia veterum grammaticorum in Euripidis Phoenissas, ex codicibus manuscriptis, praesertim Augustano, supplevit, emendavit, nunc primum editis locupletavit plus quam ducentis, notisque instruxit* [separately paginated appendix of his *Euripidis Tragoedia Phoenissae*]. Franequer.

van Rossum-Steenbeek, M. 1988. *Greek Readers' Digests? Studies on a Selection of Subliterary Papyri.* Mnemosyne Supplement 175. Leiden.

Vári, R. 1909. "Parerga Oppianea." *Egyetemes Philologiai Közlöny* 33: 17–32, 116–131.

Vater, F. 1837. *Euripidis Rhesus cum scholiis antiquis.* Berlin.

Verhasselt, G. 2015. "The Hypotheses of Euripides and Sophocles by 'Dicaearchus.'" *GRBS* 55: 608–636.

Vitelli, V. 1884. "Spicilegio Fiorentino." *Museo Italiano di antichità classica* 1: 1–32, 159–174.

Vogel, M., and Gardthausen, V. 1909. *Die griechischen Schreiber des Mittelalters und der Renaissance.* Zentralblatt für Bibliothekswesen, Beiheft 33. Leipzig.

Walz, C. 1832–1836. *Rhetores Graeci.* 9 vols. in 10. Stuttgart and Tübingen.

Wattenbach, W., and von Velsen, A. 1878. *Exempla codicum Graecorum litteris minusculis scriptorum*. Heidelberg.
Webb, R. 1994. "A Slavish Art? Language and Grammar in Late Byzantine Education and Society." *Dialogos. Hellenic Studies Review* 1: 81–103.
———. 1997. "Greek Grammatical Glosses and Scholia: The Form and Function of a Late Byzantine Commentary." In N. Mann and B. M. Olsen, eds., *Medieval and Renaissance Scholarship. Proceedings of the Second European Science Foundation Workshop on the Classical Tradition in the Middle Ages and Renaissance*, 1–17. Leiden.
Wehrli, F. 1967. *Die Schule des Aristoteles. Heft 1: Dikaiarchos*. Basel and Stuttgart.
Weil, H. 1904. *Euripide. Oreste*. Paris.
Weissmann, K. 1896. *Die scenischen Anweisungen in den Scholien zu Aischylos, Sophokles, Euripides und Aristophanes und ihre Bedeutung für die Bühnenkunde*. Bamberg.
Wendel, C. 1932. *Die Überlieferung der Scholien zu Apollonios von Rhodos*. Abhandlungen der Gesellschaft der Wissenschaften zu Göttingen, Philolog.-Hist. Klasse, Dritte Folge, Nr. 1. Berlin.
———. 1948. "Tzetzes 1." *RE* 7A: 1959–2010.
———. 1949. "Parmeniskos 3." *RE* 18:4: 1570–1572.
———. 1950. "Planudes, Maximos." *RE* 20:2: 2202–2253.
Wentzel, C. 1894a. "Apollodoros 62 [of Cyrene]." *RE* 1:2: 2886.
———. 1894b. "Apollodoros 63 [of Tarsus]." *RE* 1:2: 2886.
———. 1896. "Asklepiades 27." *RE* 2:2: 1628.
West, M. L. 1998. *Aeschyli Tragoediae cum incerti poetae Prometheo*. Rev. ed. Stuttgart.
———. 2001. *Studies in the Text and Transmission of the Iliad*. Munich.
Wilamowitz-Moellendorff, U. v. 1887. Review of Schwartz, vol. I. *Deutsche Litteraturzeitung* 31: 1111–1113. [Reprinted in Wilamowitz, *Kleine Schriften* I.173–175. Berlin 1971.]
———. 1895. *Einleitung in die Griechische Tragödie*. 2. Aufl. [= Bd. 1 of *Euripides Herakles*]. Berlin.
Willink, C. W. 1986. *Euripides. Orestes*. Oxford.
Wilson, N. G. 1966. Review of Zuntz 1965, in *Gnomon* 38: 334–342.
———. 1967. "A Chapter in the History of Scholia." *CQ* n.s. 17: 244–256.
———. 1973a. "Three Byzantine Scribes." *GRBS* 14: 223–228.
———. 1973b. *Mediaeval Greek Bookhands: Examples Selected from Greek Manuscripts in Oxford Libraries*. Cambridge, Mass.
———. 1977. "Scholarly Hands of the Middle Byzantine Period." In *La Paléographie Grecque et Byzantine* (Actes du Colloque international sur la paléographie grecque et byzantine, organisé par Jean Glénisson, Jacques Bompaire, et Jean Irigoin), 221–239. Paris.
———. 1978. Review of P. Moraux et al., *Aristoteles Graecus: Die griechischen Handschriften des Aristoteles, Erster Band, Alexandrien–London*. *CR* 28: 335–336.
———. 1983a. "A Mysterious Byzantine Scriptorium: Ioannikios and His Colleagues." *Scrittura e Civiltà* 7: 161–176.
———. 1983b. "Scoliasti e commentatori." *Studi classici e orientali* 33: 83–112.
———. 1991. "Ioannikios and Burgundio: A Survey of the Problem." In G. Cavallo et al., eds., *Scritture, Libri e Testi nelle Aree Provinciali di Bisanzio*, 447–455. Spoleto.

———. 1996. *Scholars of Byzantium*. Rev. ed. London and Cambridge, Mass.
Wirth, P. 2000. *Eustathii Thessalonicensis opera minora magnam partem inedita*. Corpus Fontium Historiae Byzantinae, 32. Berlin.
Xenis, G. 2010a. *Scholia Vetera in Sophoclis Electram*. Sammlung griechischer und lateinischer Grammatiker, 12. Berlin and New York.
———. 2010b. *Scholia Vetera in Sophoclis Trachinias*. Sammlung griechischer und lateinischer Grammatiker, 13. Berlin and New York
Zanetti, A. M., and Bongiovanni, A. 1740. *Graeca D. Marci Bibliotheca codicum manu scriptorum per titulos digesta*. Venice. Digtial images at http://cataloghistorici.bdi.sbn.it/dett_catalogo.php?IDCAT=240.
Ziegler, K. 1936. "Timachidas." *RE* 6A:1: 1052–1060.
Zuntz, G. 1938. "Die Aristophanes-Scholien der Papyri, I–II." *Byzantion* 13: 631–690.
———. 1939. "Die Aristophanes-Scholien der Papyri, III." *Byzantion* 14: 545–614.
———. 1965. *An Inquiry into the Transmission of the Plays of Euripides*. Cambridge.

INDEX OF MANUSCRIPTS

See also the listing of manuscripts on pages xvii–xxviii. Manuscripts that are named only in those lists are not indexed here.

A. mss of Euripides

Athos
  Iviron 161 (209) (W), 79
El Escorial
  E.I.17 (destroyed codex), 79
Florence
  Conventi soppressi 71 (Xb), 89, 183n69
  Conventi soppressi 98 (Yf), 72, 98–101, 104–106, 121n39, 140
  Laurentianus plut. 31.03 (Sb), 115–116, 119–148
  Laurentianus plut. 31.10 (O), 30, 35, 63, 107, 162
  Laurentianus plut. 31.17 (Lr), 139–140
  Laurentianus plut. 31.21 (Lp), 142n76
Jerusalem
  Patriarchal Library, Τάφου 36, 5–6, 28–32, 35, 61, 72, 161, 163
Milan
  Ambrosianus I 47 sup. (Zm), 39n124, 122, 141n75
  Ambrosianus L 39 sup. (G), 66
Oxford
  Auct. F.3.25 (X), 89, 183n69
  Auct. T.4.10 (Ox), 63
  Barocci 120 (Xa), 89
  Laud gr. 54 (Xo), 89, 93, 105
Naples
  Neapolitanus II.F.9 (Y), 89–103, 105, 110–111, 115–118, 123, 125–126, 128–133, 137–140, 142n77, 145, 148, 154, 156–158, 160, 199, 213, 215
  Neapolitanus II.F.37 (Yn), 105
Paris
  Parisinus gr. 2713 (B), 2, 4–6, 12, 26–28, 31, 33–34, 36–37, 61, 74, 80, 93n85, 107, 138n73, 161–164, 168–169, 171–172, 180, 183, 200, 205

Reims
  Bibliothèque Municipale 1306 (Pr), 42, 71–72, 80, 104–105, 115–118, 128–132, 134–138, 141, 144–146, 148, 159–160, 200, 203–204
Rome
  Angelicus gr. 14 (T), 5, 39n125, 89, 91, 95n91, 100n98, 117, 138n73, 183, 198–199
Salamanca
  Salamanticensis 31 (S), 47, 63, 67–69, 71, 77, 105, 107–148, 160
Turin
  Biblioteca Nazionale B.IV.13 (C), 5–6, 200
Vatican City
  Barberinianus gr. 4 (gB), 153–160
  Urbinas gr. 142 (Ta), 100n98
  Vaticanus gr. 909 (V), vii, x, 3–6, 72, 80–85, 92, 104, 107, 118, 160, 199–223
  Vaticanus gr. 1135 (R), 71, 77, 105, 115, 117, 149–152, 160
  Vaticanus gr. 1345 (Sa), 42, 67–69, 71, 77, 105, 115–117, 160
Venice
  Marcianus gr. 468 (F), 63, 72, 138n71
  Marcianus gr. 469 (Yv), 2, 44–59, 89n72
  Marcianus gr. 471 (M), vii, 4–6, 12, 26–28, 31, 34, 36–37, 61, 74, 80, 107, 161–185, 200
Vienna
  phil. gr. 119 (Rw), 34n118, 37, 67, 105, 129n54, 203–204
Wolfenbüttel
  Gudianus gr. 15 (Gr, Gu), 3n13, 42n127, 46, 67n15,, 71n23, 73, 76, 81n54, 92n85, 103, 105–106, 129n54, 131, 136–137, 140, 141n75, 148, 157, 160, 199

B. mss of other authors

Florence
  Conventi soppressi 152, 84n62
  Laurentianus plut. 32.09, 74, 167n33, 170n47
  Laurentianus plut. 69.06, 171n52

Grottaferrata
  La Badia cod. B.a.4, 170n47
Milan
  Ambrosianus C 222 inf., 78, 85n65, 86, 205n18
  Ambrosianus E 26 sup., 159n96
Oxford
  Auct. T.4.13, 167n33
  Clarkianus 39, 170n47
Paris
  Parisinus gr. 438, 167n33, 171n52
  Parisinus gr. 2659, 171n53
  Parisinus gr. 2722, 205n16
Ravenna
  Ravennas 137, 167n33, 172
Vatican City
  Ottobonianus gr. 43, 159n96
  Urbinas gr. 35, 170n47
  Vaticanus gr. 1, 170n47
  Vaticanus gr. 7, 66n11
  Vaticanus gr. 197, 159n96
  Vaticanus gr. 504, 171n53
  Vaticanus gr. 1675, 167n33–34, 170n49
  Vaticanus gr. 1818, 130n55
  Vaticanus pap. gr. 92, 132n52
  Vaticanus Pii II 21, 171n52
Vienna
  Phil. gr. 219, 113n18
Venice
  Marcianus gr. 304, 130n55
  Marcianus gr. 454, 12n41, 13n47, 170n47
  Marcianus gr. 474, 12n41, 164, 166, 172
  Marcianus gr. 476, 12n42

INDEX LOCORUM

Aeschylus
  Agamemnon 1485-1486, 73
Ammonius
  de adfin. vocab. diff. 4, 70, 124; 7, 70; *193*, 125; *233*, 71n24
Ammonius
  in Arist. Cat. 93, *1*, 154
  in Porphyr. isagogen 67, *20-21*, 152; 67, *23-68, 1*, 152
[Anastasius]
  Quaestiones aliae PG 28:773, 38, 94
Anonymus
  Misc. Philosophica (Barb. gr. 131) 18 (61, 15), 70n22
Anonymus
  περὶ ἀκυρολογίας *17 Nickau*, 71n24
Anthologia Graeca (Beckby)
  2.1, 32-35, 109; *7.43*, 109; *7.44*, 109; *7.47*, 109; *7.48*, 109
[Apollodorus]
  Bibliotheca 1.27, 149n82
Apollonius Sophista
  Lexicon Hom. 98, *20*, 93; *114, 21*, 156
Apostolis, Michael
  Paroem. cent. 9, *1*, 96
Aristides Quintilianus
  De musica 1.15, 112n15
Aristophanes
  Nubes 37, 151
[Aristotle]
  de virt. et vitiis 1250b19-24, 82n56
  de mundo 339b21-22, 140
Arsenius
  Paroem. cent. 5, *80b*, 112n15

Basilius
  de vita et miraculis sanctae Theclae 1.23, 80n53

Choeroboscus
  Epimerismi in Psalmos 6, *24-32*, 73n31; 73, *25-29*, 124-125; 99, *6*, 94; *183, 3*, 76
Chrysostomus, Ioannes
  PG 49.262, 31, 135; *61.124, 37*, 135

Constantinus Manasses
  Aristarchus and Callithea, fr. 152a, 126-127
Damascenus, Ioannes
  PG 95.609, 1, 135
Epimerismi Homerici
  in Il. 1.190, 144; *in Il. 1.483a1*, 94; ἔσσεται, 125; Ταλθύβιος, 142
Etymologicum Genuinum
  α *234*, 100; α *400*, 85; α *1364*, 41; λ *41*, 75; λ *71*, 40; ταρβῶ, 130n55
Etymologicum Gudianum
  ἠρίον, 157; θάρσος, 71n24; δύω, 132; κευθμών, 119; κῆπος, 131; κόπις, 159; ναός, 105; οἰκτρῶς, 139; ποδάγρα, 152; Ταλθύβιος, 142; τάρβος, 130n56; φέρω, 125; φυρμός, 129; χηλή, 156
Etymologicum Magnum
  βίος, 73n31; δέρρις, 146; εἰρεσιώνη, 23; κῆπος, 131; κόπις, 158-159; λάτρις, 75; τάρβος, 130n56; τραγῳδία, 109; φάσγανον, 144
Etymologicum Symeonis
  δρᾶμα, 149
Euripides
  Hecuba 70, 126
  Hippolytus 546, 207n24
  Orestes 201, 33-34
Eusebius
  Praep. evang. 1.9.14, 6-8, 94
Eustathius
  in Il. 1.25, 136; *1.115*, 123; *1.232*, 76; *1.320*, 142-143; *2.190*, 150n85; *4.123*, 158; *6.252*, 125n44; *7.191*, 145; *9.116*, 99; *10.324*, 134; *12.13*, 136n67; *17.167-169*, 124; *22.56-59*, 43n128
  in Od. 1.87, 124; *13.215*, 43n128; *21.145*, 132
Eustratius
  in Arist. EN 279, 23, 135

Geminus
  Elementa astronomica 16.3, 140
Gregorius Nazianzenus
  Orat. 18, PG 35:1004, 41-43, 133

INDEX LOCORUM   239

Gregorius Nyssenus
  ad Graecos ex communibus notionibus 3:1.30-
    32, 151n86
Herennius Philo
  de diversis verb. signif. ν 121, 159n96
  epitome 72, 125
[Herodian]
  Excerpta fr. 93 Dain, 98
  Παρεκβολαί 4, 12–15, 111n10
  Partitiones 147, 15–16, 145; 2777, 8–9, 98n95
Herodotus
  Historiae 2.16, 140; 4.42, 140
Hesiod
  Theogony 207–210, 73
Hesychius
  α 2204, 129; α 2826, 100; α 5428, 40; α 8144,
    41; α 8322–8323, 99; δ 975, 20n84; κ 2393,
    93; λ 767, 40; λ 773, 40; ο 1030, 156; π 769,
    40; π 2098, 144; τ 1526, 41
Hippocrates
  de septimanis 5, 152n88

Josephus, Flavius
  Bell. Jud. 7.345, 135

Lesbonax
  de figuris 14b, 23–25, 97
Leo VI
  Homiliae 7, 276–280, 139
Libanius
  Declam. 40.2.80, 6–8, 202n11
Lucian
  De domo 28, 149n82

Menander Rhetor
  περὶ ἐπιδεικτικῶν 361, 17–20, 82
Moeris
  τ 25, 72n29
Moschopulus
  περὶ τοῦ εἰδώλου, 108n2

Oribasius
  Collectiones medicae 5.3.10, 4–5, 99
Orion
  Etymologicum μάρψαι, 77; πηγή, 75; τάλας,
    124; τλήμων, 124

Palaephatus
  De incredibilibus 2, 83n59
Paulus, Epit. med. 6.52.3, 146
Philo
  De confusione linguarum 182–187, 129
Philoponus, Ioannes
  de opificio mundi (p. 224 Reichert), 97

Photius
  Amphilochia, epist. 146, 12–13, 154
  Bibliotheca cod. 28, 25n97; cod. 145, 25n97;
    cod. 279, 25n97
  Lexicon β 213, 41; γ 45, 41; ε 2041, 105n110; κ
    633, 93; λ 231, 40; ο 404, 156; τ 224, 72n29;
    τ 607, 41
Planudes
  Epistulae 12, 19–80, 95
  paraphrase of Constantinus Manasses, excerpt
    34, 126–127
Plato
  Cratylus 397d2–4, 94
  Euthypho 12e, 82n57
  Lysis 204c7–d1, 103
[Plato],
  Definitiones 415a9, 82n57
Plutarch
  fr. 126 Sandbach, 25
  Mor. 184a, 110n8
  Mor. 489a, 110n8
  Thes. 19, 83n59
[Plutarch]
  de Homero 1056–1057, 85
Pollux
  Onomasticon 2.235, 146; 7.48, 110n8
Polybius
  Historiae 3.37.2, 140
Proclus,
  in Pl. Rem publ. II.331, 15–18, 131n58
Psellus, Michael
  Orationes hagiographicae 3a, 565–568, 139
  Opuscula logica etc. 50, 112–115, 154
  Oratoria minora 25, 57, 69n19
[Ptolemaeus]
  de diff. vocab. 100, 159n96; 404, 29–405, 2,
    159n96

Sch. Aesch.
  Pers. 28 (rec), 134
  Prom. 36a, 105; 36c, 79; 555a, 33n115; 863, 100
  Septem 289f, 130; 370g, 72n27, 159; 534f,
    72n27; 534l, 72n27; 1025g, 72n27
Sch. Aratus
  Phaenomena 247, 70n22
Sch. Aristoph.
  Acharn. 740a, 156; 740a (Tri), 156
  Nubes 6a (Tz), 81; 176a (Tz), 79; 261 (Tz), 41;
    713 (Tz), 81; 782a, 121n35; 1120f (rec), 99
  Plutus 253a (Tz), 14n49; 447, 76; 500b (Tz),
    72n30; 659, 105; 682 (Tz). 82; 729b (rec), 157
  Ranae 53, 8n26; 320a (Tz), 20n84; 320f, 20n84;

354a (Tz), 85n65; *1144a (Tz)*, 85n65; *1225 (Tz)*, 85n65; *1328 (Tz)*, 86–88
Sch. in Basilicorum Libros I–XI
  12.1(CA).61.17, 2–3, 204n16
Sch. Batrachymyomachia
  81 *(Mosch.)*, 124n43
Sch. Eur.
  Alcestis *1*, 11n38; *233*, 19n74; *1128*, 25
  Andromache *1*, 16; *32*, 10n37, 11n38; *21*n84; *102*, 111–112; *103*, 33n115; *167*, 72–73; *229*, 25n94; *330*, 22; *362*, 22; *445*, 16; *616*, 71; *885*, 22; *1077*, 22; *1188*, 137n68
  Hecuba *1*, 67, 93, 108–109, 119–120; *2*, 93–94; *3*, 94, 109; *6*, 121; *7*, 120–121; *8*, 68, 122–123; *9*, 68, 57n16; *12*, 94–95; *13*, 23; *14*, 68; *16*, 154; *21–22*, 155; *24*, 154–155; *31*, 76, 123–124; *35*, 110; *39*, 68; *47*, 124; *59*, 124–125, 155–156; *66*, 95; *71*, 95, 126–128; *80*, 95; *83*, 125–126; *84*, 96; *85*, 96; *86*, 129–130; *87*, 96–97; *89*, 128–129; *90*, 110, 156; *91*, 136; *97*, 130–131; *98*, 136; *99*, 131; *103*, 131–132; *109*, 111. 157; *121*, 76, 89; *126*, 157n95; *130*, 110; *131*, 110–111, 132–133; *132*, 133, 158–159; *142*, 158; *143*, 68; *144*, 157–158; *145*, 103; *148*, 68; *156*, 155; *160*, 155; *164*, 130–131;*167*, 104; *168*, 72, 85, 95; *174*, 134–135; *175*, 68n17; *176*, 135; *177*, 159–160; *195*, 133–134; *209*, 135–136; *213*, 76; *254–255*, 137–138; *288*, 71n23; *292*, 136; *304*, 73, 85; *313*, 105; *334*, 121n39, 146–147; *339*, 136; *359*, 138–139; *415–431*, 52; *417*, 139; *420*, 139–140; *424*, 158; *480*, 140–142; *481*, 140; *484*, 142–143; *489*, 133–134; *543*, 144–145; *549*, 146; *553*, 145–146; *555*, 137; *567*, 71n23; *572*, 146; *609*, 75; *612*, 71n26; *616*, 131; *729*, 22, 142n76; *736*, 22; *752*, 97; *759*, 97; *788*, 82n57; *847*, 22; *852*, 90; *857*, 137; *887*, 22; *900*, 137; *973*, 97–98; *1172*, 137; *1201*, 206n26; *1220*, 80; *1271*, 11n38; *1273*, 11n38
  Hippolytus *48*, 216n31; *171*, 18–19; *191*, 15n54; *196*, 15n54; *337*, 83; *377*, 181; *384*, 83; *656*, 15n54, 81; *678*, 137n68; *820*, 84; *887*, 85; *1013–1015*, 81, 85; *1127*, 137n68
  Medea *1*, 21–22; *9*, 20; *148*, 20, 22; *167*, 22; *169*, 20; *204*, 21n88; *214*, 24, 202n9; *219*, 24, 202n9; *264*, 20, 22; *356*, 22; *380*, 22; *399*, 75; *469*, 71; *613*, 25; *687*, 25n94; *737*, 22; *1027*, 25; *1201*, 80, 206n20; subscription, 13
  Orestes *1–14*, 45; *1*, 63, 65; *2*, 67; *3*, 63; *4*, 63; *5*, 63–64; *6*, 63; *7*, 63; *8*, 64–65; *10*, 63; *11*, 64–65; *12*, 23; *13*, 65; *14–27*, 45–46; *15*, 65; *16*, 64; *25*, 41; *28–70*, 46–47; *29*, 64; *30*, 35; *32*, 41; *33*, 41, 64; *36*, 41, 65; *37*, 35; *38*, 41, 65; *41*, 41; *42*, 41; *44*, 41; *45*, 64; *49*, 64; *50*, 40; *54*, 64; *55*, 41; *57*, 34n118; *58*, 41; *59*, 41; *60*, 41; *62*, 40; *69*, 65; *71*, 65; *73*, 34n118; *76*, 181; *78*, 64; *81*, 35, 64; *82*, 142n76; *86*, 65; *90*, 40, 64; *91*, 64–66; *93*, 64; *103*, 64; *108*, 29–30, 29n111; *109*, 29n111; *115*, 29, 29n111; *116*, 29n111; *117*, 73; *119*, 65; *120*, 65; *121*, 30, 29n111; *125*, 64, 66; *126*, 64–65; *127*, 29n111; *128*, 29n111, 30, 64, 66; *131*, 29n111; *134*, 41; *142*, 29n111; *144*, 29n111; *147*, 29n111; *149*, 29n111; *152*, 40; *157*, 31; *160*, 65; *162*, 31–32, 36, 40, 81n54; *169*, 41; *174*, 29n111; *178*, 40; *183–186*, 40; *185*, 40; *186*, 40; *187*, 40; *189*, 41; *191*, 29n111; *199*, 33; *200*, 33–34, 66; *201*, 33–34; *206*, 64; *211*, 31; *212*, 64; *213*, 64; *219*, 41; *220*, 73, 98–99; *221*, 99; *223*, 99; *225*, 25n94; *226*, 64; *228*, 65; *233*, 64; *234*, 31, 36–37; *257*, 64; *264*, 65; *265*, 64; *275*, 181; *282*, 64; *291*, 100; *303*, 64; *304*, 64; *305*, 64; *314*, 19; *315*, 64–65; *325–326*, 40; *327*, 65; *328*, 41; *329*, 40; *331*, 32, 74–75; *335*, 29n111; *340*, 29n111; *341*, 64; *343*, 64; *349*, 42; *356*, 29n111; *371*, 8n26; *382*, 41; *385*, 65; *396*, 40; *411*, 29n111; *412*, 65; *414*, 200–203; *416*, 203–205; *424*, 203–205; *434*, 19; *435*, 64; *439*, 41; *452*, 40; *458*, 40; *488*, 17, 40; *714*, 17n67; *734–754*, 54; *795*, 83n60; *919*, 100; *1028*, 19; *1038*, 17n67; *1065*, 100; *1094*, 64; *1233*, 16; *1257*, 32n115; *1284*, 92, 101; *1287*, 17n67, 92. 101–103; *1371*, 23; *1384*, 21–22, 10n37; *1490*, 64; *1506*, 32n115; *1645*, 11n38; subscription, 13
  Phoenissae *21*, 66n14; *40*, 83n60; *45*, 11n38; *50*, 11n38; *101*, 181; *205*, 181; *208*, 16, 66n14; *235*, 181; *271*, 71n23; *274*, 105n110; *751*, 22; *963–976*, 47; *977–989*, 57; *991–1012*, 49; *1010*, 70; *1019–1042*, 50; *1102*, 181; *1116*, 70; *1165*, 137; *1296*, 75; *1485*, 33n115; *1747*, 22
  Rhesus *5*, 16, 20; *29*, 16; *523*, 20; *528*, 16, 20; *540*, 20; *916a*, 11n36
  Troades *9*, 10; *47*, 17; *221*, 20; *228*, 20, 23; *1079*, 22
Sch. Hesiod
  Opera *3 (Tz)*, 73n31; *491 (Tz)*, 83; *524–526*, 76
Sch. Hom.
  Iliad *1.2 (D)*, 110n6; *1.115, no. 69 (Tz)*, 123; *1.151, no 29 (Tz)*, 73n31; *1.266, no. 39 (Tz)*, 125; *1.350, no. 18 (Tz)*, 85; *1.400 (D)*, 32; *1.440, no. 95 (Tz)*, 157–158; *3.80b*, 71n25; *3.82b*, 71n25; *4.157a*, 71n25; *14.3 (D)*, 125n44;*15.137*, 77; *21.281*, 76

Odyssey 1d1, 1d2, 73n31; *8.258*, 100; *17.343*, 121n35
Sch. Lucian
  de domo 28, 149n82
Sch. Lycophron (Tzetzes)
  Alexandra 14, 88–89; *28*, 76; *157*, 85; *1328*, 158
Sch. Nicander
  Theriaca 15a, 149n82
Sch. Oppian
  Halieutica 1.59, 141; *1.234*, 75; *1.380*, 120; *1.389*, 119; *1.418 Vári*, 147; *1.567*, 121; *1.576*, 123; *2.175*, 77; *2.613*, 76; *3.3*, 134
Sch. Pindar
  Olympian 1.84g, 121n35
Sch. Soph.
  Ajax 155b, 136; *373*, 84n63
  OC 475, 23
Sch. Theocr.
  Idyll 2.95, 136
Sch. Thuc.
  Historiae 2.102.5 (Tz), 132
Septuagint
  Genesis 2:24, 138
  Job 1:12, 135
  Psalms 5:2, 134
Strabo
  Geographia 14.2.7, 84
Stobaeus
  1.17.4 (Chrysippus), 129
Suda
  α *939*, 134; β *390*, 41; β *493*, 157; γ *91*, 41; δ *1063*, 15n54; ε *732*, 25n97; ε *782*, 139; κ *792*, 23; μ *250*, 158; ο *464*, 156; σ *1576–1577*, 134; τ *1068*, 41; τ *1158*, 157

Συναγωγὴ λέξεων χρησίμων
  κ *488*, 151n87
Syncellus, Georgius
  Ecloga chronographica 199, 21–27, 83n59
Synesius
  Epistula 5 Garzya, 101–103

Thomas Magister
  Ecloga vocum Atticarum 233, 12, 98; *349, 9*, 72n29; *391, 9*, 39
Textamentum Novum
  Matthew 19:5, 139
  Mark 10:8, 139
Theodorus Dexius
  Epist. 2.18, 69–70, 204n16
Theon, Aelius
  Progymn. 96, 19ff., 137
Tzetzes, Ioannes
  Allegories of the Iliad, Proleg. 280, 147; *Proleg. 324*, 147; *16.186*, 85; *23.46*, 147
  Chiliades 1.19, 528–529, 83; *2.51, 745–747*, 85; *3.363 (scholion)*, 81; *7.113, 119–128*, 84; *10.323, 276*, 82; *11.369, 246–249*, 86; *12.397, 11*, 82; *12.399, 209*, 82; *12.409, 399–400*, 83; *12.447, 826–831*, 84
  Epist. 58, 127–128

[Zenodorus]
  τῶν περὶ συνηθείας ἐπιτομή *254, 1–2*, 134
Zonaras
  Homilia de Hypapante 7, 80n53
[Zonaras]
  Lexicon, λάτρις, 75

GENERAL INDEX

abbreviations (in manuscripts), 12n43, 83n60, 101n99, 128n53, 149n81, 164–166, 168–169, 170n47, 171, 175–176, 178–183, 191, 193–194, 205n19, 208, 211, 214, 216
Achaeus, 109–110
Aeschines (*grammaticus*), 23
Aeschrio, 23–24
Aeschylus, 1, 22, 73–74, 77, 79–80, 87–88, 115, 148, 159–160, 167, 170n47, 175, 205
  A-commentary (Φ-commentary), 33n115, 77, 79, 105, 117n33, 130, 148, 205
Alcestis, 1, 3n9, 3n12, 15, 26, 183, 222
Alexander of Aetolia, 17n56
Alexander of Aphrodisias, 9
Alexandrian library, 8–9
Alexandrian scholarship, *see* scholarship
alphabetic plays of Euripides, 3n9, 34n118, 89
Amatius, H. (Girolamo Amati), 3
Ammonius (commentator on Aristotle), 105n110, 160
Ammonius (grammarian), 39, 70
Anagnostes, Ioannes, 113n18
Andromache, 1, 3n9, 3n12, 5, 11, 22, 26, 61, 161, 173, 182–183, 187, 209, 211, 222
antiptōsis, 81
Apion, 25
Apollodorus of Cyrene, 21
Apollodorus of Tarsus, 20–21
Apollonius Rhodius, 12n41, 13, 24, 25n94
Apollonius Sophista, 72
Aratus, 9, 144
Aristarchus, 15n56, 17, 20, 64n7
Aristobulus Apostolis, *see* Arsenius
Aristonicus, 71n25
Aristophanes (of Athens), 1, 4n15, 8n26, 12n41, 13, 20n84, 21, 69n20, 72n27, 74n35, 78–79, 82, 85–87, 127, 151, 153, 160, 164, 166, 167n33, 168n42, 169, 171–172, 175, 182
Aristophanes (of Byzantium), 8–9, 11, 15–19, 22n90, 108, 120
Aristotle, 7–8, 14–15, 78, 81–82, 154, 160
Arsenius (Aristobulus Apostolis), xxviii, 1–2, 44–59, 96, 129–130
article gloss, 63
Asclepiades, 11n38

Barnes, J., 2
Callimachus, 8, 16
Cavarzeran, J., xvii, 2n5, 2n7, 4, 7n24, 15n54, 18n72, 37n119, 47, 81n55, 82–83, 84n61, 84n63, 206n21, 215n30, 216n31
Choeroboscus, Georgius, 75, 122, 156
Cobet, C. G., 3n11
commentary, 6, 8–11, 13n43, 17, 19–21, 23–24, 30–32, 33n115, 34, 38, 39n125, 60, 77–80, 89–90, 93, 98, 105, 113n16, 117n33, 118, 130, 134, 148, 154n94, 165, 170n47, 205; *see also hypomnēma*
Crates, 14, 16, 20
Creusa, 109–110
Cyrillus, 14n50

Daedalus, 150–151
Demosthenes, 9, 32n115, 202
Derveni Papyrus commentary, 9
Dicaearchus, 15
Didymus, 9–11, 13–14, 16, 20–23, 25–26, 60
Dindorf, L., 3n10, 102
Dindorf, W., 2–3, 4n15, 5n19, 44, 67, 80, 92n85, 105, 108n2, 131n60, 134n63, 139n74, 142n76, 215
Dionysius (uncertain person named in subscriptions), 13–14, 23
Dionysius Periegetes, 161, 165, 172, 176
Dionysius Thrax, 112
disambiguating gloss, 63–64
distinctions (of meanings of a word, or between words), 61–62, 67, 70–72, 82, 104–105, 125–126, 129–131, 134, 137–138, 147, 152, 157–158, 170, 200

Easter, timing of, 152
eccyclema, 18–19
education, 6–7, 14, 34, 60–63, 89, 162; *see also* teaching
enlarged letters (in minuscule script), 166–167, 173–181, 184–185, 205, 209–210, 212–214, 219
Epimerismi Homerici, 62, 70, 72, 74, 94, 121, 125, 142–144, 153
Etymologica, etymological dictionaries, 66n11, 74, 76–77, 119, 123, 130, 144, 148, 160, 181

242

GENERAL INDEX 243

Et. Genuinum, 130, 156
Et. Gudianum, 121n39, 130
Et. Magnum, 79n49, 130
Et. Symeonis, 130n56
etymology, etymologizing, 23, 39, 44, 61–62, 66n11, 73–77, 83–85, 94, 104, 112, 114, 116, 119, 121, 123–124, 130–131, 142–149, 152, 156–157, 159n96, 160, 200
Eustathius, *or* Eustathian, 34, 42–43, 76–78, 79n49–50, 85, 89n71, 95, 117, 123–124, 134, 142–143, 145, 148, 149n85, 163n11, 205
Eutecnius, 113

gloss, glossing, glossation, 2, 5–6, 9, 11, 17, 21, 27–28, 33–34, 37–42, 44–47, 58, 61n21–3, 62–65, 68n18, 69n20, 77–78, 80, 89n75, 90–93, 97, 99–100, 103n103, 107, 111n9, 112, 114, 122, 127–129, 131, 134–136, 139–140, 142, 146, 149, 153, 154n94, 157, 159–160, 169n46, 170n47, 199, 200n5, 203n13, 207–215, 217–223
glossary, 14n50, 25n94, 153n91
grammaticus, 23, 61, 89
Gregoras, Nicephorus, 121
Gregorius Nazianzenus, 97
Günther, H.-C., ix, 5–6, 12, 44, 89n72, 89n75, 90–91, 94n88, 98, 105, 139n74

Hecuba, 1–3, 22, 28, 38, 39n124, 47, 52–54, 67, 71–72, 74, 83, 91, 92–93, 104, 107, 110, 112–114, 116–117, 136, 138, 144, 148–149, 153, 165, 170, 172–173, 183, 186, 200, 211–212, 217
Helen, 89
Helladius, 25
Heracles, 34n118
Herennius Philo, 70, 125, 159n96
hermēneia, 184–185
Hermogenes, 81, 82n57, 86, 112, 155
Herodian, 25, 129–130
Hervagius, J., 2n4
Hesychius, 42
Hipparchus, 9
Hippocrates, 152
Hippolytus, 1, 3n9, 4, 26, 31, 47, 61, 82–83, 161, 170, 172–173, 182–183, 188, 207n24, 221
Homer, 8–9, 11, 12n41, 12n43, 13n47, 17–18, 27n100, 17n104, 29–30, 62, 64, 70–71, 123, 142, 145, 153, 164, 170n47, 182n67, 202
hyperbaton, 62, 135–137
hypomnēma, 8–9, 14, 38; *see also* commentary
hypothesis, 8, 15–16, 17n54, 91, 107–108, 113n17, 115n24, 170, 173, 209, 211, 214, 222–223

Iamblichus, 152n88
Icarus, 150–152
Ioannikios, 28, 132n62, 162–163, 205n18
Ion, 109–110
iota adscript, 168n40, 170–171, 177
Irenaeus, 23–25, 202
Ixion, 34n118

Kalliandros, Ioannes, 113
Kampmann, C. F., 3
King, J., 2

lacuna, in V, left by Hand A, often filled in by Hand B, 204–205, 218–220, 223
Libanius, 97, 202
Life of Aeschylus, 115
Life of Euripides, 3n13, 91, 107–108, 165
Life of Hesiod, 78
Life of Lycophron, 113n17
long mark (macron) over vowels, 183
Lycophron, 12n42

majuscule
  small (*Kleinunciale*), 12n43, 169–170
  used in minuscule manuscript, 166, 170, 173, 175–179, 181, 211–213
marginalia, 8n27, 12, 170n48
Matthiae, A., 2–3, 131n60, 134n63, 139n74, 142n76
Medea, 1, 3n9, 3n12, 11–13, 15, 21–22, 26, 28, 220
Menander, 15, 21n87
Merro, G., xvii, 11n38, 16n61
Minotaur, 83
Minucius Pacatus, 24
Molottus (Molossus), 113
Moschopulus, Manuel, *or* Moschopulean, 3, 5–6, 34, 38–42, 44n1, 45, 61–63, 66, 81, 89–93, 96–98, 100, 102, 104–105, 108n2, 118, 120n37, 123, 128, 131, 134, 136–137, 139n74, 140, 146, 148
myth, mythography, 7–8, 11, 15–16, 20, 22, 83, 87, 90, 104, 109

Neophron's *Medea*, 15
Niketas (scribe), 12n42

obelus
  dotted (as sign of omission), 207
  marking "recent" scholia in Schwartz, 18n72, 33, 67n14
Oppian
  Cynegetica, 113
  Haliectica, 79n50, 112–113, 115–116
Orestes, 1–2, 3n9, 3n12, 12, 17, 19, 38, 45, 47, 67,

72, 74, 91–93, 103n103, 104, 117, 149, 170, 173, 183, 185, 200, 211, 217
Orion (lexicographer), 74n33
Orion (mythological figure), 149

Palaeologan (era or scholarship), ix, 3–5, 28, 34, 39, 61, 63, 74, 77, 105–106, 114, 137, 144n79, 183, 199–200, 202–203, 212
Pamphilus, 21n85
paraphrase, 2, 5n19, 11, 14, 23–24, 29, 33, 37–38, 40, 44–59, 60, 62–63, 78, 96, 98, 100, 104–106, 110, 113, 122, 126, 136, 143, 185, 200, 209
Parmeniscus, 20, 21n88, 22–23
Pasiphaë, 83
Perlschrift, 165–166
Philo Judaeus, 152n88
Phoenissae, 1–2, 3n9, 3n12, 10, 27n104, 47, 72, 74, 91–92, 114, 116, 118n35, 170, 173, 182–183, 185, 186, 219
Phrancopulus, Georgius, 66
Phrynichus, 25
Piers, W., 2
Pindar, 8–9, 183n69
Planudes, Maximus, *or* Planudean, 44, 61–62, 77, 89–106, 117–118, 126–128, 129n54, 148, 199–206
Plato, 32n115, 82, 123, 170
  Cratylus, 73
Plutarch, 25
P. Oslo inv. 1662, 10
prepositional gloss, 64–65
problēma, 16, 20, 22, 66n14, 108
Proclus (commentator on Hesiod), 78
pronoun, glossed with antecedent, 65
Psellus, Michael, 62n4, 69n19, 78, 79n49, 95, 102, 139, 154, 205
pseudo-Apollodorus, 25n94
P. Würzburg 1, *see* Würzburg scholia

question-and-answer form, 66, 68n17, 81, 121, 127, 139, 147; *see also problēma*

recentiores (manuscripts of Euripides), 4, 6, 34, 37–42, 61, 63, 66–67, 71–72, 74, 77, 82, 92–93, 105, 107, 112, 117, 136, 160, 200, 204–205, 210, 215
reference symbol or marker, 27, 34, 95n89, 114, 173, 181–182, 186–188, 209, 218
relative pronoun, glosses on, 64
Rhesus, 1, 3, 11, 15, 20n82, 28, 107, 220, 223
rhetorical analysis, 21, 61, 105, 148, 163n67, 200–202, 205
rhetorical instruction, 10, 24, 62n41, 86, 160, 204

Saint Thecla, churches of, 185
schedography, 39, 44, 61n2
scholarship
  Alexandrian, 6–7, 10, 16, 17n66, 22
  ancient, ix, 7, 156
  Homeric, 8–9, 16n57, 71n24–25
scholia
  old(er) (*scholia vetera*), 3–4, 6–7, 12, 13n46, 26, 28, 39, 41, 60, 61n2, 62–63, 66, 74, 78–81, 86–87, 90, 95–96, 98, 100, 109, 112, 115n24, 126–127, 136, 137n68, 162, 200, 205
  on particular authors: Aeschylus, 42, 74, 79, 115n24, 160; Apollonius Rhodius, 12n41, 13, 24; Aristophanes, 4n15, 8n26, 13, 72n27, 74n35, 78, 86, 127, 160, 169, 182; Demosthenes, 202; Hesiod, 42, 78, 83–84; Homer, 2n5, 4n15, 62, 70, 72n27, 182n67; Lycophron, 78; Oppian, 76, 78, 112–113, 115, 117, 121, 135, 141; Pindar, 9; Sophocles, 7n24, 31n113, 33n115, 62n3, 74; Thucydides, 202
  Palaeologan, 3n13, 5, 34, 39, 61, 74, 77, 105–106; *see also* Moschopulus, Planudes, Thomas, Triclinius
  shaped, 183–184
  younger (*scholia recentiora*), 6–7, 18n72, 33, 60–62, 67n14, 127, 200, 205
  see also teachers' scholia, Tzetzes, Würzburg scholia
Schwartz, Eduard, 1n7, 4–6, 11n38, 15n54, 16n62, 17n68, 18n72, 21n54, 24n93, 31–34, 37, 44, 61n1, 67n14, 72n26, 80–81, 111n12, 162, 180–181, 200, 201n3, 203n13, 204, 205n21–22, 206–207, 212, 215, 217–218
selection, select plays of Euripides, 1, 11, 26, 153, 199, 220
sigla, of Euripides manuscripts, xvii-xxviii, 206, 215
sign
  critical signs, 9, 17, 19, 204, 220
  sign of omission (in V), 204, 207, 219–220
  see also reference symbol
Sophocles, 1, 7n24, 15, 28, 31n113, 33n115, 67, 74, 80, 84n62, 88–89, 90n78, 91, 93, 138, 162, 167, 170n47, 175, 176n62, 202
Soteridas, 14n51
Spheneas, Manuel, 115
Stephanus, P. (Paul Estienne), 2n4
subscription (to scholia), 11–14, 23, 183
Symeon (Metaphrastes), 122
Synesius, 97, 101–102

tally of pages by scribes, 172–173

Taurus, 83
teachers' scholia, 42–43, 60–77, 80, 82, 94, 90, 92–93, 104–106, 110, 112–148, 153–154, 204
teaching, teachers, 1, 6, 10–11, 13–14, 24, 28–29, 32–34, 38–39, 42–44, 60–64, 66–67, 68n17, 70, 72–74, 77, 79–80, 82, 84, 89–90, 92–93, 95, 98, 102, 104–107, 110–114, 117–118, 120, 124–125, 127, 129–130, 132, 136–137, 139–140, 144, 147–148, 153–154, 160, 162, 184–185, 199–200, 202–205
Telchines, 84, 202
Theodorus (scribe of Sa), 116
Theodorus Continuatus, 100
Theodosius, 25
Thomas Magister, *or* Thoman, 3, 5–6, 33–34, 38–42, 46, 61–63, 66, 72n29, 81, 82n57, 90–91, 99, 105, 108n2, 122, 131, 134, 137, 140–141, 148, 199
Thucydides, 10, 79, 88, 132, 202
Timachidas, 21–22
tmesis, 62, 136–137
Triclinius, Demetrius, *or* Triclinian, 3, 5, 15, 38, 39n125, 42, 52, 61, 66, 69n20, 81, 89–91, 93, 122, 138n73, 148, 183, 199, 215
truncation (for abbreviation of word), 12n43, 83n60, 181, 184, 195, 208
Tryllitsch, G. F., 3
triad plays, 1–4, 11, 26, 37–38, 39n125, 44, 61–62, 72, 74, 77, 80, 81n54, 89, 90n78, 91n82, 92n84, 105, 112, 115–116, 149, 153, 161, 206, 215, 217, 220
Troades, 1, 3, 11, 89, 199n2, 209, 215, 220, 223
Turyn, A., 3n8, 5, 44, 66n11, 89–90, 91n81, 92n84, 93, 103n104, 105–106, 113, 115–116, 117n30, 129n54, 139n74, 162–164, 199–200, 205
Tzetzes, Ioannes, *or* Tzetzean, 14, 15n54, 34, 62, 64, 72n27, 73n31, 74n35, 77–89, 105, 113, 115, 117, 123, 125–128, 132, 147–148, 157–158, 160, 163n11, 167, 200n2, 202, 205
Logismoi (lost work), 86–88
Tzetzes, Isaac, 77, 113

Valckenaer, L. C., 2, 3n8
Vater, F., 3
vita Euripidis, see Life of Euripides
vocabulary, mastery of or building, 39, 61–63, 66, 70, 72, 74, 104, 120–121, 148, 153

Würzburg scholia (P. Würzburg 1), 9, 114, 118n35

Xuthus, 109–110

Zenodotus, 16

ἄγω, 70, 124–125, 155–156
ἄδυτον, 70
ἀήρ, 146–147
ἄθλιος, 139
αἰθήρ, 146–147
ἄκουσον, 127
ἀκούω, 134–135
ἀλάστωρ, 84
ἄλλος vs. ἄλλο, 151
ἀμαθής, 82
ἀναντίρρητον, 159–160
ἀνατολή, 70
ἀνήρ, 73
ἀντέγκλισις, 140–142
ἀντινομία, 154–155
ἀντιχρονισμός, ἀντιχρονία, 141–142
ἀπό (as gloss), 64–65
ἀρτηρία, 71n23
βάκχη, 76
βίος, 72, 94
βρόμος, 145
βρώματα, 126–128
βωμός, 71n23, 155, 157–158
γενήσεται vs. ἔσται, 125–126
γνωμικόν, 137–138
δαίμων vs. θεός, 130–131
δέρις, 146
διά (as gloss), 64n8
διαπορεῖται, 66n14
διαφέρει, 70–72, 81–82, 105, 110–111, 114, 120, 122, 124–125, 128, 137, 139, 145, 147, 156–158
δίκαιον, 82
δόξα, 133–134
δοριθήρατος, 131–132
δρᾶμα, 149–150
εἰς (as gloss), 64
ἔκθλιψις, 121
ἔκλειψις, 121
ἐλεύθερος, 139–140
ἐν (as gloss), 64
ἐναντιοφανής, 203–204
ἐναντίρρητον, 159–160
ἕνεκα (as gloss), 65
ἐπιτολή, 70
ἔρημος, 76
ἑρμηνεία, 28, 184–185
ἔσται vs. γενήσεται, 125–126
ἐσχάρα, 71n23
ἑταῖρος, 120–121

εὐσεβές, 82
ζητοῦσι, 20, 66n14
ἤ (glosses on), 64
ἠθοποιΐα, 42–43
ἠλίθιος vs. ἀκόλαστος, 152
ἠρίον, 157
θεός, 94; vs. δαίμων, 130–131
θράσος/θάρσος, 71
καί (gloss on τε), 65
κανών, 42
κεῖσθαι, 154
κευθμών, 93, 119–120
κόπις, 133, 158–159
κουστωδία, κοῦστος, 151
λάτρις, 75
λέσχη, 83–84
ληρέω, 82
λυγρός, 75
λώβη, 76
μάρψαι, 77
μαστός vs. μασθός, 158
μειονέκτης vs. πλεονέκτης, 152
μνῆμα, 157
μολοττός, 112
μονῳδία, 110–111
ναός vs. βωμός, 155, 157–158
νέμεσις, 71n23
νέον, 159–160
νοβελισιμοϋπέρτατος, 122
νωβελίσσιμος, 122, 123n41
ξένος, 120–121
οἰκτρός, 139
ὁλοχερές, 13
ὀμφαλός, 74–75
ὄνυξ, 156
ὁπλή, 156
ὅσιον, 82
πανουργία, 200
παραγέγραπται, 13
παράκειται, 13
παρεπιγραφή, 21
πέλανος, 98–99
πένης, πένομαι, 80
περίφρασις, 122
πόνος, 146

προκατασκευή, 202
προλόγισις, 110
πῶς vs. πως, 132–133
ῥόθος, 145
σηκός, 70
σκηνή, 131
σκῆνος, 116, 131
σπονδεῖος, 112
σύγχυσις vs. μίξις, 128–129
συμφυΐα, 138–139
συνασπισμός, 205
συνιῶ, 134–135
σῶμα, 123
τάλας, 124
Ταλθύβιος, 142–143
τάρβος, 129–130
τάφος, 157
τε (glossed with καί), 65
τελεία ἔγκλισις (vs. ἀτελής), 111
τεῦχος, 72
τλήμων, 124
τραγῳδεῖν, τραγουδῶ, τραγούδι, 32n115
τραγῳδούμενα, 11
τρωθείς vs. βληθείς, 71
τύμβος, 157
ὑπάρχω (gloss on εἰμί), 65
ὑπερβατόν, 135–137
ὑπόνοια, 200
ὑπόστασις, 138–139
ὑποταγάτος, 121
φάσγανον, 144–145
φέρω, 70, 124–125, 155–156
φεῦ δᾶ, 75
φθόνος, 71n23
φίλος, 120–121
φλέψ, 71n23
φλοῖσβος, 145
φλυαρέω, 81, 85
χηλή, 156
ψίλος, 131–132
ψυχή, 135
ὡραῖον, 137–138
Ὠρίων, 149
ὡς (glosses on), 63–64

www.ingramcontent.com/pod-product-compliance
Lightning Source LLC
Chambersburg PA
CBHW020643230426
43665CB00008B/290